"We hold these truths

to be self-evident: that all men are created equal; that they are endowed by their creator with certain inalienable rights . . ." *Thus began the first American revolution.*

Since then, a second revolution has been under way. For two centuries, American women have been demanding *their* rights. And today the storm of their protest has broken out with renewed fury.

These selections are by women only. They include the great militants of the past and the most telling spokeswomen of the present. They cover politics, jobs, marriage, childraising, heterosexuality, lesbianism, racism, sexism and other active fronts in the war for liberation. *They will raise many men's blood pressures and almost every woman's consciousness. Strong, frank, uncompromising, these are voices that refuse to be denied.*

Other SIGNET Books of Special Interest

☐ **THE BLACK WOMAN—AN ANTHOLOGY, Toni Cade, editor.** What is the reality of being Black, being a woman, and living in America—a society that still regards the Black woman as "the slave's slave"? With this collection we at last hear her voice expressing her opinions on such subjects as politics, racism, the Black man, Black pride, and many other topics. (#Q4317—95¢)

☐ **ZULU WOMAN, by Rebecca Hourwich Reyher.** The fascinating story of a courageous woman who defied tradition and left her husband. Thus making her the first Zulu woman to get a divorce. (#Q4126—95¢)

☐ **TO BE YOUNG, GIFTED AND BLACK, by Lorraine Hansberry.** Adapted by Robert Nemiroff. By the author of **A Raisin in the Sun,** here is Miss Hansberry's unique view of the human spirit, and her unwavering belief in the possibilities innate in human nature. (#Q4339—95¢)

☐ **UP AGAINST THE LAW: THE LEGAL RIGHTS OF PEOPLE UNDER 21, by Jeanne Strouse.** A legal primer for the under-21 set which presents all the regulations concerning minors and talks about them in layman's, rather than lawyer's, language. The minor's rights as son or daughter, student, draftee are covered, as well as the laws governing him in relation to marriage, drugs, cars, employment, contracts, and arrest. (#Q4315—95¢)

Voices from
WOMEN'S
LIBERATION

Compiled and Edited by
LESLIE B. TANNER

A SIGNET BOOK from
NEW AMERICAN LIBRARY
TIMES MIRROR

Ⓢ SIGNET TRADEMARK REG. U.S. PAT. OFF. AND FOREIGN COUNTRIES
REGISTERED TRADEMARK—MARCA REGISTRADA
HECHO EN CHICAGO, U.S.A.

SIGNET, SIGNET CLASSICS, SIGNETTE, MENTOR AND PLUME BOOKS
are published by The New American Library, Inc.,
1301 Avenue of the Americas, New York, New York 10019

FIRST PRINTING, JANUARY, 1971

PRINTED IN THE UNITED STATES OF AMERICA

TO ALL SISTERS

Contents

PART 2   OBSERVATIONS ON WOMEN
BY WOMEN   99

PART 3   VOICES FROM THE
PRESENT   107

Preface

It was only in the summer of 1969 that two friends and I first talked about starting a Women's Liberation group on the Lower East Side in New York. Other groups were organizing in New York, as indeed they were beginning to organize all over the country at that time, but we wanted to get together on our own. Having attended the July Women's Conference at the New School for Social Research, we realized through the workshops the need for many small groups in which women could talk freely to one another. It is extraordinary how quickly one realizes that deeply imbedded anxieties, far from being personal hang-ups are, in fact, universally shared by women as a direct result of their oppression.

Papers were being written by other women in the movement, and we avidly read and circulated everything we could get our hands on. There was never enough to go around within our own growing group, and nowhere near enough to pass along to other women who expressed an interest in Women's Liberation. This is the point where I started to think in terms of gathering together all the papers that had helped us, that had opened up our heads to new ideas, to a totally new way of thinking. Why not make a book of these "voices" from Women's Liberation? This could also be a true form of communication between women—not something written as an exploitive kind of "jumping on the bandwagon" book that the media all too frequently grind out.

As I gathered papers and became more involved in the physical aspect of putting the book together, I became aware of the historical aspect of Women's Liberation. I found out how little I (and most women I talked to) actually knew about our own heritage. A minimal amount of research soon showed me how deliberately women had been left out of our history books. Strong, courageous, brilliant women! I became angry. I felt cheated. That's when the idea came to include

13

the "voices" from the past as well as from the present. Man has defined our world for us—religiously, politically, economically, and socially—and it is time for us to define it for ourselves. Man can no longer cheat us.

Our movement is young, but it is growing at an astonishing rate. Women may come from so-called different economic and social classes, but the single most important issue in our movement is that we recognize each other as sisters. Society (man) has isolated us and alienated us from each other. This reinforces man's control and at the same time reinforces our dependence on him. Susan B. Anthony said (in 1893), "Women have been taught always to work for something else than their own personal freedom." Eighty years later we are still being taught not only to work, but to live, for something other than our own personal freedom. If we want our Revolution to be successful we had better start working—and living—for ourselves.

In collecting these "voices" I have tried to cover as broad a range as possible to show the full spectrum of the movement, past and present. There are few biographical notes included, as I feel that "voices" rather than personalities carry the movement forward. (One reason for the spectacular growth of Women's Liberation is precisely this de-emphasis on charismatic leadership. In many of our groups, the creative as well as the shit work is shared, often by drawing lots, which does away with the leadership cult.) There has been very little editing and cutting of material, to allow women's voices to be heard as they are without conforming to manmade rules of professionalism. All women are important, and what each of us has to say is terribly important. This is what Women's Liberation is all about.

A word about the Introduction to this book. Amazingly relevant for today, it was written nearly one hundred years ago and originally introduced the classic six-volume *The History of Woman Suffrage*. The first three volumes were prepared by Elizabeth Cady Stanton, Susan B. Anthony, and Mathilda Joslyn Gage. The concluding three volumes were the joint effort of Ida Husted and Susan B. Anthony.

This classic, *The History of Woman Suffrage*, has long been out of print, and what a commentary it is that only through the prodding of today's Women's Liberation Movement will it find its rightful place in the libraries of America!

Historically, another tremendously significant document for women is the small volume, *Letters on the Equality of the Sexes and the Condition of Women*. This work was written in

1838 by Sarah Moore Grimké. At this writing, it exists in the archives of the New York Public Library, not even as a bound book, only on microfilm! Dig it! On microfilm it is one of the ten documents titled "Ten Miscellaneous Economic Reports." These are reports appearing in various European languages on economic statistics of the mid-nineteenth century. The New York Public Library had not even bothered to index the *Letters on the Equality of the Sexes and the Condition of Women* under Sarah Moore Grimké's name, and I came across it quite by chance.

To the dedicated sisters who have contributed their papers to this collection, I can say only *Venceremos!* Thank you all for your warm encouragement and help. Especially to The Group.

Unless otherwise noted, permissions to reprint the articles, papers, and essays are granted by the individual authors. On page 444 is a listing of the organizations and women's journals that have contributed substantially to this anthology. Addresses and subscription rates are included so that the reader may send for additional material.

LESLIE B. TANNER
February, 1970

Introduction

The prolonged slavery of women is the darkest page in human history. A survey of the condition of the race through those barbarous periods, when physical force governed the world, when the motto, "might makes right," was the law, enables one to account for the origin of woman's subjection to man without referring the fact to the general inferiority of the sex, or Nature's law.

Writers on this question differ as to the cause of the universal degradation of woman in all periods and nations.

One of the greatest minds of the century has thrown a ray of light on this gloomy picture by tracing the origin of woman's slavery to the same principle of selfishness and love of power in man that has thus far dominated all weaker nations and classes. This brings hope of final emancipation, for as all nations and classes are gradually, one after another, asserting and maintaining their independence, the path is clear for woman to follow. The slavish instinct of an oppressed class has led her to toil patiently through the ages, giving all and asking little, cheerfully sharing with man all perils and privations by land and sea, that husband and sons might attain honor and success. Justice and freedom for herself is her latest and highest demand.

Another writer asserts that the tyranny of man over woman has its roots, after all, in his nobler feelings; his love, his chivalry, and his desire to protect woman in the barbarous periods of pillage, lust, and war. But wherever the roots may be traced, the results at this hour are equally disastrous to woman. Her best interests and happiness do not seem to have been consulted in the arrangements made for her protection. She has been bought and sold, caressed and crucified at the will and pleasure of her master. But if a chivalrous desire to protect woman has always been the mainspring of man's dominion over her, it should have prompted him to place in her hands the same weapons of defense he has found to be most effective against wrong and oppression.

It is often asserted that as woman has always been man's slave—subject—inferior—dependent, under all forms of government and religion, slavery must be her normal condition. This might have some weight had not the vast majority of men also been enslaved for centuries to kings and popes, and orders of nobility, who, in the progress of civilization, have reached complete equality. And did we not also see the great changes in woman's condition, the marvelous transformation in her character, from a toy in the Turkish harem, or a drudge in the German fields, to a leader of thought in the literary circles of France, England, and America!

Woman's steady march onward, and her growing desire for a broader outlook, prove that she has not reached her normal condition, and that society has not yet conceded all that is necessary for its attainment.

Moreover, woman's discontent increases in exact proportion to her development. Instead of a feeling of gratitude for rights accorded, the wisest are indignant at the assumption of any legal disability based on sex, and their feelings in this matter are a surer test of what her nature demands, than the feelings and prejudices of the sex claiming to be superior. American men may quiet their consciences with the delusion that no such injustice exists in this country as in Eastern nations, though with the general improvement in our institutions, woman's condition must inevitably have improved also, yet the same principle that degrades her in Turkey *insults* her in this republic. . . .

The condition of married women, under the laws of all countries, has been essentially that of slaves. . . .

Overburdened with cares in the isolated home, women had not the time, education, opportunity, and pecuniary independence to put their thoughts clearly and concisely into propositions, nor the courage to compare their opinions with one another, nor to publish them, to any great extent, to the world.

It requires philosophy and heroism to rise above the opinion of the wise men of all nations and races, that to be *unknown* is the highest testimonial woman can have to her virtue, delicacy and refinement.

A certain odium has ever rested on those who have risen above the conventional level and sought new spheres for thought and action, and especially on the few who demand complete equality in political rights. The leaders in this movement have been women of superior mental and physical organization, of good . . . education . . . good speakers and writers, inspiring and conducting the genuine reforms of the day; everywhere exerting themselves to promote the best interests of society; yet they have been uniformly ridiculed, misrepresented, and denounced in public and private by all classes of society.

Woman's political equality with man is the legitimate outgrowth of the fundamental principles of our Government, clearly set forth in the Declaration of Independence in 1776, in the United States Constitution adopted in 1784, in the prolonged debates on the origin of human rights in the anti-slavery conflict in 1840, and in the more recent discussions of the party in power since 1865, on the 13th, 14th, and 15th Amendments to the National Constitution. . . .

Under the influence of these liberal principles of republicanism that pervades all classes of American minds, however vaguely, if suddenly called out, they might be stated, woman readily perceives the anomalous position she occupies in a republic, where the government and religion alike are based on individual conscience and judgment—where the natural rights of all citizens have been exhaustively discussed, and repeatedly declared equal.

From the inauguration of the government, representative women have expostulated against the inconsistencies between our principles and practices as a nation. Beginning with special grievances, woman's protests soon took a larger scope. Having petitioned State legislatures to change the statutes that robbed her of children, wages, and property, she demanded that the Constitutions—State and National—be so amended as to give her a voice in the laws, a choice in the rulers, and protection in the exercise of her rights as a citizen of the United States.

While the laws affecting woman's civil rights have been greatly improved during the past thirty years, the political demand has made but a questionable progress, though it must be counted as the chief influence in modifying the laws. The selfishness of man was readily enlisted in securing woman's civil rights, while the same element in his character antagonized her demand for political equality.

Fathers who had estates to bequeath to their daughters could see the advantage of securing to woman certain property rights that might limit the legal power of profligate husbands.

Husbands in extensive business operations could see the

advantage of allowing the wife the right to hold separate property, settled on her in time of prosperity, that might not be seized for his debts. . . . But political rights, involving in their last results equality everywhere, roused all the antagonism of a dominant power, against the self-assertion of a class hitherto subservient. Men saw that with political equality for woman, they could no longer keep her in social subordination, and *"the majority of the male sex,"* says John Stuart Mill, *"can not yet tolerate the idea of living with an equal."* [italics added—L.B.T.] The fear of a social revolution thus complicated the discussion. The Church, too, took alarm . . . isolated texts have been used to block the wheels of progress in all periods; thus bigots have defended capital punishment, intemperance, slavery, polygamy, and the subjection of woman. The creeds of all nations make obedience to man the corner-stone of her religious character. . . .

As the social and religious objections appeared against the demand for political rights . . . some said, "Man is woman's natural protector, and she can safely trust him to make laws for her." She might with fairness reply, as he uniformly robbed her of all property rights to 1848, he can not safely be trusted with her personal rights in 1880 . . . the calendars of our courts still show that fathers deal unjustly with daughters, husbands with wives, brothers with sisters, and sons with their own mothers. . . .

Again, it is said: "The women who make the demand are few in number, and their feelings and opinions are abnormal, and therefore of no weight in considering the aggregate judgment on the question." The number is larger than appears on the surface, for the fear of public ridicule, and the loss of private favors from those who shelter, feed, and clothe them, withhold many from declaring their opinions and demanding their rights. The ignorance and indifference of the majority of women, as to their status as citizens of a republic, is not remarkable, for history shows that the masses of all oppressed classes, in the most degraded conditions, have been stolid and apathetic until partial success had crowned the faith and enthusiasm of the few.

It is said, "the difference between the sexes indicates different spheres." It would be nearer the truth to say the difference indicates different duties in the same sphere. . . . In governing nations, leading armies, piloting ships across the sea . . . in art, science, invention, literature, woman has proved herself the complement of man in the world of thought and action. This difference does not compel us to spread our tables with different food for man and woman, nor to provide in our common schools a different course of study for boys and girls. Sex pervades all nature, yet the male and female tree and vine and shrub rejoice in the same sunshine and shade. The earth and air are free to all the fruits and flowers, yet each absorbs what best ensures its growth. But whatever it is, it requires no special watchfulness on our part to see that it is maintained. This plea, when closely analyzed, is generally found to mean woman's inferiority. . . .

Men are uniformly more attentive to women of rank, family, and fortune, who least need their care, than to any other class. *We do not see their protecting love generally extending to the helpless and unfortunate ones of earth.* [italics added—L.B.T.] Wherever the skilled hands and cultured brain of woman have made the battle of life easier for man, he has readily pardoned her sound judgment and proper self-assertion. But the prejudices and preferences of man should be a secondary consideration, in presence of the individual happiness and freedom of woman. The formation of her character and its influence on the human race, is a larger question than man's personal liking. . . .

As the power to extend or limit the suffrage rests now wholly in the hands of man, he can commence the experiment with as small a number as he sees fit, by requiring any lawful qualification. Men were admitted on property and educational qualifications in most of the States, at one time, and still are in some—so hard has it been for man to understand the theory of self-government. Three-fourths of the women would be thus disqualified, and the remaining fourth would be too small a minority to precipitate a social revolution . . . the path of duty is plain for . . . those gentlemen who fear universal suffrage for women, but are willing to grant it on property and educational qualifications . . . let those who trust the absolute right proclaim the higher principle in government, "equal rights to all." . . .

The isolated household is responsible for a large share of woman's ignorance and degradation. A mind always in contact with children . . . whose aspirations and ambitions rise no higher than the roof that shelters it, is necessarily dwarfed in its proportions. The advantages to the few whose fortunes enable them to make the isolated household a more successful experiment, can not outweigh the difficulties of the many who are wholly sacrificed to its maintenance.

Quite as many false ideas prevail as to woman's true position in the home as to her status elsewhere. Womanhood is the great fact in her life; wifehood and motherhood are but incidental relations. Governments legislate for men; we do not have one code for bachelors, another for husbands and fathers; neither have the social relations of women any significance in their demands for civil and political rights. Custom and philosophy, in regard to woman's happiness, are alike based on the idea that her strongest social sentiment is love of children; that in this relation her soul finds complete satisfaction. . . . They who give the world a true philosophy, a grand poem, a beautiful painting or statue, or can tell the story of every wandering star; a George Eliot, a Rosa Bonheur, an Elizabeth Barrett Browning, a Maria Mitchell—whose blood has flowed to the higher arches of the brain—have lived to a holier purpose than they whose children are of the flesh alone, into whose minds they have breathed no clear perceptions of great principles, no moral aspiration, no spiritual life.

Her rights are as completely ignored in what is adjudged to be woman's sphere as out of it; the woman is uniformly sacrificed to the wife and mother. Neither law, gospel, public sentiment, nor domestic affection shield her from excessive and enforced maternity, depleting alike to mother and child; —all opportunity for mental improvement, health, happiness —yea, life itself, being ruthlessly sacrificed. The weazened, weary, withered, narrow-minded wife—mother of half a dozen children—her interests all centering at her fireside, forms a painful contrast in many households to the liberal, genial, brilliant, cultured husband in the zenith of his power, who has never given one thought to the higher life, liberty, and happiness of the woman by his side; believing her self-abnegation to be Nature's law.

It is often asked "if political equality would not rouse antagonisms between the sexes." If it could be proved that men and women had been harmonious in all ages and countries, and that women were happy and satisfied in their slavery, one might hesitate in proposing any change whatever. But the apathy, the helpless, hopeless resignation of a subjected class can not be called happiness. The more complete the despotism, the more smoothly all things move on the surface. "Order reigns in Warsaw." In right conditions, the interests of man and woman are essentially one; but in false conditions, they must ever be opposed. The principle of equality of rights underlies all human sentiments, and its assertion by any individual or class must rouse antagonism, unless conceded. This has been the battle of the ages, and will be until all forms of slavery are banished from the earth.

Philosophers, historians, poets, novelists, alike paint woman the victim ever of man's power and selfishness. And now all writers on Eastern civilization tell us, the one insurmountable obstacle to the improvement of society in those countries, is the ignorance and superstition of the women. Stronger than the trammels of custom and law, is her religion, which teaches that her condition is Heaven-ordained. . . . A woman growing up under American ideas of liberty in government and religion, having never blushed behind a Turkish mask, nor pressed her feet in Chinese shoes, can not brook any disabilities based on sex alone, without a deep feeling of antagonism with the power that creates it. The change needed . . . can not be reached by remanding women to the spinning-wheel, and the contentment of her grandmother, but by conceding to her every right which the spirit of the age demands. Modern inventions have banished the spinning-wheel, and the same law of progress makes the woman of today a different woman from her grandmother.

Foreword

The preceding Introduction was written nearly one hundred years ago. It is the Introduction to the classic six-volume *The History of Woman Suffrage,* published in 1881.

The implications of that Introduction are extraordinary. If it could have been written today, how far *have* we come? Compared with Susan B. Anthony and other early feminists, *are* we so radical? A glance at the origins of our movement will show that we have a most radical heritage.

Consider a voice still earlier than that of Susan B. Anthony —the voice of Sarah Moore Grimké in 1838: "I ask no favors for my sex. . . . All I ask of our brethren is that they take their feet from off our necks."

Or the action of the very *first* Woman's Rights Convention at Seneca Falls, New York, in 1848. Having hired a hall for their meeting, the women arrived to find that the men had reconsidered the propriety of a women's convention, and had locked the doors. The women gained entry by breaking open a window, and then took over the hall for a meeting that adopted the radical Declaration of Sentiments and Resolutions. (The Declaration appears on pages 44–48 of this volume.)

Susan B. Anthony gave her feminist newspaper the title *Revolution.* That newspaper lasted only a few years, but its writings revealed a revolutionary fervor we can do well to exemplify today.

Our school history books—written by men—depict the early feminists as frustrated spinsters. A falsehood, deliberately perpetrated by opponents of the women's rights movement to ridicule and kill it. For an entire century this myth of the woman activist has persisted, but now as women search out the historical truth about themselves, the myth is being seen for the lie it is.

Our male-written history books also give the impression that the early women's rights movement was obsessed by the vote and concern over temperance. This is another historical falsehood. Listen again to the voice of Susan B. Anthony on the question of the elective franchise for women:

"The ballot is not even half the loaf; it is only a crust—a crumb."

As for the temperance crusade which swept the country in the years after 1825, that movement—far from being led by women—was started by men, run by men, and men humiliated the women by prohibiting them from voting or even speaking at the conventions. The first World's Temperance Convention held in New York in 1853 enjoined women from having any part of the proceedings, and the New York *Tribune* referred to it sarcastically as "The Orthodox White Male Saints' Convention."

The movement for women's rights may be dated from the 1840 World's Anti-Slavery Convention held in London.

Abolition societies sent delegations from many countries and the anti-slavery societies of Massachusetts and Pennsylvania sent delegations that included eight women. Among these were Elizabeth Cady Stanton, Lucretia Mott and Ann Green Phillips.

The convention met at Freemason's Hall the morning of June 12. At eleven o'clock the enormous hall was filled, and the husband of Ann Green Phillips introduced a motion that a committee be appointed to prepare a list of the members of the convention, with instructions to include in the list all persons bearing credentials from any anti-slavery body.

This motion opened the debate on the admission of women delegates.

When the original call for the convention had been sent out many months earlier, no mention was made that the convention was to be limited to men only. It had not occurred to the Englishmen of Queen Victoria's time that any woman anywhere would think of sitting with men to discuss a political matter. Then, when the abolition societies of Massachusetts and Pennsylvania wrote that women would be part of their delegations, they received letters of instruction. Women were not invited. The Victorian Englishmen assumed that the matter was settled.

It wasn't, and a number of American clergymen took a boat ahead of the women to warn the Englishmen that women were on their way to invade the proceedings. Thus, everyone was well prepared for a floor fight when Wendell Phillips rose to introduce his motion.

The debate on the motion for admitting women raged for hours.

Opponents insisted that it would be better to dissolve the convention than to permit women to sit with men on an equal basis. The motion lost by an overwhelming majority, and the American women were informed that if they wanted to attend the meetings at all they would have to sit in silence behind a curtained enclosure.

Lucretia Mott and Elizabeth Cady Stanton adjourned to their hotel near Great Queen Street. They talked about the absurdity of a World Convention proclaiming the black man's right to liberty, yet denying equal liberty to women. They agreed that on their return to the United States they would meet again and plan a public meeting of protest.

Eight years passed, and during that interval Lucretia Mott continued her involvement in the anti-slavery movement. Elizabeth Cady Stanton, having moved to Seneca Falls, in the isolated Five Fingers region of New York (where her husband had taken a job), was busy rearing children and learning what it was to be a housewife. As she herself wrote:

I now fully understood the practical difficulties most women had to contend with in the isolated household, and the impossibility of woman's best development if in contact, the chief part of her life, with servants and children. . . . The general discontent I felt with woman's portion as wife, mother, housekeeper, physician, and spiritual guide, the chaotic condition into which everything fell without her constant supervision, and the wearied, anxious look of the majority of women, impressed me with the strong feeling that some active measures should be taken to remedy the wrongs of society in general and of women in particular.

In July 1848 Lucretia Mott attended a Quaker meeting at Waterloo, New York, not far from Seneca Falls, and she and Elizabeth Cady Stanton and several other women met for the first time since the World Anti-Slavery Convention. Of this meeting, Elizabeth Cady Stanton was to write: "I poured out, that day, the torrent of my long accumulating discontent, with such vehemence and indignation that I stirred myself, as well as the rest of the party, to do and dare something."

Seated at a round mahogany table, she and Lucretia Mott prepared on July 14, 1848, this announcement that appeared in the following day's edition of the *Seneca County Courier:*

Woman's Rights Convention—A Convention to discuss the social, civil and religious rights of woman will be held in the Wesleyan Chapel, Seneca Falls, New York, on Wednesday and Thursday, the 19th and 20th of July current; commencing at 10 A.M. During the first day the meeting will be held exclusively for women, who are earnestly invited to attend. The public generally are invited to be present on the second day, when Lucretia Mott of Philadelphia and other ladies and gentlemen will address the convention.

The Seneca Falls convention issued the Declaration of Sentiments and Resolutions referred to above. It was signed by one hundred women and men. Modeled after the 1776 American Declaration of Independence, it set forth a long list of grievances. Unlike the 1776 Declaration, which was directed to "King George," the Seneca Falls Declaration was directed to "Man."

By unanimous vote, eleven out of twelve resolutions were adopted by the Seneca Falls Declaration. The resolution that failed of unanimous passage stated: "It is the duty of the women of this country to secure to themselves their sacred right to the elective franchise." A bitter debate preceded this particular resolution, and it was passed by only a slim majority.

Today, as we look back on these extraordinary proceedings, what emerges as truly extraordinary is that the least radical of the Seneca Falls resolutions—the right to the elective franchise—evoked so much bitterness and dissension.

The time was to come when the women's rights movement would devote its entire energies to winning the vote, but by then the energies of the women radicals had been spent and the entire movement would fall in terrible defeat.

We are concerned here with the early phases of the women's rights movement, and its origins were undeniably radical.

The movement spread swiftly. Two weeks after Seneca Falls, a second women's rights convention met in Rochester, New York, on August 2, 1848. Similar conventions took place in other parts of New York, then in Massachusetts, Pennsylvania, and Indiana. By 1850 the movement had spread as far west as Wisconsin and Kansas.

Devastating attacks on the movement appeared in the Establishment media and are chronicled in Anthony's *History of Woman Suffrage*. Ranging from gross ridicule and contempt to outright lies and distortions, the coverage bears an astonishing likeness to the accounts we read about the movement in the Establishment media of today.

Like the women of today, women activists relied for more honest exchanges of information on the radical press of the time—the underground papers created by the mid-nineteenth-century abolitionists. Published and edited by men, the abolitionist press failed to give the women's rights movement the coverage it merited, and the accounts that appeared—though far more honest than the Establishment media—fell just as far short of the real truth as do the accounts in the underground press of today (again published by men!)

And so it was that women began to write, edit, publish, and print their own tracts and journals. Among the early efforts were *The Una;* the *Woman's Advocate,* published by a joint stock company of women and printed entirely by women's labor; *The Lily,* published by Amelia Bloomer, with this masthead: "Devoted entirely to the Interests of Women." The most forthright journal was Anthony's *Revolution,* and her masthead read: "Men their rights, and nothing more; Women their rights and nothing less."

The conservative turn of the women's rights movement after the 1880's, the involvement by women with other reformist causes—to their own detriment—and the eventual collapse of the movement after 1920 are analyzed in detail on pages 433–43 by Shulamith Firestone.

We have learned many a lesson from the history of the struggle by women for their own rights, and surely the most important is: we must fight our own battles and not be co-opted ever again by playing a subservient role to any other cause.

My concern here is to draw parallels to the movement today, and to show the militancy of the early fighters for women's rights.

Susan B. Anthony went all the way. Early in the 1860's, she faced arrest as an accomplice on a kidnapping charge. She was harboring a fugitive mother who had taken her child from the father, a Massachusetts state senator. By any standards, justice was on the mother's side, but by law all legal rights were on the side of the husband, controlling as he did the wife's person as well as the children.

This was a time when practically any abolitionist worthy of the name was defying the Fugitive Slave Law by helping slaves escape from the South to Canada. Susan Anthony was extending the humanitarian principle to the cause of woman's rights. The woman she was helping was a slave under the law, and the law be damned. Anthony's abolitionist friends refused to see the connection. They urged her to abide by the Massachusetts law and return the child, lest she harm both the abolitionist and the woman's rights movements.

"That I should stop to ask if my act would injure the reputation of any movement never crossed my mind," she answered. "Nor will I allow such a fear to stifle my sympathies. . . . Trust me that as I ignore all law to help the slave, so will I ignore it all to protect an enslaved woman."

To William Lloyd Garrison, militant on every issue except when it touched the institution of marriage, she said: "You would die before you would deliver a slave to his master, and I will die before I give up that child to its father." And in her diary she wrote: "Very many abolitionists have yet to learn the ABC of woman's rights."

LESLIE B. TANNER

PART 1

Voices from the Past

We Are Determined
to Foment a Rebellion*

ABIGAIL ADAMS, *in a letter to Mercy Otis Warren*

(1776)

He [Mr. Adams] is very sausy to me, in return for a list of female grievances which I transmitted to him. I think I will get you to join me in a petition to Congress. I thought it was very probable our wise statesmen would erect a new government and form a new code of laws, I ventured to speak a word in behalf of our sex who are rather hardly dealt with by the laws of England which gives such unlimited power to the husband to use his wife ill. I requested that our legislators would consider our case and as all men of delicacy and sentiment are averse to exercising the power they possess, yet as there is a natural propensity in human nature to domination I thought the most generous plan was to put it out of the power of the arbitrary and tyranick to injure us with impunity by establishing some laws in our favour upon just and liberal principals.

I believe I even threatened fomenting a Rebellion in case we were not considered and assured him we would not hold ourselves bound by any laws in which we had neither a voice nor representation.

In return he tells me he cannot but laugh at my extraordinary code of laws that he had heard their struggle had loosned the bonds of government, that children and apprentices were disobedient that schools and colleges were grown turbulent, that Indians slighted their guardians and Negroes grew insolent to their Masters. But my letter was the first intimation that another Tribe more numerous and powerful than all the rest were grown discontented. This is rather too coarse a

Mercy Warren by Alice Brown (Charles Scribner's Sons, N. Y., 1896).

compliment, he adds, but that I am so sausy he wont blot it out.

So I have helped the sex abundantly, but I will tell him I have only been making trial of the disinterestedness of his virtue [and] when weighd in the balance have found it wanting.

It would be bad policy to grant us greater power say they since under all the disadvantage we labour we have the ascendancy over their hearts

> 'And charm by accepting,
> by submitting sway.'

Of Free Enquiry Considered As a Means for Obtaining Just Knowledge*

Frances Wright

(1830)

However novel it may appear, I shall venture the assertion, that until women assume the place in society which good sense and feeling alike assign to them, human improvement must advance but feebly. It is in vain that we would circumscribe the power of one half of our race, and that half by far the most important and influential. If they exert it not for good, they will for evil; if they advance not knowledge, they will perpetuate ignorance. Let women stand where they may in the scale of improvement, their position decides that of the race. Are they ignorant?—so is society gross and insipid. Are they wise?—so is the human condition prosperous. Are they foolish?—so is it unstable and unpromising. Are they free?—so is the human character elevated. Are they enslaved?—so is the whole race degraded. Oh! that we could learn the advantage of just practice and consistent principles! that we could understand, that every departure from prin-

*From *Course of Popular Lectures* (New York, 1830).

ciple, how speciously soever it may appear to administer to
our selfish interests, invariably saps their very foundation!
that we could learn that what is ruinous to some is injurious
to all, and that whenever we establish our own pretensions
upon the sacrificed rights of others, we do in fact impeach
our own liberties and lower ourselves in the scale of being!

The Prevailing Opinion of
a Sexual Character Discussed*

MARY WOLLSTONECRAFT

(1833)

To account for, and excuse the tyranny of man, many in-
genious arguments have been brought forward to prove, that
the two sexes, in the acquirement of virtue, ought to aim at
attaining a very different character: or, to speak explicitly,
women are not allowed to have sufficient strength of mind to
acquire what really deserves the name of virtue. . . . Strengthen
the female mind by enlarging it, and there will be an end to
blind obedience; but, as blind obedience is ever sought for
by power, tyrants and sensualists are in the right when they
endeavour to keep women in the dark, because the former
only want slaves, and the latter a play-thing. The sensualist,
indeed, has been the most dangerous of tyrants, and women
have been duped by their lovers, as princes by their ministers,
whilst dreaming that they reigned over them. . . .

Women are, therefore, to be considered either as moral beings, or so weak that they must be entirely subjected to the
superior faculties of men.

Let us examine this question. Rousseau declares, that a
woman should never, for a moment feel herself independent,
that she should be governed by fear to exercise her *natural*
cunning, and made a coquettish slave in order to render her a

*From *Vindication of the Rights of Woman with Strictures on Political
and Moral Subjects* (New York, 1833).

more alluring object of desire, a *sweeter* companion to man, whenever he chooses to relax himself. He carries the arguments, which he pretends to draw from the indications of nature, still further, and insinuates that truth and fortitude, the corner stones of all human virtue, shall be cultivated with certain restrictions, because with respect to the female character, obedience is the grand lesson which ought to be impressed with unrelenting rigour.

What nonsense! when will a great man arise with sufficient strength of mind to puff away the fumes which pride and sensuality have thus spread over the subject! If women are by nature inferior to men, their virtues must be the same in quality, if not in degree, or virtue is a relative idea; consequently their conduct should be founded on the same principles and have the same aim. . . .

Probably the prevailing opinion, that woman was created for man, may have taken its rise from Moses's poetical story; yet, as very few it is presumed, who have bestowed any serious thought on the subject, ever supposed that Eve was, literally speaking, one of Adam's ribs, the deduction must be allowed to fall to the ground; or only be so far admitted as it proves that man, from the remotest antiquity, found it convenient to exert his strength to subjugate his companion, and his invention to show that she ought to have her neck bent under the yoke; because she as well as the brute creation, was created to do his pleasure. . . .

I cannot discover why, unless they are mortal, females should always be degraded by being made subservient to love or lust. . . . To speak disrespectfully of love is, I know, high treason against sentiment and fine feelings; but I wish to speak the simple language of truth, and rather to address the head than the heart. To endeavour to reason love out of the world, would be to out Quixote Cervantes, and equally offend against common sense; but an endeavour to restrain this tumultuous passion, and to prove that it should not be allowed to dethrone superior powers, or to usurp the sceptre which the understanding should ever cooly wield, appears less wild.

Youth is the season for love in both sexes; but in those days of thoughtless enjoyment, provision should be made for the more important years of life, when reflection takes place of sensation. But Rousseau, and most of the male writers who have followed his steps, have warmly inculcated that the whole tendency of female education ought to be directed to one point to render them pleasing.

Let me reason with the supporters of this opinion, who have any knowledge of human nature, do they imagine that marriage can eradicate the habitude of life? The woman who has only been taught to please, will soon find that her charms are oblique sun-beams, and that they cannot have much effect on her husband's heart when they are seen every day, when the summer is past and gone. Will she then have sufficient native energy to look into herself for comfort and cultivate her dormant faculties? or, is it not more rational to expect, that she will try to please other men; and, in the emotions raised by the expectation of new conquests, endeavour to forget the mortification her love or pride has received? When the husband ceases to be a lover—and the time will inevitably come, her desire of pleasing will then grow languid, or become a spring of bitterness; and love, perhaps, the most evanescent of all passions, gives place to jealousy or vanity.

I now speak of women who are restrained by principle or prejudice; such women though they would shrink from an intrigue with real abhorrence, yet, nevertheless, wish to be convinced by the homage of gallantry, that they are cruelly neglected by their husbands; or, days and weeks are spent in dreaming of the happiness enjoyed by congenial souls, till the health is undermined and the spirits broken by discontent. How then can the great art of pleasing be such a necessary study? . . .

Love, from its very nature, must be transitory. To seek for a secret that would render it constant, would be as wild a search as for the philosopher's stone, or the grand panacea; and the discovery would be equally useless, or rather pernicious to mankind. The most holy band of society is friendship. . . .

This is, must be, the course of nature—friendship or indifference inevitably succeeds love. . . .

Letters on the Equality of the Sexes and the Condition of Woman (Addressed to Mary S. Parker, President of the Boston Female Anti-Slave Society)*

SARAH MOORE GRIMKÉ

(1838)

LETTER II

Woman Subject Only to God

Newburyport, 7th mo. 17, 1837

Woman, I am aware, stands charged to the present day with having brought sin into the world. I shall not repel the charge by any counter assertions, although, as was hinted, Adam's ready acquiescence with his wife's proposal does not savor much of that superiority in *strength of mind* which is arrogated by man. Even admitting that Eve was the greater sinner, it seems to me that man might be satisfied with the dominion he has claimed and exercised for nearly six thousand years, and that more true nobility would be manifested by endeavoring to raise the fallen and envigorate the weak than by keeping woman in subjection. I ask no favors for my sex. I surrender not our claim to equality. All I ask of our brethren is that they will take their feet from off our necks.

All history attests that man has subjected woman to his will, used her as a means to promote his selfish gratification, to minister to his sensual pleasures, to be instrumental in pro-

*From a pamphlet of the same name published by Isaac Knapp, Boston, 1838.

moting his comfort; but never has he desired to elevate her to that rank she was created to fill. He has done all he could to debase and enslave her mind; and now he looks triumphantly on the ruin he has wrought, and says, the being he has thus deeply injured is his inferior.

LETTER VIII

On the Condition of Women in the United States

Brookline, 1837

There is another way in which the general opinion, that women are inferior to men, is manifested, that bears with tremendous effect on the laboring class, and indeed on almost all who are obliged to earn a subsistence, whether it be by mental or physical exertion—I allude to the disproportionate value set on the time and labor of men and of women. A man who is engaged in teaching, can always, I believe, command a higher price for tuition than a woman—even when he teaches the same branches, and is not in any respect superior to the woman. . . . As for example, in tailoring, a man has twice, or three times as much for making a waistcoat or pantaloons as a woman, although the work done by each may be equally good. A woman who goes out to wash, works as hard in proportion as a wood sawyer, or a coal heaver, but she is not generally able to make more than half as much by a day's work.

There is another class of women in this country, to whom I cannot refer, without feelings of the deepest shame and sorrow. I allude to our female slaves. Our southern cities are whelmed beneath a tide of pollution; the virtue of female slaves is wholly at the mercy of irresponsible tyrants, and women are bought and sold in our slave markets, to gratify the brutal lust of those who bear the name of Christians. In our slave States, if amid all her degradation and ignorance, a woman desires to preserve her virtue unsullied, she is either bribed or whipped into compliance, or if she dares resist her seducer, her life by the laws of some of the slave States may be, and has actually been sacrificed to the fury of disappointed passion. Where such laws do not exist, the power which is necessarily vested in the master over his property, leaves the defenceless slave entirely at his mercy, and the sufferings of some females on this account, both physical and mental, are intense. Mr. Gholson, in the House of Delegates of Virginia, in 1832, said "He really had been under the impression that he owned his slaves. He had lately purchased four women and ten children, in whom he thought he had obtained a great bargain; for he supposed they were his own property, *as were his brood mares.*"

LETTER XIII

Relation of Husband and Wife

Brookline, 9th mo., 1837

Man has exercised the most unlimited and brutal power over woman, in the peculiar character of husband—a word in most countries synonymous with tyrant. . . . Woman, instead of being elevated by her union with man, which might be expected from an alliance with a superior being, is in reality lowered. She generally loses her individuality, her independent character, her moral being. She becomes absorbed into him, and henceforth is looked at, and acts through the medium of her husband.

There Is No Such Thing As a Sphere for a Sex*

ELIZABETH CADY STANTON *Answers Newspapers' Objections to Women's Conventions*

(Rochester, N. Y., September 14, 1848)

For those who do not yet understand the real objects of our recent Conventions at Rochester and Seneca Falls, I would state that we did not meet to discuss fashions, customs, or dress, the rights or duties of man, nor the propriety of the

*From *The History of Woman Suffrage,* vol. 1.

sexes changing positions, but simply our own inalienable rights, our duties, our true sphere. If God has assigned a sphere to man and one to woman, we claim the right to judge ourselves of His design in reference to *us,* and we accord to man the same privilege. We think a man has quite enough in this life to find out his own individual calling, without being taxed to decide where every woman belongs; and the fact that so many men fail in the business they undertake, calls loudly for their concentrating more thought on their own faculties, capabilities, and sphere of action. We have all seen a man making a jackass of himself in the pulpit, at the bar, or in our legislative halls, when he might have shone as a captain of a canal boat, or as a tailor on his bench. Now, is it to be wondered at that woman has some doubts about the present position assigned her being the true one, when her every-day experience shows her that man makes such fatal mistakes in regard to himself?

There is no such thing as a sphere for a sex. Every man has a different sphere, and one in which he may shine, and it is the same with every woman; and the same woman may have a different sphere at different times. The distinguished Angelina Grimké was acknowledged by all the anti-slavery host to be in her sphere, when, years ago, she went through the length and breadth of New England, telling the people of her personal experience of the horrors and abominations of the slave system, and by her eloquence and power as a public speaker, producing an effect unsurpassed by any of the highly gifted men of her day. Who dares to say that in thus using her splendid talents in speaking for the dumb, pleading the cause of the poor friendless slave, that she was out of her sphere? . . . The highly gifted Quakeress, Lucretia Mott, . . . has a talent for public speaking; her mind is of a high order; her moral perceptions remarkably clear; . . . and who shall tell us that this divinely inspired woman is out of her sphere in her public endeavors to rouse this wicked nation to a sense of its awful guilt, to its great sins of war, slavery, injustice to women and the laboring poor. . . .

WOMAN: The Great Unpaid Laborer of the World*

Susan B. Anthony

(c. 1848)

Although woman has performed much of the labor of the world, her industry and economy have been the very means of increasing her degradation. Not being free, the results of her labor have gone to build up and sustain the very class that has perpetuated this injustice. Even in the family, where we should naturally look for the truest conditions, woman has always been robbed of the fruits of her own toil. . . . Taught that the fruits of her industry belonged to others, she has seen man enter into every avocation most suitable to her, while she, the uncomplaining drudge of the household, condemned to the severest labor, has been systematically robbed of her earnings, which have gone to build up her master's power, and she has found herself in the condition of the slave, deprived of the results of her own labor. . . . Taught that a low voice is an excellent thing in woman, she has been trained to a subjugation of the vocal organs, and thus lost the benefit of loud tones and their well-known invigoration of the system. Forbidden to run, climb, or jump, her muscles have been weakened, and her strength deteriorated. Confined most of the time to the house, she has neither as strong lungs nor as vigorous a digestion as her brother. . . .

Woman has been the great unpaid laborer of the world, and although within the last two decades a vast number of new employments have been opened to her, statistics prove that in the great majority of these, she is not paid according to the value of the work done, but according to sex. The opening of all industries to woman, and the wage question as connected with her, are most subtle and profound questions

*From *The History of Woman Suffrage*, vol. 1.

of political economy, closely interwoven with the rights of self-government.

Declaration of Sentiments and Resolutions

The First Woman's Rights Convention*

(Seneca Falls, N. Y., July 19-20, 1848)

When, in the course of human events, it becomes necessary for one portion of the family of man to assume among the people of the earth a position different from that which they have hitherto occupied, but one to which the laws of nature and of nature's God entitle them, a decent respect to the opinions of mankind requires that they should declare the causes that impel them to such a course.

We hold these truths to be self-evident: that all men and women are created equal; that they are endowed by their Creator with certain inalienable rights; that among these are life, liberty, and the pursuit of happiness; that to secure these rights governments are instituted, deriving their just powers from the consent of the governed. Whenever any form of government becomes destructive of these ends, it is the right of those who suffer from it to refuse allegiance to it, and to insist upon the institution of a new government, laying its foundation on such principles, and organizing its powers in such form, as to them shall seem most likely to effect their safety and happiness. Prudence, indeed, will dictate that governments long established should not be changed for light and transient causes; and accordingly all experience hath shown that mankind are more disposed to suffer, while evils are sufferable, than to right themselves by abolishing the forms to which they were accustomed. But when a long train of abuses and usurpations, pursuing invariably the same object evinces a design to reduce them under absolute despotism, it is their duty to throw off such government, and to provide new guards for their future security. Such has been the pa-

*From *The History of Woman Suffrage*, vol. 1.

tient sufferance of the women under this government, and such is now the necessity which constrains them to demand the equal station to which they are entitled.

The history of mankind is a history of repeated injuries and usurpations on the part of man toward woman, having in direct object the establishment of an absolute tyranny over her. To prove this, let facts be submitted to a candid world.

He has never permitted her to exercise her inalienable right to the elective franchise.

He has compelled her to submit to laws, in the formation of which she had no voice.

He has withheld from her rights which are given to the most ignorant and degraded men—both natives and foreigners.

Having deprived her of this first right of a citizen, the elective franchise, thereby leaving her without representation in the halls of legislation, he has oppressed her on all sides.

He has made her, if married, in the eye of the law, civilly dead.

He has taken from her all right in property, even to the wages she earns.

He has made her, morally, an irresponsible being, as she can commit many crimes with impunity, provided they be done in the presence of her husband. In the covenant of marriage, she is compelled to promise obedience to her husband, he becoming, to all intents and purposes, her master—the law giving him power to deprive her of her liberty, and to administer chastisement.

He has so framed the laws of divorce, as to what shall be the proper causes, and in case of separation, to whom the guardianship of the children shall be given, as to be wholly regardless of the happiness of women—the law, in all cases, going upon a false supposition of the supremacy of man, and giving all power into his hands.

After depriving her of all rights as a married woman, if single, and the owner of property, he has taxed her to support a government which recognizes her only when her property can be made profitable to it.

He has monopolized nearly all the profitable employments, and from those she is permitted to follow, she receives but a scanty remuneration. He closes against her all the avenues to wealth and distinction which he considers most honorable to himself. As a teacher of theology, medicine, or law, she is not known.

He has denied her the facilities for obtaining a thorough education, all colleges being closed against her.

He allows her in Church, as well as State, but a subordinate position, claiming Apostolic authority for her exclusion from the ministry, and, with some exceptions, from any public participation in the affairs of the Church.

He has created a false public sentiment by giving to the world a different code of morals for men and women, by which moral delinquencies which exclude women from society, are not only tolerated, but deemed of little account in man.

He has usurped the prerogative of Jehovah himself, claiming it as his right to assign for her a sphere of action, when that belongs to her conscience and to her God.

He has endeavored, in every way that he could, to destroy her confidence in her own powers, to lessen her self-respect, and to make her willing to lead a dependent and abject life.

Now, in view of this entire disfranchisement of one-half the people of this country, their social and religious degradation—in view of the unjust laws above mentioned, and because women do feel themselves aggrieved, oppressed, and fraudulently deprived of their most sacred rights, we insist that they have immediate admission to all the rights and privileges which belong to them as citizens of the United States.

In entering upon the great work before us, we anticipate no small amount of misconception, misrepresentation, and ridicule; but we shall use every instrumentality within our power to effect our object. We shall employ agents, circulate tracts, petition the State and National legislatures, and endeavor to enlist the pulpit and the press in our behalf. We hope this Convention will be followed by a series of Conventions embracing every part of the country.

Resolutions Adopted

WHEREAS, The great precept of nature is conceded to be, that "man shall pursue his own true and substantial happiness." Blackstone in his Commentaries remarks, that this law of Nature being coeval with mankind, and dictated by God himself, is of course superior in obligation to any other. It is binding over all the globe, in all countries and at all times;

no human laws are of any validity if contrary to this, and such of them as are valid, derive all their force, and all their validity, and all their authority, mediately and immediately, from this original; therefore,

Resolved, That such laws as conflict, in any way, with the true and substantial happiness of woman, are contrary to the great precept of nature and of no validity, for this is "superior in obligation to any other."

Resolved, That all laws which prevent woman from occupying such a station in society as her conscience shall dictate, or which place her in a position inferior to that of man, are contrary to the great precept of nature, and therefore of no force or authority.

Resolved, That woman is man's equal—was intended to be so by the Creator, and the highest good of the race demands that she should be recognized as such.

Resolved, That the women of this country ought to be enlightened in regard to the laws under which they live, that they may no longer publish their degradation by declaring themselves satisfied with their present position, nor their ignorance, by asserting that they have all the rights they want. . . .

Resolved, That the same amount of virtue, delicacy, and refinement of behavior that is required of woman in the social state, should also be required of man, and the same transgressions should be visited with equal severity on both man and woman.

Resolved, That the objection of indelicacy and impropriety, which is so often brought against woman when she addresses a public audience, comes with a very ill-grace from those who encourage, by their attendance, her appearance on the stage, in the concert, or in feats of the circus.

Resolved, That woman has too long rested satisfied in the circumscribed limits which corrupt customs and a perverted application of the Scriptures have marked out for her, and that it is time she should move in the enlarged sphere which her great Creator has assigned her. . . .

Resolved, That the equality of human rights results necessarily from the fact of the identity of the race in capabilities and responsibilities.

Resolved, therefore, That, being invested by the Creator with the same capabilities, and the same consciousness of responsibility for their exercise, it is demonstrably the right and duty of woman . . . to promote every righteous cause by every righteous means . . . and this being a self-evident truth growing out of the divinely implanted principles of human nature, any custom or authority adverse to it, whether modern or wearing the hoary sanction of antiquity, is to be regarded as a self-evident falsehood, and at war with mankind.

Woman's Free Development*

ELIZABETH BLACKWELL, *in a letter to Emily Collins*

(August 12, 1848)

M y whole life is devoted unreservedly to the service of my sex. The study and practice of medicine is in my thought but one means to a great end, for which my very soul yearns with intensest passionate emotion, of which I have dreamed day and night, from my earliest childhood, for which I would offer up my life with triumphant thanksgiving . . . the true ennoblement of woman, the full . . . development of her unknown nature and the consequent redemption of the whole human race. . . .

Women are feeble . . . frivolous at present: ignorant of their own capacities, and undeveloped in thought and feeling; and while they remain so . . . humanity will continue to suffer, and cry in vain for deliverance, for woman has her work to do, and no one can accomplish it for her. She is bound to rise, to try her strength, to break her bonds . . . with quiet strength . . . with cool determination . . . let her do her duty, pursue her highest conviction of right, and firmly grasp whatever she is able to carry.

Much is said of the oppression woman suffers. . . . The exclusion and constraint woman suffers . . . has arisen naturally . . . because woman has desired nothing more, has not felt the soul too large for the body. But when woman, with matured strength, with steady purpose, presents her lofty claim, all barriers will give way. . . . If . . . society will not admit of woman's free development, then society must be remodeled. . . .

*From *The History of Woman Suffrage*, vol. 1.

To Keep a Wife in Subjection*

EMILY COLLINS

(1848)

I was born and lived almost forty years in South Bristol, Ontario County—one of the most secluded spots in Western New York; but from the earliest dawn of reason I pined for that freedom of thought and action that was then denied to all womankind. I revolted in spirit against the customs of society and the laws of the State that crushed my aspirations and debarred me from the pursuit of almost every object worthy of an intelligent, rational mind. But not until that meeting at Seneca Falls in 1848, of the pioneers in the cause, gave this feeling of unrest form and voice, did I take action. Then I summoned a few women in our neighborhood together and formed an Equal Suffrage Society, and sent petitions to our Legislature; but our efforts were little known beyond our circle. . . . Yet there was enough of wrong in our narrow horizon to rouse some thought in the minds of all.

In those early days a husband's supremacy was often enforced in the rural districts by corporeal chastisement, and it was considered by most people as quite right and proper—as much so as the correction of refractory children in like manner. I remember in my own neighborhood a man who was a Methodist class-leader and exhorter, and one who was esteemed a worthy citizen, who, every few weeks, gave his wife a beating with his horsewhip. He said it was necessary, in order to keep her in subjection, and because she scolded so much. Now this wife, surrounded by six or seven little children, whom she must wash, dress, feed, and attend to day and night, was obliged to spin and weave cloth for all the garments of the family. She had to milk the cows, make butter and cheese, do all the cooking, washing, making, and mending for the family, and, with the pains of maternity forced

*From *The History of Woman Suffrage*, vol. 1.

upon her every eighteen months, was whipped by her pious husband, "because she scolded." And pray, why should he not have chastised her? The laws made it his privilege—and the Bible, as interpreted, made it his duty. It is true, women repined at their hard lot; but it was thought to be fixed by a divine decree, for "The man shall rule over thee," and "Wives be subject to your husbands," and "Wives, submit yourselves unto your husbands as unto the Lord," caused them to consider their fate inevitable. . . . It is ever thus; where Theology enchains the soul, the Tyrant enslaves the body. But can any one, who has any knowledge of the laws that govern our being—of heredity and pre-natal influence— be astonished that our jails and prisons are filled with criminals, and our hospitals with sickly specimens of humanity? As long as the mothers of the race are subject to such unhappy conditions, it can never be materially improved. Men exhibit some common sense in breeding all animals except those of their own species.

All through the Anti-Slavery struggle, every word of denunciation of the wrongs of the Southern slave, was, I felt, equally applicable to the wrongs of my own sex. Every argument for the emancipation of the colored man, was equally one for that of woman; and I was surprised that all Abolitionists did not see the similarity in the condition of the two classes. I read, with intense interest, everything that indicated an awakening of public or private thought to the idea that woman did not occupy her rightful position in the organization of society; and, when I read the lectures of Ernestine Rose and the writings of Margaret Fuller, and found that other women entertained the same thoughts that had been seething in my own brain, and realized that I stood not alone, how my heart bounded with joy!

A Demand for the Political Rights of Women*

LUCRETIA MOTT

A discourse delivered in the Assembly buildings (Philadelphia, 1849)

Why should not woman seek to be a reformer? If she is to shrink from being such an iconoclast as shall "break the image of man's lower worship," as so long held up to view; if she is to fear to exercise her reason, and her noblest powers, lest she should be thought to "attempt to act the man," and not "acknowledge his supremacy"; if she is to be satisfied with the narrow sphere assigned her by man, nor aspire to a higher, lest she should transcend the bounds of female delicacy; truly it is a mournful prospect for woman . . . we deny that the present position of woman is her true sphere, until the disabilities and disadvantages, religious, civil, and social, which impede her progress, are removed out of her way. These restrictions have enervated her mind and paralyzed her powers. . . .

So far from her "ambition leading her to attempt to act the man," she needs all the encouragement she can receive, by the removal of obstacles from her path, in order that she may become the "true woman." . . . Let her cultivate all the graces and proper accomplishments of her sex, but let not these degenerate into a kind of effeminacy, in which she is satisfied to be the mere plaything or toy of society, content with outward adornings, and the flattery and fulsome adulation too often addressed to her. . . .

The question is often asked, "What does woman want, more than she enjoys? What is she seeking to obtain? Of what rights is she deprived? What privileges are withheld from her?" I

*From The History of Woman Suffrage, vol. 1.

answer, she asks nothing as favor, but as right; she wants to be acknowledged a moral, responsible being. She is seeking not to be governed by laws in the making of which she has no voice. She is deprived of almost every right in civil society, and is a cipher in the nation. . . . In religious society her disabilities have greatly retarded her progress. Her exclusion . . . marked out for her by her equal brother man . . . is unworthy her true dignity.

In marriage there is assumed superiority on the part of the husband, and admitted inferiority with a promise of obedience on the part of the wife. This subject calls loudly for examination in order that the wrong may be redressed. Customs suited to darker ages in Eastern countries are not binding upon enlightened society. . . .

I tread upon delicate ground in alluding to the institutions of religious associations; but the subject is of so much importance that all which relates to the position of woman should be examined apart from the undue veneration which ancient usage receives.

> Such dupes are men to custom, and so prone
> To reverence what is ancient, and can plead
> A course of long observance for its use,
> That even servitude, the worst of ills,
> Because delivered down from sire to son,
> Is kept and guarded as a sacred thing.

So with woman. She has so long been subject to the disabilities and restrictions with which her progress has been embarrassed, that she has become enervated, her mind to some extent paralyzed; and like those still more degraded by personal bondage, she hugs her chains. Liberty is often presented in its true light, but it is liberty for man. I would not go so far, either as regards the abject slave or woman; for in both cases they may be so degraded by the crushing influences around them, that they may not be sensible of the blessings of freedom. Liberty is not less a blessing, because oppression has so long darkened the mind that it can not appreciate it. I would, therefore, urge that woman be placed in such a situation in society, by the recognition of her rights, and have such opportunities for growth and development, as shall raise her from this low, enervated, and paralyzed condition to a full appreciation . . . of entire freedom of mind.

It is with reluctance that I make the demand for the political rights of women, because this claim is so distasteful to the age. Woman shrinks . . . from taking any interest in politics. The events of the French Revolution, and the claim for woman's rights, are held up to her as a warning . . . but remember that the age was marked with extravagances and wickedness in men as well as women. . . . Who knows but that if woman acted her part in governmental affairs, there might be an entire change in the turmoil of political life? It becomes man to speak modestly of his ability to act without her. If woman's judgment were exercised, why might she not aid in making the laws by which she is governed? Lord Brougham remarked that the works of Harriet Martineau upon Political Economy were not excelled by those of any political writer of the present time. . . .

Professor Walker, of Cincinnati, in his *Introduction to American Law,* says: "With regard to political rights, females form a positive exception to the general doctrine of equality. They have no part or lot in the formation or administration of government. . . . We hold them amenable to the laws when made, but allow them no share in making them. This language applied to males would be the exact definition of political slavery; applied to females custom does not teach us so to regard it."

He further says: "The law of husband and wife, as you gather it from the books, is a disgrace to any civilized nation. The theory of the law degrades the wife almost to the level of slaves. . . . The merging of her name in that of her husband is emblematic of the fate of all her legal rights. The torch of Hymen serves but to light the pile on which these rights are offered up. The legal theory is, that marriage makes the husband and wife one person, and that person is the husband. . . ."

I would ask if such a code of laws does not require change? . . . Hurlbut, in his "Essay upon Human Rights," says: "Rights are human rights, and pertain to human beings without distinction of sex. Laws should not be made for man or for woman, but for mankind. Man was not born to command, nor woman to obey." . . .

Address to the Women of Ohio*

(Salem, Ohio, April 19-20, 1850)

Said to have been written by

JANE ELIZABETH JONES

Governments, at times, manifest an interest in human suffering; but their cold sympathy and tardy efforts seldom avail the sufferer until it is too late. Philanthropists, philosophers, and statesmen study and devise ways and means to ameliorate the condition of the people. Why have they so little practical effect? . . . Let the amelioration process go on . . . the people must be instructed in the Rights of Humanity . . . we learn that rights are coeval with the human race, that every human being, no matter of what color, sex, condition, or clime, possesses those rights upon perfect equality with all others. . . .

Rights may not be usurped on one hand, nor surrendered on the other, because they involve a responsibility that can be discharged only by those to whom they belong. . . . To secure these rights, says the Declaration of Independence, "Governments were instituted among men, deriving their just powers from the consent of the governed"; and "whenever any form of government becomes destructive of those ends, it is the right of the people to alter or abolish it, and to substitute a new government. . . ." *The Government of this country, in common with all others, has never recognized or attempted to protect women as persons possessing the rights of humanity. They have been recognized and protected as appendages to men* [italics added—L.B.T.] without independent rights or political existence, unknown to the law except as victims of its caprice and tyranny. This government, having therefore exercised powers underived from the consent of the governed, and having signally failed to secure the end for which all just

*From *The History of Woman Suffrage*, vol. 1.

government is instituted, should be immediately altered, or abolished. . . .

Woman, over half the globe, is now and always has been but a chattel. Wives are bargained for, bought and sold, as other merchandise, and as a consequence of the annihilation of natural rights, they have no political existence. In Hindostan, the evidence of woman is not received in a court of justice. The Hindu wife, when her husband dies, must yield implicit obedience to the oldest son. In Burmah, they are not allowed to ascend the steps of a court of justice, but are obliged to give their testimony outside of the building. In Siberia, women are not allowed to step across the footprints of men or reindeer. . . . The Moors, for the slightest offense, beat their wives most cruelly. The Tartars believe that women were sent into the world for no other purpose than to be useful, convenient slaves. To these [precedents] our brethren sometimes refer to prove the inferiority of woman, and to excuse the inconsistency of the only Government on earth that has proclaimed the equality of man. An argument worthy its source. . . .

In conclusion, we appeal to our sisters of Ohio to arise from the lethargy of ages; to assert their rights as independent human beings; to demand their true position as equally responsible . . . with their brethren in this world of action. We urge you by your self-respect, by every consideration for the human race, to arise and take possession of your birthright to freedom and equality. Take it not as the gracious boon tendered by the chivalry of superiors, but as your *right,* on every principle of justice and equality. . . .

The Call*

Convention at Worcester, Massachusetts

(October 23-24, 1850)

A Convention will be held at Worcester, Mass., on the 23d and 24th of October next, to consider the question of Woman's Rights, Duties, and Relations. . . .

*From *The History of Woman Suffrage,* vol. 1.

The upward-tending spirit of the age, busy in an hundred forms of effort for the world's redemption from the sins and sufferings which oppress it, has brought this one, which yields to none in importance and urgency, into distinguished prominence. One-half the race are its immediate objects. . . .

Of the many points now under discussion, and demanding a just settlement, the general question of woman's rights and relations comprehends these: Her education—literary, scientific, and artistic; her avocations—industrial, commercial, and professional; her interests—pecuniary, civil, and political; in a word, her rights as an individual, and her functions as a citizen. . . .

Woman has been condemned for her greater delicacy of physical organization, to inferiority of intellectual and moral culture, and to the forfeiture of great social, civil, and religious privileges. In the relation of marriage she has been ideally annihilated and actually enslaved in all that concerns her personal and pecuniary rights, and even in widowed and single life, she is oppressed with such limitation and degradation of labor and avocation, as clearly and cruelly mark the condition of a disabled caste. . . .

The tyranny which degrades and crushes wives and mothers sits no longer lightly on the world's conscience. . . . The signs are encouraging; the time is opportune. Come, then, to this Convention. . . .

Address to the Judiciary Committee
of the Massachusetts Legislature*

MARY UPTON FERRIN

(1850)

Long have our liberties and our lives been lauded to the skies, to our amusement and edification, and until our sex has been as much regaled as has the Southern slave, with "liberty

*From *The History of Woman Suffrage*, vol. 1.

and law." But, says one, "Women are free." So likewise are slaves free to submit to the laws and to their masters. "A married woman is as much the property of her husband, likewise her goods and chattels, as is his horse," says an eminent judge, and he might have added, many of them are treated much worse. No more apt illustration could have been given. Though man can not beat his wife like his horse, he can kill her by abuse—the most pernicious of slow poisons; and, alas, too often does he do it. It is for such unfortunate ones that protection is needed. Existing laws neither do nor can protect them, nor can society, on account of the laws. If they were men, society would protect and defend them. Long, silently, and patiently have they waited until forbearance ceases to be a virtue.

Appeal from Man's Injustice*

PAULINA WRIGHT DAVIS

(Woman's Rights Convention,

Worcester, Mass., 1850)

The reformation we propose in its utmost scope is radical and universal. It is not the mere perfecting of a reform already in motion, a detail of some established plan, but it is an epochal movement—the emancipation of a class, the redemption of half the world, and a conforming reorganization of all social, political, and industrial interests and institutions. Moreover, it is a movement without example among the enterprises of associated reformations. . . .

Our claim must rest on its justice, and conquer by its power of truth. We take the ground that whatever has been achieved for the race belongs to it, and must not be usurped by any class or caste. The rights and liberties of one human being can not be made the property of another, though they were redeemed for him or her by the life of that other; for rights can

*From *The History of Woman Suffrage*, vol. 1.

not be forfeited by way of salvage, and they are, in their nature, unpurchasable and inalienable. We claim for woman a full and generous investiture of all the blessings which the other sex has solely, or by her aid, achieved for itself. We appeal from man's injustice and selfishness to his principles and affections.

Political Economy of Women*

SUSAN B. ANTHONY

(c. 1850)

There has never been, from time immemorial, much difference of opinion concerning woman's right to do a good share in the *drudgery* of the world. But in the renumerative employments, before 1850, she was but sparsely represented. In 1840, when Harriet Martineau visited this country, she found to her surprise that there were only seven vocations, outside home, into which the women of the United States had entered. These were "teaching, needlework, keeping boarders, weaving, type-setting, and folding and stitching in book-bindery." In contrast, it is only necessary to mention that in Massachusetts alone, woman's ingenuity is now employed in nearly 300 different branches of industry. It cannot be added that for doing the same kind and amount of work women are paid men's wages. The census does not include the services of the mother and daughter among the *paid* vocations, though, as is well known, in many instances they do all the housework of the family. They get no wages, and therefore do not appear among the "useful classes." They are not earners, but savers of money. A money*saver* is not a recognized factor, either in political economy or in the State census. The mother, daughter or wife is put down in its pages as "keeping house." If they were paid for their services they would be called "housekeepers," and would have their place among the paid employments.

"AUNT FANNY" WILL SPEAK*

Woman's Rights Meeting in a Barn

Frances D. Gage

(1850)

In 1850 Ohio decided by the votes of her male population to "alter and amend her Constitution." The elected delegates assembled in Cincinnati in the spring of that year.

In view of affecting this legislation the "Woman's Rights Convention" at Salem, Columbiana Co., was called in April, 1850, and memorialized the Delegate Convention, praying that Equal Rights to all citizens of the State be guaranteed by the new Constitution. In May a county meeting was called in McConnelsville, Morgan Co., Ohio. Mrs. H. M. Little, Mrs. M. T. Corner, Mrs. H. Brewster, and myself, were all the women that I knew in that region, even favorable to a movement for the help of women. Two of these only asked for more just laws for married women. One hesitated about the right of suffrage, I alone in the beginning asked for the ballot, and equality before the law for all adult citizens of sound minds, without regard to sex or color. The Freemasons gave their hall for our meeting, but no men were admitted. I drew up a memorial for signatures, praying that the words "white" and "male" be omitted in the new Constitution. I also drew up a paper copying the unequal laws on our statute books with regard to women. We met, Mrs. Harriet Brewster presiding. Some seventy ladies of our place fell in through the day. I read my paper, and Mrs. M. T. Corner gave a historical account of noted women of the past. It was a new thing. At the close, forty names were placed on the memorial. For years I had been talking and writing, and people were used to my "craziness." But who expected Mrs. Corner and others to take such a stand! Of course, we were heartily abused.

*From *The History of Woman Suffrage*, vol. 1.

This led to the calling of a county meeting at Chesterfield, Morgan County. It was advertised to be held in the M. E. Church. There were only present some eight ladies, including the four above mentioned. We four "scoffers" hired a hack and rode sixteen miles over the hill, before 10 A.M., to be denied admittance to church or school-house. Rev. Matthews had found us shelter on the threshing-floor of a fine barn, and we found about three or four hundred of the farmers, and their wives, sons, and daughters, assembled. They were nearly all "Quakers" and Abolitionists, but then not much inclined to "woman's rights." . . .

The farmers' wives brought huge boxes and pans of provisions. Men and women made speeches, and many names were added to our memorial. On the whole, we had a delightful day. It was no uncommon thing in those days for Abolitionist, or Methodist, or other meetings, to be held under the trees, or in large barns, when school-houses would not hold the people. But to shut up doors against women was a new thing.

In December of 1851 I was invited to attend a Woman's Rights Convention at the town of Mount Gilead, Morrow Co., Ohio. A newspaper call promised that celebrities would be on hand, etc. I wrote I would be there. It was two days' journey, by steamboat and rail. The call was signed "John Andrews," and John Andrews promised to meet me at the cars. I went. It was fearfully cold, and John met me. He was a beardless boy of nineteen, looking much younger. We drove at once to the "Christian Church." On the way he cheered me by saying "he was afraid nobody would come, for all the people said nobody would come for his asking." When we got to the house, there was not one human soul on hand, no fire in the old rusty stove, and the rude, unpainted board benches, all topsy-turvy. I called some boys playing near, asked their names, put them on paper, five of them, and said to them, "Go to every house in this town and tell everybody that 'Aunt Fanny' will speak here at 11 A.M., and if you get fifty to come and hear, I will give you each ten cents." They scattered off upon the run. I ordered John to right the benches, picked up chips and kindlings, borrowed a brand of fire at the next door, had a good hot stove, and the floor swept, and was ready for my audience at the appointed time. John had done his work well, and fifty at least were on hand, and . . . I said my say, and before 1 P.M., we adjourned appointing another session at 3, and one for 7 P.M., and three for the following day. . . .

Sojourner Truth*

Reminiscences by Frances D. Gage

(Convention at Akron, Ohio,
May 28-29, 1951)

The leaders of the movement trembled on seeing a tall, gaunt black woman in a gray dress and white turban, surmounted with a sun-bonnet, march deliberately into the church, walk with the air of a queen up the aisle, and take her seat upon the pulpit steps. . . .

Morning, afternoon, and evening exercises came and went. Through all these sessions old Sojourner, quiet and reticent as the "Lybian Statue," sat crouched against the wall on the corner of the pulpit stairs, her sun-bonnet shading her eyes, her elbows on her knees, her chin resting upon her broad, hard palms. At intermission she was busy selling the "Life of Sojourner Truth," a narrative of her own strange and adventurous life. . . .

The second day the work waxed warm. . . . There were very few women in those days who dared to "speak in meeting"; and the august teachers of the people were seemingly getting the better of us. . . . Some of the tender-skinned friends were on the point of losing dignity, and the atmosphere betokened a storm. When, slowly from her seat in the corner rose Sojourner Truth, who, till now, had scarcely lifted her head. . . . She moved slowly and solemnly to the front, laid her old bonnet at her feet, and turned her great speaking eyes to me. There was a hissing sound of disapprobation above and below. I rose and announced "Sojourner Truth," and begged the audience to keep silence for a few moments.

The tumult subsided at once, and every eye was fixed on this almost Amazon form, which stood nearly six feet high, head erect, and eyes piercing the upper air like one in a dream.

*From *The History of Woman Suffrage*, vol. 1.

At her first word there was a profound hush. She spoke in deep tones, which, though not loud, reached every ear in the house, and away through the throng at the doors and windows.

"Where there is so much racket there must be somethin' out of kilter. I think that between the Negroes of the South and the women at the North, all talkin' about rights, the white men will be in a fix pretty soon. But what's all this here talkin' about?

"That man over there says that woman needs to be helped into carriages, and lifted over ditches, and to have the best place everywhere. Nobody ever helps me into carriages, or over mud-puddles, or gives me any best place."

And raising herself to her full height, and her voice to a pitch like rolling thunder, she asked:

"And ain't I a woman? Look at me! Look at my arm [and she bared her right arm to the shoulder, showing her tremendous muscular power]. I have ploughed, and planted, and gathered into barns, and no man could head me! And ain't I a woman? I could work as much and eat as much as a man— when I could get it—and bear the lash as well! And ain't I a woman? I have borne thirteen children, and seen most all sold off to slavery, and when I cried out with my mother's grief, none but Jesus heard me! And ain't I a woman?

"Then they talk about this thing in the head; what do they call it? ["Intellect," whispered some one near.] That's it. What's that got to do with woman's rights or Negroes' rights? If my cup won't hold but a pint, and yours holds a quart, wouldn't you be mean not to let me have my little half-measure full?"

The cheering was long and loud. She continued:

"Then that little man in black there, he says women can't have as much rights as men, 'cause Christ wasn't a woman! Where did your Christ come from?"

Rolling thunder couldn't have stilled that crowd, as did those deep, wonderful tones, as she stood there with outstretched arms and eyes of fire. Raising her voice still louder, she repeated.

"Where did your Christ come from? From God and a woman! Man had nothin' to do with Him."

Turning again to another objector, she took up the defense of Mother Eve. . . . "If the first woman God ever made was strong enough to turn the world upside down all alone, these women together [and she glanced her eye over the platform] ought to be able to turn it back, and get it right side up again! And now they are asking to do it, the men better let 'em."

Amid roars of applause, she returned to her corner. . . . I have never in my life seen anything like the magical influence that subdued the mobbish spirit of the day, and turned the sneers and jeers of an excited crowd into notes of respect and admiration.

Women Must Be Educated with a View to Action*

HARRIET MARTINEAU, *in a letter to*
Paulina Wright Davis
(1851)

Ever since I became capable of thinking for myself, I have clearly seen . . . that there can be but one true method in the treatment of each human being, of either sex, of any color, and under any outward circumstances, to ascertain what are the powers of that being, to cultivate them to the utmost, and *then* to see what action they will find for themselves. . . . It has certainly never been done for women. . . .

Women, like men, must be educated with a view to action, or their studies can not be called education, and no judgment can be formed of the scope of their faculties. The pursuit must be life's business, or it will be mere pastime or irksome task.
. . .

My conviction always was, that an intelligence never carried out into action could not be worth much; and that, if all the action of human life was of a character so tainted as to be unfit for women, it could be no better for men, and we ought all to sit down together, to let barbarism overtake us once more.

My own conviction is, that the natural action of the whole human being occasions not only the most strength, but the highest elevation; not only the warmest sympathy, but the deepest purity. The highest and purest beings among women seem now to be those who, far from being idle, find among their restricted opportunities some means of strenuous action; and I can not doubt that, if an active social career were open to all women, with due means of preparation for it, those who are high and holy now, would be high and holy then, and would be joined by an innumerable company of just spirits from among those whose energies are now pining and fretting in enforced idleness, or unworthy frivolity, or brought down into pursuits and aims which are anything but pure and peaceable. . . .

I Groaned for Forty Years*

MEHITABEL HASKELL

(Worcester Convention, October 15-16, 1851)

Perhaps, my friends, I ought to apologize for standing here. Perhaps I attach too much importance to my own age. This meeting, as I understand it, was called to discuss Woman's Rights. Well, I do not pretend to know exactly what woman's rights are; but I do know that I have groaned for forty years, yea, for fifty years, under a sense of woman's wrongs. I know that even when a girl, I groaned under the idea that I could not receive as much instruction as my brothers could. I wanted to be what I felt I was capable of becoming, but opportunity was denied me. I rejoice in the progress that has been made. I rejoice that so many women are here; it denotes that they are waking up to some sense of their situation. . . .

*From *The History of Woman Suffrage*, vol. 1.

Remove the Legal Shackles from Woman*

Ernestine Rose

(Second National Convention in Worcester, 1851)

Even here, in this far-famed land of freedom, under a Republic that has inscribed on its banner the great truth that "all men are created free and equal, and endowed with inalienable rights to life, liberty, and the pursuit of happiness"—a declaration borne, like the vision of hope, on wings of light to the remotest parts of the earth, an omen of freedom to the oppressed and down-trodden children of man—when, even here, in the very face of this eternal truth, woman, the mockingly so-called "better half" of man, has yet to plead for her rights, nay, for her life. For what is life without liberty, and what is liberty without equality of rights? And as for the pursuit of happiness, she is not allowed to choose any line of action that might promote it; she has only thankfully to accept what man in his magnanimity decides as best for her to do, and this is what he does not choose to do himself. . . .

At marriage she loses her entire identity, and her being is said to have become merged in her husband. Has nature thus merged it? Has she ceased to exist and feel pleasure and pain? . . . What an inconsistency, that from the moment she enters that compact, in which she assumes the high responsibility of wife and mother, she ceases legally to exist, and becomes a purely submissive being. Blind submission in woman is considered a virtue, while submission to wrong is itself wrong, and resistance to wrong is virtue, alike in woman as in man.

But it will be said that the husband provides for the wife, or in other words, he feeds, clothes, and shelters her! I wish I had the power to make every one before me fully realize the degradation contained in that idea. Yes! he *keeps* her, and so

*From *The History of Woman Suffrage*, vol. 1.

he does a favorite horse; by law they are both considered his property. . . .

Again, I shall be told that the law presumes the husband to be kind, affectionate, and ready to provide for and protect his wife. But what right, I ask, has the law to presume at all on the subject? What right has the law to entrust the interest and happiness of one being into the hands of another? And if the merging of the interest of one being into the other is a necessary consequence on marriage, why should woman always remain on the losing side? Turn the tables. Let the identity and interest of the husband be merged in the wife. . . .

We have hardly an adequate idea how all-powerful law is in forming public opinion, in giving tone and character to the mass of society. To illustrate my point, look at that infamous, detestable law, which was written in human blood, and signed and sealed with life and liberty, that eternal stain on the statute book of this country, the Fugitive Slave Law. Think you that before its passage, you could have found any in the free States—except a few politicians in the market—base enough to desire such a law? No! no! Even those who took no interest in the slave question, would have shrunk from so barbarous a thing. But no sooner was it passed, than the ignorant mass, the rabble of the self-styled Union Safety Committee, found out that we were a law-loving, law-abiding people! Such is the magic power of Law. . . . Hence . . . the reason why we call on the nation to remove the legal shackles from woman, and it will have a beneficial effect on that still greater tyrant she has to contend with, Public Opinion.

Carry out the republican principle of universal suffrage, or strike it from your banners and substitute "Freedom and Power to one half of society, and Submission and Slavery to the other." . . .

No! there is no reason against woman's elevation, but there are deep-rooted, hoary-headed prejudices. The main cause of them is, a pernicious falsehood propagated against her being, namely, that she is inferior by her nature. Inferior in what? What has man ever done, that woman. . . could not do? . . .

On Medical Education of Women[*]

HARRIOT K. HUNT

(Westchester, Pennsylvania, Convention, June 2, 1852)

1st. *Resolved,* That the present position of medical organizations, precluding women from the same educational advantages with men, under pretext of delicacy, virtually acknowledges the impropriety of his being her medical attendant.

2nd. *Resolved,* That we will do all in our power to sustain those women who, from a conviction of duty, enter the medical profession, in their efforts to overcome the evils that have accumulated in their path, and in attacking the strongholds of vice.

. 3rd. *Resolved,* That the past actions and present indications of our medical schools should not affect us at all; and notwithstanding Geneva and Cleveland Medical Colleges closed their doors after graduating one woman each, and Harvard, through the false delicacy of the students, declared it inexpedient to receive one who had been in successful practice many years, we would still earnestly follow in peace and love where duty points, and leave the verdict to an enlightened public sentiment.

*From *The History of Woman Suffrage,* vol. 1.

A Dissolution of the Existing Social Compact*

Elizabeth Oakes Smith
(Syracuse National Convention, September, 1852)

My friends, do we realize for what purpose we are convened? Do we fully understand that we aim at nothing less than an entire subversion of the present order of society, a dissolution of the whole existing social compact? Do we see that it is not an error of today, nor of yesterday, against which we are lifting up the voice of dissent, but that it is against the hoary-headed error of all times—error borne onward from the foot-prints of the first pair ejected from Paradise, down to our own time? . . .

We are said to be a "few disaffected, embittered women, met for the purpose of giving vent to petty personal spleen and domestic discontent." I repel the charge; and I call upon every woman here to repel the charge. . . .

Bitterness is the child of wrong; if any one of our number has become embittered . . . it is because social wrong has so penetrated to the inner life that we are crucified thereby. . . . All who take their stand against false institutions, are in some sense embittered. The conviction of wrong has wrought mightily in them. Their large hearts took in the whole sense of human woe, and bled for those who had become brutalized by its weight, and they spoke as never man spoke in his own individualism, but as the embodied race will speak, when the . . . time shall come. . . .

*From *The History of Woman Suffrage*, vol. 1.

A Plan of Action*

MATILDA JOSLYN GAGE

(Syracuse National Convention,

September, 1852)

This Convention has assembled to discuss the subject of Woman's Rights, and form some settled plan of action for the future. . . . Women are now in the situation of the mass of mankind a few years since, when science and learning were in the hands of the priests, and property was held by vassalage. The Pope and the priests claimed to be not only the teachers, but the guides of the people; the laity were not permitted to examine for themselves; education was held to be unfit for the masses, while the tenure of their landed property was such as kept them in a continual state of dependence on their feudal lords.

It was but a short time since the most common rudiments of education were deemed sufficient for any woman; could she but read tolerably and write her own name it was enough. Trammeled as women have been by might and custom, there are still many shining examples, which serve as beacon lights to show what may be attained by genius, labor, energy, and perseverance combined.

Although so much has been said of woman's unfitness for public life, it can be seen, from Semiramis to Victoria, that she has a peculiar fitness for governing. In poetry, Sappho was honored with the title of the Tenth Muse. Helena Lucretia Corano, in the seventeenth century, was of such rare scientific attainments, that the most illustrious persons in passing through Venice, were more anxious to see her than all the curiosities of the city; she was made a doctor, receiving the title of Unalterable. Mary Cunity, of Silesia, in the sixteenth century, was one of the most able astronomers of her time. Anna Maria Schureman was a sculptor, engraver, musician, and painter.

*From *The History of Woman Suffrage*, vol. 1.

With the learning, energy, and perseverance of Lady Jane Grey, Mary and Elizabeth, all are familiar. Mrs. Cowper was spoken of by Montague as standing at the head of all that is called learned, and that every critic veiled his bonnet at her superior judgment. . . . Caroline Herschell shares the fame of her brother as an astonomer. The greatest triumphs of the present age in the drama, music, and literature have been achieved by women, among whom may be mentioned Charlotte Cushman, Jenny Lind, the Misses Carey, Mrs. Stowe, and Margaret Fuller. Mrs. Somerville's renown has long been spread over both continents as one of the first mathematicians of the present age.

Self-reliance is one of the first lessons to be taught our daughters; they should be educated with our sons, and equally with them, taught to look forward to some independent means of support, either to one of the professions or the business best fitted to exercise their talents. Being placed in a position compelling them to act has caused many persons to discover talents in themselves they were before unaware of possessing.

Let us look at the rights it is boasted women now possess. After marriage the husband and wife are considered as one person in law, which I hold to be false from the very laws applicable to married parties. Were it so, the act of one would be as binding as the act of the other, and wise legislators would not need to enact statutes defining the peculiar rights of each; were it so, a woman could not legally be a man's inferior. Such a thing would be a veritable impossibility. One-half of a person can not be made the protection or direction of the other half. Blackstone says "a woman may indeed be attorney for her husband, for that implies no separation from, but rather a representation of, her lord. And a husband may also bequeath anything to his wife by will; for it can not take effect till the coverture is determined by his death." After stating at considerable length the reasons showing their unity, the learned commentator proceeds to cut the knot, and show they are not one, but are considered as two persons, one superior, the one inferior, and not only so, but the inferior in the eye of the law as acting from compulsion.

A Revolution in Human Society*

Mariana Johnson

(Westchester, Pennsylvania, June 2, 1852)

The position in which woman has been placed is an anomaly. On the one hand she is constantly reminded of duties and responsibilities from which an angel might shrink. The world is to be saved by her prayers, her quiet and gentle efforts. Man, she is told, is ruled by her smiles; his whole nature subdued by the potency of her tears. Priests, politicians, and poets assure her with flattering tongue, that on her depend the progress and destiny of the race. On the other hand, she is told that she must lovingly confide in the strength and skill of man, who has been endowed with superior intellectual powers; that she must count it her highest honor to reflect upon the world the light of his intelligence and wisdom, as the moon reflects the light of the sun!

We may congratulate one another on this occasion in view of the cheering indications so manifest on every hand that the ignorance and darkness which have so long brooded over the prospects of woman, are beginning to give place to the light of truth. In the summer of 1848, in the village of Seneca Falls, a small number of women, disregarding alike the sneers of the ignorant and the frowns of the learned, assembled in Convention and boldly claimed for themselves, and for their sex, the rights . . . so long withheld by man. Their courageous words were the expression of sentiments which others had felt as deeply as themselves, but which the restraints imposed by long-established custom had taught them to suppress. But now the hour had come, and the world stood prepared for the reception of a new thought, which is destined to work a revolution in human society, more beneficent than any that has preceded it. The seeds of truth which that Convention planted in faith and hope were not left to perish. . . .

*From *The History of Woman Suffrage*, vol. 1.

Woman at length is awaking from the slumber of ages. Many of the sex already perceive that knowledge, sound judgment, and perfect freedom of thought and action are quite as important for the mothers as for the fathers of the race. They weary of the senseless talk of "woman's sphere." . . . Woman begins to grow weary of her helpless and dependent position, and of being treated as if she were formed only to cultivate her affections, that they may flow in strong and deep currents merely to gratify the self-love of man.

She does not listen with delight, as she once did, when she hears her relations to her equal brother represented by the poetical figure of the trellis and creeping tendril, or of the oak and the gracefully clinging vine. No, she feels that she is. like him, an accountable being. . . . She sees the glaring injustice by which she has long been deprived of all fair opportunity to earn an independent livelihood, and thus, in too many instances, constrained to enter the marriage relation, as a choice of evils, to secure herself against the ills of impending poverty. The wrong she so deeply feels she is at length arousing herself to redress.

What Does Woman Want?*

Ann Preston

(Westchester, Pennsylvania, Convention, 1852)

The question is repeatedly asked by those who have thought but little upon the subject of woman's position in society. "What does woman want more than she possesses already? Is she not beloved, honored, guarded, cherished? Wherein are her rights infringed, or her liberties curtailed?"

Glowing pictures have been drawn of the fitness of the present relations of society, and of the beauty of woman's dependence upon the protecting love of man, and frightful visions have been evoked of the confusion and perversion of nature

*From *The History of Woman Suffrage*, vol. 1.

which would occur if the doctrine of the equal rights of man and woman was once admitted.

The idea seems to prevail that movements for the elevation of woman arise, not from the legitimate wants of society, but from the vague restlessness of unquiet spirits; not from the serene dictates of wisdom, but from the headlong impulses of fanaticism. . . .

We ask that woman shall have free access to vocations of profit and honor, the means of earning a livelihood and independence for herself! As a general rule, profitable employments are not considered open to woman. . . .

Their pursuits are to be determined, not by their inclination, judgment, and ability, as are those of man, but by the popular estimate of what is proper and becoming. In Turkey public delicacy is outraged if a woman appears unveiled beyond the walls of the harem; in America a sentiment no less arbitrary presumes to mark out for her the precise boundaries of womanly propriety; and she who ventures to step beyond them, must do it at the peril of encountering low sneers, coarse allusions, and the withering imputation of want of feminine delicacy.

Even for the same services woman generally receives less than man. The whole tendency of our customs, habits, and teaching, is to make her dependent—dependent in outward circumstances, dependent in spirit. . . .

Those who are best acquainted with the state of society know that there is, at this time, a vast amount of unhappiness among women for want of free outlets to their powers; that thousands are yearning for fuller development, and a wider field of usefulness. The same energies which in man find vent in the professions, and in the thousand forms of business and study, must find an ennobling channel in woman, else they will be frittered away in trifles, or turned into instruments to prey upon their possessor. . . .

It is recognized, in reference to man, that his judgment, opportunities, and abilities are the proper measure of his sphere. "The tools to him who can use them." But the same principles are not trusted in their application to woman, lest, forsooth, she should lose her feminine characteristics, and, like the Pleiad, forsake her native sphere! . . .

We demand for woman a more complete physical, intellectual, and moral education. . . .

We believe that woman, as an accountable being, can not innocently merge her individuality in that of her brother, or accept from him the limitations of her sphere. In all life's great extremities she also is thrown upon her inward resources, and stands alone. Man can not step in between her and the "accusing angel" of her own conscience; alone in the solitude of her spirit she must wrestle with her own sorrows; none can walk for her "the valley of the shadow of death!" . . .

The Women Want Their Rights*

SOJOURNER TRUTH

(Broadway Tabernacle, September 6-7, 1853)

I come forth to speak about Woman's Rights. . . . We have all been thrown down so low that nobody thought we'd ever get up again; but we have been long enough trodden now; we will come up again. . . .

I was thinking, when I see women contending for their rights, I was thinking what a difference there is now, and what there was in old times . . . in the old times the kings of the earth would hear a woman. There was a king in the Scriptures; and then it was the kings of the earth would kill a woman if she came into their presence; but Queen Esther came forth, for she was oppressed, and felt there was a great wrong, and she said I will die or I will bring my complaint before the king. Should the king of the United States be greater, or more crueler, or more harder? But the king, he raised his sceptre and said: "Thy request should be granted unto thee—to the half of my kingdom will I grant it to thee!" . . . The women want their rights as Esther. . . .

Now, women do not ask half of a kingdom, but their rights, and they don't get them. When she comes to demand them, don't you hear how sons hiss their mothers like snakes, because they ask for their rights; and can they ask for anything less? . . . But we'll have our rights; see if we don't; and you can't stop us from them; see if you can. You may hiss as much as you like, but it is coming. Women don't get half as much rights as they ought to; we want more, and we will have it. . . .

*From *The History of Woman Suffrage*, vol. 1.

The Pulpit Has a Bad Influence*

ABBY KELLY FOSTER

(Cleveland National Convention,
October 6-8, 1853)

I want to say here that I believe the law is but the writing out of public sentiment, and back of that public sentiment, I contend lies the responsibility. Where shall we find it? "'Tis education forms the common mind." Now if we can ascertain who has had the education of us, we can ascertain who is responsible for the law, and for public sentiment. Who takes the infant from its cradle and baptizes it "in the name of the Father, Son, and Holy Ghost;" and when that infant comes to childhood, who takes it into Sabbath-schools; who on every Sabbath day, while its mind is "like clay in the hands of the potter," moulds and fashions it as he will; and when that child comes to be a youth where is he found one-seventh part of the time; and when he comes to maturer age does he not leave his plow in the furrow and his tools in the shop, and one-seventh part of the time go to the place where prayer is wont to be made? . . . for we are taught that we must not think our own thoughts, but must lay our own wills aside, and come to be moulded and fashioned by the priest. . . .

It is the pulpit, then, which has the entire ear of the community, one-seventh part of the time. If you say there are exceptions, very well, that proves the rule. If there is one family who do not go to church, it is no matter, its teachings are engendered by those who do go; hence I would say, not only does the pulpit have the ear of the community one-seventh part of the time of childhood, but it has it under circumstances for forming and moulding and fashioning the young mind, as no other educating influence can have it. The pulpit has it, not only under these circumstances; it has it on

*From *The History of Woman Suffrage*, vol. 1.

occasions of marriage . . . on occasions of sickness and death, when all the world beside is shut out, when the mind is most susceptible of impressions from the pulpit, or any other source.

You may tell me, that it is woman who forms the mind of the child; but I charge it back again, that it is the minister who forms the mind of the woman. It is he who makes the mother what she is; therefore her teaching of the child is only conveying the instructions of the pulpit at second hand. If public sentiment is wrong on this . . . the pulpit is responsible for it, and has the power of changing. The clergy claim the credit of establishing public schools. Granted. Listen to the pulpit in any matter of humanity, and they will claim the originating of it, because they are the teachers of the people. Now if we give credit to the pulpit for establishing public schools, then I charge them with having a bad influence over those schools. . . .

Disappointment Is the Lot of Woman*

LUCY STONE

(Convention at Cincinnati, October 17-18, 1855)

From the first years to which my memory stretches, I have been a disappointed woman. When with my brothers, I reached forth after the sources of knowledge, I was reproved with "It isn't fit for you; it doesn't belong to women." Then there was but one college in the world where women were admitted, and that was in Brazil. I would have found my way there, but by the time I was prepared to go, one was opened in the young State of Ohio—the first in the United States where women and Negroes could enjoy opportunities with white men. I was disappointed when I came to seek a profession worthy an immortal being—every employment was closed to me, except those of the teacher, the seamstress, and the housekeeper. *In education, in marriage, in religion, in everything, disappointment is the lot of woman. It shall be the*

*From *The History of Woman Suffrage*, vol. 1.

*business of my life to deepen this disappointment in every
woman's heart until she bows down to it no longer* [italics
added—L.B.T.]. I wish that women, instead of being walking
show-cases, instead of begging of their fathers and brothers
the latest and gayest new bonnet, would ask of them their
rights.

The question of Woman's Rights is a practical one. The
notion has prevailed that it was only a ephemeral idea; that
it was but women claiming the right to smoke cigars in the
streets, and to frequent bar-rooms. Others have supposed it a
question of comparative intellect; others still, of sphere. Too
much has already been said and written about woman's sphere.
Trace all the doctrines to their source and they will be found
to have no basis except in the usages and prejudices of the age.
This is seen in the fact that what is tolerated in woman in one
country is not tolerated in another. In this country women
may hold prayer-meetings, etc., but in Mohammedan countries it is written upon their mosques, "Women and dogs, and
other impure animals, are not permitted to enter." Wendell
Phillips says, "The best and greatest thing one is capable of
doing, that is his sphere." . . . Leave women, then, to find
their sphere. And do not tell us before we are born even, that
our province is to cook dinners, darn stockings, and sew on
buttons. We are told woman has all the rights she wants; and
even women, I am ashamed to say, tell us so. They mistake
the politeness of men for rights—seats, while men stand in
this hall to-night, and their adulations; but these are mere
courtesies. We want rights. The merchant, the house-
builder, and the postman charge us no less on account of our
sex; but when we endeavor to earn money to pay all these,
then, indeed, we find the difference. Man, if he have energy,
may hew out for himself a path where no mortal has ever
trod, held back by nothing but what is in himself; the world
is all before him. . . . But the same society that drives forth
the young man, keeps woman at home—a dependent—
working little cats on worsted, and little dogs on punctured
paper; but if she goes heartily and bravely to give herself to
some worthy purpose, she is out of her sphere and she loses
caste. Women working in tailor-shops are paid one-third as
much as men. Some one in Philadelphia has stated that
women make fine shirts for twelve and a half cents apiece;
that no women can make more than nine a week, and the sum
thus earned, after deducting rent, fuel, etc., leaves her just
three and a half cents a day for bread. Is it a wonder that
women are driven to prostitution? Female teachers in New

York are paid fifty dollars a year, and for every such situation there are five hundred applicants. . . . The present condition of woman causes a horrible perversion of the marriage relation. It is asked of a lady, "Has she married well?" "Oh, yes, her husband is rich." Woman must marry for a home. . . .

The widening of woman's sphere is to improve her lot. Let us do it, and if the world scoff, let it scoff—if it sneer, let it sneer. . . .

Civil and Political Existence of Women*

ELIZABETH CADY STANTON

(A letter to Lucy Stone, National Convention, Cooper Institute, 1856)

We may continue to hold our Conventions, we may talk of our right to vote, to legislate, to hold property, but until we can arouse in woman a proper self-respect, she will hold in contempt the demands we now make for our sex. We shall never get what we ask for until the majority of women are openly with us; and they will never claim their civil rights until they know their social wrongs. . . . How is it that woman can any longer silently consent to her present false position? How can she calmly contemplate the barbarous code of laws which govern her civil and political existence? How can she devoutly subscribe to a theology which makes her the conscientious victim of another's will, forever subject to the triple bondage of the man, the priest, and the law? How can she tolerate our social customs, by which womankind is stripped of all . . . virtue, dignity, and nobility? How can she endure our present marriage relations, by which woman's life, health, and happiness are held so cheap, that she herself feels . . . no individuality of her own. . . . She patiently bears all this because in her blindness she sees no way of escape. Her bondage, though it differs from that of the Negro slave, frets and chafes her just the same. She too sighs and groans in her chains; and lives but in the hope of better things to come. She looks to heaven; whilst the more philosophical slave sets out for Canada. . . .

Marriage, as we now have it, is opposed to all God's laws. It is by no means an equal partnership. The silent partner loses everything. On the domestic sign, the existence of a second person is not recognized by even the ordinary abbreviation, Co. There is the establishment of John Jones. Perhaps his partner supplies all the cents and the senses—but no one knows who she is or whence she came. If John is a luminous body, she shines in his reflection; if not, she hides herself in his shadow. But she is nameless, for a woman has no name! She is Mrs. John or James, Peter or Paul, just as she changes masters; like the Southern slave, she takes the name of her owner. Many people consider this a very small matter; but it is the symbol of the most cursed monopoly on this footstool; a monopoly by man of all the rights, the life, the liberty, and happiness of one-h lf of the human family—all womankind. For what man can honestly deny that he has not a secret feeling that where his pleasure and woman's seems to conflict, the woman must be sac. 'ficed; and what is worse, woman herself has come to think so too. . . . This sentiment pervades the laws, customs, and religions of countries, both Christian and heathen. Is it any wond'r then, that woman regards herself as a mere machine, a to. or men's pleasure? Verily is she a hopeless victim of his morb 'ly developed passions. . . .

Call yourselves . . . wor n, you who sacrifice all that is great . . . for an ignoble peace, who betray the best interests of the race for a temporary ease? . . . What mean these asylums all over the land for the deaf and dumb, the maim and blind, the idiot and the raving maniac? What all these advertisements in our public prints, these family guides, these female medicines. . . . Do not all these things show to what a depth of degradation the women . . . have fallen, how false they have been to the . . . instincts of their nature. . . .

The first step in this improvement is the elevation of woman. . . .

This Is the Negro's Hour*

Elizabeth Cady Stanton

(New York, December 26, 1865)

"This is the negro's hour." Are we sure that he, once entrenched in all his inalienable rights, may not be an added power to hold us at bay? Have not "black male citizens" been heard to say they doubted the wisdom of extending the right of suffrage to women? Why should the African prove more just and generous than his Saxon compeers? If the two millions of Southern black women are not to be secured in their rights of person, property, wages, and children, their emancipation is but another form of slavery. . . . We who know what absolute power the statute laws of most of the States give man, in all his civil, political, and social relations, demand that in changing the status of the four millions of Africans, the women as well as the men shall be secured in all the rights, privileges, and immunities of citizens.

It is all very well for the privileged order to look down complacently and tell us, "This is the negro's hour; do not clog his way; do not embarrass the Republican party with any new issue; be generous and magnanimous; the negro once safe, the woman comes next." Now, if our prayer involved a new set of measures, or a new train of thought, it would be cruel to tax "white male citizens" with even two simple questions at a time; but the disfranchised all make the same demand, and the same logic and justice that secures suffrage to one class gives it to all. The struggle, of the last thirty years has not been merely on the black man as such, but on the broader ground of his humanity. Our Fathers, at the end of the first revolution, in their desire for a speedy readjustment of all their difficulties, and in order to present to Great Britain, their common enemy, an united front, accepted the compromise urged on them by South

*From *The History of Woman Suffrage*, vol. 2.

Carolina, and a century of wrong, ending in another revolution, has been the result of their action. This is our opportunity to retrieve the errors of the past and mould anew the elements of Democracy. The nation is ready for a long step in the right direction; party lines are obliterated, and all men are thinking for themselves. If our rulers have the justice to give the black man suffrage, woman should avail herself of that new-born virtue to secure her rights; if not, she should begin with renewed earnestness to educate the people into the idea of universal suffrage.

Petition of the Smith Sisters[*]

(Glastonbury, Connecticut, 1878)

The Petition of Julia E. Smith and Abby H. Smith, of Glastonbury, to the Senate of the State of Connecticut:

This is the first time we have petitioned your honorable body, having twice come before the House of Assembly, which the last time gave a majority that we should vote in town affairs; but it was negatived in the Senate.

We now pray the highest court in our native State that we may be relieved from the stigma of birth. For forty years since the death of our father have we suffered intensely f being born women. We cannot even stand up for the princi ples of our forefathers (who fought and bled for them) without having our property seized and sold at the sign-post, which we have suffered four times; and have also seen eleven acres of our meadow-land sold to an ugly neighbor for a tax of fifty dollars—land worth more than $2,000. And a threat is given out that our house shall be ransacked and despoiled of articles most dear to us, the work of lamented members of our family who have gone before us, and all this is done without the least excuse of right or justice. We are told that it is the law of the land made by the legislature and done to us, two defenceless women, who have never broken these laws, made by not half the citizens of this State. And it was said in our Declaration of Independence that "Governments derive their just powers from the consent of the governed."

[*]From *The History of Woman Suffrage*, vol. 3.

For being born women we are obliged to help support those who have earned nothing, and who, by gambling, drinking, and the like, have come to poverty, and these same can vote away what we have earned with our own hands. And when men meet to take off the dollar poll-tax, the bill for the dinner comes in for the women to pay. Neither have we husband, or brother, or son, or even nephew, or cousin, to help us. All men will acknowledge that it is wrong to take a woman's property without her consent as to take a man's without his consent; and such wrong we suffer wholly for being born women, which we are in no wise to blame for. To be sure, for our consolation, we are upheld by the learned, the wise and the good, from all parts of the country, having received communications from thirty-two of our States, as well as from over the seas, that we are in the right, and from many of the best men in our own State. But they have no power to help us. We therefore now pray your honorable body, who have power, with the House of Assembly, to relieve us of this stigma of birth, and grant that we may have the same privileges before the law as though we were born men. And this, as in duty bound, we will ever pray.

Julia and Abby Smith
Glastonbury, Conn., Jan. 29, 1878

A Female Soldier*

(1865)

There is a female here appealing for five months' back pay due her as a soldier in the army. Her name is Mary E. Wise. She is an orphan, without a blood relative in the world, and was a resident of Jefferson Township, Huntington County, Indiana, where she enlisted in the 34th Indiana Volunteers under the name of William Wise. She served two years and eighteen days as a private, participating in six of the heaviest engagements in the West, was wounded at Chickamauga and Lookout Mountain, at the latter place severely in the side. Upon the discovery of her sex, through her last wound, she was sent to her home in Indiana. When she arrived there, her step-mother refused her shelter, or to assist her in any way. Having five months' pay due from the Government, she

*From *The History of Woman Suffrage,* vol. 2.

started for Washington, in the hope of collecting it, arriving in this city on the 4th instant. Here her troubles have only increased. She can not get her pay. Her colonel probably, under the circumstances, not deeming it necessary, failed to give her a proper or formal discharge, with the necessary papers. In her difficulties she has, repeatedly, endeavored to refer her case to the President, but, not having influential friends to back her, she has been disappointed in all her efforts to see him, and the Department can pay her only upon proper or formal discharge papers, etc. So she is here, without friends or means, wholly dependent upon the bounty of the Sanitary Commission.

Women As Soldiers*

(1866)

There are many and interesting records of women who served in Iowa, Ohio, Michigan, Minnesota, Illinois, Indiana, Kansas, New York, and Pennsylvania Regiments, in the armies of the Potomac, the Cumberland, the Tennessee, in cavalry, artillery, on foot. A woman was one of the eighteen soldiers sent as a scout at Lookout Mountain—whose capture was deemed impossible—to ascertain the position of General Bragg's forces; and a woman performed one of the most daring naval exploits of the war. It was a woman of Brooklyn, N.Y., who, inspired with the idea that she was to be the country's savior, joined the army in spite of parental opposition, and during the bloody battle of Lookout Mountain, fell pierced in the side, a mortal wound, by a minie ball. Elizabeth Compton served over a year in the 25th Michigan cavalry; was wounded at the engagement of Greenbrier Bridge, Tennessee, her sex being discovered upon her removal to the hospital, at Lebanon, Kentucky, where, upon recovery, she was discharged from the service. Sophia Thompson served three years in the 59th O.V.I. Another woman soldier, under the name of Joseph Davidson, also served three years in the same company. Her father was killed fighting by her side at Chickamauga. A soldier belonging to the 14th Iowa regiment was discovered by the Provost-Marshal of Cairo, to be a woman. An investigation being ordered, "Charlie"

*From *The History of Woman Suffrage*, vol. 2.

placed the muzzle of her revolver to her head, fired, and fell dead on open parade-ground. No clue was obtained to her name, home, or family.

Frances Hook, of Illinois, enlisted with her brother in the 65th Home Guards, assuming the name of "Frank Miller." She served three months, and was mustered out without her sex being discovered. She then enlisted in the 90th Illinois, and was taken prisoner in a battle near Chattanooga. Attempting to escape she was shot through one of her limbs. The rebels in searching her person for papers, discovered her sex. They respected her as a woman, giving her a separate room while she was in prison at Atlanta, Ga. During her captivity, Jeff Davis wrote her a letter, offering her a lieutenant's commission if she would enlist in the rebel army, but she preferred to fight as a private soldier for the stars and stripes. rather than accept a commission from the rebels. This young lady was educated in a superior manner, possessing all the modern accomplishments. After her release from the rebel prison, she again enlisted in the 2d East Tennessee Cavalry. She was in the thickest of the fight at Murfreesboro, and was severely wounded in the shoulder, but fought gallantly and waded the Stone River into Murfreesboro on that memorable Sunday when the Union forces were driven back. Her sex was again disclosed upon the dressing of her wound, and General Rosecrans was informed, who caused her to be mustered out of the service, notwithstanding her earnest entreaty to be allowed to serve the cause she loved so well.

"Frank" found the 8th Michigan at Bowling Green, in which she again enlisted, remaining connected with this company. She said she had discovered a great many women in the army, one of them holding a lieutenant's commission, and had at different times assisted in burying women soldiers, whose sex was unknown to any but herself.

Anna Ella Carroll: Military Genius*

(Editorial from the *National Citizen*, Syracuse, N. Y., September, 1881)

THE CONTRAST.—"Look on this picture and on that." While President James A. Garfield lay dying, another Ameri-

*From *The History of Woman Suffrage*, vol. 2.

can citizen, one to whom the country owes far more than it did to him, was stricken with an incurable disease. But in this case no telegram heralded the fact; no messages were cabled abroad; few newspapers made comment, and yet had it not been for the wisdom of this person whom the country forgets, we should have possessed no country today.

Anna Ella Carroll lies at her home near Baltimore, stricken with paralysis—perhaps already beyond the river. As the readers of the *National Citizen* well know, when the nation was in its hour of extreme peril, with a nearly depleted treasury, with England and France waiting with large fleets for a few more evil days in order to raise the blockade, with President, Congress, and people nearly helpless and despair-in᠎ ᠎ere arose this woman, who with strategic science far in advance of any military or naval officer on land or sea, pointed out the way to victory, sending her plans and maps to the War Department, which adopted them. Thus the tide of battle was turned, victory perched on the Union banner, and in accordance with the President's proclamation, the country united in a day of public thanksgiving.

But that woman never received recognition from the country for her services. The Military Committee of various Congresses has reported in her favor, but no bill securing her even a pension has ever been passed, and now she is dying or dead. . . .

Miss Carroll says: "I am sure you retain your kind interest in the matter, and will be gratified by the last action of Congress, which is a complete recognition of my public service, on the part of military men; both Confederate and Union brigadiers belonging to the Military Committee."

While this bill was in no sense commensurable with the services rendered by Miss Carroll to the country, yet as the main point was conceded, it was believed it would secure one more consonant with justice at the next session of Congress.

The nation is mourning Garfield with the adulation generally given monarchs; General Grant is decorating his New York "palace" with countless costly gifts from home and abroad; yet a greater than both has fallen, and *because she was a woman*, she has gone to her great reward on high, unrecognized and unrewarded by the country she saved. Had it not been for her work, the names of James A. Garfield and of Ulysses S. Grant would never have emerged from obscurity. Women, remember that to one of your own sex the salvation of the country is due, and never forget to hold deep in your hearts, and to train your children to hold with reverence the name of ANNA ELLA CARROLL.

Egged at Jacksonville*

ABIGAIL SCOTT DUNIWAY

(1878)

In June, 1878, a convention met in Walla Walla, Washington territory, for the purpose of forming a constitution for the proposed new State of Washington, and in compliance with the invitation of many prominent women of the territory I visited the convention and was permitted to present a memorial in person, praying that the word "male" be omitted from the fundamental law of the incubating State. But my plea (like that of Abigail Adams a century before) failed of success, through a close vote however—it stood 8 to 7—and men went on as before, saying, as they did in the beginning: "Women do not wish to vote. If they desire the ballot let them ask for it." . . .

I went to Southern Oregon in 1879, and while sojourning in Jacksonville was assailed with a shower of eggs (since known in that section as "Jacksonville arguments") and was also burned in effigy on a principal street after the sun went down. Jacksonville is an old mining town, beautifully situated in the heart of the Southern Oregon mountains, and has no connection with the outside world except through the daily stagecoaches. Its would-be leading men are old miners or refugees from the bushwhacking district whence they were driven by the civil war. The taint of slavery is yet upon them and the methods of border-ruffians are their hearts' delight. . . . But that raid of the outlaws proved a good thing for the woman suffrage movement. It aroused the better classes, and finally shamed the border ruffians by its own reaction. When I returned to Portland a perfect ovation awaited me. Hundreds of . . . women who had not before allied them-

*From *The History of Woman Suffrage,* vol. 3.

selves with the movement made haste to do so. The newspapers were filled with severe denunciations of the mob, and "Jackson-villains," as the perpetrators of the outrage were styled, grew heartily disgusted over their questionable glory.

. . .

On the Fourth of July of this year [1885] a grand celebration was held at Vancouver, on Washington soil, the women of Oregon having resolved in large numbers that they would never again unite in celebrating men's independence day in a State where they are denied their liberty. . . . Boys and girls rode in the liberty-car and represented the age of the government. . . . The New Declaration of Independence was read by Josie De Vore Johnson . . . the Oregon Woman Suffrage Association . . . adopted the following resolutions:

Resolved, That while we deplore the injustice that still deprives the women of Oregon of the liberty to exercise their right to the elective franchise, we rejoice in the record the women of Washington are making as citizens, as voters and . . . we congratulate them upon their newly acquired liberties. . . . And we are further

Resolved, That if our own fathers, husbands, sons and brothers do not at the next session of the Oregon legislature bestow upon us the same electoral privileges which the women of Washington already enjoy, we will prepare to cross the Columbia river and take up our permanent abode in this "land of the free and home of the brave."

The Indifference of Women*

ALICE STONE BLACKWELL

(Convention held Washington, D. C., February 13-19, 1898)

It is often said that the chief obstacle to equal suffrage is the indifference and opposition of women, and that whenever the majority ask for the ballot they will get it. But it is a simple historical fact that every improvement thus far made in their condition has been secured, not by a general demand from the majority, but by the arguments, entreaties and "continual coming" of a persistent few. In each case the advocates of progress have had to contend not merely with the conservatism of men, but with the indifference of women, and often with active opposition from some of them.

When a man in Saco, Maine, first employed a saleswoman the men boycotted his store, and the women remonstrated with him on the sin of which he was guilty in placing a young woman in a position of such publicity. When Lucy Stone tried to secure for married women the right to their own property, they asked with scorn, "Do you think I would give myself where I would not give my property?" When Elizabeth Blackwell began to study medicine, the women at her boarding house refused to speak to her, and those passing her on the streets would hold their skirts aside so as not to touch her. It is a matter of history with what ridicule and opposition Mary Lyon's first efforts for the education of women were received, not only by the mass of men, but by the mass of women as well. In England when the Oxford examinations were thrown open to women, the Dean of Chichester preached a sermon against it, in which he said: "By the sex at large, certainly, the new curriculum is not asked for. I have ascertained, by extended inquiry among gentlewomen, that, with true feminine instinct, they either entirely distrust or else look with downright disfavor on so wild an innovation and interference with the best traditions of their sex." Pundita Ramabai tells us that the idea of education for girls is so unpopular with the majority of Hindoo women that when a progressive Hindoo proposes to educate his little daughter it is not uncommon for the women of his family to threaten to drown themselves.

All this merely shows that human nature is conservative. . . . The persons who take a strong interest in any reform are always comparatively few . . . and they are habitually regarded with disfavor, even by those whom the proposed reform is to benefit. . . .

Many changes for the better have been made during the last half century . . . relating to women. Everybody approves of these changes now, because they have become accomplished facts. But not one of them would have been made to this day if it had been necessary to wait until the majority of women asked for it. . . . In the light of history

the indifference of most women and the opposition of a few
must be taken as a matter of course. . . .

Can Women Be Fighters?*

LAURA CLAY

(National Convention, Washington, D. C.,
February 13-19, 1898)

It is by no means self-evident that women are naturally
unfitted for fighting or are unwarlike in disposition. The
traditions of Amazons† and the conduct of savage women
give room to believe that the instinct for war was primitively
very much the same in both sexes. Though the earliest
division of labor among savages known to us is that of assigning war and the chase to men, yet we have no reason to
believe that this was done by way of privilege to woman; but
in the struggle for tribal supremacy that tribe must have
ultimately survived and succeeded best which exposed its
women the least. Polygamy, universal among primitive races,
would in a degree sustain population against the ravages
among men of continual warfare, but any large destruction
of women must extinguish a tribe that suffered it. So those
tribes which earliest engrafted among their customs the

*From *The History of Woman Suffrage*, vol. 4.

†Female warriors of Brazil who ruled over a large territory and proved
invincible in battle. Their weapons were bows and arrows. Once a
year they admitted to their company for a limited time the men of the
neighboring tribe, who at the expiration of their period were sent
away with presents. All male children born were killed in infancy,
female children being brought up by their mothers. One explanation
for the origin of the tribe is that the females abandoned the males of
the tribe and sought to establish a settlement in the region of the
Jamunda River, but being followed by disconsolate husbands and
lovers, pity caused them to relent to the extent of making a pact with
the discarded ones to admit them to their society on sufferance once
a year. (*Women of America*, John Larus, 1907)

exclusion of woman from war were the ones that finally survived. . . .

Military genius among women has appeared in all ages and people, as in Deborah, Zenobia, Joan of Arc and our own Anna Ella Carroll. The prowess of women has often been conspicuous in besieged cities. . . . It is well known that in the late war many women on both sides eluded the vigilance of recruiting officers, enlisted and fought bravely. Who knows how many of such women there might have been if their enlistment had been desired and stimulated by beat of drum and blare of trumpet and "all the pomp and circumstance of glorious war?" But no State can afford to accept military service from its women, for while a nation may live for ages without soldiers, it could exist but for a span without mothers.

For the Sake of Liberty*

CARRIE CHAPMAN CATT

(Thirty-second annual convention of the suffrage association held in Washington, D. C., February 8-14, 1900)

A survey of the changes which have been wrought within the past hundred years in the status of women—educational, social, financial and political—fills the observing man or woman with a feeling akin to awe. No great war has been fought in behalf of their emancipation; no great political party has espoused their cause; no heroes have bled and died for their liberty; yet words fail utterly to measure the distance between the "sphere" of the woman of 1800 and that of the woman of 1900. How has the transformation come? What mysterious power has brought it?

On the whole . . . women of the present rejoice at every right gained . . . yet when the plea is made that the free, self-respecting, self-reliant, independent, thinking women of

*From *The History of Woman Suffrage*, vol. 4.

this generation be given the suffrage, the answer invariably comes back, "When women as a whole demand it, men will consider it." This answer carries with it the apparent supposition that all the changes have come because the majority of women wanted them, and that further enlargement of liberty must cease because the majority do not want it. Alas, it is a sad comment upon the conservatism of the average human being that not one change of consequence has been desired by women as a whole, or even by a considerable part. It would be nearer the truth to say women as a whole have opposed every advance.

The progress has come because women of a larger mold . . . than the average have been willing to face the opposition of the world for the sake of liberty. . . . The sacrifice of suffering, of doubt, of obloquy, which has been endured by the pioneers in the woman movement will never be fully known or understood. . . .

There are two kinds of restrictions upon human liberty—the restraint of law and that of custom. No written law has ever been more binding than unwritten custom supported by popular opinion. At the beginning of our century both law and custom restricted the liberty of woman.

It was the edict of custom which prohibited women from receiving an education, engaging in occupations, speaking in public, organizing societies, or in other ways conducting themselves like free, rational human beings. It was law which forbade married women to control their own property or to collect their own wages, and which forbade all women to vote. The changes have not come because women wished for them or men welcomed them. . . .

There are a few fanatics who, if they could, would force the women of this generation back into the spheres of their grandmothers. There are some pessimists who imagine they see all natural order coming to a speedy end because of the enlarged liberties and opportunities of women. . . .

The way before us is difficult at best, not because our demand is not based upon unquestioned justice, not because it is not destined to win in the end, but because of the nature of the processes through which it must be won. In fact the position of this question might well be used to demonstrate that observation of Aristotle that "a democracy has many striking points of resemblance with tyranny. . . ."

Conditions of Wage-Earning Women*

Gail Laughlin

(Convention held in Washington, D. C., February 8-14, 1900)

"Wage-earner" among women is used in a broad sense. All women receiving money payment for work are proud to be called wage-earners, because wage-earning means economic independence. The census of 1890 reports nearly 400 occupations open to women, and nearly 4,000,000 women engaged in them. But government reports show the average wages of women in large cities to be from $3.83 to $6.91 per week, and the general average to be from $5.00 to $6.68. In all lines women are paid less than men for the same grade of work, and they are often compelled to toil under needlessly dangerous and unsanitary conditions. . . .

How are these evils to be remedied? By organization, suffrage, co-operation among women, and above all, the inculcation of the principle that a woman is an individual, with a right to choose her work, and with other rights equal with man. Our law-makers control the sanitary conditions and pay of teachers. Here is work for the women who have "all the rights they want." When one of these comfortably situated women was told of the need of the ballot for working women, she held up her finger, showing the wedding ring on it, and said, "I have all the rights I want." The next time that I read the parable of the man who fell among thieves and was succored by the good Samaritan, methought I could see that woman with the wedding ring on her finger, passing by on the other side.

It is said that every woman who earns her living crowds a man out. That argument is as old as the trade guilds of the thirteenth century, which tried to exclude women. The

*From *The History of Woman Suffrage*, vol. 4.

Rev. Samuel G. Smith of St. Paul, who has recently declared
against women in wage-earning occupations, stands today
just where they did seven hundred years ago. . . .

The Economic Basis of Woman Suffrage*

ELIZABETH SHELDON TILLINGHAST

(Convention held in Washington, D. C.,
February 8-14, 1900)

However we may explain it, and whether we like it or not,
woman has become an economic factor in our country and
one that is constantly assuming larger proportions. The question is now what treatment will make her an element of
economic strength instead of weakness as at present. The
presence of women in business now demoralizes the rate of
wages even more than the increase in the supply of labor.
Why? Principally because she can be bullied with greater
impunity than voters—because she has no adequate means
of self-defense. This seems a hard accusation, but I believe
it to be true.

Trade is a fight—an antagonism of interests which are
compromised in contracts in which the economically stronger
always wins the advantage. There are many things that contribute to economic strength besides ability, and among them
the most potent is coming more and more to be the power
which arises from organization expressing itself in political
action. Without political expression woman's economic value
is at the bottom of the scale. She is the last to be considered,
and the consideration is usually about exhausted before she
is reached.

She must do better work than men for equal pay or equal
work for less pay. In spite of this she may be supplanted at
any time by a political adherent, or her place may be used

*From *The History of Woman Suffrage*, vol. 4.

as a bribe to an opposing faction. Women are weak in the
business world because they are new in it; because they are
only just beginning to learn their economic value. . . .

For these reasons women are . . . economically weaker than
men. Does it appeal to any one's sense of fairness to give
the stronger party in a struggle additional advantages and
deny them to the weaker one? Would that be considered
honorable—would it be considered tolerable—even among
prize fighters? . . . And yet these are practically the conditions
under which women do business in forty-one of our States.

While the State does not owe any able-bodied sound-
minded . . . woman a living, it does owe them all a fair . . .
opportunity to earn their own living, and one that shall not
be prolonged dying. I do not claim that woman suffrage
would be a panacea for all our economic woes. But I do
claim that it would remove one handicap which women
workers have to bear. . . .

The Winning of Educational Freedom*

HARRIET MAY MILLS

(Convention held in Washington, D. C.,
February 8-14, 1900)

Abigail Adams said of the conditions in the early part of
the nineteenth century: "Female education in the best families
went no farther than reading, writing and arithmetic and,
in some rare instances, music and dancing." A lady living in
the first quarter of the century relates that she returned from
a school in Charleston, where she had been sent to be
"finished off," with little besides a knowledge of sixty different
lace stitches. . . .

The majority of women were content, they asked no change;
they took no part in the movement for higher education
except to ridicule it. This, like every other battle for freedom

*From *The History of Woman Suffrage*, vol. 4.

which the world has seen, was led by the few brave, strong souls who saw the truth and dared proclaim it. In 1820 the world looked aghast upon "bluestockings." Because a young woman was publicly examined in geometry at one of Emma Willard's school exhibitions, a storm of ridicule broke forth at so scandalous a proceeding. It was ten years after Holyoke was founded before Mary Lyon dared to have Latin appear in the regular course, because the views of the community would not allow it. Boston had a high school for girls in 1825, which was maintained but eighteen months, Mayor Quincy declaring that "no funds of any city could stand the expense." The difficulty was that "too many girls attended." . . .

Elizabeth Blackwell applied to twelve colleges before she gained admittance to the Geneva (N.Y.) Medical School in 1846, and secured the first M. D. ever given to a woman in this country. Today, 1,583 women are studying medicine. Not so full a measure of freedom has been won in law or theology. In 1897, 131 women were in the law schools, 193 in the theological schools, but women are still handicapped in these professions. . . .

Unfortunately, educational freedom has not been followed by industrial freedom. Of the leading colleges for women but four have women presidents; but one offers a free field to women on its professional staff. In the majority of co-educational colleges which give women any place as teachers, they appear in small numbers as assistant professors and, more often, as instructors. . . .

Educational freedom without political freedom is but partial. Minerva sprang fully armed from the head of Jove; not only had she wisdom, but she had the spear and the helmet in her hands—every weapon of offense and defense to equip her for the world's conquest. Standing on the threshold of the new century, we behold the woman of the future thus armed. . . . Educational freedom must lead to political freedom.

Working Woman's Need of the Ballot*

FLORENCE KELLEY

(Convention held in Washington, D. C., February 8-14, 1900)

No one needs all the powers of the fullest citizenship more urgently than the wage-earning woman, and from two different points of view—that of actual money wages and that of her wider needs as a human being and a member of the community.

The wages paid any body of working people are determined by many influences, chief among which is the position of the particular body of workers in question. Thus the printers, by their . . . powerful organization, their solidarity and united action keep up their wages in spite of the invasion of their domain by new and improved machinery.

In the garment trades . . . the presence of a body of the disfranchised . . . undoubtedly contributes to the economic weakness of these trades. Custom, habit, tradition, the regard of the public, both employing and employed, for the people who do certain kinds of labor, contribute to determine the price of that labor, and no disfranchised class of workers can permanently hold its own in competition with enfranchised rivals. But this works both ways. It is fatal for any body of workers to have forever hanging from the fringes of its skirts other bodies on a level just below its own; for that means continual pressure downward, additional difficulty to be overcome in the struggle to maintain reasonable rates of wages. Hence, within the space of two generations there has been a complete revolution in the attitude of the trades-unions toward the women working in their trades. . . . The workingmen . . . see . . . that there can not be two standards of

*From *The History of Woman Suffrage*, vol. 4.

work and wages for any trade without constant menace to the higher standard. . . .

But this same menace holds with regard to the vote. The lack of the ballot places the wage-earning woman upon a level of irresponsibility compared with her enfranchised fellow workingman. By impairing her standing in the community the general rating of her value as a human being, and consequently as a worker, is lowered. In order to be rated as good as a good man in the field of her earnings, she must show herself . . . more steady, or more trustworthy, or more skilled, or more cheap in order to have the same chance of employment. . . .

Finally, the very fact that women now form about one-fifth of the employees in manufacture and commerce in this country has opened a vast field of industrial legislation directly affecting women as wage-earners. The courts in some of the States, notably in Illinois, are taking the position that women can not be treated as a class apart and legislated for by themselves, as has been done in the factory laws of England and on the continent of Europe, but must abide by that universal freedom of contract which characterizes labor in the United States. This renders the situation of the working woman absolutely anomalous. On the one hand, she is cut off from the protection awarded to her sisters abroad; on the other, she has no such power to defend her interests at the polls, as is the heritage of her brothers at home. This position is untenable, and there can be no pause in the agitation for full political power . . . until these are granted to all the women of the nation.

PART 2

Observations on Women by Women

Observations on Women by Women

With respect to the formation of the foetus in the womb, we are very ignorant; but it appears to me probable, that an accidental physical cause may account for this phenomenon, and prove it not to be a law of nature.

MARY WOLLSTONECRAFT, 1833

I have faced every form of disability because I am a woman, have met defeat after defeat, till the iron has entered my soul.

ELIZA CONNOR, 1889

Of all kinds of aristocracy, that of sex is the most odious and unnatural . . . subjugating everywhere, moral power to brute power.

ELIZABETH CADY STANTON, 1869

The only name given, by which the country can be saved, is that of WOMAN.

LUCY STONE, 1867

We mean treason; we mean secession, and on a thousand times grander scale than was that of the South. We are plotting revolution; we will overthrow this bogus Republic and plant a government of righteousness in its stead.

VICTORIA WOODHULL, 1871

While woman's intellect is confined, her morals crushed, her health ruined, her weaknesses encouraged, and her strength punished, she is told that her lot is cast in the paradise of women; and there is no country in the world where indulgence is given her as a substitute for justice.

HARRIET MARTINEAU, 1837

Women are so overworked that they have no time to think, they are joined to their wash-tubs. But the children of these overworked women are coming on, young girls matrimonially inclined, who fear the avowal of a belief in suffrage would injure their chances. Their motto should be "Liberty first, and union afterwards."

ABIGAIL DUNIWAY SCOTT, 1895

The only way for women to get their rights is to take them. If necessary let there be a domestic insurrection. Let young women refuse to marry, and married women refuse to sew on buttons, cook, and rock the cradle until their liege-lords acknowledge the rights they are entitled to.

BELVA A. LOCKWOOD, 1878

By law, public sentiment, and religion from the time of Moses down to the present day, woman has never been thought of other than a piece of property, to be disposed of at the will and pleasure of man.

SUSAN B. ANTHONY, 1860

The strong natural characteristics of womanhood are repressed and ignored in dependence, for so long as man feeds woman she will try to please the giver and adapt herself to his condition.

ELIZABETH CADY STANTON, 1869

I am not going to question your opinions. I am not going to meddle with your beliefs. I am not going to dictate to you mine. All I say is examine; enquire. Look into the nature of things. Search out the ground of your opinions, the *for* and the *against*. Know *why* you believe, understand *what* you believe, and possess a reason for the faith that is in you.

FRANCES WRIGHT, 1829

From the cradle to the grave she is subject to the power and control of man. Father, guardian, or husband, one conveys her like some piece of merchandise over to the other.

ERNESTINE ROSE, 1851

The wrongs of woman have too long slumbered. They now begin to cry for redress. Let them, then, not *ask* as *favor*, but *demand* as *right*, that every civil obstacle be removed out of the way.

LUCRETIA MOTT, 1850

I plant myself on the basis of the Declaration of Independence and insist, with our Revolutionary sires, that taxation without representation is tyranny. Well, here am I, an independent American woman, educated for and living by the practice of medicine. I own property, and pay taxes on that property. I demand of the Government that taxes me that it should allow me an equal voice with the other tax-payers in the disposal of the public money.

HARRIOT K. HUNT, 1853

From the marriage hour woman is presented only in a series of dissolving views. First, she stands beside her husband radiant in girlish beauty. She worships. One side of the lesson is well learned, that of entire dependence. Not once has she dreamed that there must be mutual dependence and separate fountains of reciprocal life. In the next scene the child wife appears withering away from life ? from the heart she is not large or noble enough to fill—pining in the darkness of her home-life, made only the deeper by her inactivity, ignorance, and despair. . . . In another view she has passed the season of despair, and appears as the heartless flirt, or that most to be despised being, a married coquette, or as beauty of person has faded away, she may be found turning to a quiet kind of hand-maiden piety and philanthropy.

PAULINA WRIGHT DAVIS, 1852

With women dependency is interiorized: she *is* a slave even when she behaves with apparent freedom; while man is essentially independent and his bondage comes from without. . . . it is asserted that *men* oppress *women,* the husband is indignant; he feels that *he* is the one who is oppressed—and he is; but the fact is that it is the masculine code, it is the society developed by the males and in their interest, that has established woman's situation in a form that is at present a source of torment for both sexes.

SIMONE DE BEAUVOIR, 1949

Our society is not a community, but merely a collection of isolated family units. Desperately insecure, fearing his woman will leave him if she is exposed to other men or to anything remotely resembling life, the male seeks to isolate her from other men and from what little civilization there is, so he moves her out to the suburbs, a collection of self-absorbed couples and their kids. Isolation enables him to try to maintain his pretense of being an individual by becoming a "rugged individualist," a loner, equating non-cooperation and solitariness with individuality.

VALERIE SOLANAS, 1967

Today's woman, armed with her ballot, her diploma, her union card, faces a dizzily complex world; inevitably she is often confused and paralyzed by it. Whatever its hazards, it is doubtful if the world which women face today can appear to them any more hostile or bewildering than that which confronted the early nineteenth-century woman with aspirations. . . . It might help if we remembered more often, not only the lonely vigils of Washington at Valley Forge and Lincoln in the White House, but the doubts and fears that racked an Angelina Grimké or Elizabeth Cady Stanton when she stood up to make her first public speech in the tiny Wesleyan chapel at Seneca Falls.

ELEANOR FLEXNER, 1959

It is clear, by tracing the history of economic "progress" of women, that we have been used and abused. The myths that are promoted about the NEW AMERICAN WOMAN, of career and fashion model stereotype, are counter-balanced by the MYTH OF THE TOTAL HOUSEWIFE. Women's position has *changed some,* but *improved little.*

LYN WELLS, 1969

Oppression is an on-going activity. If women are a political class and women are being oppressed, it must be that some other political class is oppressing the class of women. Since the very definition of women entails that only one other class could be relevant to it, only one other class could possibly be oppressing women: the class of men.

TI-GRACE ATKINSON, 1969

What the women's movement has to do is to develop a self-defined class of women based on equality among all. If we keep within our class the hierarchal structure which results from our displacement among men our struggles will be doomed to failure. It is within our power to change the nature of the female class itself and to destroy the premises on which our class was set up in the first place. For if we do not change it we cannot be expected to attract the great masses of women. We cannot be unified. We will not move out.

BARBARA MEHRHOF, 1969

The whole notion of sacrifice and surrender pervades every part of a woman's life. A "good mother" is one who continually ignores her own needs and desires in favor of those of her family. A "good wife" is always there behind her husband, making him look good, helping him out, cheering him on, ironing his shirts, raising his children. A "good woman" puts her man's sexual pleasure before her own—"after all, men need sex more."

VIRGINIA BLAISDELL, 1969

In almost every industry and every occupation women are paid less than men. Women are massed in the lower paying major occupations. In industries and businesses with a wide spectrum of jobs women are found in the lower paying jobs. Women are hired for the lower paying jobs; women are paid less for doing the same job as men; women are passed over for on-the-job training, upgrading; women are denied advancement. Why? What excuses are given for this discrimination?

JOAN JORDAN, 1968

The movement is supposed to be for human liberation: how come the condition of women inside is no better than outside?

MARGE PIERCY, 1970

Marriage is in the same state as the Church: both are becoming functionally defunct as their preachers go about heralding a revival, eagerly chalking up converts in a day of dread. And just as God has been pronounced dead quite often but has this way of resurrecting himself, so everyone debunks marriage, yet ends up married.

SHULAMITH FIRESTONE, 1970

Engels, on the nineteenth-century family system, said, "Man is the capitalist; woman is the means of production, the factory; children are labor." Today's system of marriage is again "just a way to get cheap labor—economics is all it is."

GLORIA STEINEM, 1970

The liberation of women can only be achieved if *all four* structures [Production, Reproduction, Sexuality, Socialization] in which they are integrated are transformed.

JULIET MITCHELL, 1969

Militant women in the 1970s may be spurned and spat upon as the suffragists were during the decade before the vote was won for women in 1920. But it might be recognized that such militant women will win legal, economic, and political rights for the daughters of today's traditionalist Aunt Bettys, just as our grandmothers won the vote that women can exercise today.

ALICE S. ROSSI, 1970

One of the areas where the criminal law operates most discriminately is prostitution. Despite the fact that a recent New York law makes the "John," or customer, guilty as well as the prostitute, the New York District Attorney's office sees fit not to prosecute the male customer but only the woman he exploits.

DIANE SCHULDER, 1970

They [women] are confined to conditions of economic dependence based on the sale of their sexuality in marriage, or a variety of prostitutions. Work on a basis of economic independence allows them only a subsistence level of life—often not even that.

KATE MILLET, 1970

The basic American institution for oppressing females is marriage, and this institution exists for the purpose of extorting domestic and personal services, including production and care of offspring, who become subordinates of the male-supremacist state.

SUZIE OLAH, 1970

PART 3

Voices from the Present

MANIFESTOS, ACTIONS, AND STRATEGY

Redstockings Manifesto

I. After centuries of individual and preliminary political struggle, women are uniting to achieve their final liberation from male supremacy. Redstockings is dedicated to building this unity and winning our freedom.

II. Women are an oppressed class. Our oppression is total, affecting every facet of our lives. We are exploited as sex objects, breeders, domestic servants, and cheap labor. We are considered inferior beings, whose only purpose is to enhance men's lives. Our humanity is denied. Our prescribed behavior is enforced by the threat of physical violence.

Because we have lived so intimately with our oppressors, in isolation from each other, we have been kept from seeing our personal suffering as a political condition. This creates the illusion that a woman's relationship with her man is a matter of interplay between two unique personalities, and can be worked out individually. In reality, every such relationship is a *class* relationship, and the conflicts between individual men and women are *political* conflicts that can only be solved collectively.

III. We identify the agents of our oppression as men. Male supremacy is the oldest, most basic form of domination. All other forms of exploitation and oppression (racism, capitalism, imperialism, etc.) are extensions of male supremacy: men dominate women, a few men dominate the rest. All power structures throughout history have been male-dominated and male-oriented. Men have controlled all political, economic and cultural institutions and backed up this control with physical force. They have used their power to keep women in an inferior position. *All men* receive economic, sexual, and psychological benefits from male supremacy. *All men* have oppressed women.

IV. Attempts have been made to shift the burden of responsibility from men to institutions or to women themselves. We condemn these arguments as evasions. Institutions alone do not oppress; they are merely tools of the oppressor. To blame institutions implies that men and women are equally victimized, obscures the fact that men benefit from the subordination of women, and gives men the excuse that they are forced to be oppressors. On the contrary, any man is free to renounce his superior position provided that he is willing to be treated like a woman by other men.

We also reject the idea that women consent to or are to blame for their own oppression. Women's submission is not the result of brainwashing, stupidity, or mental illness but of continual, daily pressure from men. We do not need to change ourselves, but to change men.

The most slanderous evasion of all is that women can oppress men. The basis for this illusion is the isolation of individual relationships from their political context and the tendency of men to see any legitimate challenge to their privileges as persecution.

V. We regard our personal experience, and our feelings about that experience, as the basis for an analysis of our common situation. We cannot rely on existing ideologies as they are all products of male supremacist culture. We question every generalization and accept none that are not confirmed by our experience.

Our chief task at present is to develop female class consciousness through sharing experience and publicly exposing the sexist foundation of all our institutions. Consciousness-raising is not "therapy," which implies the existence of individual solutions and falsely assumes that the male-female relationship is purely personal, but the only method by which we can ensure that our program for liberation is based on the concrete realities of our lives.

The first requirement for raising class consciousness is honesty, in private and in public, with ourselves and other women.

VI. We identify with all women. We define our best interest as that of the poorest, most brutally exploited woman.

We repudiate all economic, racial, educational or status privileges that divide us from other women. We are determined to recognize and eliminate any prejudices we may hold against other women.

We are committed to achieving internal democracy. We will do whatever is necessary to ensure that every woman in our movement has an equal chance to participate, assume responsibility, and develop her political potential.

VII. We call on all our sisters to unite with us in struggle.

We call on all men to give up their male privileges and support women's liberation in the interest of our humanity and their own.

In fighting for our liberation we will always take the side of women against their oppressors. We will not ask what is "revolutionary" or "reformist," only what is good for women.

The time for individual skirmishes has passed. This time we are going all the way.

July 7, 1969

REDSTOCKINGS
P.O. Box 748
Stuyvesant Station
New York, N. Y. 10009

Southern Female Rights Union Program for Female Liberation

1. We demand free, non-compulsory, public childcare. The public schools must be extended to include all children from birth. Free and adequate care must be available on a fulltime (24 hours every day of the year) basis for infants and children of all ages, regardless of parents' income. All meals, medical and dental care, clothing, and equipment must be available for the children in the schools, so that no child is deprived by their parents' inadequate support. An equal number of females and males in all positions must staff the schools. Tracking and counseling, textbooks, games, equipment, and instruction must be free of sexual (and racial) discrimination at all levels of public education.

2. We demand an adequate guaranteed annual income (minimum $2400) for every *individual* (not family) in this country. Recognizing the failure of the local or national economy to provide jobs for people, particularly women, each person must be guaranteed an adequate income whether they can find work or not. Inadequate or part-time salaries must be supplemented to meet the guaranteed income level. There must be an end to the present welfare system that forces women to be beggars, and still have nothing, or to remain in intolerable marriage situations.

3. We demand an end to sexual (and racial) discrimination in hiring, firing, wages, and job-training. All-male occupations must be opened to equal numbers of women—professional, mechanical, construction, trucking, public defense (police, firemen).

4. We demand free self-defense instruction for females of all ages in the public schools. Considering the heinous crimes by men against thousands of females every year, something must be done. Through miseducation and the lack of physical

training for young females, women become weak and unable to defend themselves or another person in trouble. Crimes against women will stop only when women are no longer helpless and defenseless, and no longer dependent on men for their protection. Karate is the most practical method for learning the physical and psychic responses to attack.

5. We demand that the present hormonal birth control pills be withdrawn from the market as deadly. Women who have been harmed by these pills while being used as human guinea pigs must be compensated. Nothing can be done for those who have died and will die of blood clots and cancer. Further, the brainwashing by the government about overpopulation must stop. The problem is an unequal division of resources, not too many people. Safe contraceptives must be developed for women who want to use them. Contraceptives and sterilization for men should be encouraged.

6. We demand that the television, radio, and newspaper industries establish a new code of ethics, removing from advertisements, news shows, and commentaries all discriminatory allusions to females. Serials, cartoons, and stories which feed off the stereotype images of the "empty-headed" woman, the "fickle" woman, the "bitch," the "sexpot," and the "happy" housewife armed with the tools of household slavery, must be discontinued. Let's see as many men as women washing the clothes and dishes, cleaning the house (not as a joke, but seriously). Let's see women washing the car and pole-vaulting. People identify with the models portrayed in the news media.

Some of these demands are very "costly", those in power will say. As it is now, women pay the costs in a lifetime of endless, unthanked labor and suffering, and personality disintegration; children pay the cost in malnutrition, mental disorders, misery, and sometimes brutal mistreatment, even death. These programs can be paid for by taxing the rich. There is just one problem. Our legislators and administrators *are* the rich or are closely tied to them. No one in power will *give* us our human rights. We women must fight and *act* upon our demands. We must *take* our human rights. It will be a long, hard fight.

The November 21, 1969 issue of *Time* Magazine reported: "Although 51% of Americans are female, women face many of the problems of a minority. Only 1% of the nation's engineers are women, 3% of its lawyers, 7% of its doctors. For the same jobs, women's pay is often less than half that of men, and nearly ⅕ of employed women with a B.A. have jobs in such categories as clerks, factory workers and cooks. Moreover, the status of American women is, in many ways, deteriorating:

Median wages and salaries of fully employed men were $4713 in 1957, compared with $3,008 for women. In 1968, men's income had risen to about $7,800, or 65%, while women's had gone up to $4,550, or 51%. The gap is widening.

In the past ten years women have lost 50 seats in state legislatures. Margaret Chase Smith is the lone woman in the U.S. Senate, and there are only ten Congresswomen, compared with 17 in 1960."

The U.S. Department of Commerce, Bureau of the Census reports the following comparative statistics for men and women in the labor force, 1960.

Occupation	PERCENTAGE OF WOMEN (Of total working women)	INCOME/ANNUAL		No./workers-millions	
		Female	Male	Female	Male
Professional	13%	$4358	$7115	3	5
Managers, Officials, and proprietors	5%	3514	7241	1	5
Clerical	31%	3586	5247	7	3
Factory workers	15%	2970	4977	4	9
Sales	7%	2389	5842	2	3
Service	15%	2340	4089	3	3
Private household	10%	1156	....	2	....

MEDIAN ANNUAL WAGES BY SEX AND RACE

Workers	Annual wage
White Males	$5137
Non-White Males	3075
White Females	2537
Non-White Females	1276

Men often ask, scornfully, why women don't get out of the house and go to work. The above statistics tell a part of the story why. The charts do not list other job categories to which women are relegated such as prostitution, playbunnies, go-go girls, and marriage. No statistics are given for the poor subsistence women are given for their jobs as housewives and mothers.

The division of labor and resources by sex constitutes a system of SEXISM, which is the oldest form of institutionalized oppression. The roots of sexism have long been obscured by the dialectics of history. Different races and nationalities have been oppressed for centuries at a time, continuing into these times, but the subjugation of the female sex by the male has gone on for tens of thousands of years. Eons of time and the dialectical interactions of civilizations have served to hide the caste oppression of females by means of ancient traditions, refined and modified, or exaggerated and rigidified.

Sexism can not be revealed by any superficial or traditional examination of society. To understand sexism, we must re-examine the foundations of civilization. To destroy sexism, we must fight, as females, collectively for the unity of human-kind. We must change attitudes and material conditions.

SOUTHERN FEMALE RIGHTS UNION, 1024 Jackson Avenue, Room 3, New Orleans, La., 70130
For Roxanne Dunbar or Martha Atkins

Lilith's Manifesto*

1. The biological dichotomy of sex needs no reinforcement by differential cultural mores. Whatever qualities pertain to humanity pertain to it as a species. If assertiveness, for example, is a virtue in man, it is a virtue also in woman; if forbearance is a virtue in woman, it is likewise a virtue in man. (If you, brother, can't get a hard-on for a woman who doesn't grovel at your feet, that's *your* hangup; and sister, if you can't turn on to a man who won't club you and drag you off by the hair, that's yours. Keep your hangups the hell out of this revolution.)

2. The mutilation of individual whole human beings to fit the half-size Procrustes' beds society assigns selectively to "men" and to "women" serves a purpose far more contrary to the pursuit of freedom than simple divisiveness; because *all* persons can be consigned to one or the other category and their personalities trimmed, by differential social experience, to fit the mold considered appropriate to their sex, *none* can escape; half the human race receives indoctrination and training in the exercise of dominance over others, while the other half receives reciprocal conditioning to servility, all being given to presuppose that a pattern of authority and submission to au-

*From *WOMEN: A Journal of Liberation* (Fall, 1970), © 1970 by Women: A Journal of Liberation, Inc.

thority is the universal, inevitable, and biologically determined order of social relationships.

3. All known societies have thus utilized the clear and all-inclusive dichotomy of sex as the chief vehicle for early and continuous limitation on the essentially liberatory free play of human imaginings and aspirations, perverting a benign natural phenomenon to service of the social status quo. Bourgeois society only inherited this tradition—anti-revolutionary by definition—and modified it to suit the special needs and conditions of capitalism; socialist societies have done no more than modify it likewise to their ends. The pursuit of freedom demands that it be utterly transcended.

4. By the nature of revolution as such, not all the forces engaged in it are committed to its fullest possible consummation. That commitment, however, defines the vanguard, whatever other elements may, in the vicissitudes of movement, usurp or be displaced into its position. Should leadership be retained by forces of but limited vision, the revolution must be cut tragically short of its full potential, for commitment to the lesser goals such a pseudo-vanguard does envision will turn against the revolution at the very moment it stands poised to overreach them.

5. It is unthinkable that the revolution now in process be allowed to suffer such curtailment. Heretofore, disappointed survivors of a truncated revolution have known, at least, that the seeds of future revolt remained; no power was capable of exterminating them. The proliferating technology of biochemical manipulation now robs us of even that bitter consolation; no state power, capitalist or socialist, is to be entrusted with it; we can afford no less than total liberation. *This* revolution has got to go for broke: power to no one, and to every one; to each the power over his/her own life, and no others.

Why OWL (Older Women's Liberation)?

In general, the Women's Liberation Movement is a young movement. Statistics on age are not available but observation indicates the average age of women participating in the movement to be around 25. Older women in the movement are exceedingly rare. OWL (women 30 and above), unlike the younger women's liberation groups, was consciously created by women who:

1) felt different from the main body of the movement because of age, life experiences, family commitments and goal orientations.
2) felt that we had experienced long years of personal oppression and participated in the events of life (child birth, child rearing, marriage, divorce, homemaking and careers) that many of the younger groups theorized about.
3) felt that our special skills and knowledge could be utilized for the benefit of the movement.

OWL addresses itself to problems that do not often arise at other meetings. *Problems* like:

1) How does one live equitably with a husband when the relationship is not egalitarian?
2) How does one bring up children in an oppressive society?
3) How does a mother relate to adolescent sons who are attempting to reach male maturity by emulating male stereotyped role models?
4) How does one raise a daughter?
5) Problems of rearing children when there is one parent.
6) Problems of alimony.
7) How to cope with aging and dependent parents.
8) How to pursue a job, career or *anything* while raising a family.
9) How to participate in the movement if one's husband objects.
10) How to change from 20 to 40 years of behavioral response.

We of OWL believe that we can speak to a broad segment of Amerikan women. Having shared the problems of housewives, of the poor, of the dependent, OWL is developing programs that will speak to all our needs. Programs like:

1) Pay for housewives, the housewives' bill of rights
2) Divorce referral service
3) Transitional communes
4) Job training, employment services

5) Child care, total health care

Sisters, join with us to create a new society.

Women Support Panther Sisters*

New Haven, Connecticut. On Saturday, November 22, a coalition of Women's Liberation, the Black Panther Party and the Welfare Rights Organization staged an inspiring demonstration in support of 14 New Haven Panthers in prison. Led by members of Women's Liberation and Welfare Rights, thousands of black and white radicals marched through crowded streets of New Haven and held a militant rally in front of the Court House. This was the first large action planned and led by Women's Liberation.

The 14 Panthers have spent the last 6 months in jail without a trial on charges of conspiracy, murder and kidnapping, in connection with the death of Alex Rackley, a former Panther, last Ma . The Panthers claim these are trumped-up charges, designed to keep them off the street, out of their communities and away from the people they want to serve. There have been similar incidents all over the country.

Five of the 14 Panthers are women: 2 of the women—Rose Smith and Loretta Luce—are pregnant; 1 woman—_____ Carter—recently gave birth un.. armed guard. Her physical condition was so poor, she spent 30 hours in labor and the baby was delivered by Caesarian section. The women have been denied the right to physical exercise, fresh air, and proper clothing. Rose has gained only 1 pound in the 6 months of her pregnancy spent in jail. They have not been able to sleep as lights have flooded their cells day and night. Their babies will be taken away from them by the state, denying the wishes of the Black Panther community to raise the children in a Panther commune.

The speakers at the rally were two Panther women, a Young Lord woman, and a woman from Women's Liberation. Their raps dealt with the specific issues of the demonstration, political repression, the true nature of the "system" and the relation of all these to women.

Throughout the march and rally, cries of "Right On!" echoed in reply to exhortations to "Free Our Sisters, Free

*From WOMEN: A Journal of Liberation (Winter, 1970), © 1970 by Women: A Journal of Liberation, Inc.

Ourselves, Power to the People!"; "Fuck Harvard, Fuck Yale, Get Those Panthers Out of Jail!"; "Out of the House, Out of the Ghetto, Out from Under, Women Unite!" and, in short, to make a revolution in America NOW!

Women conceived of and led the march and rally to support our sisters and brothers who are political prisoners and to raise the issues of the particular oppression of women in our society. We wanted to make the following points: 1) Women are committed to the struggle to radically change America in solidarity with our brothers, black and white; 2) Women are committed to playing a leadership role in this struggle; 3) Women are committed to raising issues which are particularly relevant to women in the struggle.

Free Our Sisters, Free Ourselves

(Leaflet distributed at demonstration to support the Panther sisters, New Haven, Conn., November 22, 1969)

Jean Wilson, Maude Francis, Peggy Hudgins, Erica Huggins, Francis Carter, Loretta Lukes and Rose Smith are being held, without bail, in Niantic State Prison Farm. They have not been tried or charged with any crime. Our sisters are young, black, and members of the Black Panther Party.

Francis Carter, Loretta Lukes and Rose Smith are pregnant, and due to give birth in December.

WHAT'S BEING DONE TO THESE WOMEN?
They are deliberately kept in bad health; searchlights shine in their faces, sirens sound outside their windows day and night, so they can't sleep.

They are badly fed, denied fresh air and exercise, and were allowed maternity clothes only a month ago.

They are kept in solitary confinement, denied the right to speak to other women, or to choose lawyers to defend them.

They will be forced to give birth under armed guard, attended by prison doctors who don't care at all about them: Rose

Smith weighed 133 when she was thrown into jail six months ago. She is now eight months pregnant, and has gained only one pound.

If the babies manage to be born alive, and survive under these conditions, the State of Connecticut intends to:
    call our sisters "unfit" mothers
    take away their babies
    decide who will raise their babies.

Francis Carter, Loretta Lukes and Rose Smith are being tortured because they are BLACK
        because they are PANTHERS
        because they are WOMEN

And what these women are suffering is an extension and reflection of generally how rotten things are for all women, like on the job, alone in the home.

WE DEMAND: *With the mothers, that the Black Panther Party be allowed to care for these children as is the desire of the Black Panther women and men.*
    We reject the State's definition of "fit" mother, family unit, and "suitable" home.
    The State, by its tortuous treatment of our Panther sis has proved itself to be an "unfit" guardian for these childre
    We insist that a mother is NOT "unfit" because she does not accept the status quo.

WE DEMAND: *That our three pregnant sisters be released on their own recognizance,* and that reasonable bail be set for all of the Panthers in jail.

WE DEMAND: An end to the torture of these women, adequate diet, exercise and clothing, an end to the isolation and sleepless nights.

WE DEMAND: Their right to prenatal and maternal care by doctors of their choice, their right to give birth without armed guard.

WE DEMAND: Immediate freedom for the Connecticut Panthers, and all political prisoners.

AND WHAT IS THEIR CRIME?

They have begun to construct concrete programs which help women.
—Free health programs
—Free Breakfast for Children programs
—Free day-care programs
—Free clothes for women and children who need them

These women had to stand up alone to begin these things. We will no longer have to stand up alone—*now when we rise up —we rise up together.*

We will show the prisons, the courts, and the state that we will not tolerate the oppression of our sisters anywhere, in any way, shape or form.

Pass the Word, Sister

(Leaflet distributed at demonstration to support Panther sisters, New Haven, Conn., November 22, 1969, by Women's International Terrorist Conspiracy from Hell [WITCH])

Erika Huggins.
Frances Carter.
Rose Smith.
Loretta Luckes.
Margaret Hudgins.
Maud Frances.

6 sisters in prison.
3 sisters pregnant.
2 sisters almost in labor.
All have been falsely accused
of conspiracy and murder.
None have been tried
or found guilty.
All 6 are black.

All 6 are Panthers.
All 6 are sisters.

CONFINEMENT: 1. The act of
shutting within an enclosure;
the act of imprisoning.
2. The state of being restrained
or obliged to stay indoors.
3. A woman's lying-in;
childbirth.
Standard
College
Dictionary

How does Niantic State
Woman's Farm treat women
in confinement?
They are:
isolated from other prisoners;
denied sleep by the continual
noise of walkie-talkies
and constant bright lights;
denied their constitutional right
to prepare their case;
denied their legal right
to choice of counsel.

How does Niantic State
Woman's Farm prepare women
for their confinement?
They are:
denied their choice of doctors;
denied information about childbirth;
denied their choice of method
of childbirth; deprived of proper diet,
exercise, medication & clothing.

Rose Smith weighed 132 pounds
at the start of her pregnancy.
Now—7 months pregnant—
after Niantic's prenatal care,
Rose Smith weighs 133 pounds.

Guards will be there
when the babies are born.

Guards will be there
to take them away.
The State will decide
who's "fit" and who's "not fit"
to guard and be guardian
of mother and child.

Children oppressed:
on welfare, in orphanages,
in schools, in foster homes;
by poverty, by routine,
by racism, by male supremacy.

Therefore,
WITCH curses the State
and declares it unfit.

WITCH knows our suppressed history:
that women who rebel are not only
jailed, napalmed, & beaten, but also
raped, branded & burned at the stake.

We women are:
in jail at Niantic
in the mud of Vietnam
in the slums of the cities
in the ghetto-sinks of suburbia
at the typewriters
of the corporations
at the mimeograph machines
of the Left
in the water at Chappaquidick
in the brutalizing beds of Babylon

We are going to stop
all confinement of women.

WITCH calls down destruction
on Babylon
Oppressors:
the curse of women is on you.

DEATH TO MALE CHAUVINISM.

Congress to Unite Women—What Women Want

(Workshops program for Saturday, November 22, 1969, New York)

Description of some topics to be considered by the workshops:

1 EARLY CHILDHOOD: CARE & EDUCATION
More and better child care facilities are an absolutely urgent need, to make the liberation of women real. It is imperative we activate present laws in this area or find further possibilities for political action, immediately, for the benefit of: working mothers, non-working mothers, fathers, the changing family structure, equal partnership between men and women regardless of income, the growing needs of today's children, who live in a complex, pluralistic society. Do you agree or disagree?

2 EDUCATION (with stress on secondary & higher)
To open the door to true equality for women today, we must equalize higher education opportunities across the board, in: aptitude evaluation; college-entrance requirements; "women's studies"—substituting facts for mystiques and myths; course planning; study and vocational counseling; graduate school qualifications; loans and fellowships; professional training quotas; double-standard social regulations on campus; female role models; faculty nepotism rules; "continuing education" for women returning to work. Do you agree or disagree?

3 EMPLOYMENT
Damaging inequality hits the working woman in: salaries, legal rights and restrictions, sexist typecasting, unwritten laws of behavior, authority, access to information, amount of work expected, time structuring, status, getting credit, value to employer and prospective employers, use of capabilities, growth potential, the ceiling on her aspirations. Do you agree or disagree?

4 FAMILY STRUCTURE

Central to family structure is the institution of marriage. We will examine how women are forced into marriage and how this institution constitutes legal slavery, as well as the myth that marriage and family structure benefit women. Also to be discussed will be the economic function of the family unit and its importance in maintaining male supremacy.

5 THE "FEMININE IMAGE"

Our stereotyped image—most blatantly seen in the presentations of the mass media, academic fields, etc.—is in fact in everybody's head. Women did not create this set of stereotypes. Who produces and reinforces this image? Why? Who benefits? From our awareness that it is not to our advantage to perpetuate this "Feminine Image" we see the need to work together to create a new and fully-human concept of Woman.

6 HOW WOMEN ARE DIVIDED: Class, Racial, Sexual, and Religious Differences

If sisterhood between women were a fact, it would not be necessary to hold this conference. This workshop will explore the specific ways we are divided, with the hope that understanding this may help us to find out how we can work together and who and what is responsible for the division.

7 LOVE AND SEX

Tracing briefly the history of the concept of love, and the institution of heterosexual sex down through the ages—especially in western society; relationship between love in sex and love in religion; theories of sex and how they are used to degrade and exploit women; the semantics of love in sex; the concept of love as a reaction to, and defense against, oppression; female fantasies and media reinforcement of male fantasies; would women's liberation lead to the end of sex or to better sex?

8 THE NATURE AND FUNCTION OF A FEMINIST GROUP

Why we need a group (the superiority of collective to individual action; the "consciousness" and "stability" of a group versus the "spontaneity" of a purely mass movement); structure—the ways in which a group organizes to insure a maximum of efficiency, to create power for itself, and to develop skills and abilities in each of its members. The ways in which individual responsibility and self-discipline are encouraged and utilized by the group. Equality and the lot system in a leader-less group. Resistance to the idea of a group.

9 POLITICAL POWER

The movement of women's liberation requires re-examination of all institutions, both political and those not now considered political, in terms of how they keep women politically power-less. The concept of individual liberation is an illusion. The goals of the women's liberation movement can only be achieved by means of a united political struggle.

10 REPRODUCTION AND ITS CONTROL

This group will discuss: the freedom to choose whether to bear children as a woman's basic human right, and as a pre-requisite to the exercise of the other freedoms she may win; elimination of all laws and practices that compel women to bear children against their will (professional practices, public and private attitudes, and legal barriers limiting access to contraception and abortion), research in extrauterine gesta-tion.

11 THE SEX-ROLE SYSTEM

Despite technological advances, humanity has made no prog-ress in interpersonal relationships. This workshop will explore the alternatives to the traditional female and male sex roles and how to cope with the hostilities that one encounters when one dares to have an identity independent of those sex roles. We will attempt to redefine male and female roles—or, better yet, eliminate them altogether.

12 WOMEN AND THE LAW

Review of the bases of the Supreme Court decisions—as late as 1961—that women are not "persons" in the legal sense, with discussion of what legislative measures are necessary to accomplish equal protection of the law, civil rights, and af-firmative action programs on behalf of women. Please bring ideas.

Saturday Afternoon at the Congress to Unite Women

Evelyn Leo

I was in the school building only about 10 minutes when there was a commotion in the hall. Bill Baird had pushed his way into the building, followed by a TV cameraman, grinding away, men with floodlights and a few women, who were responsible for his being there. He came on with a big "pity me" attitude, reciting that he was in debt for $50,000, was awaiting a jail sentence, had done more for women on the abortion issue than any woman who was in that building. His rap was that he wanted to address the Congress NOW and he just would not take no for an answer. To me this was typical of the sexual relationship with men: when they wanted intercourse NOW, it had to be NOW. However, he was pushed a little, talked to for some time about the fact that it was a private meeting, that a vote had been taken by the women at the Congress and a decision had been reached that there were to be no men present and that was it, and he would have to leave.

He left, but only after trying to shout down and coerce the women who engaged in conversation with him. I was told that when he was outside he was angry with the women who had put him up to it. He was put down and I suppose eventually had to put it on women.

After this and before the workshops started again, all the women were called into the auditorium and there was a discussion about what had taken place with Bill Baird and how that situation should be handled if it happened again. The women were almost split in half about why not only Bill Baird, but men in general were not allowed at the Congress.

I next went to the workshop on "How Women are Divided: Class, Racial, Sexual and Religious Differences." The first exchange that took place is worth noting. A black woman said

127

she had been at the workshop that morning and went on to complain about what a waste it had been because everyone was talking around the subject and not at it, etc. A white woman responded and said, "It was not as black as you are painting it." Need I say more.

It seemed to me that the most divisive factor between women is competition between women for men. I am beginning to see this as the main one, because it then spirals into so many others, i.e., becoming the sex object, taking on the sex image, being manipulated as a sex object, coming on strong as the sex object so that you will be assured of your security through some man. MAN *is the symbol of Everywoman's security and you* BETTER *fight for him.*

The discussion about why it was difficult to bring certain women, the black woman, suburban housewife, older woman, into Woman's Lib, was more revealing about the divisive factors between women than any other topic. It brought out more strongly that the economics of living was what kept most women from having the guts to get involved.

Suburban housewives see Woman's Lib as a demand that they leave their husbands. They also see it as demanding that they take issue with politics, the war, free love, etc. They are not willing to do this because where would they get their bread if they challenged their man. Older women were pictured as being too inflexible in their attitudes; but again this goes back to economic factors, because their free daughters would not necessarily stick around to help them and support them in their old age. As one woman said, with much anger, these are real threats, not to be treated lightly or with contempt.

I think, for me, one of the most beautiful things that came out of this workshop was that black women are way ahead of white women on taking issue with society, on standing independent of and with men. They are together and they are stronger because they have had to take the lead and they have learned to cope with the loss of those things the white woman takes for granted as being hers. Other white women have told me that their black women friends had expressed this reaction to Woman's Lib.

My feeling, upon reflection on this workshop, is that our group has dealt with all the subjects that came up in discussion and that it is not necessary to have such a large gathering in order for the individual woman to reach the same insights. The small group can achieve the same goal. The large Congress is necessary for the actions that take place afterwards.

I also think that we women who are in Woman's Lib must get the message across that we want to take the woman out of her role solely as sex object and put her in the role of human being first. That we are not asking her to set aside the good things in her life but only to destroy the things that are destroying her as a human being.

There are a lot more issues going around inside my head which I have to sort out. I find it even more difficult to separate the political from the Woman's Lib issues, but again, found agreement that we women must not allow our energies to be watered down by running after each and every issue but must necessarily determine first if we are helping Everywoman.

Again, and this may be premature, we must not only consider new freedoms for women but at the same time must consider new roles for men. This may even be an automatic process which results from defining new styles for women.

Women Unite for Revolution*

The Congress to Unite Women is a historic event in the unfinished revolution for women's liberation. Over 500 women from the eastern United States met in New York November 21-23 to set up a Congress to Unite Women. A Continuing Committee was established to carry out the decisions of the Congress and to set in motion procedures for a permanent nation-wide coalition for women's liberation.

The Congress to Unite Women is committed to the liberation of all women now. We know that only with power can we end the oppression of women. Together, in a united Congress we will fight for what is good for women.

1. With regard to early childhood education and care: We demand nation-wide free twenty-four-hour-a-day child care centers for all children from infancy to early adolescence, regardless of their parents' income or marital status, with child care practices decided by those using the centers. To encourage the breakdown of sex role stereotypes, these centers must be staffed equally by women and men. Their wages should be equal to those of public school teachers.

*From *Woman's Monthly* (November 28, 1969).

Until these free child care centers are established, we demand immediate national and state legislation for deduction of child care expenses from income before taxes.

2. In the field of education, we are against the tracking system. We believe high school and college guidance counseling must not restrict individuals to sex-determined roles. Home economics, shop, and other vocational courses must be made available to all without regard to sex. History texts and anthologies of literature must be changed to represent fairly and correctly the achievements of women. Workshops on women's problems should be conducted for parents, teachers, and teachers-in-training, and be included in adult and continuing education courses.

Women, regardless of marital status or pregnancy, must be guaranteed the right to attend school.

We demand a women's studies section in all public libraries and school and university libraries.

We encourage the academic community to restructure language to reflect a society in which women have equal status with men.

Educational institutions must no longer be exempt from Title VII of the 1964 Civil Rights Act.

We demand the elimination of nepotism rules from colleges and universities.

We demand that all educational institutions set up day care centers for all students, faculties, and staff.

Woman's study programs should be established in all colleges and universities.

3. On the subject of employment, we demand that working hours be made flexible for both men and women.

We demand legal steps to open trade schools and unions to women.

We support ACLU Women's Rights Project, and intend to create dossiers analyzing individual companies and the per cent of women hired in each job category.

Part-time employment must be made available for women who want it.

All women are oppressed as women and can unite on that basis; however, we acknowledge that there are differences among women—male-created—of economic and social privilege, race, education, etc., and that these differences are real, not imaginary. Such divisions must be eliminated. They can only be eliminated by hard work and concrete action, not by rhetoric.

POLITICAL POWER. The Congress to Unite Women announces the formation of a women's political power block to fight for women's liberation. We now expand the definition of political to include women's "personal" lives, meaning both the structure of government in the present society, and new alternatives on which women unite. While we demand representation on all such bodies in proportion to our numbers (presently 51%), we see this only as a means to an even larger end—the total liberation of women by every avenue available.

1. We will work against people in politically powerful positions who have demonstrated that they oppose our interest.

2. We are determined to get priority in political attention for our issues, particularly child care, abortion, civil rights, and the Equal Rights amendment.

SEX ROLES. We must proceed on the assumption that there are *no* biological bases for any sex-role differentiation beyond the basic reproductive functions. If we are truly free we will soon find out what differences there are, if any.

Children should be given *human* models to emulate, not just male and female models.

We must each have the courage to fight to live our own beliefs in undifferentiated sex roles.

WOMEN & THE LAW. We resolve to direct attention to two issues now:

1. The Civil Rights Act of 1964 includes sex in only Title VII, which covers employment. There is no provision for penalty against discrimination or enforcement of the act. There is no money available for suits, which must be instituted at the expense of the plaintiff.

2. An Equal Rights Amendment is essential. While the 14th Amendment guarantees equal protection under the law to all persons who are citizens, the Supreme Court has refused to rule on the issue of whether women are persons.

ABORTION. The Congress to Unite Women recognizes women's basic human right to decide whether to have children and opposes in the courts, in the legislature and in direct action all attitudes, practices, and laws that would compel any woman to bear a child against her will. We not only demand the *total* repeal *now* of all laws restricting access to contraception, sterilization, and abortion, and in the free public provision of such birth control services in all hospitals and clinics; but, concomitantly, we insist that appropriate safeguards be developed so that women are not coerced or in any way pressured into birth control, sterilization or abortion.

We protest the derogatory image of women presented by the media. This Congress deplores the misrepresentation of the movement for women's liberation to the women of America.

What Can Be Learned

A Critique of the Miss America Protest

(November, 1968)

CAROL HANISCH

The protest of the Miss America Pageant in Atlantic City in September told the nation that a new feminist movement is afoot in the land. Due to the tremendous coverage in the mass media, millions of Americans now know there is a Woman's Liberation Movement. Media coverage ranged from the front pages of several newspapers in the United States to many articles in the foreign press.

The action brought many new members into our group and many requests from women outside the city for literature and information. A recurrent theme was, "I've been waiting so long for something like this." So have we all, and the Miss America protest put us well on our way.

But no action taken in the Women's Liberation Struggle will be all good or all bad. It is necessary that we analyze each step to see what we did that was effective, what was not, and what was downright destructive.

At this point in our struggle, our actions should be aimed primarily at doing two inter-related things: 1) awakening the latent consciousness of women about their own oppression, and 2) building sisterhood. With these as our primary immediate goals, let us examine the Miss America protest.

The idea came out of our group method of analyzing women's oppression by recalling our own experiences. We were watching *Schmearguntz,* a feminist movie, one night at our meeting. The movie had flashes of the Miss America contest in it. I found myself sitting there remembering how I had felt at home with my family watching the pageant as a child, an adolescent, and a college student. I knew it had evoked powerful feelings.

When I proposed the idea to our group, we decided to go around the room with each woman telling how she felt about the pageant. We discovered that many of us who had always put down the contest still watched it. Others, like myself, had consciously identified with it, and had cried with the winner.

From our communal thinking came the concrete plans for the action. We all agreed that our main point in the demonstration would be that all women were hurt by beauty competition—Miss America as well as ourselves. We opposed the pageant in our own self-interest, e.g. the self-interest of all women.

Yet one of the biggest mistakes of the whole pageant was our anti-womanism. A spirit of every woman "do her own thing" began to emerge. Sometimes it was because there was an open conflict about an issue. Other times, women didn't say anything at all about disagreeing with a group decision; they just went ahead and did what they wanted to do, even though it was something the group had definitely decided against. Because of this egotistic individualism, a definite strain of anti-womanism was presented to the public to the detriment of the action.

Posters which read "Up Against the Wall, Miss America," "Miss America Sells it," and "Miss America Is a Big Falsie" hardly raised any woman's consciousness and really harmed the cause of sisterhood. Miss America and all beautiful women came off as our enemy instead of as our sisters who suffer with us. A group decision had been made rejecting these anti-woman signs. A few women made them anyway. Some women who had opposed the slogans were in the room when the signs were being made and didn't confront those who were making the anti-woman signs.

A more complex situation developed around the decision of a few women to use an "underground" disruptive tactic. The action was approved by the group only after its adherents said they would do it anyway as an individual action. As it turned out, we came to the realization that there is no such thing as "individual action" in a movement. We were linked to and were commited to support our sisters whether they called their action "individual" or not. It also came to many of us that there is at this time no real need to do "underground" actions. We need to reach as many women as possible as quickly as possible with a clear message that has the power of our person behind it. At this point women have to see other women standing up and saying these things. That's why draping a women's liberation banner over the balcony that night and yelling our message was much clearer. We should have known, however, that the television network, because it was not competing with other networks for coverage, would not put the action on camera. It did get on the radio and in newspapers, however.

The problem of how to enforce group decisions is one we haven't solved. It came up in a lot of ways throughout the whole action. The group rule of not talking to male reporters was another example.

One of the reasons we came off anti-woman, besides the posters, was our lack of clarity. We didn't say clearly enough that we women are all FORCED to play the Miss America role —not by beautiful women but by men who we have to act that way for and by a system that has so well institutionalized male supremacy for its own ends.

This was none too clear in our guerilla theater either. Women chained to a replica, red-white-and-blue-bathing-suited Miss America could have been misinterpreted as against beautiful women. Also, crowning a live sheep Miss America sort of said that beautiful women *are* sheep. However, the action did say to some women that women are *viewed* as auction-block, docile animals. The grandmother of one of the participants really began to understand the action when she was told about the sheep, and she ended up joining the protest.

There is as great a need for clarity in our language as there is in our actions. The leaflet that was distributed as a press release and as a flyer at the action was too long, too wordy, too complex, too hippie-yippee-campy. Instead of an "in" phrase like "Racism with Roses" (I still don't know exactly what that means), we could have just called the pageant RACIST and everybody would have understood our opposition on that point. If we are going to reach masses of women, we must give up all the "in-talk" of the New Left/Hippie movements—at least when we're talking in public. (Yes, even the word FUCK!) We can use simple language (*real* language) that everyone from Queens to Iowa will understand and not misunderstand.

We should try to avoid the temptation to say everything there is to say about what is wrong with the world and thereby say nothing that a new person can really dig into and understand. Women's liberation itself is revolutionary dynamite. When other issues are interjected, we should clearly relate them to our oppression *as women*.

We tried to carry the democratic means we used in planning the action into the actual *doing* of it. We didn't want leaders or spokesmen. It makes the movement not only *seem* stronger and larger if everyone is a leader, but it actually *is* stronger if not dependent on a few. It also guards against the time when such leaders could be isolated and picked off one way or another. And of course many voices are more powerful than one.

Our first attempt at this was not entirely successful. We must learn how to fight against the media's desire to make leaders and some women's desire to be spokesmen. Everybody talks to the press or nobody talks to the press. The same problem came up in regard to appearances on radio and television shows after the action. We theoretically decided no one should appear more than once, but it didn't work out that way.

The Miss America protest was a zap action, as opposed to person to person group action. Zap actions are using our presence as a group and/or the media to make women's oppression into social issues. In such actions we speak to men as a group as well as to women. It is a rare opportunity to talk to men in a situation where they can't talk back. (Men must begin to learn to listen.) Our power of solidarity, not our individual intellectual exchanges, will change men.

We tried to speak to individual women in the crowd and now some of us feel that it may not have been a good tactic. It put women on the spot in front of their men. We were putting them in a position which we choose to avoid ourselves when we don't allow men in our discussion groups.

It is interesting that many of the non-movement women we talked to about the protest had the same reaction as many radical women. "But I'm not oppressed," was a shared response. "I don't care about Miss America," was another. If more than half the television viewers in the country watch the pageant, somebody cares! And many of us admitted watching it too, even while putting it down.

It's interesting, too, that while much of the Left was putting us down for attacking something so "silly and unimportant" or "reformist", the Right saw us as a threat and yelled such things as "Go back to Russia" and "Mothers of Mao" at the picket line. Ironically enough, what the Left/Underground press seemed to like best about our action was what was really our worst mistake—our anti-woman signs.

Surprisingly and fortunately some of the mass media ignored our mistakes and concentrated on our best points. To quote from the *Daily News,* ". . . some women who think the whole idea of such contests is degrading to femininity, took their case to the people. . . . During boardwalk protest, gals say they're not anti-beauty, just anti-beauty contest." Shana Alexander wrote in a *Life* magazine editorial that she "wished they'd gone farther." Together *Life* and the *Daily News* reach millions of Americans.

We need to take ourselves seriously. The powers that be do. Carol Giardina of Gainesville, Florida, was fired from her job because of her activities in women's liberation and her participation in the protest. Police cars were parked outside the planning meeting one night. The next day we got a call from the mayor of Atlantic City questioning us about just what we planned to do. Pepsi-Cola is withdrawing as a sponsor of the pageant. They produce a diet cola and maybe see themselves as next year's special target.

Unfortunately the best slogan for the action came up about a month after when Roz Baxendall came out on the David Susskind show with "Every day in a woman's life is a walking Miss America Contest." We shouldn't wait for the best slogan; we should go ahead to the best of our understanding. We hope all our sisters can learn something as we did from our first foray.

Women's Liberation Fights Washington, D. C., Health Crisis*

Sept. 1969 After doing abortion counseling for over a year and angered by arbitrary interpretations of law by doctors, psychiatrists and hospital boards, D. C. Women's Liberation and Citywide Welfare Alliance and the Medical Com-

*From *WOMEN: A Journal of Liberation* (Winter, 1970), © 1970 Women: A Journal of Liberation, Inc.

mittee for Human Rights sent telegrams to city health officials asking them to meet to clarify regulations of abortion in D. C. The group demanded that the city make public statistical information on actual conditions. The telegrams were not answered, but the women went to D. C. General Hospital where cops stopped them at the main gates. Inside, 190 interns and residents were holding their own press conference to announce 33 demands and threatening a heal-in (acceptance of all patients on need rather than availability of services). Police, uptight about the women who had arrived, refused to let the press go in to meet the doctors. The doctors then walked out of the hospital to hold a press conference in the street. This *appeared* to be a joint press conference, but actually the doctors were at that time outraged by the women's abortion literature. The next day WL, CWA and MCHR sat in with the Director of Public Health to set up a committee of their coalition with health professionals to draft policy suggestions. Mayor Washington activated a task force on health resources made up of elite professionals and experts who held closed meetings. WL, CWA, and MCHR disrupted and entered several meetings in process. The task force voted them into the group, but Mayor Washington told Women's Liberation to get off the task force or it would be disbanded. D. C. women interpreted the Mayor's action as an attempt to make WL the scapegoat and to break up a coalition between black and white women. Women's Liberation was finally invited to work with the subcommittees of the task force and they accepted in order to: "educate ourselves about the workings of the health system, to make contact within the medical systems with whatever radical energy did exist, to legitimize ourselves as a group willing to commit ourselves seriously to the untangling and eventual resolving of the issues, to dramatize the lethargy and apathy of the task force, to control the general direction of the task force, to make an analysis which will not be made by vested interests of the professional elite."

Women Destroy Draft Files*

An anti-war, anti-imperialist raid on a draft board took place in New York City in July. Destroyed were at least 6,500 1-A files, most of the cross reference system, and the "1" and "A"

*From *WOMEN: A Journal of Liberation* (Winter, 1970), © 1970 Women: A Journal of Liberation, Inc.

keys on typewriters. Pictures of one week's war dead were pasted up and a note was left to the workers at the draft board explaining that women had done the action and why they had done it.

The women then appeared, as they had promised they would, at a demonstration in Rockefeller Center on July 3. They stated that they wanted to make clear the connection between overseas corporate involvement and American military and political intrusions into the affairs of Asia, Africa, and Latin America; and that corporations such as Dow, Standard Oil, Shell, and Chase Manhattan bear much responsibility for U. S. domination of those areas from which we profit. Although the police knew which women were the participants in the action, six were arrested, including two who had had nothing to do with the action. The women had been tossing shredded 1-A files into the air amid lunchtime crowds.

Funeral Oration for Traditional Womanhood*

KATHIE AMATNIEK

You see here the remains of a female human being who during her all too short a lifetime was a familiar figure to billions of people in every corner of the world. Although scientists would classify this specimen within the genus species of homo sapiens, for many years there has been considerable controversy as to whether she really belonged in some kind of sub-species of the genus. While the human being was distinguished as an animal who freed himself from his biological limitations by developing technology and expanding his consciousness, traditional Womanhood has been recognized, defined and valued for her biological characteristics only and those social functions closely related to her biological characteristics.

As human beings, both men and women were sexual creatures and they shared their sexuality. But the other areas of

*From Notes from the First Year (June, 1968).

humanity were closed off to Traditional Womanhood . . . the areas which, as has already been noted, were more character-istically human, less limited by biology. For some reason, man said to woman: you are less sexual when you participate in those other things, you are no longer attractive to me if you do so. I like you quiet and submissive. It makes me feel as if you don't love me, if you fail to let me do all the talking . . . if you actually have something to say yourself. Or else, when I like you to be charming and well-educated . . . entertain-ment for me and an intelligent mother for my children . . . these qualities are for me and for me alone. When you con-front the world outside the home—the world where I operate as an individual self as well as a husband and father—then, for some reason, I feel you are a challenge to me and you become sexless and aggressive.

If you turn me off too much, you know, I'll find myself another woman. And if that happens, what will you do? You'll be a nobody, that's what you'll be. An old maid, if I haven't deigned to marry you yet. A divorced woman . . . with some children, no doubt. Without me, you won't even have your sexuality anymore, that little bit of humanity which I have allowed you. And even if you manage to solve that problem in some kind of perverse way, it's going to be hard for you.

What kinds of jobs can you get to keep yourself in com-fort? I control those few interesting, challenging ones. And I control the salaries on all the other kinds of jobs from which my fellow men who work at them will at least get the satisfac-tion of more *pay* than you. And I control the government and its money which, you can bet your tax dollar, isn't going to get allotted for enough good nursery schools to put your children into so you can go out to work. And because of all these things, there can always be another woman in my life, when you no longer *serve* my needs.

And so Traditional Womanhood, even if she was unhappy with her lot, believed that there was nothing she could do about it. She blamed herself for her limitations and she tried to *adapt*. She told herself and she told others that she was happy as half a person, as the "better half" of someone else, as the mother of others, powerless in her own right.

Though Traditional Womanhood was a hardy dame, the grand old lady finally died today—her doctor said, of a bad case of shock. Her flattering menfolk had managed to keep her alive for thousands of years. She survived the Amazon challenge. She survived the Lysistrata challenge. She survived the Feminist challenge. And she survived many face-liftings. She was burning her candle at one end on a dull wick and she went out slowly, but she finally went . . . not with a bang but a whimper.

There are some grounds for believing that our march today contributed to the lady's timely demise and this is partly the reason we have decided to hold her funeral here. The old hen, it turns out, was somewhat disturbed to hear *us*—other women, that is—asserting ourselves just this least little bit about critical problems in the world controlled by men. And it was particularly frightening to her to see other women, we women, asserting ourselves together, however precariously, in some kind of solidarity, instead of completely resenting each other, being embarrassed by each other, hating each other and hating ourselves.

And we were even attempting to organize ourselves on the basis of power . . . that little bit of power we are told we have here in America . . . the so-called power of wives and mothers. That this power is only a *substitute* for power, that it really amounts to nothing politically, is the reason why all of us attending this funeral must bury Traditional Womanhood tonight. We must bury her in Arlington Cemetery, however crowded it is by now. For in Arlington Cemetery, our national monument to war, alongside Traditional Manhood is her natural resting place.

Now some sisters here are probably wondering why we should bother with such an unimportant matter at a time like this. Why should we bury Traditional Womanhood while hundreds of thousands of human beings are being brutally slaughtered in our names . . . when it would seem that our number one task is to devote our energies directly to ending this slaughter or else solve what seem to be more desperate problems at home?

Sisters who ask a question like this are failing to see that they really do have a problem as women in America . . . that their problem is social, not merely personal . . . and that their problem is so closely related and interlocked with the other problems in our country, the very problem of war itself . . . that we cannot hope to move toward a better world or even a truly democratic society at home until we begin to solve our own problems.

How many sisters failed to join our march today because they were afraid their husbands would disapprove? How many more sisters failed to join us today because they've been taught to believe that women are silly and a women's march even sillier? And how many millions of sisters all across America failed to join us because they think so little of themselves that they feel incapable of thinking *for* themselves . . . about the war in Vietnam or anything else? And if some sisters come to conclusions of their own, how many others of us fail to express these ideas, much less argue and demonstrate for them, because we're afraid of seeming unattractive, silly, "uppity"? To the America watching us, after all, we here on this march are mere women, looking silly and unattractive.

Yes, sisters, we have a problem as women all right, a problem which renders us powerless and ineffective over the issues of war and peace, as well as over our own lives. And although our problem is Traditional Manhood as much as Traditional Womanhood, we women must begin on the solution.

We must see that we can only solve our problem together, that we cannot solve it individually as earlier Feminist generations attempted to do. We women must organize so that for man there can be no "other woman" when we begin expressing ourselves and acting politically, when we insist to men that they share the housework and child-care, fully and equally, so that we can have independent lives as well.

Human qualities will make us attractive then, not servile qualities. We will want to have daughters as much as we want to have sons. Our children will not become victims of our unconscious resentments and our displaced ambitions. And both our daughters and sons will be free to develop themselves in just the directions they want to go as human beings.

Sisters: men need us, too, after all. And if we just get together and tell our men that we want our freedom as full human beings, that we don't want to live just through our man and his achievements and our mutual offspring, that we want human power in our own right, not just "power behind the throne," that we want neither dominance or submission for anybody, anyplace, in Vietnam or in our own homes, and that when we all have our freedom we can truly love each other.

If men fail to see that love, justice and equality are the solution, that domination and exploitation hurt everybody, then our species is truly doomed; for if domination and exploitation and aggression are inherent biological characteristics which cannot be overcome, then nuclear war is inevitable and we will have reached our evolutionary deadend by annihilating ourselves.

And that is why we must bury this lady in Arlington Cemetery tonight, why we must bury Submission alongside Aggression. And that is why we ask you to join us. It is only a symbolic happening, of course, and we have a lot of real work to do. We have new men as well as a new society to build.

Questions I Should Have Answered Better: A Guide to Women Who Dare to Speak Publicly

SALLY MEDORA WOOD

Part I: Prepare Yourself

Learning to speak in public is one thing; learning to speak about women's liberation is quite another, as I found to my dismay. Approaching my first talk prepared with ample amounts of information and self-confidence, I was struck— devastated is perhaps a more accurate term—by the intensity of the audience's personal reactions to me, and by their seemingly illogical questions. I've thought and learned a lot since then, and my point in writing this paper is to let you who are contemplating speaking about women's liberation to un-initiated audiences know what you might be getting into, and what you might do about it.

When speaking for women's liberation, as when any action is taken before an audience, the participants become objec-tified. That is, the audience does not relate to them as human beings, but as who or what they symbolically portray. The steel company representative stands symbolically for the whole steel company although everyone understands, intellectually, that he or she is only one person who works for the steel company. Likewise the poor black man represents all poor black men, and all the feelings the audience has about the group as a whole are projected upon him. But while everyone is not emotionally involved with the steel company or with a poor black man, everyone is emotionally involved with at least one woman. Thus the experience of objectification, while certainly not unique to the women's liberation speaker, hits her particularly hard due to the intense emotional involvement on the part of her audience.

Moreover, the women's liberation speaker must be aware that she and the ideas she presents are a personal threat to most of her audience. The liberation of women—and the subsequent liberation of men—is a frightening idea. To uninitiated women, it says that their values and the very mode of their lives is hypocritical; to men it points out quite definitely that the time has come to move over—and fast. For some women, of course, the experience will be an exciting and liberating one, but for many the initial exposure is frightening.

The most important thing to do while speaking is to take yourself seriously. You will be hassled and attacked for the reasons discussed above. The amount of hostility will increase with your audience's awareness that what you are proposing is not just a reform movement, but a restructuring of society in which everyone must take part. Don't ask for sympathy in the face of their hostility. Stand up and answer. The oppression of women is serious; you are to be taken seriously.

Perhaps your first chance to practice being tough, yet human, will take place even before your talk begins. Often when the speaker is introduced, especially when she is introduced by a man, references will be made to her appearance, boyfriends, husband, or children which are intended to show that she is in actuality firmly entrenched in a "woman's place," and therefore not really important.

Here is pretty little Miss _____ who is going to tell you all about something called women's liberation.

or

I want to introduce Mrs. _____ who is speaking about women's liberation. Now don't any of you guys get any ideas, because her husband is sitting right down there in the audience.

These gems will be followed by appreciative chuckles from the men and perhaps some of the women in the audience. Don't laugh or smile as it's obviously not funny. On the other hand, it is probably ineffective (however satisfying) to sock the program chairman in the jaw or to scream obscenities at him. If you're totally enraged, you've lost control of the situation. Wait until the last chuckle has died down and then say in clear definite tones that it is not clear to you what your appearance (or your husband, etc.) has to do with your credentials as a speaker. Say it firmly, and then begin your talk. Don't get into a verbal exchange with the program chairman (that's not what you're there for) and don't seize the opportunity to explain why your being pretty is irrelevant unless your audience is both knowledgeable about and favorable to women's liberation. If you make your point later, it will become self-evident why your appearance is not under consideration, and why the program chairman is a racist (sexist).

When speaking before women's groups, and being introduced by women, the program chairman sometimes includes a description of your "credentials" as a woman (married, engaged, children, etc.) so as to prove that you are really one of them. It might be effective to say something like:

I didn't come here because of my children (husband, etc.). I am here because we are all women; we are oppressed; and we must fight our oppression together.

You must prove you are "one of them" through creating awareness of your common plight, rather than your matching numbers of children.

Many of these problems of objectification, fear, and introduction can be avoided or lessened when talking to small groups of women. But however greater the effectiveness of small female groups, there are many opportunities that should not be passed up where larger, mixed groups are involved.

Part II: Question and Answer

The seeming irrationality of the questions asked by people in the audience is directly related to the simple fact that most of them don't understand much about and don't believe in women's liberation. For example even the most straightforward question like, "What is the point of women's liberation?" is profoundly illogical to the believer, particularly if she is under the impression that she has just spent twenty minutes explaining it in detail. For the explanation involves volumes of social analysis concerning the entire society, yet the questioner is in the society (in fact has just heard her speech) and can not see what to her is so painfully obvious. And it's hard for the believer to go back eons of time to when she didn't understand either, and try again to answer the question sensibly.

But however impossible these questions are, they are being asked seriously, and represent people that have to be reached and communicated with. Agreeing with sisters after a speech or discussion that "those people were just insane" might relieve some emotional tension, but it is not the way to get the revolution going. It must be remembered that while the old man in the back who leeringly asked about the speaker's sexual hang-ups is never going to be convinced that women should be other than whores, all the women in the audience will be watching and learning about women's liberation from her answer. And they will not be careless in their observations. We must not be careless in our answers.

Short, complete, concise answers are much better than long involved rhetoric. And, it's important to listen carefully to the question, for the most brilliant answer is useless if it is out of place. Listen carefully for questions beneath the question. For example, implied in the question, "What's wrong with being feminine?" are the questions "What's wrong with being masculine?" and, more personally, "What's wrong with me?" The answer, if it is to be effective, must apply to all of these.

Most probably your answers to these questions won't be the same as mine, but at least you'll know that these questions do exist and can prepare yourself. The questions were selected and answered in reference to a sexually mixed audience which was politically moderate and almost totally unexposed to women's liberation. Almost all of the questions were actually asked, and this is especially true of the more outrageous ones, as I couldn't have thought of those anyway.

What do you have against Motherhood?

Nothing. It's just that I'm for fatherhood too. I think that both the mother and the father should share equally in caring for and enjoying the children. It is unfortunate that many men work long hours and almost never see their children, except when they are presented clean and sweet smelling for an evening romp and a good night kiss. A father would know his children better if he had a chance to see them in all circumstances—the good as well as the bad. The mother could then enjoy her children more too, because if responsibility for them were shared, she wouldn't feel so burdened by them. Equality of responsibility is very hard to achieve in the nuclear family, and this is one reason for the interest in communal situations.

Don't you think that some women just like to stay at home and take care of children? I mean, some women wouldn't be happy doing anything else. [Asked by a male who obviously hopes he has one like that.]

Yes, I think that some women just like to stay home and take care of children. And I think some men do too. More men probably would if it were generally socially acceptable for them to do so. I have no argument with the women who genuinely like to be full time housewives and mothers.

However, I think that many women, who both love and like their children, get bored and restless in a life filled with diapers and dishes. They feel guilty, for their boredom implies that they are not good mothers. I would hope these women would admit their need to do something else and go ahead and do it. Everyone thinks a woman who doesn't want to stay at home and have children is somehow not a real woman. And likewise, a man who *wants* to stay home is somehow not a real man. It seems to me that people should develop their capacities and choose their life work on the basis of potential and interest, not on the basis of sex. It's almost as absurd as saying that all people with brown hair should do menial work, while all those with blond hair should do professional work, regardless of the individual capacities involved.

But the mother is the one who carries the child and feeds it. It's only logical that she should be the one to take care of it.

It's true that the mother carries the child in her body, and that the father's sperm must join with the egg to produce a child. Perhaps in times when no other food was available, the mother had to breast feed the child until he or she could eat regular food. But today, when breast feeding is a matter of choice, it is totally ridiculous that infant and child care should be relegated on the basis of sex. It would make as much sense to say that because the woman has put forth so much effort to carry the child for nine months, the man should care for it from then on.

Both mother and father are equally responsible for the child and should care for it equally. It's as simple as that.

It says in the Bible that "Man was created for the glory of God, and woman for the glory of man." What do you think of that?

It proves to me beyond a doubt that men (and not women) wrote the Bible.

Don't you think that men and women are just innately different?

I don't know. At this point the question is not an empirical one. There is no way to test it in a controlled environment as all women and all men have been highly socialized. Moreover, even if innate difference were proved, it would go against all of our democratic principles to say that because of this difference one sex should be oppressed by the other.

Well, if you don't think that women's place is in the home, where do you think it is?

I don't think that either men or women have "places" as you say. Each person should find her or his own place according to interest and ability. I don't think that sex should confine a person to a "place" in society.

Women are free now. Just last week _____ [a woman] did _____ [something a man usually does]. Why don't you just do what you want and forget it?

Legally, the Civil Rights Act of 1964 prohibited all discrimination against people because of sex in places of employment where there are 25 or more employees. However, both *rules* and *conventions* serve to carry on sexual discrimination.

In terms of *rules,* employers refuse to hire women for high paying, responsible positions. Others refuse to hire engaged women, or women with small children. The average woman's salary for 1967 was $3000.00 less than men's in the *same job categories*. Sexually differentiated help wanted ads in newspapers serve to illustrate this point, as do quotas for women in school admission

policies. Colleges traditionally have discriminated against
women by instituting hours for women students and not
for men students.

In terms of *convention* there are strong barriers to
overcome. Women who have achieved in traditionally
masculine fields are generally noted as special exceptions.
Articles about a particular "lady engineer" or "lady doctor" reflect this bias. It would seem silly to write a newspaper article about a "male doctor" or a "male president."
Many talented and capable young women are deterred
from professional excellence by the fear of being thought
"unladylike" or "unwomanly." Women who have
achieved responsible positions are scarred by the experience. In short, my answer is that it simply isn't possible
to do what you want and forget discrimination against
women—especially if you're a woman.

Personal statement from a woman in the audience: I did ___
*[a remarkable accomplishment—president of 3 companies,
holder of 5 Ph.D.s, etc.]. Here I am. I made it without any
women's liberation. I relied on myself. If you let yourself be
discriminated against you will be; it's just up to you.*

As you say, if you let yourself be discriminated against
you will be. It sounds like a running battle. The battle
is easier and more effective when all women fight it together. The situation is not that certain individuals are
keeping women down and thus only individuals need to
fight. The whole society is set up to keep women down,
and that's something we all have to change together.

*I'm a woman, and I'm already liberated. What's wrong with
you? [Asked by hip-looking woman.]*

I don't see how anyone, man or woman, can be liberated
in a society that discriminates against 53% of its population. Perhaps if you've found a way to live totally apart
from the society, it's possible. The fact that you're standing there tells me you've not done that. What do you
mean when you say you're liberated? [Listen and see
what she says.]

*Revolution yes, but what does that have to do with women's
liberation? [Inevitably asked, one way or the other, by movement men.]*

In the past it's had little or nothing to do with it, which is exactly the problem. Although revolution in some countries has made some *changes* in the status of women, I know of no country where women are truly liberated. Revolution, if it is successful, must make changes in life style as well as in societal structure. Revolution can not create a free society if one half of the population's role is to serve the other half. Women's liberation is revolutionary because when we reach the state where women are no longer in subservient roles changes will have been made in people's life style and in societal structure. Alteration of the family structure alone will affect the entire economy.

The goal of women's liberation is not to be like men. We don't want to be dominating and brutal oppressors any more than we enjoy being the dominated and brutalized oppressed. We want a different society for all people, not just a bigger share in this one.

Women are discriminated against here, but it's just because it's a small town in a backward part of the country. It's not true in other places, is it? [*Asked by hip teeney-bopper yearning to see the world.*]

Yes. As far as job discrimination goes, figures show clearly that it is a country-wide phenomenon. The media portray women only in limited sex and motherhood roles all over the country. Incidentally the first state to give women the vote was Wyoming, which is not generally thought of as being in the forefront of new ideas and social change.

What's the difference between women's liberation and a ladies' tea group? It seems to me that this is just a tea group for hippie and intellectual left wing women.

The purpose of a tea group is social and companionable conversation. The purpose of women's liberation is revolution.

What's wrong with you? Can't you get a man? [*This will be spoken only by the most candid. It will be thought by many.*]

I sincerely hope that I never "get a man" with all of the subterfuge, dishonesty, and competitiveness that phrase implies. I don't think men should be sexual objects any more than women should be. Making a person into an object to be "gotten" takes away some of that person's humanity, and puts barriers between people.

I want to be judged on my own merits rather than on my husband's or boyfriend's.

[However you choose to answer this question, don't feel that you have to show your "credentials" as a woman to defend yourself. Saying that you're happily married and have 12 children doesn't convince anybody, even if it's true. It just implies that you accept their definition of you as their kind of woman, even while you talk of liberation.]

Are you bitter because you're unloved?

Yes. If you felt that half of the country was trying to put you down, wouldn't you feel unloved too?

What's wrong with being feminine?

I think femininity and masculinity are both myths. "Feminine" is supposed to mean all that is soft, gentle, and helpless and "masculine" is supposed to represent qualities of hardness, strength, and resourcefulness. In actuality, people—both male and female—have both kinds of qualities. It's enough trouble for me to try to be the best kind of person I know how to be without trying to figure out if I'm "masculine" or "feminine."

What don't you go home [where you belong] and solve your own sexual hang-ups?

I don't live in a vacuum. I don't think any individual living in this society can avoid having sexual hang-ups. So if everybody has them, we may as well solve them together.

Well, you're attractive enough. Why don't you just relax and enjoy it?

I enjoy having people think me attractive, myself included. But most of the men who look at me aren't concerned with my attractiveness, or lack of it. They see me only as a collection of sexual parts walking down the street for their amusement. This enrages me and makes me want to kill them, which is not quite the sentiment for effective relaxation.

Why doesn't women's liberation believe in wearing bras?

Women's liberation isn't for or against bras *per se:* some women find them comfortable, some women don't. We're against the idea that any woman who doesn't wear a bra, i.e., who shows her body as it is, is considered to be a whore, slut, or sexually promiscuous.

[Note: The following two questions were asked on the same evening of two women's lib. women, one of whom had on a dress, and one of whom wore jeans. Moral: it doesn't matter what you wear, but be prepared to defend it.]

Why do you wear stockings like that [patterned] and have that long hair if you don't want to be considered a sexual object?

I enjoy making myself attractive to both men and women, including myself. The process of objectification, by definition, originates in the perceiver and not in the perceived.

Why do you wear jeans and try to look so grubby? It doesn't bother me *you understand, but it really hurts your cause. [Asked by a woman who was obviously bothered.]*

Every person has the right to decorate her or himself as she or he chooses. Our cause—for it's your cause too—is not hurt by freedom of choice, but is strengthened when people are free of conventions that are stifling.

What do you think of alimony payments? [Asked suspiciously, by a male].

I think it's silly for a woman to receive support payments just because she's a woman. In some cases where children have to be supported, then certainly the father and mother both should contribute. But the concept of alimony payments in general is one of those so called "special privileges" that make men and women unequal, and I think that the time has come to stop.

Why do you hate men?

I hate men who oppress women. I hate men who look down on women and think of them in terms only of making babies, making men happy, and being made. I hate men who discriminate against women in employment, salary scales, and school admission. I hate men who assume that it is their right to make laws that control women (abortion laws, laws having to do with birth control information, etc.). I hate them because in doing these things they assume that I am less than human. I do not hate men who don't do these things.

Why are you so full of hate?

Because the society is so full of oppression.

What does your husband think of woman's liberation?

You'll have to ask him. [Sometimes, especially in small groups of women, I think it is meaningful to answer this question. Some women want to know if you've worked out a way to work toward liberation with your man, and if perhaps they might do it, too. In large groups the question is too often asked teasingly, or is a request for a male stamp of approval.]

Why aren't there any men in the women's liberation movement? Isn't this segregation?

Yes, it is. However the pattern of our society is such that women are separated from each other through their competition for men. We have to learn to respect each other and value each other as individuals, and we can't begin to learn this unless we are alone together. In addition, to my knowledge there has never been an instance of an oppressor taking the initiative to free the oppressed. If women are to be liberated, we will have to liberate ourselves.

Toward the end of the session, an exasperated and baffled onlooker will inevitably explode with, "Well, what do you [people] want, anyway?"

First of all, in the words of Sarah Grimké, pioneer feminist,

I ask no favors for my sex. I surrender not our claim to equality. All I ask of our brethren is that they will take their feet from off our necks, and permit us to stand upright on the ground which God has designed us to occupy.

> (*The Equality of the Sexes and*
> *the Conditions of Women.*
> Boston: 1838)

Secondly—now in 1970—we want free 24-hour-a-day child care centers, staffed by both males and females and available to every parent so that women can be free to meet together and to begin to learn how to participate as equals in the society. We want equal pay for equal work, an end to job discrimination, and paid maternity leave. We want the legalization of abortion, overhaul of marriage and divorce laws, and free birth control information so that women can control their own bodies. We want the problems of working fathers to be discussed as much as those of working mothers. We want equal educational opportunity at all levels, free education at all levels, courses in women's history and inclusion of women's history in regular textbooks, and a thorough re-study of female psychology. We want equal political representation, free medical and dental care for all people, and no more media portrayal of women as sex machines.

Ultimately, we want all women, regardless of economic class or political position, to struggle against their oppression and to create a life situation in which all people, male and female, will be humane and responsible to each other and in which each person will have an equal say in the functioning of the society.

Address comments, criticisms, requests, gripes, questions, etc., to

Sally Medora Wood, 406 Forrest Ave., Chattanooga, Tenn. 37405

Feminist Consciousness Raising and "Organizing"

Kathie Sarachild

(Outline prepared for a Lake Villa Conference workshop, November, 1968)

I. The "bitch session" cell group
    A. On-going consciousness expansion
        1. Personal recognition and testimony
            a. Recalling and sharing our bitter experiences
            b. Expressing our feelings about our experiences both at the time they occurred and at present
            c. Expressing our feelings about ourselves, men, other women
            d. Evaluating our feelings
        2. Personal testimony—methods of group practice
            a. Going around the room with key questions on key topics
            b. Speaking out experience—at random
            c. Cross examination
            d. Others ????
        3. Relating and generalizing individual testimony
            a. Finding the common root when different women have opposite feelings and experiences
            b. Examining the negative and positive aspects of each woman's feelings and her way of dealing with her situation as a woman
    B. Classic forms of resisting consciousness, or: How to avoid facing the awful truth
        1. Anti-womanism
        2. Glorification of the oppressor

3. Excusing the oppressor (and feeling sorry for him)
4. False identification with the oppressor and other socially privileged groups
5. Shunning identification with one's own oppressed group and other oppressed groups
6. Romantic fantasies, Utopian thinking and other forms of confusing present reality with what one wishes reality to be
7. Thinking one has power in the traditional role—can "get what one wants", has power behind the throne, etc.
8. Belief that one has found an adequate personal solution or will be able to find one without large social changes
9. Self cultivation, rugged individualism, seclusion, and other forms of go-it-alonism
10. Self-blame!!
11. Ultra-militancy & others??? . . .

C. "Starting to Stop"—overcoming repressions and delusions
  1. Daring to see, or: Taking off the rose-colored glasses
     a. Reasons for repressing one's own consciousness
        1) Fear of feeling the full weight of one's painful situation
        2) Fear of feeling one's past wasted and meaningless
           a.) Wanting others to go through the same obstacles
        3) Fear of despair for the future
        4) Fear of hope (fake hope)
        5) Others
     b. Analyzing which fears are valid and which invalid
        1) Examining the objective conditions in one's own past and in the lives of most women throughout history
        2) Examining objective conditions for the present
     c. Discussing possible methods of struggle
        1) History of women's struggle and resistance to oppression

      2) Possibilities for individual struggle at present

      3) Group struggle

  2. Daring to share one's experiences with the group

    a. Sources of hesitancy

      1) Fear of personal exposure (fear of being thought stupid, immoral, weak, self-destructive, etc. by the group)

      2) Feeling of loyalty to one's man, boss, parents, children, friends, "the Movement", etc.

      3) Fear of reprisal if the word gets out (losing one's man, job, reputation, etc.)

      4) Fear of hurting the feelings of someone in the group

      5) Others . . . ???

    b. Deciding which fears are valid and which invalid

    c. Structuring the group so that it is relatively safe for people to participate in it

D. Understanding and developing radical feminist theory

  1. Using above techniques to arrive at an understanding of oppression wherever it exists in our lives—our oppression as black people, workers, tenants, consumers, children or whatever as well as our oppression as women

  2. Analyzing whatever privileges we may have—the white skin privilege, the education and citizen of a big power nation (imperialist) privilege or whatever and seeing how these help to perpetuate our oppression as women, workers, etc.

E. Consciousness-raiser (organizer) training—so that every woman is a given bitch session cell group herself becomes an "organizer" of other groups

  1. The role of the consciousness-raiser "organizer"

    a. Dares to participate

    b. Dares to expose herself, bitch, etc.

    c. Dares to struggle

  2. Learning how to bring theory down to earth, in terms of personal experience, etc.

  3. Learning to "relate" to

    a. Sisters in the group

    b. Other women

    c. Friends and allies

        d. Enemies
      4. Particular problems of starting a new group
II. Consciousness-raising actions
    A. Zap actions
      1. Movie benefits, attacks on cultural phenomenon
        and events, stickers, buttons, posters, films, etc.
    B. Consciousness programs
      1. Newspapers, broadsides, storefronts, women's
        liberation communes, literature, answering mail,
        others . . . ???
    C. Utilizing the mass media
III. Organizing
    A. Helping new people start groups
    B. Intra-group communication and actions
      1. Monthly meetings
      2. Conferences

MYTHS ABOUT WOMEN

The Myth of the Vaginal Orgasm*

ANNE KOEDT

Whenever female orgasm and frigidity is discussed, a false distinction is made between the vaginal and the clitoral orgasm. Frigidity has generally been defined by men as the failure of women to have vaginal orgasms. Actually the vagina is not a highly sensitive area and is not constructed to achieve orgasm. It is the clitoris which is the center of sexual sensitivity and which is the female equivalent of the penis.

I think this explains a great many things: First of all, the fact that the so-called frigidity rate among women is phenomenally high. Rather than tracing female frigidity to the false assumptions about female anatomy, our "experts" have declared frigidity a psychological problem of women. Those women who complained about it were recommended to psychiatrists, so that they might discover their "problem"—diagnosed generally as a failure to adjust to their role as women.

The facts of female anatomy and sexual response tell a different story. There is only one area of sexual climax, although there are many areas for sexual arousal; that area is the clitoris. All orgasms are extensions of sensation from this area. Since the clitoris is not necessarily stimulated sufficiently in the conventional sexual positions, we are left "frigid."

Aside from physical stimulation, which is the common cause of orgasm for most people, there is also stimulation through primarily mental processes. Some women, for example, may achieve orgasm through sexual fantasies, or through fetishes. However, while the stimulation may be psychological, the orgasm manifests itself physically. Thus, while the cause is psychological, the *effect* is still physcial, and the orgasm necessarily takes place in the sexual organ equipped for sexual climax—the clitoris. The orgasm experience may also differ in degree of intensity—some more localized, some more diffuse and sensitive. But they are all clitoral orgasms.

All this leads to some interesting questions about conventional sex and our role in it. Men have orgasms essentially by friction with the vagina, not the clitoral area which is external and not able to cause friction the way penetration does. Women have thus been defined sexually in terms of what pleases men; our own biology has not been properly analyzed. Instead, we are fed the myth of the liberated woman and her vaginal orgasm—an orgasm which in fact does not exist.

What we must do is redefine our sexuality. We must discard the "normal" concepts of sex and create new guidelines which take into account mutual sexual enjoyment. While the idea of mutual enjoyment is liberally applauded in marriage manuals, it is not followed to its logical conclusion. We must begin to demand that if certain sexual positions now defined as "standard" are not mutually conducive to orgasm, they no longer be defined as standard. New techniques must be used or devised which transform this particular aspect of our current sexual exploration.

FREUD—A FATHER OF THE VAGINAL ORGASM

Freud contended that the clitoral orgasm was adolescent, and that upon puberty, when women began having intercourse with men, women should transfer the center of orgasm to the vagina. The vagina, it was assumed, was able to produce a parallel, but more mature, orgasm than the clitoris. Much work was done to elaborate on this theory, but little was done to challenge the basic assumptions.

To fully appreciate this incredible invention, perhaps Freud's general attitude about women should first be recalled. Mary Ellman, in *Thinking About Women*, summed it up this way:

Everything in Freud's patronizing and fearful attitude toward women follows from their lack of a penis, but it is only in his essay *The Psychology of Women* that Freud makes explicit . . . the deprecations of women which are implicit in his work. He then prescribes for them the abandonment of the life of the mind, which will interfere with their sexual function. When the psychoanalyzed patient is male, the analyst sets himself the task

of developing the man's capacities; but with women patients, the job is to resign them to the limits of their
sexuality. As Mr. Rieff puts it: For Freud, "Analysis
cannot encourage in women new energies for success and
achievement, but only teach them the lesson of rational
resignation."

It was Freud's feelings about women's secondary and inferior
relationship to men that formed the basis for his theories on
female sexuality.

Once having laid down the law about the nature of our
sexuality, Freud not so strangely discovered a tremendous
problem of frigidity in women. His recommended cure for a
woman who was frigid was psychiatric care. She was suffering
from failure to mentally adjust to her "natural" role as a woman. Frank S. Caprio, a contemporary follower of these ideas,
states:

. . . whenever a woman is incapable of achieving an
orgasm via coitus, provided her husband is an adequate
partner, and prefers clitoral stimulation to any other form
of sexual activity, she can be regarded as suffering from
frigidity and requires psychiatric assistance. (*The Sexually
Adequate Female*, p. 64.)

The explanation given was that women were envious of men—
"renunciation of womanhood." Thus it was diagnosed as an
anti-male phenomenon.

It is important to emphasize that Freud did not base his
theory upon a study of woman's anatomy, but rather upon his
assumptions of woman as an inferior appendage to man, and
her consequent social and psychological role. In their attempts
to deal with the ensuing problem of mass frigidity, Freudians
created elaborate mental gymnastics. Marie Bonaparte, in *Female Sexuality,* goes so far as to suggest surgery to help women
back on their rightful path. Having discovered a strange connection between the non-frigid woman and the location of the
clitoris near the vagina,

it then occurred to me that where, in certain women, this
gap was excessive, and clitoridal fixation obdurate, a
clitoridal-vaginal reconciliation might be effected by surgical means, which would then benefit the normal erotic
function. Professor Halban, of Vienna, as much a biolo-
gist as surgeon, became interested in the problem and

worked out a simple operative technique. In this, the suspensory ligament of the clitoris was severed and the clitoris secured to the underlying structures, thus fixing it in a lower position, with eventual reduction of the labia minora (p. 148).

But the severest damage was not in the area of surgery, where Freudians ran around absurdly trying to change female anatomy to fit their basic assumptions. The worst damage was done to the mental health of women, who either suffered silently with self-blame, or flocked to the psychiatrists looking desperately for the hidden and terrible repression that kept from them their vaginal destiny.

LACK OF EVIDENCE?

One may perhaps at first claim that these are unknown and unexplored areas, but upon closer examination this is certainly not true today, nor was it true even in the past. For example, men have known that women suffered from frigidity often during intercourse. So the problem was there. Also, there is much specific evidence. Men knew that the clitoris was and is the essential organ for masturbation, whether in children or adult women. So obviously women made it clear where *they* thought their sexuality was located. Men also seem suspiciously aware of the clitoral powers during "foreplay," when they want to arouse women and produce the necessary lubrication for penetration. Foreplay is a concept created for male purposes, but works to the disadvantage of many women, since as soon as the woman is aroused the man changes to vaginal stimulation, leaving her both aroused and unsatisfied.

It has also been known that women need no anesthesia inside the vagina during surgery, thus pointing to the fact that the vagina is in fact not a highly sensitive area.

Today, with extensive knowledge of anatomy, with Kinsey, and Masters and Johnson, to mention just a few sources, there is no ignorance on the subject. There are, however, social reasons why this knowledge has not been popularized. We are living in a male society which has not sought change in women's role.

ANATOMICAL EVIDENCE

Rather than starting with what women *ought* to feel, it

would seem logical to start out with the anatomical facts regarding the clitoris and vagina.

The Clitoris is a small equivalent of the penis, except for the fact that the urethra does not go through it as in the man's penis. Its erection is similar to the male erection, and the head of the clitoris has the same type of structure and function as the head of the penis. G. Lombard Kelly, in *Sexual Feeling in Married Men and Women,* says:

> The head of the clitoris is also composed of erectile tissue, and it possesses a very sensitive epithelium or surface covering, supplied with special nerve endings called genital corpuscles, which are peculiarly adapted for sensory stimulation that under proper mental conditions terminates in the sexual orgasm. No other part of the female generative tract has such corpuscles. (Pocket Books, p. 35.)

The clitoris has no other function than that of sexual pleasure.

The Vagina—Its functions are related to the reproductive function. Principally, 1) menstruation, 2) receive penis, 3) hold semen, and 4) birth passage. The interior of the vagina, which according to the defenders of the vaginally caused orgasm is the center and producer of the orgasm, is:

> like nearly all other internal body structures, poorly supplied with end organs of touch. The internal entodermal origin of the lining of the vagina makes it similar in this respect to the rectum and other parts of the digestive tract. (Kinsey, *Sexual Behavior in the Human Female,* p. 580.)

The degree of insensitivity inside the vagina is so high that "Among the women who were tested in our gynecologic sample, less than 14% were at all conscious that they had been touched." (Kinsey, p. 580.)

Even the importance of the vagina as an *erotic* center (as opposed to an orgasmic center) has been found to be minor.

Other Areas—Labia minora and the vestibule of the vagina. These two sensitive areas may trigger off a clitoral orgasm. Because they can be effectively stimulated during "normal" coitus, though infrequent, this kind of stimulation is incorrectly thought to be vaginal orgasm. However, it is important to distinguish between areas which can stimulate the clitoris, incapable of producing the orgasm themselves, and the clitoris:

Regardless of what means of excitation is used to bring the individual to the state of sexual climax, the sensation is perceived by the genital corpuscles and is localized where they are situated: in the head of the clitoris or penis. (Kelly, p. 49.)

Psychologically Stimulated Orgasm—Aside from the above mentioned direct and indirect stimulations of the clitoris, there is a third way an orgasm may be triggered. This is through mental (cortical) stimulation, where the imagination stimulates the brain, which in turn stimulates the genital corpuscles of the glans to set off an orgasm.

WOMEN WHO SAY THEY HAVE VAGINAL ORGASMS

Confusion—Because of the lack of knowledge of their own anatomy, some women accept the idea that an orgasm felt during "normal" intercourse was vaginally caused. This confusion is caused by a combination of two factors. One, failing to locate the center of the orgasm, and two, by a desire to fit her experience to the male-defined idea of sexual normalcy. Considering that women know little about their anatomy, it is easy to be confused.

Deception—The vast majority of women who pretend vaginal orgasm to their men are faking it to, as Ti-Grace Atkinson says, "get the job." In a new best-selling Danish book, *I Accuse* (my own translation), Mette Ejlersen specifically deals with this common problem, which she calls the "sex comedy." This comedy has many causes. First of all, the man brings a great deal of pressure to bear on the woman, because he considers his ability as a lover at stake. So as not to offend his ego, the woman will comply with the prescribed role and go through simulated ecstasy. In some of the other Danish women mentioned, women who were left frigid were turned off to sex, and pretended vaginal orgasm to hurry up the sex act. Others admitted that they had faked vaginal orgasm to catch a man. In one case, the woman pretended vaginal orgasm to get him to leave his first wife, who admitted being vaginally frigid. Later she was forced to continue the deception, since obviously she couldn't tell him to stimulate her clitorally.

Many more women were simply afraid to establish their right to equal enjoyment, seeing the sexual act as being primarily for the man's benefit, and any pleasure that the woman got as an added extra.

Other women, with just enough ego to reject the man's idea

that they needed psychiatric care, refused to admit their frigid-ity. They wouldn't accept self-blame, but they didn't know how to solve the problem, not knowing the physiological facts about themselves. So they were left in a peculiar limbo.

Again, perhaps one of the most infuriating and damaging results of this whole charade has been that women who were perfectly healthy sexually were taught that they were not. So in addition to being sexually deprived, these women were told to blame themselves when they deserved no blame. Look-ing for a cure to a problem that has none can lead a woman on an endless path of self-hatred and insecurity. For she is told by her analyst that not even in her one role allowed in a male society—the role of a woman—is she successful. She is put on the defensive, with phony data as evidence that she better try to be even more feminine, think more feminine, and reject her envy of men. That is, shuffle even harder, baby.

WHY MEN MAINTAIN THE MYTH

1. *Sexual Penetration Is Preferred*—The best stimulant for the penis is the woman's vagina. It supplies the necessary friction and lubrication. From a strictly technical point of view this position offers the best physical conditions, even though the man may try other positions for variation.

2. *The Invisible Woman*—One of the elements of male chauvinism is the refusal or inability to see women as total, separate human beings. Rather, men have chosen to define women only in terms of how they benefited men's lives. Sexually, a woman was not seen as an individual wanting to share equally in the sexual act, any more than she was seen as a person with independent desires when she did anything else in society. Thus, it was easy to make up what was con-venient about women; for on top of that, society has been a function of male interests, and women were not organized to form even a vocal opposition to the male experts.

3. *The Penis as Epitome of Masculinity*—Men define their lives greatly in terms of masculinity. It is a *universal*, as op-posed to racial, ego boosting, which is localized by the geography of racial mixtures.

The essence of male chauvinism is not the practical, eco-nomic services women supply. It is the psychological su-periority. This kind of negative definition of self, rather than positive definition based upon one's own achievements and development, has of course chained the victim and the oppressor both. But by far the most brutalized of the two is the victim.

An analogy is racism, where the white racist compensates his feelings of unworthiness by creating an image of the black man (it is primarily a male struggle) as biologically inferior to him. Because of his power in a white male power structure, the white man can socially enforce this mythical division.

To the extent that men try to rationalize and justify male superiority through physical differentiation, masculinity may be symbolized by being the *most* muscular, the most hairy, the deepest voice, and the biggest penis. Women, on the other hand, are approved of (i.e., called feminine) if they are weak, petite, shave their legs, have high soft voices, and no penis.

Since the clitoris is almost identical to the penis, one finds a great deal of evidence of men in various societies trying to either ignore the clitoris and emphasize the vagina (as did Freud), or, as in some places in the Mideast, actually performing clitoridectomy. Freud saw this ancient and still practiced custom as a way of further "feminizing" the female by removing this cardinal vestige of her masculinity. It should be noted also that a big clitoris is considered ugly and masculine. Some cultures engage in the practice of pouring a chemical on the clitoris to make it shrivel up into proper size.

It seems clear to me that men in fact fear the clitoris as a threat to their masculinity.

4. *Sexually Expendable Male*—Men fear that they will become sexually expendable if the clitoris is substituted for the vagina as the center of pleasure for women. Actually this has a great deal of validity if one considers *only* the anatomy. The position of the penis inside the vagina, while perfect for reproduction, does not necessarily stimulate an orgasm in women because the clitoris is located externally and higher up. Women must rely upon indirect stimulation in the "normal" position.

Lesbian sexuality could make an excellent case, based upon anatomical data, for the extinction of the male organ. Albert Ellis says something to the effect that a man without a penis can make a woman an excellent lover.

Considering that the vagina is very desirable from a man's point of view, purely on physical grounds, one begins to see the dilemma for men. And it forces us as well to discard many "physical" arguments explaining why women go to bed with men. What is left, it seems to me, are primarily psychological reasons why women select men at the exclusion of women as sexual partners.

5. *Control of Women*—One reason given to explain the Mideastern practice of clitoridectomy is that it will keep the women from straying. By removing the sexual organ capable of orgasm, it must be assumed that her sexual drive will diminish. Considering how men look upon their women as property, particularly in very backward nations, we should begin to consider a great deal more why it is not in the men's interest to have women totally free sexually. The double standard, as practiced for example in Latin America, is set up to keep the woman as total property of the husband, while he is free to have affairs as he wishes.

6. *Lesbianism and Bisexuality*—Aside from the strictly anatomical reasons why women might equally seek other women as lovers, there is a fear on men's part that women will seek the company of other women on a full, human basis. The establishment of clitoral orgasm as fact would threaten the heterosexual *institution*. For it would indicate that sexual pleasure was obtainable from either men *or* women, thus making heterosexuality not an absolute, but an option. It would thus open up the whole question of *human* sexual relationships beyond the confines of the present male-female role system.

BOOKS MENTIONED IN THIS ESSAY

Sexual Behavior in the Human Female, Alfred C. Kinsey, Pocket Books

Female Sexuality, Marie Bonaparte, Grove Press

Sex Without Guilt, Albert Ellis, Grove Press

Sexual Feelings in Married Men and Women, G. Lombard Kelly, Pocket Books

I Accuse (Jeg Anklager), Mette Ejlersen, Chr. Erichsens Forlag (Danish)

The Sexually Adequate Female, Frank S. Caprio, Fawcett Gold Medal Books

Thinking About Women, Mary Ellman, Harcourt Brace Jovanovich, Inc.

Human Sexual Response, Masters and Johnson, Little, Brown

Also see:
The ABZ of Love, Inge and Sten Hegeler, Alexicon Corp.

On Being Natural*

DEE ANN PAPPAS

Always be yourself, be natural," school teachers say to us. "Have the natural look," the fashion books say. Lady Clairol spends millions in advertising to convince women they can dye their hair and yet "be natural." The great philosophical injunction of Socrates, "Know Thyself," does not seem to apply to the woman of the mass media. There is no quest for her. There is no search to fathom the mystery within. She is not urged to stand alone before the universe. Instead, she is told to be, to exist and to procreate.

One of the stumbling blocks to woman's consciousness is her fear of failing to fulfill what she believes to be nature's will. But evidence exists which proves that "being natural" in reality means obeying society, not nature. Let us consider the findings of the biological and social sciences to discover what is natural about the sexes and their roles.

BIOLOGICAL SCIENCES

Attempts to find a causal relationship between biological givens and sex roles concentrate on hormone study. Hormones, secreted by key glands, are the body's messengers. They influence growth, digestion and reproduction. Male hormones are called androgens; the female are called progesterone. Males and females possess both types of hormones, but in differing amounts at different times of their lives.

The hormones have definite effects on the body. One androgen, testosterone, produces aggressive behavior in rats. It has also been used in small doses on women who have severe menstrual problems to counter-balance the effects of higher amounts of progesterone which causes discomfort. The female hormone, progesterone, enters the brain and affects brain

*From *WOMEN: A Journal of Liberation* (Fall, 1969), © 1969 Women: A Journal of Liberation, Inc.

function (Hamburg 1965). It can produce general anesthesia (Merryman 1954) and convulsive seizures (Woolley & Timiras 1962) when injected into female rats in large amounts. At first glance, the dominant behavior produced seems to substantiate the mythic difference between males and females: aggression and passivity.

This pattern is further reinforced by studies of the behavior of testosterone on female monkeys. It was found in earlier studies of old world monkeys that males and females display marked differences in behavior. When Young, Goy and Phoenix (1964) injected pregnant monkeys with testosterone, the "masculinized" female offspring, who had pseudomale genitalia, participated in rough and tumble play in much the same manner as the normal male monkeys. Although the effects of the hormone diminished in time, some masculinized females showed these effects for up to three years.[1]

In spite of results like these which seem to support the theory of hormones determining sex roles, the investigators are conservative in their conclusions. Hamburg and Lunde commenting on the above experiment in "Sex Hormones in the Development of Sex Differences" believe it "unlikely that the early exposure of hypothalmic cells to androgen would established fixed, complex patterns of aggressive behavior for a lifetime."[2] They believe it might create readiness to learn aggressive patterns. These scientists are more interested in how the hormones affect developmental potential. For example, young males are rewarded for rough play. In later life, when hormone levels may be different, the social conditioning has already produced the male role. Directions are set by hormones, but sex roles are learned: "In the delivery rooms of many hospitals it is the custom to wrap the new born baby in either a pink or blue blanket, depending on the sex as determined by the genitalia. From this moment on, the child's maleness or femaleness is constantly reinforced. It is difficult then to determine the extent to which the child's learning of his sex role may be influenced by underlying biological predispositions."[3]

Another study by Money (1961) and Hampson and Hampson (1961) reveals yet another interesting conclusion about biology and learning. Hormonal imbalance in pregnant women sometimes produces children of confused sexuality. Injections of androgens to prevent miscarriages in some women produces children who have internal female organs, but the external genitalia are distorted. The clitoris is so enlarged that it resembles a penis and the labial folds are fused. These children are mistakenly reared as males for years. When these pseudo-hermaphrodites were studied, Money, Hampson and Hampson advanced the thesis that gender role was entirely the result of the learning process which is independent of chromosomal, gonadal or hormonal sex. These children conceived of themselves in their learned sex roles and had great difficulty readjusting to their proper sexual identity. These researchers went so far as to suggest that humans are actually psychosexually neutral at birth.[4] Others like Beach and Diamond (1965) take issue with this position but do admit: "Nevertheless sexual predisposition is only a potentiality setting limits to a pattern that is greatly modifiable by ontogenetic experiences."[5] In other words, the life experiences of the individual can modify a pattern given by sexual predisposition.

Recently scientists have discovered that the triggering of puberty is done, not by the endocrine system, but by the brain. This means that environmental influences could have an effect on the functioning of the pituitary gland. Population studies show that the average age of puberty is decreasing. Thus it seems highly possible that the environment may affect its functioning.

These conclusions suggest that female babies are taught how to conceive of their role. They are not "naturally" passive. Hormones will ready the body for its reproductive function, but this need not lead a woman to accept the accompanying conclusions about her job-staying power, her ability to do math, or her emotional stability.

SOCIAL SCIENCES

Margaret Mead, noted anthropologist, has gathered material about cultures which lead to helpful insights into the questions we are discussing. Her studies demonstrate the variety of ways cultures conceive of sex roles. She considered seven cultures in the South Seas in her book *Male and Female*. Three of the cultures will be discussed here.[6]

Among the Arapesh tribe a spirit of cooperation exists. These are a mild people who live in a poor mountain area in which there is rarely enough to eat. The Arapesh, however, are committed to helping one another. The males and females are primarily interested in growing things: children, trees, animals. According to Mead, the Arapesh male would be considered feminine by our standards because he has a large role in child care.

The cannibal Mundugumor, on the other hand, project a

completely different pattern for the behavior of the sexes. They live on the banks of a swift river and take advantage of the poorer people who live in the bush nearby. They spend their time quarreling and headhunting. Their social organization stresses the belief that every man's hand is against everyone else's. The women are as aggressive as the men. Childhood is not a positive experience for these people. Pregnancy is resented; children are an imposition. Often children are sent to other tribes as hostages. The behavior of the women would be considered aggressive and masculine by people in our culture.

The Tchambuli live beside a lovely lake in New Guinea. The women in this culture are hard workers. They fish and go to market and manage the functioning of life there. Men, on the other hand, do little all day but carve, paint and learn dance steps. They tend to gossip as well. These people present almost the reversal of the sex roles in American culture.

Mead concludes from this: "These three situations suggest, then, a very definite conclusion. If these temperamental attitudes which we have traditionally regarded as feminine—such as passivity, responsiveness and a willingness to cherish children—can so easily be set up as the masculine pattern in one tribe, and in another to be outlawed for the majority of men, we no longer have any basis for regarding such aspects of culture as sex linked."[7] She ~oes on to assert: "Human nature is almost unbelievably maleable."[8]

But Mead's conclusions about the male limit women forever to the roles of housewife and mother. She says: "The recurrent problem of civilization is to define the male role satisfactorily enough—whether it be to build gardens, to raise cattle, to kill game or enemies . . . so that the male may in the course of his life reach a solid sense of irreversible achievement, of which his childhood knowledge of the satisfaction of childbearing has given him a glimpse. In the case of the woman it is only necessary that they be permitted by the given social arrangements to fulfill their biological role, to attain this sense of irreversible achievement. If women are to be restless and questioning, even in the face of childbearing, they must be made so through education."[9]

Mead seems to be aware of the implications of her research, but she hesitates to apply it to her own time. She fails to consider the new dimensions of a culture in which women are educated and in which child-rearing does not occupy so many years of a woman's life. She fails to cope with the concept of social change. (This is amply documented in Betty Friedan's *The Feminine Mystique*.)

There is a need to examine the sociological evidence which seems to refute our conclusions. How do we account for cultures which have *tried* to abolish sex role differentiation and yet have failed?

In 1956 M. E. Spiro studied the Israeli kibbutzim.[10] Freedom of women was to be one of the primary purposes of founding the kibbutzim. In the beginning women shared equally in all phases of the work. But as the kibbutzim grew older and the birth-rate increased, more and more women were forced to leave the so-called "productive" parts of the economy to enter service branches. The end result was that the women found themselves in the same roles from which they had hoped to be freed. They found themselves cooking or sewing or laundering or caring for children for eight hours a day. Some women were very unhappy with these results and confessed that they believed their lives to be failures. Why did this occur?

In 1949 Mead suggested that the problems of kibbutz women stemmed from an under-evaluating of the feminine role. D'Andrade in "Sex Differences and Cultural Institutions" shares Mead's view and adds that a cultural under-evaluation of women cannot be corrected by abolishing the traditional female role. D'Andrade betrays his bias in this statement. He is operating under the functionalist approach in anthropology which holds that male and female roles are what a culture says they are. He never faces up to new possibilities. He fails to ask why women and men could not share respons ilities, such as child-rearing, which limit mobility. Implicit in D'Andrade's approach is the idea that sex roles will remain functionally the same because of the historic development of sex role differentiation from the division of labor in primitive times when the female's reproductive function did severely limit her. The kibbutz experiment failed, not because they went too far, but because they did not go far enough. The concept of the male sex role was never challenged.

WHY MALE AND FEMALE SEX ROLES
HAVE REMAINED BASICALLY UNCHANGED

It is now useful to turn to a very interesting study by H. R. Hays called *The Dangerous Sex: The Myth of Feminine Evil*. A consideration of this book is important for several reasons. First, Hays provides a possible answer to the problem identified by Mead, D'Andrade and others, namely, that men universally have greater difficulty adjusting to their roles.[11] Second, Hays arrives at an important reason why women have failed to play a larger role in history. Finally, Hays reveals to women the actual negative aspects of the myths about woman's nature.

Hays' argument is based on Freud's notion that anxiety behavior and the ritual behavior of primitive cultures are similar. According to Hays, because children, preliterates and the mentally ill express basic drives and tendencies without the censorship of civilization, it is possible to see striking resemblances among them all.[12] For Hays the primitive culture projects into its customs the universal birth and early life experience of the male child. As civilization evolves, the social institutions reflect the earlier customs of the primitive society.

It is Hays' thesis that the primitive male child (as well as the modern child) finds his mother to be strange, different from himself. Because the child cannot cope with this fear, he develops ambivalent feelings about the mother and her genitals.

Most of the primitive rituals which concern women reflect fear of menstruation and pregnancy on the part of the males. When a Surinam Negro women is menstruating, she must live in solitude. She must warn anyone who approaches her with the cry, "I am unclean." During menses Siberian Samoyed women are not allowed to cook for men. The Nootka of the Canadian Northwest coast give a girl her private eating utensils at her first period and she must eat alone for eight months. The Australians of Queensland take the girl who menstruates for the first time to a shady place where she is buried to the waist in a deep hole. A hedge of branches and twigs is set about her with an opening toward which she must face. A fire is started in front of her. She must remain in the squatting position as part of the purification ceremony. In Uganda a menstruating woman can make her husband sick by touching his personal belongings. A woman pregnant for the first time among the Indians of Costa Rica can infect a whole neighborhood. She is blamed for any deaths and her husband must pay damages. In the Hebrew tradition, menstruating women are forbidden to work in a kitchen, sit at meals or drink from a glass used by others. Sexual contact at that time of month is a sin.

Women, according to many myths, have been created by castration—the vulva is seen as a wound. This image, interestingly enough, appears also in the fantasies of mentally ill males. In New Guinea, carvings show images of women with a crocodile attacking the vulva, or a hornbill plunging its beak into the organ, or a penis-like snake emerging from it. These details suggest that men fear that they too will be castrated. It is Hays' view that the resulting fear of women has its source in these early patterns in childhood and in primitive cultures.

Men cope with these anxieties in many ways. The primitive male builds secret societies which exclude women. Initiates participate in rituals which symbolically portray the birth of the new member by the older man. Often the initiate is made to handle the genitals of other society members.

Hays claims such patterns do not disappear with civilization. The Christian religion—based on male anxiety from the Hebrew tradition—takes the fear of the female to even greater extremes. During the Middle Ages celibacy (which is related to fear of the female) produced such strong anxieties that both self-castration and sodomy existed. In modern times, men's fraternities, smokers and drinking clubs are similar in function to men's houses in primitive cultures. Both are off limits to women and both hold seasonal initiation rites.

Hays sees that male attitudes toward working women also reflect male fears. He concludes: "Everything tends to show that male attitudes toward working women are involved with ideas about their masculinity. All the material we have been discussing indicates that men have been fragile in their sex life. . . . The man in a highly developed society equates his work and his achievement with his potency. When women compete with him, his ego suffers."[13]

If there is a myth about the "inherent nature" of women, perhaps it is male created. If this idea is an over-simplification on Hays' part (it is difficult to doubt him; he is very convincing), at least he has suggested a direction for more fruitful study. If Hays is correct, then many problems can be seen in a new light. We can develop ways of socializing young males which could lessen fears of women. We can also now understand another dimension of the women's suffrage movement. We can also better understand why the addition of the word "sex" to the 1964 Civil Rights Act was accompanied by joking and condescension by the male members of Congress.[14]

Hays makes a strong plea for social change. He obviously admires women greatly. His methods for change, however, are not searching enough and they lead back to the individual male for solution: "It is time he learned to accept his existentialist anguish; it is time he realized the menace of the female lies within himself. And when he is ready to accept her as a partner in work and love, he may even begin to find out what she is like."[15] Hays is to be commended for his research and his observations. But the twentieth century has shown that social change does not occur by waiting for people to change their minds. Social change occurs through deep struggle and full consciousness of the true meaning of politics. But here consciousness is blocked again by another conception of what is "natural" in human beings.

HUMAN NATURE: ANOTHER FALLACY

The beliefs people hold about human nature are also stumbling blocks to political consciousness. Just as a woman's false conception of her "nature" can keep her from personal fulfillment, so the underlying belief in the human being's basic corruptibility and competitiveness underlies the assumptions about mankind on which our own capitalist country rests. "Power corrupts. Absolute Power corrupts absolutely." Are these qualities inherent in human beings or, as we have seen in the case of women, are they conditioned to conform to the goals of a culture?

Opposing conceptions of human nature underlie the two economic systems: capitalism and communism. The capitalist believes himself to be the realist: "Look, our basic nature is competitive. The struggle for survival is built into the growth of nature. The strong survive; the weak perish. Each man seeks his own selfish interest. If you have a revolution, you substitute one form of oppression for another. That's the way it is and ever shall be."

The Marxist does not accept this interpretation of human nature. He believes that systems not men create oppression in the world. Children can be raised to fulfill new values. In short, he believes a new, more humane image is not only inevitable but essential for the continuance of the world. Unless social priorities are reordered, human potential will be crushed by bombs or ecological catastrophe.

Is it possible that people who claim to be "nonpolitical" or who refuse to sully themselves in politics think this way because they hold a faulty view of man's potential? Is it possible that they do not understand that we can build a new conception of politics? Would people who believe that man is not "inherently" anything join together to overthrow a system which arises from such faulty assumptions about human nature?

CONCLUSION

When considering what is "natural" in human beings, we are left, ultimately, with a question. Science has not progressed enough to fully understand the effects of hormonal balance, genetic action and the effects of social conditioning. I have tried to show that the ideas we are putting forward as the basis of our struggle have not taken us outside the bounds of what is "naturally" possible. The answers to these questions end in choices and the prices to be paid for them. We recognize that few characteristics are inherent. The problem is to study patterns to discover which forms produce the most unalienated individuals.

If this assembled argument is correct, then every woman must know that to go beyond the act of child-rearing and a second place in history is to risk threatening the whole social order. The full selfhood of women is a threat. The choice and its price are real. But there are allies who know that a larger struggle for human fulfillment envelops us all. The woman's question may be, for the first time in history, the actual vanguard of change.

FOOTNOTES

[1]Hamburg, David A. & Lunde, Donald T., "Sex Hormones in the Development of Sex Differences in Human Behavior," in Maccoby, Eleanor, *The Development of Sex Differences*, California, 1966, p. 14.

[2]*Ibid.*

[3]*Ibid.*, p. 15.

[4]*Ibid.*, p. 16.

[5]*Ibid.*, p. 17.

[6]Mead, Margaret, *Male and Female*, (Laurel Edition, 1968), pp. 76-97.

[7]Cited in D'Andrade, Roy G., "Sex Difference and Cultural Institutions," in Maccoby, Eleanor, *op. cit.*, pp. 190-91.

[8]*Ibid.*

[9]Mead, *op. cit.*, p. 168.

[10]Cited in D'Andrade, *op. cit.*, pp. 178-180.

[11]*Ibid.*, p. 200.

[12]Hays, H. R., *The Dangerous Sex: The Myth of Feminine Evil*, New York, 1964, p. 33.

[13]*Ibid.*, p. 283.

[14]Bird, Caroline, *Born Female*, New York, 1969, pp. 1-5.

[15]Hays, *op. cit.*, p. 295.

The Myth of Women's Inferiority*

EVELYN REED

One of the conspicuous features of capitalism, and of class society in general, is the inequality of the sexes. Men are the masters in economic, cultural, political and intellectual life, while women play a subordinate and even submissive role. Only in recent years have women come out of the kitchens and nurseries to challenge men's monopoly. But the essential inequality still remains.

This inequality of the sexes has marked class society from its very inception several thousand years ago, and has persisted throughout its three main stages: chattel slavery, feudalism and capitalism. For this reason class society is aptly characterized as male-dominated. This domination has been upheld and perpetuated by the system of private property, the state, the church and the form of family that served men's interests.

On the basis of this historical situation, certain false claims regarding the social superiority of the male sex have been propagated. It is often set forth as an immutable axiom that men are *socially* superior because they are *naturally* superior. Male supremacy, according to this myth, is not a social phenomenon at a particular stage of history, but a natural law. Men, it is claimed, are endowed by nature with superior physical and mental attributes.

An equivalent myth about women has been propagated to support this claim. It is set forth as an equally immutable axiom that women are *socially* inferior because they are *naturally* inferior to men. And what is the proof? They are the mothers! Nature, it is claimed, has condemned the female sex to an inferior status.

This is a falsification of natural and social history. It is not nature, but class society, which lowered women and elevated men. Men won their social supremacy in struggle

*From *Problems of Women's Liberation* by Evelyn Reed, New York, Merit Publishers, 1969. Due to its length, this paper is here reprinted in part.

against and conquest over the women. But this sexual struggle was part and parcel of a great social struggle—the overturn of primitive society and the institution of class society. Women's inferiority is the product of a social system which has produced and fostered innumerable other inequalities, inferiorities, discriminations and degradations. But this social history has been concealed behind the myth that women are naturally inferior to men.

It is not nature, but class society, which robbed women of their right to participate in the higher functions of society and placed the primary emphasis upon their animal functions of maternity. And this robbery was perpetrated through a twofold myth. On the one side, motherhood is represented as a biological affliction arising out of the maternal organs of women. Alongside this vulgar materialism, motherhood is represented as being something almost mystical. To console women for their status as second-class citizens, mothers are sanctified, endowed with halos and blessed with special "instincts," feelings and knowledge forever beyond the comprehension of men. Sanctity and degradation are simply two sides of the same coin of the social robbery of women under class society.

But class society did not always exist; it is only a few thousand years old. Men were not always the superior sex, for they were not always the industrial, intellectual and cultural leaders. Quite the contrary. In primitive society, where women were neither sanctified nor degraded, it was the women who were the social and cultural leaders.

Primitive society was organized as a matriarchy which, as indicated by its very name, was a system where women, not men, were the leaders and organizers. But the distinction between the two social systems goes beyond this reversal of the leadership role of the two sexes. The leadership of women in primitive society was not founded upon the dispossession of the men. On the contrary, primitive society knew no social inequalities, inferiorities or discriminations of any kind. Primitive society was completely equalitarian. In fact, it was through the leadership of the women that the men were brought forward out of a more backward condition into a higher social and cultural role.

In this early society maternity, far from being an affliction or a badge of inferiority, was regarded as a great natural endowment. Motherhood invested women with power and prestige—and there were very good reasons for this.

Humanity arose out of the animal kingdom. Nature had

endowed only one of the sexes—the female sex—with the organs and functions of maternity. This biological endowment provided the natural bridge to humanity, as Robert Briffault has amply demonstrated in his work *The Mothers*. It was the female of the species who had the care and responsibility of feeding, tending and protecting the young.

However, as Marx and Engels have demonstrated, all societies both past and present are founded upon labor. Thus, it was not simply the capacity of women to give birth that played the decisive role, for all female animals also give birth. What was decisive for the human species was the fact that maternity led to labor—and it was in the fusion of maternity and labor that the first human social system was founded.

It was the mothers who first took the road of labor, and by the same token blazed the trail toward humanity. It was the mothers who became the chief producers; the workers and farmers; the leaders in scientific, intellectual and cultural life. And they became all this precisely because they were the mothers, and in the beginning maternity was fused with labor. This fusion still remains in the languages of primitive peoples, where the term for "mother" is identical with "producer-procreatrix."

We do not draw the conclusion from this that women are thereby naturally the superior sex. Each sex arose out of natural evolution, and each played its specific and indispensable role. However, if we use the same yardstick for women of the past as is used for men today—social leadership—then we must say that women were the leaders in society long before men, and for a far longer stretch of time. . . .

Perhaps the least known activity of primitive women is their work in construction, architecture and engineering. Briffault writes:

> We are no more accustomed to think of the building art and of architecture than of boot-making or the manufacture of earthenware as feminine occupations. Yet the huts of the Australian, of the Andaman Islanders, of the Patagonians, of the Botocudos; the rough shelters of the Seri, the skin lodges and wigwams of the American Indian, the black camel-hair tent of the Bedouin, the "yurta" of the nomads of Central Asia all are the exclusive work and special care of the women.
> Sometimes these more or less movable dwellings are extremely elaborate. The "yurta" for example is some-

times a capacious house, built on a framework of poles, pitched in a circle and strengthened by a trellis-work of wooden patterns, the whole being covered with a thick felt, forming a dome-like structure. The interior is divided into several compartments. With the exception of the wood, all its component parts are the product of the Turkoman woman, who busies herself with the construction and the putting together of the various parts.

The "pueblos" of New Mexico and Arizona recall the picturesque sky-line of an oriental town; clusters of many-storied houses rise in terraced tiers, the flat roof of one serving as a terrace for that above. The upper stories are reached by ladders or by outside stairs, and the walls are ornamental crenellated battlements . . . courtyards and piazzas, streets, and curious public buildings that serve as clubs and temples . . . as their innumerable ruins testify. (*Op. cit.*)

The Spanish priests who settled among the Pueblo Indians were astonished at the beauty of the churches and convents that these women built for them. They wrote back to their European countrymen:

No man has ever set his hand to the erection of a house . . . These buildings have been erected solely by the women, the girls, and the young men of the mission; for among these people it is the custom that the women build the houses. (Quoted by Briffault, *op. cit.*)

Under the influence of the missionaries, men began to share in this labor, but their first efforts were greeted with hilarity by their own people. As one Spanish priest wrote:

The poor embarrassed wretch was surrounded by a jeering crowd of women and children, who mocked and laughed, and thought it the most ludicrous thing they had seen—that a man should be engaged in building a house! (*Ibid.*)

Today, just the opposite is laughed at—that women should engage in the building and engineering trades!

do you know this girl?*

Sometimes she wonders if *anybody* knows her.

When she was younger, everything seemed possible. The world was an exciting place and magazines, movies, books, even her tired, unhappy mother promised romance to come. Sometimes she got very lonely and could hardly wait for that special guy to find her.

In high school she learned about "adolescence," "puppy love," "mature love," "personality," and "charm." She and her friends thought that in order for the right guy to come along, they had to make up the right way, make the right jokes, and know the latest gossip. They began to believe that life always happened in a certain way. The loneliness inside never left her or her friends. But they never talked about it when they were together. They talked about guys and worked harder and harder for dates.

Now, the only excitement at work for the girls is men— dating, flirting, engagements, break-ups, showers, marriage, a teasing relationship with the boss. No matter how big her paycheck is, it's never quite enough to insure the perfect appearance to catch the perfect man. She realizes that the men at the office only like her because she tries to do things the way *they* like. When the boss remembers her name, it's only flattery to get extra work from her. The loneliness never ends. The boredom never ends.

What's wrong with a place that doesn't let women be who they really are? Women are used by this society. There isn't time in the rat-race to be real whole people, and we're forced to define ourselves in terms of men—girlfriends of men, wives of men, mothers of men, sexual objects for men. Who wants us to spend all our money on clothes and cosmetics? Who wants us to believe a woman's place is in the home? Who encourages us to see ourselves as passive, emotional, good listeners, etc., instead of independent, strong, thinking, with lives of our own? Men are pressured to play certain roles, too. We're beginning to think about our lives and how school, church, parents, TV, newspapers, movies, magazines teach us not to question the way things are, how these help make a society which ruins many lives—not only those of girls behind typewriters in the US but also those of boys behind machine guns in Vietnam.

To answer these questions, we must get together. Women's Liberation.

*From *Women's Liberation Newsletter,* vol. 1, no. 3 (October, 1969).

FAMILIES—DAY CARE

Functions of the Family*

LINDA GORDON

Many people, noticeably those who want to sell us things like Virginia Slims, like to congratulate women on how far we've come. In fact we've only come to another beginning: the perception of our oppression in relation to a new perception of the possibilities of liberation. Part of that new perception is a critique of the inadequacy of earlier women's liberation theory: Suffragettes asked only for equal legal and political rights for women, and thus allowed a potentially radical women's movement to be swallowed by bourgeois liberalism. Advocates of sexual freedom thought that birth control and the destruction of Puritan morality would free us, but their rebellion too has been absorbed by America's flexible capitalism, and sexual freedom has been transformed into just another, more sophisticated form of repression.

In socialist countries the situation of women is no doubt freer; there is less pressure on women to play certain roles and more room for them to define themselves. But not much more. After fifty years, two generations, of socialism in the USSR, women's overall participation in the society has increased, but her basic definition—child-bearer, child-raiser; sexual object first, productive worker second—has not changed.

I want to try to explore the function of the family in our present system and to suggest how the women's liberation movement ought to relate to the family. Families themselves are a cluster of many different functions and we should think and talk about them that way—in terms of what they offer

*From *WOMEN: A Journal of Liberation* (Fall, 1969), © 1969 Women: A Journal of Liberation, Inc.

concretely, and in what alternative ways those same functions could be served.

1. Families have harnessed men to provide sustenance for children, on the basis of each man providing for his own biological children. This is not inevitable. Why couldn't a group of men and women provide for many children and adults who do not "produce" but do other useful things for society—study, teach, grow up, paint, etc? They could, but not in a society based on capital as the measure of a man's worth, a society that needs to evaluate people in terms of their contribution to the Gross National Product.

2. Families free men to work by harnessing women to raise children, each woman with one man's children. This is not only unnecessary, but destructive. It keeps women and children isolated, deprives children of the company of men most of the time, and deprives women of the company of adults, which is enough to turn an adult brain into mush—if you're not a mother and don't believe it, try spending 48 hours with children only. Why couldn't some people care for many children? Or better still, why not end the debilitating division of labor and have a community in which all adults spend some time helping children? This, again, can't happen in a society based on capitalist values in which child care will always be low-paid and low-prestige.

3. Families have repressed sexuality so that it would interfere as little as possible with the work that men are programmed to do, without, however, completely destroying it to allow for continued reproduction. Originally, sexual fidelity was imposed upon women because in a system of private property it was necessary to ensure that inherited property remain in the man's family. With the birth of capitalism, when greater work was needed for the accumulation of capital, a special ethic—Puritanism—strengthened the sexual repression. Women in families are trained to see themselves primarily as mothers and reproducers, not as enjoyers of sex; women outside families are pressured to carry themselves primarily as sex objects—in order to catch a man and enter a family and "relax" into motherhood. Thus the family structure completely limits the alternatives of most women even before they marry. One cannot escape the sexual repression by choosing not to marry, or even by choosing to be celibate. All human personalities develop in response to the environment and if one

is not completely determined by it, one is equally determined by the necessity to fight it constantly. That determinism relaxes only when the whole society ceases to prescribe roles for people. We can be free of sexual repression only by collective effort.

4. Families have supported oppression by separating people into small, isolated units, unable to join together to fight for common interests. More, families tend to hide the very existence of common interests by training people to consider that their worries are personal and private, when in fact they are social. Being programmed to turn all one's affection towards spouse and children, people lose consciousness of the possibility of affection among a larger community. Families promote individualism and the false linking of one's personal identity with private property, private space, etc. The problem is more severe for women than men because they are often isolated at home for long hours, while men enjoy the camaraderie of fellow workers. (Have you ever noticed that the worst thing about washing dishes is that you're usually alone in the kitchen while everyone else is talking in the living room?)

5. Families make possible the super-exploitation of women by training them to look upon their work outside the home as peripheral to their "true" role. In industrial society women workers have consistently accepted less pay for equal work (scabbed, in other words) because (a) they were not usually responsible for the chief support of the family, (b) they considered themselves inferior, (c) they were trained into passivity, (d) they were not accustomed to solidarity with other women.

The necessary condition for this phenomenon was the devaluation of the work done in the home. In earliest times all manufacturing and agriculture was done in or near the home, and usually by women. Men took the technology created by women and applied it to hunting, fishing and other forms of food-gathering. When the development of agriculture presented the possibility of gaining wealth from it, men seized control of the process of cultivation, although graciously allowing women to continue to do much of the work. With the beginnings of a money economy, and the possibility of gaining wealth from manufacture, men took that over as well. Women usually continued to do the work of industry but lost all control over the products of their labor. Industrialism added the final fillip to the expropriation of women, and most men as well, by removing all important work from home to factory. Housewives today need not even make bread or clothing. They produce nothing; they are essentially janitors and mothers.

Since the activities of cleaning and child-bearing do not produce capital, they are of no value, and woman's work is despised. It is hardly surprising then that woman is despised, and when she goes out to the factory she considers herself less valuable than a man. We see this low self-esteem consistently in the lives of middle class and bourgeois women as well: they entertain themselves with volunteer work for insignificant charities, serve as chauffeurs for their children, etc. Despite their capitalist values, they do not think their time is worth money. Traditionally women's movements have fought to get women out of their home. It is equally important to point out to women who prefer to or have to be full-time housewives that their work is dignified, skilled, and important; that it deserves a salary just as much as that of their husband in the office or factory.

6. Families have chained women to their reproductive function by implying that, first, sex is inevitably connected with reproduction and, second, that the woman who bears a child must be primarily responsible for its rearing. The first connection is being broken down, but as a matter of principle, we must continue to demand free birth control devices and abortion for all women. The second assumption is almost never challenged. Politicians are always telling us that youth are the future of a society; why don't we call them on it? The state, big businesses, schools and all public institutions should be required to provide for children. Simultaneously smaller communities of friends should *practice* community responsibility for children. No woman should have to deny herself any opportunities because of her special responsibilities to her children.

7. What is worse for children, families have enforced responsibility for children by making private property of them. To insist that children are not the property of their parents is not to deny that children may want and benefit from the *special* love of a small number of adults, adults who cherish certain children above others. Indeed, the fact that we often confuse the issue of parental love with parental proprietorship merely reminds us of how much love itself has become a

commodity in our capitalist society. Love is not ownership. Property in human beings is slavery. In early industrial and agricultural societies, children are often valuable because they can be put to work to help provide for the family. In these societies children are slaves in a sense closer to the convention. In affluent, bourgeois society the services that children provide are often psychological: they are to be what their parents always dreamed of being, or they are to maintain the family name and tradition. Frustrated parents, especially mothers, must pour their creative energy into hopes and nagging directed at the child. It is very, very difficult for most women, including myself, to conceive of a society in which children do not *belong* to someone or ones. To make children the property of the state would be no improvement. Mass, state-run day care centers are not the answer. It seems absolutely essential to find ways of raising children in a community that is close and reliable but without possessiveness.

8. Families have helped to stifle even the dream of liberation by conditioning people into roles and then defining these roles as "fulfillment." A mother is forced to think of herself as "mother" and to approach the whole world as "mother." She accepts and makes self-fulfilling the conventional expectations of what mothers are like—warm, selfless, ordinary, boring, comforting. Unmarried women are equally forced into roles: career woman, loose woman, man-hater, gay divorcee. Men, too, adopt roles: aggressive go-getter, rambunctious youth, lady killer, misunderstood artist, and so on. Some of these roles are infantile and exploitative; others are not so oppressive as those forced on women. To be aggressive, for example, if that means approaching the world and the people in it openly, self-confidently and curiously, is merely to be less repressed than most women. There is no doubt that many men have more freedom to do what they want with their lives than women. But it is equally clear that in terms of freedom to *be* what you want, to define oneself, men are just as oppressed as we, though they perceive it less.

9. Families perpetuate themselves and their bad values by educating children to see them as the only model for adult life.

In its political sense the word "family" is only a shorthand for the many functions it performs. We must demystify the institution by revealing its functions and purposes. In brief, families provide a means of mobilizing and pacifying the population in the interests of production, consumption and stability—in other words, profit. Through the family, manpower is mobilized into the labor force as cheaply as possible by using womanpower as free or underpaid labor. Sex is prevented from becoming free or playful, for real play subverts. Consumption is maximized by drawing people into competition with each other and never-ending emulation of television ideals. Children are cared for at the expense of women's lives, thus creating conditions of greatest repression for the children and minimizing the dangers of their rebellion against the absurdity of the lives of adults who never do anything really interesting or useful.

Early socialist theorists claimed that the entry of women into the labor force, combined with the abolition of private ownership of the means of production, would ultimately liberate women. Some of them perceived that the family was in itself an institution of oppression, but believed that it would with.... ...... One Bolshevik theorist, Alexandra Koslontai, argued against this simplisticness—not surprisingly, since she was a woman and not spinning her theories solely out of the abstractions of economic determinism. Juliet Mitchell pointed out, "The liberation of women remains . . . (for Bebel and Engels) an adjunct to socialist theory, not structurally integrated into it." More, they did not see that the liberation of women might demand a different strategy for the entire struggle for socialism: and that the "socialism" that emerged out of men's movements, out of a struggle that did not serve the particular needs of a sex conditioned to oppression, might be a very distorted socialism indeed.

The purpose of this is not to attack the socialist revolutions of the past, for all socialist women must be glad they occurred. However, a strong, independent women's liberation movement will make it more likely that our revolution will represent all of us. But it is crucial to remember, also, the pitfalls of single-issue organizing and theorizing. Women's oppression in all societies is a complex phenomenon, a bundle of different oppressions any one of which alone would be evil. Any one of them alone, too, might be alleviated without doing us much good ultimately. The system gave us the vote and equal rights, and it still exploits us all, woman and man. The system could give us equal wages, equal education, and could probably provide day care centers and jobs for us all.

If it were clever enough, it is possible that the system could survive the destruction of the family. To say that the nuclear family serves the interests of the capitalist ruling class, as I tried to argue above, is not to say that the nuclear family is the *only* institution that could perform the functions of mobilizing and pacifying the population. We know of alternative structures that could contain, mold, and exploit people equally well. Consider the society of ancient Sparta, for example, based on slavery and without family living. Men lived together with men and women lived with women, old people and children—enslaved by the state instead of by fathers and husbands.

In contemporary society men and women could be equal—equally harnessed to the demands of consumption, technology and imperialism. Men organized into monkish business clubs could be forced to channel more sublimated energy into production for oppression. Child care could be given over to large nurseries and schools (probably still run by women), as well adapted as families to the task of brainwashing children. Without marriage, that is without the private ownership of women, there could be collective ownership of women, without sexual equality *or* liberation from one-dimensional roles as sex objects. Women could win the freedom to produce children only at will, with partners (or injections) of their choice, and with state-provided facilities for their care, without making themselves whole human beings.

The role of the family in a class society is thus a complicated one, and simple condemnation will not get us anywhere. Still, it is absolutely clear that the nuclear family is an institution of privatization and exploitative division of labor which could not coexist with the kind of true socialism that the women's liberation movement envisions. The nuclear family must be destroyed, and people must find better ways of living together. Furthermore, this process must precede as well as follow the overthrow of capitalism, for unless some brave souls develop new living patterns now, the pressures towards retrenchment that seem to follow most revolutions may stifle our advance.

Whatever its ultimate meaning, the break-up of families *now* is an objectively revolutionary process. Despite the system's exploitation and profiting off of hippies, young working women, and college students, and despite the seeming stupidity and pain of the countless divorces, remarriages and divorces, these social forces are unleashed by the disintegration of the society and are accelerating it.

It follows from this that the women's liberation movement should support and encourage women and young people who are leaving parents, leaving husbands, trying to avoid marriage and/or pregnancy. But it would be foolish to make it our program, as some have suggested, to advocate the destruction of families. That would be like making it our program to abolish capitalism: an ideal is not a program. Families are not an abstract institution, persisting out of habit. They have developed historically, to be sure, and have a tradition supporting them, but they remain because they are useful. Families are not a vice to be exorcised. A frontal propaganda assault on the family is of limited usefulness. The reactionary role of families should be part of the political education offered in all the literature and actions of the women's movement. But it is crucial not to reify the family: it is not the enemy, it is merely one time-worn structure used by the enemy for the purpose of enforcing one segment of the capitalist division of labor. The radical thrust of the women's movement lies mainly in the fact that it challenges not just the structures, but divisions of labor on all levels, down to the tiniest minutiae of daily life. Families will be finally destroyed only when a revolutionary social and economic organization permits people's needs for love and security to be met in ways that do not impose divisions of labor, or any external roles, at all.

Out of the Shadows

Rita Van Lew

The old ego wants me to talk about myself, to seek out whys, and wherefores, only to induce sympathy. The old ego and the new self have fought and the new self has just about put down for good the old ego, and with it self-pity. The old ego has to go, because it has a false foundation, a foundation built on the myths passed down from generation to generation by the Puritans. Now, all of us Sisters and Brothers know where the Puritans and Pilgrim Fathers were coming from. You may have been taught in school that these people came here in order to have religious freedom. We know these people came out of jails and were outcasts of that particular society and those that ran the show or maneuvered themselves into positions of policy-making of Government were extremists as far as the physical being and the spiritual being were concerned. Or, God and man were at such extremes with each other according to these people that the being that had been created by this Supreme being was completely contrary to all that this Supreme being stood for; remember, I said according to these people.

Because these people were not the best educated (low-class, poor, unable to secure an education), they depended on their policy-makers (upper-class, doctors, lawyers, and preachers) to set the guidelines.

Of *course* these policy-makers used the fear that was in the hearts and minds of the people. Where knowledge could and would have been, but was not, because of social standing (low-class, no money to acquire) fear was in its place. *Fear of the unknown.* So, the policy-makers, or founding fathers had only to use this fear to keep the people (lower-class) in line.

To make sure the preacher had a job, he had to have a congregation. A congregation of guilt-ridden (fear filled) sinners. And instead of implanting in their hearts the knowledge of the love of God, a love that surpasseth all understanding, and freeing their minds, he continued to hold their minds in the grip of fear. Therefore, "obeying them that had rule over you" meant the people (lower-class) had to succumb to all that the Government (leaders, policy-makers, upper-class) chose to impose upon it, or receive hell fire and damnation.

It has been a matter of life and death to the upper-class to use all methods available to keep the lower-class in line. For once we secure knowledge and confirmation within ourselves, and toss off the fear of centuries, the upper-class will no longer have its place at the top. Which is not our problem really. So, we toss off the chains of fear of the unknown.

Because we the lower-class have worked with our hands, minds and hearts joined together and made or created things, clothing, bread, homes, gardens, and we are not in complete extremes with things we make, we know and understand them. If we know and understand things that we make, then we ask ourselves, how could God make us and we be in such a state of rejection? When we make or create, we know the qualities of our products and these products are a part of us. And we have a definite attachment for our creations (love, maybe). Knowledge has replaced fear. We know more about God (the unknown), and we know more about ourselves, and we begin to see how our fear was used against us.

We see that among other things being used against us, there were myths that were tied into our fear that held first place with the upper-class in keeping us quiet and confused and fearful.

All trusted reports of our previous cultures give no record of confusion within the family; the communal family. I think we are familiar with the set-up: the man and his wives and children and grandparents all living together, all caring for one another's needs, and the children belonging to all in the commune and being cared for by all. The wives working together for a common purpose. The older folk sitting in counsel, passing knowledge. Tell me it didn't work, or that it was immoral. Tell me that by us accepting this Capitalist Government's rulings as to what is morally right or wrong and what is best for us hasn't caused us more heartache and pain than our Creator intended us to have.

You might say at this point, why am I talking about the poor family (poor Blacks and Whites, Reds, and Yellows) and its living and sleeping habits. The reason is that nobody else will. Nobody that knows what they are talking about or will be truthful about it.

We are not rich upper-class. We don't eat steaks and salads and swallow vitamins all the time. We can't afford it, not even when the National Nutritionists say that we should drink a quart of milk, eat one portion of red meat, two yellow vegetables and get so much Vitamin C per person each day. We know we can't afford it. What we do eat and what is good for us, despite what the nutritionists say, is what we can afford, and we like what we eat, and for us it works. So much so, that "they" have termed it Soul food. What baffles them is that we didn't starve to death, but instead we thrived on it.

What I'm trying to get around to saying is that we come out of the shadows and admit that we as adults have not attained happiness on the upper-classes diet of Monogamy (one husband, one wife and children living as separate families). This is not the diet for us. Please recall that the Cinderella story is a myth and not a real way of life, especially for the lower-classes.

Divide and Conquer—

Because our ancestors (products of slaves who had been separated from families—I mean men from women that they loved, women and men from children that they loved; being forced to father or give birth to children to persons of their owners' choosing, not their own—where was all the significance that they now place on Monogamy?) accepted the pattern of their master, the Capitalist, as the new way of life for themselves, we now have a sad state of affairs, family wise.

Because we have been lied to, we grew up looking to be someone's one and only, taking love but not giving it. A great dream, but an impossibility.

In a person's lifetime we are expected to love only one person. Or is it to love one at a time? Or do we now know and admit that even if we had been allowed to grow up freely, without the fear and the myths, there are numerous loves in one's lifetime and loves of varying depths, some loves that can endure a lifetime, some that once seemed the deepest that in time seem only to have been a passing fancy?

Now, according to what we've been taught one should not engage in sex of any form until we are legally (according to the laws of this land) married. We all realize how serious marriage is, once we've made the move. We as parents are very proud of our daughters who succeed in marrying before there is visible proof that they have experimented with sex. Or I should say attempted to learn about sex. But are we being fair to our children? Yes, we say. This is what our parents imposed on us, and it's good enough for our children (we say). But we wish so many times that life could have been different for us.

In making a revolution, in education, jobs and housing and the class system, why don't we do this for our children? Tell them the truth. Instead of the myths, place facts in their place. Tell your daughters and sons all you know about life. Tell them that it is not a sin or immoral to give birth to or father a child out of wedlock. The wrong would be in bringing an unloved child into the world, and of course a loved child would be cared for, if not by its natural mother, then by someone else, but there is always a place for a child. Tell your children that the upper-class has set the rules regarding legitimacy, in order to control the economy. Always remind your sons and daughters that the lower-class to which we belong are the backbone of this economy. Were it not for our free labor, blood, sweat and guts, this country would not be what it is today.

Being that all of our adult life involves sex, or is affected by sex, we should begin our adulthood with at least a base for being lovers, wives, husbands and parents. Having a general knowledge of the physical anatomy is not enough.

If you're not afraid of being truthful to yourself, tell yourself, if you can, which piece you got that was worth getting married for. Certainly not the first piece, and if you think a little bit, you will realize that without sex there could be no marriage, but marriage should not be solely for sex.

A suggestion. Expose your children to different types of contraceptives if it is economically inconvenient for a pregnancy to occur. Tell them the health hazards. Tell them that sex should only occur between two people who agree. Tell them to know their reasons for wanting and agreeing to have sex with anyone. Show them how *love* is given and received.

When sons come to you with questions as to why they find themselves wanting to love and to care for more than one woman (and they know this feeling from the feeling of just wanting to have sex by this time), you won't add to any guilt feelings that might be there, but you will remind them that this was the custom of our past culture and that it can work.

When your daughters come to you full of fear because they want to love and care for someone who already has one wife or one family, you can say to her that there is always room for more love, that this was the custom of our past culture that worked for the family.

Let's make a real revolution for ourselves and children.

If you don't help solve the problem, then maybe you are a part of the problem.

Let's get off the property kick (ownership of other human beings)!

P.S. I cannot speak for other women now, but for myself. As a poor black woman, I have chosen to live with one man and to make our relationship as pleasant as possible. When I'm happy he is, because I am; and when he's happy, I am because he is. I know that if the time comes when we no longer make each other happy, the relationship will end. Each one of us would be *free* to *choose* another partner.

Producing Society's Babies*

VICKI POLLARD

Women today are re-examining the myth of motherhood in the context of the women's liberation movement. Women are oppressed because society defines them in terms of their roles as wives and mothers. In order to break this bondage, we must think about the conditioning we've undergone, so that we can be free to choose among a wide range of alternatives which offer fulfillment.

Some women's liberation groups are advocating that women should not enter into any family arrangements at this time, and that we should stop having children. This is far too simple an answer for one of the most complex questions a woman raised in this society must face. In our society there are unfortunately no viable alternatives to the things that the family provides (warmth, security, child-rearing). To expect women to take off and leave their families with no other means of raising children (no child care centers, no collective facilities) would be utopian and unrealistic at best. It is necessary to offer the alternative of not having children to women who otherwise might never have considered this. However it is dangerous to use this as a mass demand for women whose lives are built around their families. I feel that it is more valid to raise demands that render the nuclear family inoperative.

If we in women's liberation are really intent on eradicating women's oppression and changing the relationships between people, and between people and the institutions that control their lives, then we cannot wait until the day after the revolution to begin to create a new society. We must constantly work for more meaningful relationships and life styles. Because most women in this society and many in our movement are still having children, and certainly women will produce offspring after the revolution, it is important to see how women

*From *WOMEN: A Journal of Liberation* (Fall, 1969), © 1969 Women: A Journal of Liberation, Inc.

are manipulated and what image is forced on them during the period of pregnancy and childbirth. From the moment a woman becomes pregnant in our society, her life is radically and permanently altered. This does not have to be the case.

Doctors are always enemies of women. They are an ultra-conservative group resisting any kind of social change. They consistently adopt an infuriating and patronizing attitude toward women. This is especially true of most obstetricians who elect to play the role of father and god to their patients, forcing women into the role of helpless, stupid, ridiculous little girls. The way we are treated by doctors is symptomatic of the conditioning we get in all aspects of our lives. Obstetricians are almost always men; we are therefore forced to give up all control of what happens to us and our bodies to a man who makes all the decisions for us. If a woman questions what is happening to her, her doctor will tell her not to worry, to depend on him, he'll take care of everything. He often tells her how painful it will be, but that she won't have to feel a thing because he'll sedate her. If she asks what drugs will be used on her, he insists that that decision must be made by him at the last minute.

In most countries in Europe, women who are pregnant routinely go to a six weeks' training course to learn exactly what is taking place inside their bodies, what they can expect the labor and birth to be like, the effects of each of the drugs available, and the kinds of exercises that they can do to make the childbirth easier. In this country where research is done on everything under the sun, no one has figured out anything to make birth easier for a woman. And the methods developed in other countries are ignored here because they are too much trouble for doctors, so busy making money. It takes more time for a doctor to stay by a patient who is undergoing labor in natural childbirth who will be awake and curious about what is going on than it would take him to sedate her and have a nurse call when the appropriate moment has come. Natural childbirth implies a personal involvement on the part of the doctor—a commitment that most physicians in this country are unwilling to make. They prefer instead the time-saving rationalization that the doctor-patient relationship should remain objective and devoid of feeling.

My experience with pregnancy was painful and brutal until finally, when I was almost six months pregnant, we found a rare sympathetic doctor. (At the time in the entire city of Baltimore, there were only four obstetricians known to encourage full participation in childbirth by both husband

and wife.) My first doctor baffled me completely. I don't know what kind of conditioning he was into, but whatever it was, it wasn't pleasant! For example, he said to me, "O.K., get your ass up on this table now," and "I guess I'd better check your tits out to make sure they're healthy."

I questioned him about natural childbirth. He thought it was total nonsense and believed in drugging every woman as much as possible. When I indicated that we obviously weren't thinking along the same lines, he gave me the name of the doctor who was supposed to be the best natural childbirth man in the city.

This second doctor showed his disrespect for women in much more subtle ways. Although he believed in slightly fewer drugs than the first doctor, in reality, he didn't much believe in natural childbirth either. But instead of honestly telling me this, he manipulated me. He asked if I wanted natural childbirth. I said yes. He said, "Fine. But I just want to warn you that short, stocky women have exactly the wrong kind of build for natural childbirth, so don't get all emotionally involved in doing it." A little later he asked if I was interested in breastfeeding. When I replied yes, he went into the same song and dance all over again. "Fine. But women with large breasts have a very difficult time breastfeeding their babies, so don't get all emotionally involved in doing it." Both these statements are blatant lies. But I, being in a state of semi-terrified awe of this white-haired father-figure, believed everything he said and went home from the appointment in tears because I was so sure I wouldn't be able to breastfeed my baby.

Happily he only made me come see him once a month, because after every appointment I cried. (Doctors in this country force patients to see them at least twice as often as is really necessary, and most women in Europe see obstetricians about one-third as often as Americans do.) He had decided that I should gain no weight at all in my pregnancy, so that I would be thin and "attractive to your husband" after I gave birth. So each month when he weighed me and found I had gained some, he would berate me as if I were a child who had done something really terrible.

Finally I found my doctor who, possibly because he's European, believes firmly in trained childbirth. But what happens to women who have no training to have their babies? They have heard over and over again stories of the horror of childbirth; they have even seen in movies such as *Gone With the Wind* the sweating and the screaming of poor distraught women. Women cannot help being terrified when they enter the hospital which warns them they're sick, which reminds them that they are surrounded by death. As the terror and tension builds up, the pain increases and finally shots of various drugs are given. What women are never told by their dishonest doctors during pregnancy is that for a certain percentage of their labor, no drugs can be given because they would impede the progress of the descending infant. And when drugs eventually are used, instead of really helping her handle the pain, they make the woman completely lose control of herself, and she becomes like a wounded animal. Pregnancy *does* become the horrendous experience she imagined it would be.

Possibly the worst effect is that women, after an ordeal like this, feel they have martyred themselves to have the baby. This does two things to the woman. Because she is angry and resentful, she turns against her husband, blaming him for what has happened to her. This reinforces her feelings that responsibilities are all left up to her, and she can't depend on her husband for anything that has to do with the child. Also she feels that because she has suffered so much to have this baby, the baby owes her a great deal. This is the first step in regarding the baby as a piece of property. And this is why so many women spend so much of their time telling their children about all the pain they endured having them.

Natural childbirth has been glorified as the most beautiful moment in a woman's life. This is unfortunate because it leads to the idea that motherhood is the ultimate experience in a woman's life. However, natural childbirth training does help women do what doctors won't do. It teaches women how to control their own bodies and how to help themselves in childbirth rather than depending on some man. Having a baby means using muscles that are otherwise rarely used. A woman doesn't know how to use these muscles unless she practices regularly before her labor. It's as ridiculous to expect a woman in modern, urban society to have a baby with no training as it would be to expect a person to run five miles without ever building up to it. But doctors will not tell you this because they see women as objects whose purpose is to produce babies, and they never question the fact that women should suffer in childbirth.

Trained childbirth doesn't mean that all women will have a painless experience. Many women have been so badly frightened about childbirth and about their own bodies that they will always have a difficult time. But all women will have a much easier birth than they would have had without the training. They will be able to make any necessary decisions for themselves throughout the birth, and feel that they are in control.

One of the worst things that happens to a woman when she announces that she is pregnant is that she is congratulated and praised as if she has accomplished the most difficult task in the world. People suddenly look at her in a totally new way. She is seen as being of great worth, possibly for the first time in her life. Women who have been leading active, working lives are made to feel as if only *now* are they finally settling down to the real business of life.

This is when the concept of child-rearing as the woman's role is actualized. It is easy to develop a false sense of pride and gratification if we are constantly being made to feel that we are performing the most important task of our lives. At the same time husbands are systematically excluded from having anything at all to do with the pregnancy. Even if a man feels a deep interest in sharing the kinds of things that happen in a pregnancy, he is continually left out.

My husband accompanied me to my doctor's appointments and suffered all kinds of embarrassing jokes about the fact that he was always the only man in the waiting room, about his long hair and beard, and about anything else the doctor could dig up. Later, in a fit of anger when I informed him that I was switching doctors, the obstetrician showed the depth of his hostility to my husband's wanting to share my experience. He screamed at me that any husband who was all that intent on being in the delivery room at the time of the birth was truly psychotic!

Three major things happen to husbands during pregnancy and childbirth that are extremely crucial because of the patterns that are thereby established for the functioning of the marriage. One is that doctors tell women that it is unhealthy to have intercourse both six weeks before and six weeks after the birth date. This is ridiculous. There is absolutely no medical reason for not making love even hours before the birth. And after the baby arrives, it is only necessary to wait two weeks as protection against infection. Doctors order this because they have decided that all women are frail creatures who basically hate sex and therefore all of them would prefer being told they should abstain. So rather than deal with each woman's feelings individually, doctors make the simplest possible rule that has no basis in truth. This is terrible for both partners, but it is particularly painful psychologically for the husband. Just at the time when he is feeling most left out of things, when he is most insecure about losing his wife to the child, and just when husband and wife should be closest, he is excluded. Men react to this by opting out of the family altogether. Statistics show that more husbands have their first extra-marital affair during their wife's pregnancy than at any other time.

Another preposterous rule is that the husband is not allowed in either the labor room or the delivery room. The reason given is that some men faint, so therefore it is necessary to make this rule for all men. He is forced to stay in the waiting room, a place so alienating that jokes are constantly being made about it. Here too, at a time when the husband should enjoy fully the birth of his child, he is left out. He reacts during the hours he is forced to wait by forming an alliance with the other excluded men, another form of opting out of the family.

Then after the baby is born it is kept in the nursery, and the father can do no more than gawk at it through a thick pane of glass. For several days the birth is totally unreal to him. (Forcing women to leave their babies in nurseries is another manipulation of women. The inane reason given for this is that the nurses are close by to see if anything goes wrong with the infant. But how can two nurses for some twenty or more children possibly listen to every cough and every sneeze the way a new mother does?)

It is impossible to allow a husband to play no part whatsoever in the pregnancy and childbirth of his baby and then demand that he share equally in the child-rearing. The pattern has already been established, and this has been done at an extremely sensitive time in the man's life. Also for the woman, this separation from her husband leads to her substituting the child in his place.

Trained childbirth is again an important alternative, because it is based on both the wife and the husband fully participating. The husband attends all the classes and learns as much about what the birth will be like as his wife does. There is no chance of his fainting because he will have seen slides and movies and be prepared for what he will see. Also he will be almost as busy as his wife; he coaches her in breathing and pushing and he assists by rubbing her back, as well as providing emotional support. He plays a vital role in the labor and the birth.

Many husbands and wives participate in trained childbirth but do not plan to extend this role-sharing into the process of child-rearing. Of course it will be much easier for a woman to demand that her husband take an equal part in the responsibility for raising the child if he has enjoyed his role from the beginning. But women have to constantly demand that their husbands continue to share equally in the care of the child, and more than that, women have to teach men that they have the same instinct for child-rearing as women do. If the responsibilities are shared, both people can take pleasure in their child.

Many radicals do a great deal of talking about their politics, but they seem to lack seriousness because they do nothing to change their own lives in accordance with their beliefs. The women's liberation movement has such a revolutionary force because it absolutely necessitates a change in life style. In order for our movement to succeed, we must take the initiative in making basic changes in our private lives. We can not keep ourselves abstract from the struggle against women's oppression. Therefore, if women do decide to have children, it is essential that they demand of society that they be allowed to do so in a liberated way.

On Day Care

Louise Gross and Phyllis MacEwan*

INTRODUCTION

Day care has become one of the central issues of the Women's Liberation Movement. It is quite clear that free and public day care centers would be an important means for liberating women from the traditional tasks of child rearing. It has been suggested—and in some places carried out—that women should demand day care services from the large institutions in which they work or study and from the large corporations which profit from and expand into the communities in which they live.

The authors of this discussion paper think it is a mistake to view day care solely as an issue of Women's Liberation.

*From WOMEN: A Journal of Liberation, © 1970 Women: A Journal of Liberation, Inc.

We would like to assert that day care centers in which children are raised in groups by men and women could be as important for the liberation of children as it would be for the liberation of women. Group child care—if well conceived—has a radical potential through the impact it could have on children's early development. It is therefore necessary that people in the movement gain a deeper understanding of the day care center as an environment for child rearing.

We consider this paper to be an introduction to the problems of existing day care centers and the possibilities for future centers. Although we have pointed out some specific areas for radicalizing a day care center, we certainly have not developed a comprehensive model describing what an ideal day care program would look like.

We hope to develop this paper into a more thorough pamphlet and we welcome groups that are presently organizing day care centers or teachers who are working in centers to send us their ideas and suggestions.

WHY DAY CARE HAS EXISTED IN THE U. S.

Historically in the United States full-day care programs, as contrasted to half-day nursery schools, have been provided in periods of economic stress—during World War II and the depression—when women were required in the work force.[1] These programs were created primarily as a service to the corporations which needed woman-power, not as an educational and social opportunity for children. Although wartime day care centers often became educational opportunities for children, their rapid closing following World War II was a clear indication that these centers had not been organized primarily to benefit children or even to liberate women. Rather they had been organized to facilitate the carrying out of needed production.

In the past few years there has been an upsurge of state and national government interest in developing day care facilities for welfare mothers. This current interest parallels the expansion of day care during earlier periods of economic crisis. Today the main impetus behind the new drive for day care is the goal of lowering welfare costs by channeling welfare recipients into "desirable" occupations (like key punch operating). In both periods the official drive for day care has been motivated by the "needs" of the economy rather than by a concern for the welfare of either women or children.

WHY DAY CARE HAS NOT DEVELOPED IN THE U. S.

The underlying reason for the failure of day care programs to develop in this country exists in the traditional ideology that young children and their mothers belong in the home. Even today a strong bias exists against the concept that day care is potentially good for children and mothers. That women should *have* to work and therefore *have* to put their children in day care centers are circumstances which are generally considered to be necessary evils in this society.[2]

THE DEMAND FOR DAY CARE OF THE WOMEN'S LIBERATION MOVEMENT

The current demand for day care by the Women's Liberation Movement springs from a rejection of the ideology which says that women belong in the home. Yet the Movement's present demand parallels the historical attitude toward day care in its non-child-centered approach. The primary reason for demanding day care is the liberation of women. While recognizing that day care is essential for women's liberation, the authors want the Movement to further recognize that day care is essential for the liberation of children. Group child care, in contrast to the more isolating private home environment, has the potential of providing an environment in which children will have more opportunity to develop social sensitivity and responsibility, emotional autonomy and trust, and a wider range of intellectual interests.

The struggle for day care centers must be considered a people's liberation issue, not just a women's issue, because children are people. Both men and women who are concerned with children's development must demand day care.

WHAT IS A DAY CARE CENTER LIKE TODAY?

The majority of existing U.S. day care centers, which are run as profit-making enterprises, are glorified baby sitting services—dumping grounds—where children are bored most of the time. In these centers children are emotionally brutalized; they learn the values of obedience and passivity. They are programmed through a daily routine in which opportunities for personal choice and meaningful social relationships with adults and other children are minimal. Eating and naptime are managed in a mass production style which values efficiency over dignity. The adults as well as the children become routinized and enslaved to the daily schedule.

In contrast, there are a few day care centers where children have meaningful social and educational experiences, and where they participate in nonalienating play/work activities. In these centers self-directed learning and discovery are valued, and curriculum is developed in terms of the children's interests. Social cooperation is based on a rational group-problem-solving approach, rather than on rules impersonally established. Eating and resting activities are designed to be responsive to children's individual and group needs, rather than to meet the efficiency goals of the day care operation.

WHY WE MUST DEMAND SPACE AND MONEY AND NOT THE DAY CARE CENTERS THEMSELVES

We feel the differences among existing day care centers reflect a conflict in values and attitudes toward human development. This conflict in the care and education of young children is directly related to conflicting values and attitudes expressed in the economic and political behavior of adults. Values in competitive enterprise and individual rather than social achievement, respect for private property, adoration of the nuclear family—are attitudes that are nurtured in childhood and expressed in adult society.

As radicals we must understand that *our* goals for children are in conflict with those of the institutions—corporations and universities—from whom we will be demanding day care services. This implies that when we make demands for day care they should be solely in terms of money and space. The corporations and universities should have no control.

THE HIDDEN CURRICULUM

In organizing day care centers, we need to become aware of how values and attitudes are translated into programs for young children. We need to be aware of the existence of the day care center curriculum—hidden or explicit—and how it affects children's development.

It is well documented that attitudes toward work, race, sex (including male/female roles), initiative, and cooperation are being formed during the first five years of life. It follows that as radicals, concerned with developing a radical consciousness on these issues, we need to be seriously concerned with what happens inside the day care center.

The kind of interaction that takes place between the child and the human and physical environment (be it a home or a day care center) affects the kind of capacities that the child will have as an adult. The capacity to feel deeply and be sensitive toward other people, the capacity to trust oneself and use one's initiative, the capacity to solve problems in a creative and collective way—these are all capacities that can be given their foundation or stifled in the first five years.

By the age of 4, children are assimilating the idea that a woman's place is in the home. Three- and four-year-old children are already learning that it's better to be white. They are learning to follow directions and rules without asking why. They are learning how to deny their own feelings and needs in order to win approval from adults.

These are examples of learnings that most commonly result from early childhood experiences. These are elements of the hidden curriculum that usually characterize the child's environment in our society.

THE CHILD'S PERSPECTIVE

To a young child curriculum in a day care center is everything that he or she experiences: painting a picture, having to take a nap, experimenting with sand and water, wetting your pants or making it there on time, listening to an interesting story, eating lunch, riding a trike, being socked in the nose and having it bleed, observing one teacher being bossed by the other teacher, being told that blue is called blue, figuring out a hard puzzle, being hugged by the teacher, watching a building be demolished, seeing the mother guinea pig give birth, having everyone sing "Happy Birthday" to you, hammering a nail hard, and waiting to be picked up.

Although as adults we can place these events into categories of social, intellectual, emotional and physical experiences, for the young child each event is experienced in a total way. That is, the experience of painting a picture simultaneously involves emotional, intellectual, physical, and even social capacities. Emotionally a child may be using paint to express feelings of anger, loneliness, contentment, or boredom. Intellectually a child may be using the paint to discover what happens when different colors are mixed or learning how to write different letters. Physically, the child uses the paint brush to explore her/his own coordination, movement, and rhythm. Socially, painting can give the child an opportunity to be alone, with a friend, or in a group—depending on how the teacher has structured the painting experience.

The adult can seldom know the value that a particular experience has for a particular child. The same experience (e.g. painting a picture) will have a different value for different children, a different value to the same child at different times.

THE TEACHER'S IDEOLOGY

The teacher's values and attitudes form the base from which the structure and therefore the style of the group are formed. A single activity such as "juice time" illustrates how a teacher's goals and attitudes affect the way the situation is structured. One teacher might have three-year-olds pour their own juice from a pitcher, whereas another would have the children take already-filled cups from a tray. What underlies the difference? Presumably both teachers know that three-year-olds are in the process of developing muscle as well as eye-hand coordination. Also, three-year-olds are usually concerned with becoming independent and self-sufficient. By letting children pour their own juice the teacher is structuring the situation to allow for growth—however groping—in the areas of self-reliance and manual dexterity. By filling cups for the children, the other teacher is structuring the situation for maximum efficiency and neatness: to keep the routine running smoothly. One teacher uses juice time as an opportunity for children to gain some control over their activity, while the other teacher uses juice time to take control. In the first case the child gets to act upon the environment, while in the second case the child is treated as a passive recipient.

The traditional "housekeeping corner" of the nursery school and day care center is another dramatic illustration of how the teacher's values expressed in actions can have impact.

Let us take two teachers who have undergone similar training in early childhood education and have learned that the housekeeping corner provides an opportunity for children to "act out" adult roles thus contributing to their "ego growth" and "sex identification." One of the teachers sets up a housekeeping corner which encourages girls to be Mommy, the Housewife, and boys to be Daddy, the Worker. The other teacher sets up an area in the classroom in which both boys and girls are given opportunities to cook, play with dolls and trucks, sew, hammer, build with blocks, wash clothes and dishes, dress up as doctors, firemen and firewomen, construction workers, and other interesting occupations. In other words, one teacher uses the housekeeping corner to promote the learning of traditional stereotyped roles, while the other transforms the housekeeping corner into an area where children can explore and test out various adult activities.

MEN IN THE DAY CARE CENTER/
WORK IN THE DAY CARE CENTER

Another way that children learn the traditional stereotyped roles is through observing that almost all day care teachers are women. The children quickly comprehend the concept that there is "women's work" and "men's work." This in itself would be sufficient argument for us to insist that men be included at all levels in the day care staff.

Furthermore, without including men in the day care program, the demand for day care runs the risk of contradicting the goals of women's liberation. Women should not demand simply that there be special institutions for child care, but also that men take an equal role in child care.

There is another good reason that *both* men and women should be involved in the day care center. Teaching/working/playing with children can be an extraordinarily creative and non-alienating job. What often makes the caretakers of young children—teachers and mothers—feel apologetic about their occupation and what deprives men of the opportunity of working with children is the fact that our society considers child care "women's work"—a low-status/cheap labor occupation biologically relegated to the weaker, "sensitive" sex.

A day care program which had a sexually integrated staff—and salaries in keeping with the value of this work—would make child-rearing a desirable and rewarding occupation. Finally, it seems self-evident that it's best for children—emotionally, socially and politically—that they be cared for equally by both men and women.

SOME CONCLUSIONS

Day care is a people's liberation issue. Women, of course, will gain from a good day care program, but in the final analysis women's liberation depends on an entire transformation of society, not just on one institution. However, that one institution, if radically structured, can help obtain that transformation of society. The way children develop is part of that transformation.

In order to develop a radically structured day care program

we must not allow any control to be in the hands of the universities and corporations. Our demand to these institutions for day care must be a demand solely for space and money. Control must rest with those who struggle for and use the day care center.

One of our prime tasks in that struggle is to develop an awareness of what a good day care program can be. We have simply attempted to make clear in this paper that day care is a complex issue.[3] The self-education which the movement must undergo on day care should be as thorough as on more obviously political issues.

FOOTNOTES

[1] For example, the Kaiser Child Service Centers in Portland, Oregon, which served more than 4,000 children from Nov. 8, 1943 to Sept. 1, 1945.

[2] Today in the U.S. there are 4 million working women who have children under the age of 6 years, out of a total of 30 million working women. There presently are enough day care facilities to take care of 500,000 children. Compared to a number of other western industrialized countries the U.S. is backward in the field of day care. (Figures from *New York Times,* Oct. 16, 1969)

[3] There are numerous implications of day care organizing which we have not included in this paper such as the questions of developing the day care center as a base for community political action, the day care center as a place to organize parents around their children's rights in the public school system, and the whole issue of day care for infants and collective child-rearing.

SUGGESTED READINGS & SOURCES OF LITERATURE RELATED TO DAY CARE

Boguslawski, Dorothy. *Guide for Establishing & Operating Day Care Centers for Young Children.* Child Welfare League of America, Inc.: N. Y., N. Y., 1968.

Burgess, Evangeline. *Values in Early Childhood Education.* Department of Elementary-Kindergarten-Nursery Education, National Education Association, 1965.

Dittman, Laura (Ed.). *Early Child Care: The New Perspective.* N. Y.: Atherton Press, 1968.

Federal Panel on Early Childhood, *Good References on Day Care,* U.S. Department of Health, Education & Welfare,

(Social & Rehabilitation Service, Children's Bureau), July, 1968.

Hartley, Ruth et al. *Understanding Children's Play*. N. Y.: Columbia University Press, 1952.

Hunt, J. McV. *Intelligence and Experience*. N. Y.: Ronald Press Company, 1961.

Hymes, J.L. *Teaching the Child Under 6*. N. Y.: Prentice-Hall, 1963.

Jones, Betty & Prescott, Elizabeth. *Group Day Care as a Child-Rearing Environment: An Observational Study of Day Care Program*. Pasadena, Calif.: Children's Bureau, Social Security Administration, U.S. Department of Health, Education, & Welfare, 1967.

Kritchevsky, Sybil & Prescott, Elizabeth. *Planning Environments for Young Children*. National Association for the Education of Young Children, Washington, D.C., 1969.

Moustakas, Clark. *The Authentic Teacher*. Cambridge, Mass.: Doyle Publishing Company, 1966.

Piaget, Jean. *The Language & Thought of the Child*. N. Y.: Meridian Books, 1955.

U.S. Department of Labor, Women's Bureau *Report of a Consultation on Working Women and Day Care Needs*, 1968 (free) and *Working Mothers and the Need for Day Care Services*, 1968 (free).

Warner, Sylvia Ashton. *Teacher*. N. Y.: Bantam Books, 1963.

The Abortion Problem*

CAROL DRISCOLL

It should not come as a shock to realize that women can never hope to be liberated in any sense if they are denied the right to control their bodies, especially their reproductive organs. One of the fears that reveals itself in the bulk of anti-abortion reform writing is that wholesale promiscuity will grip our women if the laws are repealed. We believe this fear is a manifestation of our society's obsession with imposing arbitrary standards of conduct on its members. To

*From *WOMEN: A Journal of Liberation* (Winter, 1970), © 1970 Women: A Journal of Liberation, Inc.

safeguard these standards it is necessary to create a deterrent to misconduct, i.e. the fear of becoming pregnant and bearing an illegitimate baby inhibits many women from experimenting in sex as they know an abortion is not available to them. This sophomoric approach loses its punch after a look at the estimated illegal abortion figures in the U.S.—800,000 to 1,000,000 annually. It can also be inferred that women are regarded largely as mindless, biological creatures, who, if entrusted with the freedom to control their biological processes would ignore the concomitant responsibility to use this freedom in their own best interests.

American women have been troubled for years (especially following the sexual revolution) by their ambivalent feelings toward sex. And while there has been an increasing acceptance of pre-marital sex, pregnancy as a result of nonprocreative sex is still regarded as highly suspicious. Married women are urged to plan their families, but any failure in contraceptive measures is likely to produce a feeling of helpless acceptance by the woman who accidentally conceives. Some of the unwillingness and ambivalency toward viewing abortion as the most logical means of supplementary birth control come from the uncomfortable to odious associations women have with the term "criminal abortions." Crime is usually equated with that which is bad or immoral; hence, if abortion is illegal it can be thought of as sinful or evil.

With a deeper understanding of the muddled history of our present abortion laws we can see how abortion came to be regarded as criminal and we can examine the ethic of the act more realistically in terms of a personal decision. It is important to know that the criminal distinction grew out of our society's needs at a time when it was useful to condemn abortion and that in light of present day needs and realities, such as overpopulation, that need no longer exists.

Historically, one of the most vigorous and influential opponents of abortion is the Catholic Church. Early Christianity held, with some exceptions, that murder was not involved in the abortion if the fetus was not "animated." This state refers to the precise moment that human life begins in the womb, but the exact time of *this* event was never defined. The ancient Greeks believed that animation occurred 40 days after conception for a male child and 80 or 90 for a female. It was never explained how fetal sex was determined. In the 13th century, English law-makers replaced the animation concept with another demarcation line known as "quickening," again, never clearly defined. Meanwhile, abortion continued to be a thorn in the side of the Church. The debate raged until 1869 when Pope Pius IX eliminated the distinction between the non-animated and animated fetus and proclaimed all abortions punishable as murder, arguing that abortion violates the so-called natural law of God. This natural law, therefore, has been in canonical existence for little more than 100 years! We can't account for all the political reasons behind the radical shift in Catholic thinking, except to assert with some conviction that the new posture was vital to the Church's ambition to increase the fold. It was around this time that the development of birth control devices and their widespread usage began to threaten Catholic population. This political consideration was supported by the Church's longstanding aversion toward sexual activity as a means for anything but the propagation of the species, especially Catholic species. It was perfectly obvious to the Catholic hierarchy that a clarification of the Church's position on birth control was long overdue.

In the United States, we simply change a few of the central characters and the story repeats itself. Connecticut was the first state to pass an abortion law in 1821. This law outlawed abortion of a fetus after it had quickened. By 1860 the statute was broadened to forbid all abortions except when "necessary to preserve the life of such women." As with the Catholic Church, it is not erroneous to say that the economic benefits to be derived from population expansion (man-power to fill the factories and fields) during the years after the Civil War were a conclusive factor in curtailing the common law which did not consider abortion before the quickening criminal. Since 1821 all the states have enacted abortion laws which are equally restrictive as those in Connecticut, although some have made attempts to liberalize their laws.

Many women agree that our present abortion laws are anachronistic, discriminating, and unjust. Few will allow themselves to think in terms of abortion on demand. It is therefore important to discuss the merits of both abortion reform and repeal. This year California, North Carolina and Colorado made legal abortions more available to some by passing reform laws. In essence, the reform allows abortion on specific psychiatric grounds as opposed to exclusively physical considerations of health. According to Larry Plagenz ("Modern Hospital," July, 1969) the number of abortions in some California hospitals has increased six-fold while some hospitals have stopped performing abortions altogether. Meanwhile, the state-wide rate of 100,000 illegal abortions continues unabated. Los Angeles General Hospital still receives

about 7 to 10 women daily—just as many as before the reform law—who are the victims of illegal abortions. Dr. George
Cunningham, Chief of the Bureau of Maternal and Child
Health stated in the same article that, "Hospitals that want
to can make the procedure for obtaining an abortion complicated, time-consuming and expensive. One method is to require statements from two psychiatrists when the law requires
only one." Another example, in California the law requires a
hospital committee of at least two doctors to review requests
for abortion (up to 13 weeks pregnant) and stipulates that
for committees of three or less a unanimous vote is required,
though for larger committees a majority vote is sufficient.
Hence some hospitals will limit the Committee to three members and permanently install one dissident doctor effectively
giving him permanent veto power. The facts dealing with the
reform law in California clearly demonstrate how very conservative and limiting this law can be and is. It puts the power
to interpret the law entirely in the hands of the hospitals who
are fiercely proprietary about that power, and yet are curiously
unwilling to wield it in the interests of women.

It is estimated that up to 1,000,000 women yearly have
illegal abortions, and it is further estimated that approximately
350,000 women suffer from postoperative complications resulting from illegal abortions, most of which are performed by
incompetent quacks under deplorable conditions. Fifty percent of the deaths in New York City for the past several years
associated with pregnancy and birth resulted from illegal
abortions. Two decades ago the common indications for legal
abortion were serious disease of the heart, lung, or kidney.
Happily, because of advances in medical science, women are
rarely endangered by such threats to their lives. Consequently,
the physician has been forced to evaluate his patient's well
being on a less absolute basis. Many times the doctor is willing
to allow for other indications when judging the over-all health
status of his private patient. The clinic patient who does not
have her own doctor is less fortunate. The voluntary hospital
(community, non-profit) which treats both private and clinic
patients aborts three times as many private patients as it does
clinic patients. This institution also does 20 times as many
therapeutic abortions as does the municipal hospital which
sees only clinic patients. One of the reasons cited for this
glaring inequity is that the doctors in municipal hospitals
rigidly adhere to the letter of the law in determining the
threat to a woman's life, while doctors of private patients are
more inclined to accept full responsibility for their welfare

and stretch a point or two when defining what constitutes a serious threat. The clinic patient lacks this resource and few sympathetic, understanding allowances are made for her total well-being. This reluctance of doctors to extend themselves for clinic patients is being challenged in every phase of medicine. It is not necessary to belabor the point here. The reform laws however permit these discriminatory practices to thrive by delegating the ultimate responsibility for making the decision to the doctor who often abdicates with clinic patients. The repeal of the abortion laws would resolve the dilemma by taking the decision out of his hands.

What is in store for the woman who decides that she will have an abortion? Procuring a legal abortion is a complicated and frustrating business, sometimes as traumatic as having it done illegally. In Massachusetts, for example, abortions are obtainable (but not always obtained) because of the ambiguity of our state law which states that only *unlawful* abortions are illegal. What has come to be "standard medical practice" are abortions based on danger or impairment to physical or mental health. These are the criteria established by the medical community as the statute is so vague as to permit abortion on nearly any grounds. The OB/GYNs in Massachusetts have interpreted the abortion law to suit their purposes, i.e. keep the abortion rate down, and have been able to keep the lid on hospital policy. The governing boards of most hospitals defer to OB/GYNs in the matter of abortion controls as they feel this is strictly their bailiwick. The final decision is made by the Chairman of the Department and entirely subject to his whims. It is possible to terminate a pregnancy in this state, but the experience can be a harrowing one for a woman who does not want to be labeled psychotic. Very few therapeutic abortions are performed for reasons of physical health as we have previously pointed out. At this writing six major hospitals in the Boston area have been known to do therapeutic abortions, but the protocol for eligibility varies from hospital to hospital.

The ground rules for eligibility are laid down by the National Association of OB/GYNs who decides the number of abortions per live births to be performed each year. The implications of this power are staggering and extend not only to women but to doctors and hospitals as well. The latter are compelled to stay within the established limits out of fear of jeopardizing their standings. Medical people piously assert that they are unwilling to make full use of the existing law for fear of being flooded with abortion requests. This is no doubt true. However, there are solutions to that problem. Doctors privately feel that the practice of performing abortions is not stimulating and interesting to the residents and medical students who are studying in the teaching hospitals. Unquestionably true. Perhaps then the local community hospitals could be persuaded to relieve the burden and no one hospital need earn the reputation of an "abortion mill." It is important here to amplify one fact: it is the medical profession who decides what is to become "standard medical practice." Therefore, it is the profession who has outlawed abortion in any setting but a hospital in-patient one. There are always alternatives. In Rumania and parts of Yugoslavia women go home two hours after the operation and do not take up valuable hospital beds. In Eastern Europe there are special clinics set up which handle abortions exclusively. One clinic in Prague with 28 beds devoted to abortions interrupted 1,800 pregnancies in 1965 and with 96 beds cared for 2,184 deliveries. In Czechoslovakia during the same year there was one maternal death for 80,000 abortions.

The two most current methods of abortion are the D&C and the Suction method. D&C stands for dilation and curettage—dilation of the cervix and scraping of the womb with a curette. The cervix is dilated by means of graduated dilators (each one being 1 mm. larger in dimension than the previous one) starting at 2 mm. and proceeding up to about 12 mm., in cases of up to ten weeks pregnancy, and to 14 mm. at 12 weeks. The classical method of removing the fetus from the dilated womb is by a gentle scraping of the internal uterine wall with a curette. This instrument is a metal loop with either a sharp, blunt or serrated edge, mounted on a thin, long handle. Naturally great care must be exercised with this instrument as a rupture of the uterine wall is always possible in inexperienced hands.

Since the D&C is the most highly acclaimed method of abortion, it was surprising to find the following description of the Suction method in the January 1969 issue of "Scientific American": "After dilation of the cervix, a metal, glass or plastic tube with a lateral opening near the end is inserted into the uterus and moved about to dislodge the embryo from the uterine wall; the fragments are then drawn out by means of a vacuum pump connected to the tube. This technique is easier, quicker, and less traumatic than the D&C." This method has not been adopted in America possibly because it would make the "grave surgical procedure" posture less defensible. It is well within the realm of possibility for abortions to be done effectively in a doctor's office using the suction tube method at a reasonable fee. Women are penalized for abortions. The price of a purely medically indicated D&C is about $200 while the cost of a therapeutic abortion using the same technique is around $500 or whatever the traffic will bear. Blue Cross/Blue Shield pays for a therapeutic abortion and welfare covers its recipients.

After 16 weeks of pregnancy, a hysterotomy or Caesarean section is performed. This procedure involves cutting through the abdominal wall and is regarded as major surgery. The above techniques are the only ones that are medically sanctioned.

The fourth and fifth most common methods of abortion, catheters and saline injections, are usually employed by nurses and midwives. A catheter procedure (the preferred method of the two) is performed by introducing a plastic tube into the uterus through the cervix, thereby stimulating a "spontaneous" abortion. The danger of this technique is apparent if the procedure is not performed by a highly skilled person. Essentially, any intrusion into the uterus by an amateur is very dangerous. There are a number of chemical agents used in an effort to abort. The agents taken by mouth are rarely effective unless they are given in toxic doses large enough to cause serious illness to the woman. Injection of over-the-counter chemical agents into the cavity of the uterus are effective in producing an abortion if they reach the fetus or if they damage the cervix or vagina and thus lead to infection or hemorrhage. Most are highly poisonous once they reach the bloodstream. Other crude techniques include taking extremely hot baths, severe or prolonged exercise, and violence to the lower abdomen. Even though we understand the plight of the desperate pregnant woman, all of the above methods should be avoided at all costs, especially the last three which are both dangerous and ineffectual.

For pregnant women seeking counsel, there are several agencies, all of them badly overworked, who do abortion counseling. Planned Parenthood is one source of information regarding therapeutic abortion; another source is the Medical Committee for Human Rights which does a limited referral business. But for the majority of women, who are not eligible for a therapeutic abortion, the only recourse is the underground, illegal abortionist, if they have money, or self-mutilation, if they don't. The efforts of the Clergy Consultation Service, a referral agency for illegal abortions, are commendable, but they are limited for lack of resources and staff. In addition, there have been recent crackdowns against such services.

Most women simply "ask around." This approach works sometimes in the big city where the illegal abortionists are to be found. But what do rural women do? The drawback of "asking around" is that you are generally referred to the abortionist of a friend of a friend of a friend and that means pot luck. The risk involved is usually not a deterrent to a woman who is determined to have an abortion. She must, however, have money to avail herself of the services of a reasonably competent abortionist. The going rate is anywhere from $200 to as high as $1,000. The exorbitant fees are justified by the risk an abortionist runs in breaking the law. Again, for the woman with no money all doors are closed except for a self-abortive attempt. Clearly, for the majority of women, an illegal abortion is the only solution to an unwanted pregnancy and it is often unavailable to them. They are forced to reckon with compulsory pregnancies and bearing children who inherit the legacy of being unwanted.

For many women the problem of an unwanted pregnancy will never occur. But it should be the goal of all women to raise the decision to have a child to a personal, private level and to strip the abortion act of its degradation. It is looked upon as degrading because to a large extent women are considered creatures whose major means of fulfillment lies in their biological functions. Most of the condemnation comes from the male segment of society who fear abortion as a potential threat to their male supremacy. Most men are unable to live with women except as wives and mothers. One way of insuring that a woman knows her place is to limit her activities with many children. Women regard abortion with mixed emotions. The process of female identification begins early in life; our culture raises motherhood to an exalted level. A more subtle restraint is the damaging psychological effect that the possibility of an unwanted pregnancy has for women. Despite the reliability of contraceptive measures, there is the eternal fear of becoming pregnant and the inability to control this leaves women feeling trapped psychologically. For the woman burdened by a large family, this fear sometimes turns her off sex completely. The problem is a seemingly insoluble one, particularly to men who neither bear nor raise children. We are suggesting that women make it their problem.

Editorial note: N.Y. Abortion Repeal (legalizing abortion) went into effect on July 1, 1970. Despite this seeming victory, what's coming down remains the same. Points made in this article are still true—the medical profession (men) still control abortion (women).

HIGH SCHOOL WOMEN

How to Get Along with Friends*

A-NEETA HARRIS

To get along with friends these days isn't very easy because of the class struggle and color. Also by people trying to be better than other people, but they're no better. I am in the class struggle, also the color struggle and many others which are embarrassing to mention.

What is embarrassing is how boys and girls use each other. Black boys say black girls play hard to get while the white girls are easy to have. Negro girls who try to be white are easy to get from what I see. They say if a boy asks you for some you'd better take it because you don't get nothing else. This is when someone really wants a boyfriend bad and wants to be like the other kids.

I feel that a black girl should be herself, not try to be like anyone else. I have learned this through my mother who is together and my sister and my home teacher who tells me things that I see for myself the next day. This is how I learned about class struggle right in my schoolroom of almost all black girls. Since I am black skinned and poor, I have had to fight against the black girls who call themselves upper-class.

I think that no one has a real friend unless his or her mind is together. I haven't a best friend because I don't trust in them and I don't believe in some of the other things they believe in. I can't really tell you how to get along with friends because I don't even get along with friends.

I have people in my class that think they are better than anyone else. Then there are those who believe in liquor,

*Written by a 13-year-old black woman who lives in Mount Vernon, New York (March, 1970).

drugs, cigarettes and many other things that I don't believe in. The only people I believe in are the ones with their minds together.

Black Women in Junior High Schools*

LA-NEETA HARRIS

We are trying to get sex education in our Junior High School because girls (mostly black girls) should learn to protect themselves from boys or other men on the streets. A lot of girls (black) are ashamed of themselves especially to hear about themselves. They also are afraid of getting pregnant but they still go on NOT knowing or caring until they do get pregnant. They say you have to hang around with the crowd or some person may say they are chicken or can't be in the crowd. These girls that get pregnant may have to leave their homes because some poor mothers or families will not be able to support them. We should have this education because a lot of girls can stay in school and have better homes. Parents who are scared don't like to tell their daughters. So this should be their chance to decide and make up their own minds and get their heads together—about a lot of things. Some people say what you don't know won't hurt you but it will and can affect many of these girls. They have schools to help these girls after they get pregnant but this is not helping us be free before we get pregnant. Sex is also a part of our life. It was harder for our parents, but we don't suffer as much as they did. But for our rights we all must suffer. We have got to move on schools before they move on us. Sex education should be taught in school.

*Written by a 13-year-old black girl, who lives in Mount Vernon, New York (March, 1970).

High School Women's Liberation

An interview with three high school students by Nanette Rainone, creator of the WBAI-New York City radio program Womankind. *The three students are Pam Charney, Bronx High School of Science, Judy Stein, High School of Music And Art, and Paula Marcus, one of the first group of thirteen women who entered the previously all-male Stuyvesant High School (fall of 1969). The interview, given in full, was broadcast on December 31, 1969.*

NANETTE: Pam, why did you start a women's liberation group at the Bronx High School of Science? Did the idea come from inside or outside?

PAM: I've always been interested and really curious about what women's liberation meant. When I was eight years old, my mother gave me *The Feminine Mystique* one summer. I read it but I didn't understand it. It made me very curious and when I started dating I realized that something was drastically wrong. At first I thought something was wrong with me. Then I realized it wasn't me. And I began to look at the system at which point I found that my cousin was in a women's lib group and I met some people who motivated me to start thinking this way.

This fall we had Moratorium activities and the girls started petitions at school. We had a meeting. No one was willing to do any of the work so the girls finally volunteered. Then three guys got up and suddenly said they were doing everything. We were supposed to write a pamphlet. I went over to them and they said I could type it. At which point I got very upset, stormed off and of course wrote the pamphlet myself. I asked a couple of girls if they wanted to start a women's lib group in the school—and to my utter shock they said yes!

NANETTE: Judy, what is happening at the High School of Music and Art?

JUDY: Well, now we sit around and talk about how women's lib affects us. We are trying to look for things in the high schools that we can change such as courses that aren't co-ed. Like in our school, the hygiene courses are divided and they tell the boys how the girls think and tell the girls how to go on dates, how to talk to boys. And we're thinking of how we can start a women's studies program—an elective.

NANETTE: What kind of a reception have you had among the women in your school?

JUDY: At the first two meetings there were over fifty women, including members of the faculty, who wanted to become members of the group. The working group is smaller, the people who come every week.

Once we had 170 women come when we had a speaker from the Margaret Sanger clinic to speak about contraceptives. But I think most everyone in the school is interested in some way and that they would support any action we might take.

PAM: The reaction at Bronx Science is sort of mixed. When you say women's lib—it's sort of a curse word and people will laugh and giggle. If you pin them down, 'though, I think if you talk seriously to them on an individual basis, they agree that they're scared to agree. In fact that's one of the things we're trying to hit now. The main thing that's wrong in our school is the basic relationship between almost all the men and women in the school which perpetuates the whole image—they don't treat each other as individuals as much as a girl or as a boy. We're trying to attack this by putting up posters with facts. We're trying to get the Feminist Theater to come—though our principal is very upset about that . . . .

NANETTE: Why is that?

PAM: At first he was scared it was going to be obscene and when we promised him it wouldn't be, he still got upset. You see, he thinks that since the Board of Education hasn't come out and said it gives full support to sex education in the schools—he's scared to touch the topic. You see, we have to get the Faculty Advisor to give a blow-by-blow account of what goes on on stage . . . .

JUDY: The one problem we have is that we have to give an account to the principal of every move we make—every leaflet we have printed . . . .

NANETTE: Does every group have to do that?

JUDY: They all do. In the leaflet we made when the Sanger speaker was coming, the first two lines were in big letters: YOU DON'T HAVE TO GET PREGNANT. He called everyone in the Board of Education. . . . They all talk out of both sides of their mouths . . . . Out of one side they say, of course we agree with what you're doing. Out of the other side they say, our jobs are at stake in all this.

But we want to organize in the schools where there are so many girls around.

NANETTE: Now let me turn to Paula. Why did you choose to be among the first thirteen girls to go to a previously all-male school—Stuyvesant High?

PAULA: Well because . . . I really didn't think about it. I couldn't imagine what it was going to be like. And I think if I'd known I'd never have gone there. Now it's too late and there's nothing I can do about it.

NANETTE: Why wouldn't you have gone?

PAULA: Because it's too much for me. I have enough problems of my own and I don't need 2,400 other problems.

NANETTE: There are 2,400 boys I take it?

PAULA: Yes.

NANETTE: How have the boys received you at the school?

PAULA: It all depends. Like the older boys—juniors and seniors—just ignore me 'cause I'm a freshman.

NANETTE: You're too young?

PAULA: Yes, I'm too young, I just wouldn't understand. And the freshman are afraid of me because they're insecure themselves. Like I feel I'm being bombarded by all sides because like each individual is so insecure they all find one place to throw all their insecurities at—and that's me.

NANETTE: Do you think that's because you're a girl?

PAULA: Yeah, that reinforces it, I think.

NANETTE: You told me before that when you want to talk in history class all the boys tell the teacher not to let you talk.

PAULA: Yeah, it's because I'm a girl and a girl's supposed to sit there and look pretty and not ask any questions and ask all the boys the right answers, I guess. Also, like they think I'm invading, like I'm attacking their masculinity by being intelligent—or even just spouting garbage.

NANETTE: You're all going to special high schools. One would assume then that you're all preparing for college and careers. But do you feel in school that your future role is seen as different from the future roles of the boys? That on the one hand they're preparing for a career and that you're up to something different?

JUDY: In Music and Art it's funny . . . there are so many more girls than boys, the ratio is about four to one. So that in the orchestra the double bass player and the trumpet player are girls and we don't have any classes which are just girls except hygiene. So the roles are very mixed up. When you talk to the girls they say, "Look, there's nothing here that's against me." It's hard for the girls to look out beyond the school. Another thing, they say, "I sleep with all the boys I want, I'm liberated."

So in Music and Art I don't think it's blatant that they're preparing us for two different roles.

PAM: We have a different situation at Bronx Science. First of all, it is two-thirds male. Second of all, the test you need to get in means it's mostly upper-class, white, predominantly Jewish. Most of the kids are following in their parents' footsteps . . . as far as what they want out of life. This is true in everything . . . . Except every once in a while you'll hear a girl who'll say to you, "I want to be anything but a housewife. I don't want to be anything like my mother." But the majority really flaunt, you know, short skirts and laugh about the teacher who makes passes at them and things like that, which I guess is kind of sad.

NANETTE: Do you all think you'd rather go to an all-girls school?

PAULA: I went to an all-girls school. No, there I felt even more strongly the sense of how the girls were competing against each other. They don't even realize that, like, they have a common goal, a need to help each other and help themselves—instead of doing that they're fighting against each other. But they were all in seventh or eighth grade and were going to junior high, being a big girl now.

Also, in Stuyvesant, like I was so amazed I was talking to some guys about what I was going to do when I grew up and got out of Stuyvesant High School, and they said, "Oh, well, why are you worrying about that? Aren't you going to get married and have children?" And I said, "No, I don't think I want to get married and have children." They said that also because of their religion. This guy said to me, "It's written in the Torah, it's written in the Torah." Like, you're not supposed to go to college and learn anything and be anyone. You're supposed to have kids and take care of ME.

NANETTE: What about you, Judy and Pam, would you prefer an all-girls school?

JUDY: No. First of all, if you go to an all-girls school, you have to get into dating and mixers, people getting you blind dates, the most disgusting kind of situation. Also, I think that it's only by being with boys all the time, by being in their classes, seeing that I can do just as much as they can, that I can think just as well—it proves that there's nothing superior about them, and if you grow up all your life in an all-girl environment, you're going to believe all the myths that they tell you. Also, I think that it's easier in an all-girls school for them to give you a lot of little feminine courses. Like in all-girls schools they can just give everyone stenography and things like that—they don't do that as often in co-ed schools.

NANETTE: Well it's true that traditionally all the all-girls high schools were commercial [secretarial]—oh, except Hunter, which is a special academic high for girls. Brooklyn Tech, Bronx Science, and Stuyvesant were the better academic highs—you need a test to get in—and they were traditionally all-male, but there was the exception of Hunter.

If you could propose some changes for your school, what changes would you institute?

PAULA: Like we don't have gym classes.

NANETTE: That's in Stuyvesant, you don't have gym classes?

PAULA: Yeah, because something about some kind of rules that boys and girls aren't allowed to compete in sports—like this is really ridiculous. The boys open the doors for me and want to hold my books going home on the subway. It's ridiculous, I'm a strong person and I'm gonna get weak if I don't move my body. And so I think it would be so good for all these people if I had a gym class with them. Of course the first few gym classes everyone would be giggling and laughing. But then after a while it would be so much better 'cause they wouldn't be so uptight about seeing me and seeing my body—or so uptight about themselves, about being a boy and being a girl. . . .

Also, like in Stuyvesant we have a lot of mechanical arts, all these shops and they think it's funny that I have to take them too, because they say, "Oh, you're not gonna be a carpenter or a plumber." They say, "Well, maybe it's good for you to be a plumber so if your sink gets stuck washing all your dishes . . . but otherwise you're not gonna need it." But I feel also that shops aren't gonna do them any good and it's very hard for them to see that when I'm against something like shop it's not because I don't want to take it, it's because I don't think anyone should have to take it.

PAM: There's a lot in our school I'd like to change. First of all, the gym classes. We have a very good physical education department at our school. I took gym, but I like to take gym in a way—so that when I get out my body is fit. I know that Judy takes judo outside of school. I'm thinking of taking it in the spring, but I think that should be available in the school. Now, in the city, girls should be able to walk around as unafraid as a man can.

NANETTE: I know that the gym classes are kept separate for males and females at all the schools, but do you think that boys are getting a different kind of physical education than you are?

JUDY: Oh, definitely. Every term they keep teaching us how to throw a basketball and then a lot of dancing. You know that's fun, but we do only *three* pushups. We're not allowed to use the ropes in the gym.

PAM: In our school we're allowed to use the ropes. . . .

JUDY: They generally don't make us physically fit. Also, the girls have to wear gym suits and they have to be freshly pressed and the teachers say, "You have to go home and wash your white socks until they're snow white."

PAM: There's a contradiction in our school. The guys can wear anything they like, just as long as they wear shorts. We have to wear a uniform with the sneakers and the right socks.

PAULA: It takes half the gym period to check everyone to make sure your sneakers are white.

When I went to Science I still had my sneakers from the summer. They were perfectly good but they were dingy because you can't get the city dirt out of your sneakers. So the teacher told me, "No, you'll have to get a new pair of sneakers or you'll have to whitewash those."

PAM: You know what they do. The guys can do whatever they want to do in gym class, they have all the activities open, the boys do whatever they want and they get marked for it. They tell us "We can't let the girls do that. If we let you do that nobody would do anything." And they organize us into teams and check list everything that we do. It's so silly, why can't we have that basic freedom the guys have? So you point out this contradiction to them and they say, "It's perfectly all right, don't bother about that."

JUDY: But I think it goes beyond gym classes. I don't think there should be a class in the city that's not co-ed, and this involves just as much home economics courses as engineering courses.

Because for instance, the government put out a pamphlet about careers opening to women and they picked out things in the craft skills that don't require any physical strength— things like aircraft mechanics, tool and die workers, all sorts of fields that are really opening up and that are very high paying and they also have the prestige of being a skilled job. The government pamphlet said, "Women come into these fields, we really need you." So a group of us did a survey and found out that none of the courses which teach those skills are open to women. Either they're given in all-boys schools, or when they're given in co-ed schools, girls aren't allowed to take the courses. For skilled jobs you need either training or experience—so obviously no girl is going to be able to get the training in New York City and that's just not fair. Why should a girl have to take a job as a secretary? You get better pay and more prestige at skilled crafts. Instead of letting girls become mechanics they have to take stenography and typing. We think that is ludicrous.

PAULA: You see but . . . it's not their [the schools] fault. That is the way everyone looks upon women . . . that they're going to be secretaries. All these jobs and employers, of course they're going to want men . . . so women aren't going to want crafts jobs, they're going to want to be secretaries.

PAM: But you have to start somewhere though.

JUDY: But if you say it's nobody's responsibility . . .

PAULA: Yeah, I know, it's everybody's fault!

NANETTE: What about the academic courses, a history or English course, for example?

PAM: I have a good story about that. At my school some girls are really getting into women's lib. So some of the social studies teachers have been sort of bombarded. Things come up in class like "This country went to ruin when women got the vote." Then all the boys in the class applaud.

NANETTE: Did a student say, "This country . . . ."

PAM: No, that teacher said it.

NANETTE: Did he give reasons?

PAM: It's a joke, but he mentioned it often enough. . . . That's one class. . . . We were talking about when the slaves had just been freed, how the white man in the South was so hostile to the upcoming group. So I made the analogy about women now. . . . Everyone got very uptight. After class, I went up to the teacher and asked him why we hadn't done a lesson on women since we were doing all the minority groups. So he said, "Well, there's no information. . . ." So I reeled off the names of books. He said, "OK, you do a report and maybe we'll talk about it." Of course I'm doing it because he said he'd use it for all his classes—which means that many kids are going to see the work I do.

Another girl I know is in a class with three other girls and their teacher hasn't been too excited either with the facts they've been throwing at him. He gave them the same answer. So I guess the only way is to do the report and make them accept it, just so the information is gotten. So women know there once were matriarchies on the earth at one time and they were very powerful and not evil structures at all.

JUDY: I think people in general don't realize the part women played in history and about their oppression and teachers don't either. When you bring it up they all think it's funny and they don't pay any attention to it at all. Or—I know some of the teachers are so chauvinistic—the men—that they don't want to discuss it anyway.

PAM: Also, how many women writers do you study in English?

NANETTE: Well, how many are there, which is another problem.

PAM: My teacher was saying he only knew of three American women writers that he respected at all.

NANETTE: Who were they?

PAM: It was Willa Cather. . . .

NANETTE: Emily Dickinson, maybe?

PAM: No. . . .

NANETTE: He doesn't respect her? With his standards we're lucky to have any.

PAULA: In my English class, my teacher always has this big thing about women's rights. I'm the only girl in that class. Whenever I speak out he always says, "Miss Marcus, be quiet. Equal rights for men, equal rights for men." So one day he gave me the class, he said, "Go up there and talk about women's rights." Everyone thought it was really funny. And they didn't think I was serious about it, but I was damned serious. So after the class, many of the guys were really angry at me, they thought I was . . . well. . . .

NANETTE: You can find a substitute word.

PAULA: It was so strange. This one guy came up to me and said, "Paula, I've never heard any girl ever talk like that before. For all I know, you're the only girl in all America that feels that way."

NANETTE: What about some issues outside the high school? In the groups you've started in school, do you want to bring in issues that don't have to do with the schools in particular?

PAM: Well, there are just so many issues in the high school. . . . It's hard to say, "OK, besides all the things we're doing let's also do all the other things. . . ." The whole culture is male-dominated to the extent that anywhere you turn you see your oppression in detail. In fact, in our group we're going to do a study of our school—statistics—which we're sure will be very interesting.

NANETTE: What kinds of things are you looking for?

PAM: Well, everything. For one thing, how many boys and how many girls in each grade? . . . In senior year you take an elective—a science elective—what we're curious about is —you're always told if you're a girl and you go into science, it will be the life sciences. It's always assumed. We'd like to see how many girls are taking biology and life sciences as an elective and how many girls are not taking chemistry and physics electives. How many girls have taken positions of power, because you've been trained you're not as a girl expected to. . . .

NANETTE: Positions of power? You mean head of student government?

PAM: Yes, authoritative figure. Even within the teachers' ranks, how many teachers are there—there are more women teachers than men—but how many women are heads of departments? How many of them are men and how many are women? And executive positions in the school—the secretaries are women. There are so many things if you just look.

NANETTE: Early in the conversation, Pam, you mentioned something about dating. I wonder if all of you have special thoughts on the subject of dating. Pam, you said you started dating this summer and were horrified, or something to that effect. I wondered what you meant by that? How do you feel, Judy and Paula?

PAULA: It was funny. I was going out with this guy and I told him that my sister was interested in women's lib. And he said, "Well, don't go to any of those women's lib peoples' houses by yourself." So like it was funny and I laughed, but I began thinking about it and like that's really sick, because everyone takes this sort of attitude—women's lib, ha ha ha. And it isn't funny. It just goes to show how he thinks— subconsciously—about the whole thing. That really surprised me. So I talked to him and he said, "I was just kidding." But I don't think he was.

PAM: I'd been dating before the summer, but it was during the summer sometime when I realized how dating was part of an oppression because the whole culture. . . . You're gonna date and you're gonna find the right man, and he's gonna marry you and you're going to be his good little wife and wait home for him . . . do the dishes and clean the house. Oh, such a sweet person you'll be. And make love to him. . . . You're there and you're his. The beginning of the training is dating. A guy takes you out, he picks you up at the door, he escorts you home so you're safe and you make him something to eat, clean up. . . . And it's just the start of it if you're gonna date that way and most guys want to date that way. Once you reject that, it's hard to find a guy to take you seriously.

NANETTE: You find that if you act the aggressor and call the boy up, for example, he rejects you?

PAM: Well, it depends. Some guys get turned off if you act the aggressor. Some guys say, "It's all right as a favor." But I was referring more to things like paying for dates. Like a guy's always going to pay for you. . . .

JUDY: He rents you!

PAM: Look, if you want to be with him as much as he wants to be with you—but he's paying because he wants to be with you—Well, I'm not going out with anyone I don't want to be with and if I want to be with him I'm perfectly willing to pay, because otherwise you come home and he walks you to the door and you know what's on his mind . . . you know what he wants tonight . . . whether it's on the sofa or whether he thinks he'll get it next month. . . . Like it's really a bad scene. I don't want to sell myself. . . .

JUDY: I knew that before I got into women's lib, I dated and I was always very mixed up. I didn't know what it was that bothered me so much about it, except that I used to feel very obligated to the guys that took me out and I should be very thankful to them. . . . But when I realized a lot of things about being a woman . . . like now I still don't like the idea of dating, but when I do go out with guys I always pay my own way, I open the door for myself, I'll go meet him if it's nearer to his house instead of having him come pick me up. I feel a lot better, I don't feel guilty for dating and I can enjoy it. But it's funny, sometimes we'll get to a door and the guy'll look at me and he won't know what to do. I think it's a lot easier to accept it if you just realize—would I act this way if I was with my girl friends . . . and I figure if I would do this with any girl then certainly I can do it with this guy, because he's just my friend the way they are.

PAULA: Well, in my school I feel so self-conscious, partly because I'm a teenager. My official teacher is always telling me that I shouldn't wear pants because it's not feminine. If I'm walking down the hall how will anyone know that I'm a girl, if I'm wearing pants. So I said, "I really don't care if anyone knows I'm a girl or not; in fact, maybe it's better if they don't know." So like when I'm in my classes, the desks are really strange and I have long legs and my legs go up to my chin. So I'm always looking at my legs 'cause they're right down there and I'm so conscious of them. I'm always exploring them and seeing how skinny they are and like they're really bothering me. So I told my sister and she said, "Paula, why are you so worried about your legs, you're not selling your body to anyone." So I was talking to my friend Roland and he said, "Well, I think you have nice legs." I don't want him to tell me that I have nice legs, I wanted him to tell me that it's not important, and it's not important to him. And he said, "Well, it is very important to me. When I see a girl walking down the hall I want to know if she's a ballet dancer and I can tell by the way the leg is shaped."

NANETTE: How many ballet dancers is he likely to see?

PAULA: He said, "I don't like to see two trunks of a tree walking down the hall." Like this is so crazy. I don't care what his body looks like. It's him I'm interested in.

Also, in school all these girls wear all these beautiful clothes, and I come in with my jeans, because in the morning I don't really care, and besides *I* go to school, it isn't my blue jeans that go to school.

My English teacher, in the spring when I was wearing sandals to school, said, "Miss Marcus, does your mother realize you're coming to school barefoot?" So I thought that he couldn't see my shoes and I said, "I am wearing sandals." And he said, "It's really not appropriate for a girl to wear pants to school." He told me I should wear shoes and stockings. The next day I wore shoes and stockings and a dress. He said, "Miss Marcus, *today* I could fall in love with you." You see, not yesterday. Yesterday, that wasn't Paula.

JUDY: In Music and Art—we were the first school to be able to wear pants in the city. . . . The girls all dress pretty hip. And they come up to me and say, "I don't wear a bra. I don't wear make-up. How can you say I'm exploiting my body?" So it's very hard for them to understand these things.

NANETTE: One last question. How do you envision your futures? What do you see yourselves doing in terms of a career, and how do you picture your social lives? Do you expect to marry and have children?

PAM: I'm not sure of a lot of that yet. As far as what I want to do personally. I'm very into something called alternative futures, which I can't go into now. It's planning for the future with what we have without destroying any more. I'll go into science. I don't know if it will be a life science. Although everyone's pushing me that way—"I knew when you were a child that's what you'd go into." I don't know and I'm not pretending I do.

I think I'll always be interested in woman's role one way or another, because I'm a woman. . . . I'm a human being, and I'm treated like a woman more than like a human being.

As far as a family—I don't know how I could even think of it now. Besides it's being very much in the future, I'm still in the midst of realizing so many contradictions I didn't think existed. I think it's going to be a long time before I recognize all the contradictions that exist within the family.

So I wouldn't set one up until I felt that I understood all the contradictions.

JUDY: Well, as far as my future goes, I know that I'm going to work for the rest of my life and I want to be an environmental designer, which is a form of city planning. It's a field that's opening up, so I think it's important for women to go into it.

Something that's a horrible controversy is marriage. It's something you never questioned—to get married and have children—and maybe it's just six months ago that I realized maybe that's not what I want to do. That's the kind of thing it will take me a long time to work out. But right now I'm beginning to feel maybe I don't want to get married and maybe I don't even want to have children, but that I'm not sure of.

PAULA: About working. I'm sure I'm gonna work. It's not only being a woman in the United States, but I can't stand the city. And I don't want to work in the city. So I was talking to someone about communes and working on a farm . . . then I'll have to go into agriculture. About marriage. About having children. I don't know. I was thinking about that and I told a friend I didn't want to have children and she got so upset and she asked me why, and she felt that I needed a psychiatrist. . . . But I don't know what I want to do and I've got plenty of time to worry about that.

NANETTE: Right. And thank you all for coming by.

So on New Year's Eve, the last day of 1969, I wanted to introduce you to the newest development in women's liberation: the high school groups. Happy New Year!

CONSCIOUSNESS RAISING

False Consciousness*

JENNIFER GARDNER

That people are unaware of the oppression of women is a serious problem, but one that will be resolved as our movement grows and makes its presence felt. The problem of false consciousness, however, is harder to solve, and ultimately more dangerous, since our consciousness will determine our goals and our strategy.

Of all the wrong theories about who oppresses women, the most confusing and insidious is the theory that women oppress themselves. This false consciousness takes two forms.

First, women are put down for submitting to unequal, unrespectful treatment without fighting back. Second, they are accused of courting their own oppression. That is, they are accused of behaving in such a weak, passive, dependent way with men that men cannot possibly treat them as equals.

The first attitude is most common among women who feel that they have tried to be strong and independent, who look around them and notice that other women appear perfectly satisfied being weak and dependent. These other women seem to have made a conscious and ignoble bargain with life, sacrificing their dignity in return for protection and keep. Let us examine this bargain, and try to understand what the elements of choice really are.

Any woman, in any social class, who tries to insist on equality in relationships with men must be prepared to face the consequences of being a single woman in our society. She must face the difficulties of travelling alone, of being an obligation to her married friends, of knowing she can depend on no one for help and companionship when she wants them.

*From *Tooth and Nail* (October, 1969).

These problems are real, not psychological, not in her mind. It is not a question of women being taught to believe that being single is undesirable. It is truly difficult for most un-attached women to operate comfortably and effectively in a male chauvinist culture.

For many women, marriage means even more than the op-portunity to avoid being single. It is also the only way out of a boring and alienating job—a job which, moreover, is likely to require that she concede her dignity to men anyway. If, for example, she is a secretary or waitress, and fails to placate the men who are her superiors or customers, chances are she will find herself job-hunting again.

Her only chance for respect—partial and phony though it is—is to have a family. Society has closed other roads to all but a few. Discrimination against women in jobs is a fact. Women's work is low-paid work. And for a woman with apparent opportunities for better-paying, less boring work, sexual discrimination in the professions and in graduate schools becomes important.

For most women, the consequences of losing—even of attempting—an individual struggle with a man are severe: poverty, isolation, even death, depending on the man's tem-perament and the woman's own class situation. Sure, every time we don't struggle we make it harder for a woman who does. But only when we have a movement, only when women can offer each other real support, can we begin to make such demands on each other. To blame women for not struggling is to forget what the risks of struggle are for us all.

The second form of this false consciousness—the theory that women are oppressed because they go around asking for it—is most dangerous to our movement. It implies that a man oppresses a woman simply as a reaction to the woman's own expectations, and that he will stop as soon as she shows him she has some self-respect. The theory denies a basic reality—that men benefit in real ways—socially, economically, sexually and psychologically—from male supremacy.

Our oppression is not in our heads. We will not become un-oppressed by "acting unoppressed." Try it—if you have the economic independence to survive the consequences. The result will not be respect and support. Men will either not like you—you are a bitch, a castrator, a nag, a hag, a witch; or they will accuse you of not liking them—you don't care about me; you don't love me; you are selfish and hostile.

True, women suffer (because they are oppressed) from feelings of inferiority and self-hatred. True, too, that believing themselves to be inadequate and to deserve their place in a different and lower class from men, women have often thought themselves unjustified in demanding their freedom. In other words, the fact that women sometimes blame themselves for their situation may prevent them from becoming strong fighters on their own behalf. Surely one important task of our movement is to make it come clear to ourselves and to all women that our low social, economic and sexual status results not from any natural inferiority but from actual, recognizable, analyzable oppression, however subtle in form. But we cannot stop there; the elimination of self-blame, the birth of self-respect, is not the elimination of oppression. Feeling convinced of the justice of our demands is not, alas, the same as having those demands met.

The job of our movement, then, is not to blame ourselves or any other women for passivity, weakness, dependence, or any other qualities that women seem to display. Nor is it simply to strengthen ourselves for personal confrontations. Our job is to provide the vision of liberation and the hope, through our collective strength, of finally overthrowing male supremacy—everywhere.

Resistances to Consciousness

IRENE PESLIKIS

Thinking that our man is the exception and, therefore, we are the exception among women.

Thinking that individual solutions are possible, that we don't need solidarity and a revolution for our liberation.

Thinking that women's liberation is therapy. This, whether or not you belong to the organization, implies that you and others can find individual solutions to problems, for this is the function of therapy. Furthermore the statement expresses anti-woman sentiment by implying that when women get together to study and analyze their own experience it means they are sick but when Chinese peasants or Guatemalan guerillas get together and use the identical method they are revolutionary.

Thinking that some women are smart and some women are dumb. This prevents those women who think they're smart and those women who think they're dumb from talking to each other and uniting against a common oppressor.

Thinking that because we have an education privilege and can talk in abstracts we are somehow exempt from feeling oppression directly and talking about it honestly and, therefore, think of personal experience as something low on the ladder of values (class values).

Thinking that women consent to their own oppression (or anyone for that matter). This is a statement which puts the blame on the oppressed group rather than on the oppressor class which ultimately uses brute force to keep the oppressed where they are. It is an anti-women and anti-people statement.

Thinking that only institutions oppress women as opposed to other people. This implies that you have not identified your enemy, for institutions are only a tool of the oppressor. When the oppressor is stopped he can no longer maintain his tools and they are rendered useless. Present institutions and our feelings about them should be analyzed in order to understand what it is we want or don't want to use in the new society.

Thinking in terms of them and us. This implies that you are setting yourself off or apart from women (the people). In doing this you neglect to recognize your own oppression and your common interests with other people, as well as your stake in revolution.

Thinking that male supremacy is only a psychological privilege with "ego" benefits as opposed to a class privilege with sexual and economic benefits. The former implies a considerable amount of individual variation among men, thereby permitting you to find an individual solution to the problem.

Thinking that the relationships among men and women are already equal and thus immersing yourself in utopian fantasies of free love in spite of the fact that the objective conditions deny it. Love between men and women, free or unfree, is millennial, not real; and if we want it, we will have to struggle for it.

Thinking you can educate the people. This implies that you are educated and you will get a revolution going by teaching other people what you know. Education does not bring on revolutions; but consciousness of our own oppression and struggle might. Unfortunately formal education and political consciousness do not usually coincide. Even formal education in Marxism-Leninism tends to make people think that they know more than they really know. When we think of what it is that politicizes people it is not so much books or ideas but experience.

Dependency in Marriage: Oppression in Middle-class Marriage

Evelyn Leo

Married women are dependent upon their husbands financially and so the woman's life becomes defined through the husband's ability to provide for her. The husband's income dictates the couple's standard of living. Should he be successful her life is relatively comfortable, with luxuries added, and she will live in a "good neighborhood" and have all the material things a two-car family implies. When the wife's education would enable her to earn a better income than her husband, the couple must still live on his income because society relegates the woman to the role of housewife and mother and prevents her from functioning independently. More often than not, the type of work the woman can obtain would be boring anyway, and if she chooses to stay home all the time, hers is a choice of the lesser of two evils. Of course, should the husband run into hard times, she is then permitted to help by obtaining a job. This work must be to help out, but not for her own enjoyment or satisfaction. Working in this situation becomes an extension of her role as husband's helpmate.

The adult woman in the marriage relationship serves in a secondary capacity. The man can set his schedule exclusively to his own needs, safe in the knowledge that there will always be someone at home—waiting and looking after everything. In return for his support she must continue to be helpless and passive, usually reacting only with tears against her helplessness. In reality, she feels rage and frustration that she must wait, like a child, for her husband to decide when her requests are legitimate, and then wait for him to grant them.

Woman, because of her dependent relationship, totally accepts her husband's values and becomes the object through which his goals and attainments are manifested. The woman is simply a reflection of her husband. She *is* Mrs. So. and So; he *does* so and so. She is just a housewife—*his* wife. The interior of the home represents her, as it must, since it is usually the only creative outlet she has. But the size and the price of the home represents him—his success. The people she sees socially are most often his friends and business contacts.

Women are raised in a manner that conditions them to accept this dependent role, which places them in a secondary position in relation to men and the larger society. This dependency is not, as society would have us believe, based on woman's "natural" physical weakness, or on an instinctive desire for dolls, or on any other characteristic that is attributed to woman as being her natural state. Her dependency comes as a result of reacting to all the cultural pressures, implicit and explicit, which are brought to bear on her. These pressures start at an early age. The girl-child is "programmed" for a passive role. She is taught that girls don't fight, and she is given dolls to play with. She is conditioned to be "girlish" by being given frilly dresses to wear, which usually hamper robust physical activity. She is told to play with girls because boys are too rough. If a girl shows too much aggression or independence she is encouraged to modify this behavior and to be more passive. Aggression is reserved for males, in the family and out of it.

The little girl's father adores her, but only if she is acquiescent, passive, and a "good girl," i.e., stays within the role society permits her. More important, she is indoctrinated to obtain what she desires *through the male*. If she behaves seductively, cute and with feminine wile, she is sure to get what she wants from father. He is her protector and the supplier of her material needs. Subsequently, later in life, another man will be her "Daddy" and she will continue in her dependent role.

Since the husband benefits by his wife's dependency, he encourages her helplessness further. Should she become involved in her own individual activity, this would upset the convenient balance that has been established, and he would be called upon to share homemaking responsibilities. The husband would have to contend with another person's schedule and would no longer be completely free to function as a freewheeling, independent person, married but free. The wife, however, is home-bound because she must be there with the children. If she voices displeasure at being in the home constantly, cooking and cleaning and having conversations on the four-year-old level, he simply cannot understand how she can be unhappy. He lets her know that she is lucky to be out of the rat-race world and therefore should appreciate her role as housewife (servant).

As a matter of fact, since she is helpless—it is difficult for someone to use muscles in the body and brain that have lain dormant for so long—she has to accept his definition of her existence as being gratifying. If she wants activities outside the home she can indulge in the activities society has relegated to her—bridge, bingo, charities, etc. As long as the activities she chooses do not intrude on the world of men they are safe for her to engage in.

It is not surprising that when her children have become independent and she is stirred to "do something," i.e., have a career, paint creatively, run her own business, she is psychologically immobilized. She has never been attuned to her own individualistic style of functioning. She is so used to functioning for others that she has immense guilt to overcome before she can feel free to spend time on herself. Again, at this stage of her life, her husband encourages her helplessness. He subtly lets her know that he disapproves of her knocking herself out. "Why don't you stay home and take it easy," he says. He pretends to listen to plans she comes up with for some personal career or project, but when he realizes she is serious he puts his foot down—on her.

For most women today it is easier to accept this relationship; she dependent, he independent. The husband, after all, is supporting her and she finds her existence rather comfortable. But at what price? She has become an adult version of the child, dependent on the male for her interests, her thinking, her decision-making, and her self-definition. She has become incapable of self-fulfillment because she has never learned what that means in terms of her own individuality. The course of her entire adult life, from beginning to end, is determined by her choice of a husband because she is culturally obligated to allow him to take the lead in career, geographic location, friends, entertainment, interests, and her so-called comforts in life.

Something is terribly wrong with this dependent status of women. They are bound up with another human being in a closely intertwined relationship, yet they are carried along in a parasitic manner, never reaching their full potential as human beings, never using their own free choice or functioning as an individual within the marriage relationship. Something must be done to change this unequal, unfair, and oppressive situation in marriage.

About My Consciousness Raising

Barbara Susan

Politics has been around for a long time, so have radical political movements. Yet so far no political movement has come up with a political analysis that is especially relevant to us women. I can only guess that it is because the method of arriving at an analysis that talks in abstractions about other people will always exclude the people who are being directly oppressed by those doing the analysis. At Redstockings we've been developing a way of analyzing political problems that is relevant to us as women. Our method is not abstract. Each woman talks about herself and her own feelings and experiences. If our method works, we will have an analysis that is not only relevant to women but to all people because it will be an analysis based on the realities of our lives.

Traditionally our feelings are one of the few things allowed to us women. Over a period of centuries they've become highly developed. It's time we started using them to our own advantage. Feelings and intuition may be one of the keys for forming a political analysis that is relevant to us.

The first consciousness raising session that I attended was

about housework. We went around the room and each woman in turn told how she felt about housework and how she felt when she was standing over the dishes or stove, or what happened when she asked her husband or a man she was living with to do the dishes. It came to my turn and I explained how my husband always helped with the housework. If I was tired he'd cook dinner and sometimes even do the dishes. Yet I'd still start to boil every time I'd get in front of the sink or stove. I listened to other women also telling about how their men "helped" with the housework.

I began to get sick at the thought of these liberal men "helping" their wives with the housework. When we did other things like go to the beach or go out for ice cream he didn't help, he shared. It was only a matter of helping when it came to doing things that he didn't like to do.[1] The group began to feel that something was wrong with the whole idea of men "helping" women with the housework. It meant that he was helping me with *my* job. Every time he'd help and I'd say "thank you" I was reinforcing the idea that it was my job! Regardless of whether I worked or not housekeeping was my job. It became pretty clear after hearing many women speak that this thing about helping was no petty detail of our personal lives. It became clear that it was a political fact. Listen to men talk about housework or better yet ask them how they feel about it. I'll bet that most of them say that they "help out." This is not just a matter of semantics. It is important because it keeps us having the job of housework as our job . . . as woman's job. There were several things that were very surprising to me at this consciousness raising session, not the least of which was the conspicuous absence of men. It was quite pleasant to talk without them. There was no need to argue about whether or not the problems we felt were real. Also, that constant undercurrent of competition that almost all of us feel when in the presence of men was almost totally absent. We were able to begin to find new ways of relating to each other.

After doing consciousness raising for a while Redstockings developed a procedure for it that we find useful. We direct our talk to one particular question at a time in order to formulate an analysis based on our real experiences and so that any generalizations we might come to will be based on fact. We go around the room, each sister taking a turn. In this way everyone has a fair chance to speak and be totally heard. When a sister gives testimony the other women in the

[1] *Politics of Housework*, Patricia Mainardi.

group can ask questions in order to clarify in their own minds what a sister is saying. Sometimes women interrupt a testimony to say how their own experiences are related directly to those of the woman speaking. When everyone has spoken we go around the room making generalizations and trying to find out what the connections are between our experiences and how they relate one to the other.

Consciousness raising is not a form of encounter group or psychotherapy. I've been involved in both and I can tell you they are very different. Therapy was useful to me in certain ways. It helped me develop a sense of self-worth and come to the understanding that I wasn't a bad person or useless. My experience in therapy helped me have a better image of myself and I even started to look better and dress in a more attractive way. In short I had more confidence in myself.

Eventually I left therapy. I noticed that men paid more attention to me. They related very well to me as a sexy young eligible woman. Yet, when it came to my ideas, my needs as a human being and my work, their attention span was not very long. Oh I got more attention but it wasn't the kind I wanted. Slowly I began to lose my studied casual look. (It took quite an effort and expense to maintain.) Slowly, I noticed that men were not talking to me with that same concerned attentiveness. It seems that therapy had neglected a very important part of my education. It hadn't made clear to me that anything was wrong with the social and economic conditions in which we live. It had only made clear that I hadn't adapted to them in a way that would be useful to me. It hadn't made clear that the relationships which cause us to have problems are in large measure predetermined by a political atmosphere and that the present political atmosphere is destructive. Therapy had made me believe that I was different from other women (in this case different meant better).

In retrospect therapy had separated me from my sisters by calling them "most women" and me "special." It had neglected to tell me that my newly acquired feeling of self-worth was only going to propel me headlong into another struggle because although I felt worthy I was still a woman and very few other people were going to recognize my worth. Not only weren't they going to recognize my worth, but I was going to be penalized for fighting for my rights. I was labelled crazy, masochistic, etc. But this time I was not completely fooled.

I got into the women's movement and began to see that other women were also called crazy. The relief at finding I was not alone was incredible. I was stunned. Here were women who were strong. And what's more they were smart and had ideas about how things ought to be. It had been very effective in therapy calling me different from my sisters, trying to make me believe that I could find an individual solution without changing the external political conditions. It had effectively separated me from my sisters and even made me start to hate them. It put me in the position of not being able to identify with other women. I was identifying with men, which seems quite natural to me since they were the ones who got all the goodies.

In the women's movement and especially in consciousness raising I saw women who recognized that there was no such thing as a personal way of solving their problems so long as male supremacy in all its formal and informal forms still existed. Here were women looking for solutions based on their own collective experience. . . . They were talking about their personal experiences and analyzing them in terms of social structures rather than in terms of their own weaknesses. They were not, as therapy often does, blaming women for being passive and in a rut. They were trying to find out exactly what that rut was and how they were forced into it so that it could be changed. They were trusting to their own minds and experiences to understand oppression . . . not as an abstraction . . . not as something that happened to other women, but as a fact of their lives.

Once I became aware of my own personal oppression I was much more motivated to act both individually and collectively to change the situation in which I lived. Acting however brings repercussions and I can easily see how people resist consciousness raising especially since some of the personal actions it leads to are very painful to deal with. During one long session on abortion it became very clear to me that sex was only half shared by men and women together. The half they shared was the good part. If an unwanted pregnancy was the result of a sexual act between a man and woman, it became the woman's problem, as if she had done it to herself. The question was always "What are *you* going to do about it?"

My husband and I had agreed that when and if we had children we would share equally in bringing them up. But we had never even considered the other half of that which meant that we should share equally in contraception. Up to now I had been taking pills but I was getting nervous about having my body controlled by chemicals whose effects are still uncertain. I asked my husband if he would use condoms half the time if I would use a diaphragm the other half. Previously I had been very sympathetic to the male argument about condoms cutting down on pleasure and being uncomfortable. Since I hadn't used a diaphragm in so long it was easy for me to see that diaphragms could cut down on pleasure (you have to stop and put them in) and that twenty-four hours later when you have to take them out and wash them in your friendly office lavatory you didn't feel too comfortable either. My husband acted like I had demanded the supreme sacrifice. He said condoms were terrible to use (I guess that meant diaphragms were pleasant) and they felt awful. He also felt terribly embarrassed when he had to go to the drugstore to buy them (I guess vaginal jelly just appears). He said he'd rather not make love at all than use one. After several weeks of bitter hassling, he realized I wasn't kidding and finally came around. Consciousness raising had brought me into direct and unpleasant conflict with men.

A collective action also came out of the same session on abortion. We came to realize that it was not only the abortion laws that had to be repealed, but that something was wrong with the whole idea of men calling themselves experts on problems that they would never have to face. In fact we found that we were opposed to the whole idea of experts. Out of this came the abortion hearing at the Methodist Church (March 1969) in which we set ourselves up as experts on the abortion question by virtue of the fact that we were women. We invited all women who wanted to join us on the panel to do so because they were experts too.

Consciousness raising is a way of forming a political analysis on information we can trust is true. That information is our experience. It is difficult to understand how our oppression is political (organized) unless we first remove it from the area of personal problems. Unless we talk to each other about our so called personal problems and see how many many of our problems are shared by other people, we won't be able to see how these problems are rooted in politics. When we talk about politics we don't mean in the limited sense of political parties such as the Democratic and Republican or economic systems like capitalism and socialism. We also see male supremacy as a political system in as much as all men are in collusion in forcing women into inferior and unproductive positions. Rare is the man who will support a woman vis-a-vis another man. There is a tacit agreement among men that women should do only certain kinds of work, (housework, childcare, nursing, clerical work, etc.) and that woman are incapable of controlling their own lives and therefore must be helped (controlled) by men. This "understanding" that men have is reinforced by our so called democratic legal system, prostitutes are criminals but their clients aren't (in New York State), women cannot accuse their husband of rape, etc.

In order for us to form a powerful political movement it must be a movement which answers to the needs of all women. We recognize that at the present time there are economic, class and racial differences among women which keep us from coming together politically. It is our hope that consciousness raising in groups of women who are not the same will help us to understand each other and help us all in building a movement which answers to the needs of more than just the most privileged woman. Our analysis is an expanding one, it changes as more and more women enter the movement and contribute their knowledge and experience thereby widening and correcting our understanding of oppression.

Sex Roles and Their Consequences*

BETSY WARRIOR

RESEARCH IN FEMALE AND MALE DIFFERENCES
RECOGNITION OF FEMALES IN HISTORY

Looking back through history, it would seem that women have contributed very little in relation to what man's contribution has been. This should be a surprising fact, considering half the world's population is female.

In 1904 Ellis made a study of British genius. He had 1,030 subjects, out of this group only 55 were female. In 1903 J. Mc K. Cattel compiled a list of the 1,000 most out-

*From No More Fun and Games (February, 1969).

standing persons in history. Out of this 1,000 only 32 were female. Of these women some were only listed because they were royalty, not on account of great personal merit.

In 1913 Castle made a study of 868 females in history, and found that the most prominent were not distinguished by their individual merit, but by the fact that they happened to be the wives or mothers or mistresses of famous men, or they were of royal birth.

All this and other similar accounts would lead us to have a very low opinion of the capabilities of women, in comparison to men.

In past eras, men (and women too) just took it for granted: females were inferior to males. Because of biological differences probably.

More observant people spotted glaring contradictions in this supposition, which led to a great deal of research and investigation into female and male differences. Sociologists, psychiatrists, anthropologists, psychologists, biologists, behavioral scientists, and others have contributed statistics and findings in the area of sex differences that lead to very different conclusions.

Keeping in mind the historical performance of adult females mentioned previously, let us look at the performance records of girls in school. Our first striking paradox shows up.

In all studies of school achievement one fact consistently comes out. Girls as a whole always do better than boys as a group do.

Given the academic achievement pattern of the girls as compared to the boys, one would expect women to far outshine men in adult achievement, but we've just seen that the opposite is true.

To come to this conclusion investigators used a great variety of tests, criteria, and methods for measuring school success.

It was also shown that girls are less often retarded than boys, and they are more often above average intellectually than boys. Yet out of 1,030 geniuses in the Ellis study only 55 were female!

A typical example of what research findings have been is a survey by Northby (1958) in which 12,826 subjects were used. They were 83 per cent of the students that graduated from the entire state of Connecticut in 1956. The students were divided into ten categories.

Of the top category, 72 per cent were girls and only 28 per cent were boys. In the very bottom tenth the boys made up 64 per cent of the group, while the girls were only 36 per cent of it.

All these statistics indicate that females aren't living up to their potential. Somewhere along the line their abilities are frustrated, misused, abused, discouraged, atrophied, or lack means of expression.

One theory used to explain the striking superiority of girls in academic achievement is the fact that girls mature more quickly than boys. But this has been disproved by the evidence that mental and physical characteristics aren't connected.

One explanation for the difference between school performance and later performance by females is that people who are docile, submissive, and passive (as females are supposed to be) aren't likely to assume positions of leadership, or have the necessary competitiveness to make a place at the top for themselves.

In 1964 Ames and Ilg made a study of 33 boy-girl pairs. They were carefully matched for age, social and economic status, and I.Q. The girls scored much higher than the boys on all the four types of tests given.

Outside the purely academic area, women do better than men in tasks involving manual dexterity. This showed up on tests like the O'Connor Finger Dexterity Test, the O'Connor Tweezer Dexterity Test and the Purdue Pegboard. In memory tests using the procedure of reproducing exactly a series of numbers, words or drawing a geometric figure after a brief study, or reciting something that has been read aloud, the rule of female superiority shows up again.

In quick perceptual response to detail, the difference between female and male is large and unquestionable, and it shows up at all grade and age levels. A summary of data from several sources by Schneider and Paterson (1942), showed that only about 20 per cent of the males exceed the mean for females.

There has been another type of finding in sex difference, but it only shows at a higher age and grade level. This is in schoolwork involving problem-solving with numbers and spatial relationships. On a high-school level differences in math and science favored the boys.

However, tests by McAndrew in 1943, and other studies show that at the preschool and primary level there is no difference between the sexes in abilities like comprehending causal relationships which underlie achievement in science and math.

At a symposium on sex differences in Berkeley, California D. W. Taylor gave evidence that the difference between boys and girls in the area of problem-solving is largely a matter of attitude toward problems and is a result of training.

The fact that males are more proficient, at higher grade and age levels only, in math and science means that this is something that develops as part of the educational process itself.

It seems that as females are exposed to the outer environment, they adopt a defeatist attitude toward problem-solving, or what psychologists prefer to call traits of passive-acceptance, docility and submissiveness.

COGNITIVE STYLE

Cognitive style is the way a person reacts to outer stimuli, such as sights, sounds and things touched. Each person has a different style in utilizing this perceptual stimuli in solving problems.

Investigations into the cognitive style of individuals have given much evidence to substantiate the theory of attitude difference formed by contact with the culture.

There is a high correlation between cognitive style and personality (temperament). The difficulty females have in problem-solving is related to the Witkin finding that the total structure of a situation influences females more than it does males.

In cognitive tests women proved to be significantly more field-dependent than males. This means in tests trying to grasp a perceptual pattern embedded in a visual field, females had a harder time disregarding the background than males did. Males showed much more field-independence.

In tilting chair experiments, females utilized a procedure of passive-acceptance. They assumed at first that the room was upright, instead of utilizing different cognitive clues to figure out the situation. Males did much better in orientation tests. The success was from their ability to keep an object isolated from compelling background forces. This is field-independence.

Some of the personality traits related to field-independence are: actively dealing with one's environment, instead of passively accepting it, self-esteem, self-acceptance, and self-realization.

Children higher on field-dependence were found to come from homes where more coercive procedures were used, more stress was placed on conformity, and children were pushed more consistently towards goals and standards set by the parents.

The significantly higher scores for females on field-dependence do not show up until adulthood. This shows that females are forced to adopt roles which society thinks are fitting for them. They are coerced into conforming to a sex role not of their choosing. The damage done by this shows up in the lack of problem-solving ability in females, as well as in many other areas.

The field-independent type, carried to the extreme, is the simple man of action who scorns complexities, and does not even see fine distinctions, a rigid authoritarian with an intolerance for ambiguity. In fact the higher the person scores on masculinity, the more apparent the Fascist traits become in the personality. A scale called the F scale (pre-Fascism) was devised to measure the personality variable directly. A high scorer on this scale is characterized by: repression rather than awareness of his own unacceptable motives, externalization or projection which leads him to suspect and blame others and to avoid introspection, conventionalism or conformity, an orientation toward others in terms of power rather than love (the instrumental goal-oriented behavior), rigidity rather than flexibility.

The field-dependent female bears great resemblance to the children who display withdrawn behavior, rather than using aggressive action to deal with their environment. The apathy and depression of these children is abundantly clear. This was not behavior that made trouble for the parents or the community. It was the behavior of the hopeless, despair and defeat.

These children did not risk overtures that could bring rebuff, or initiatives that might end in defeat. They trusted no one and expected little but rejection. In effect they withdrew from life.

Dreams must substitute for action, fantasy for reality. At least in dreams hopes can always be fulfilled, and defeat is only the fate of the villain. But dreams build no self-confidence, and fantasy teaches no pitfalls.

These are the children who may in a few years join the growing number of mentally ill. When life demands action they cannot act. The most typical responses to reality were to deny, to run away from it, then submit passively to the consequences.

There is to all this what amounts to almost an abnegation

of living. An acceptance of defeat so complete that *action is irrelevant*.

Defeatism is a spiritual poison too often encouraged by their experiences in the family. When they meet with defeat and indifference in the community too, it is hard to see where incentive for change can come from.

These personality traits aren't found only among females, but are characteristic of all oppressed groups.

INTERESTS AND VALUES

In the area of motivation and interest, great differences between men and women show up again. In the Allport-Vernon Study of Values, men showed greater interest in economic, political and theoretical values, they were motivated by a desire for practical success, influence and power over others were their goals for living.

Women showed a strong interest in aesthetic, social and idealistic values, and were motivated by a concern for the welfare of others as a goal for living.

Strong evidence shows that the much lower aspirations of females aren't because of a lesser need to accomplish, but because their aspirations aren't aroused as men's are, in a competitive money-oriented society. This is reflected in the different values and motivations of women and men.

Another contributing factor to the lower goal aspirations in women is that they have less self-assurance, less self-confidence, and a lower opinion of themselves in general.

This remarkable fact should be quite surprising, considering girls have consistently done much better in school than boys. Knowing the girls' superior performance in school one would expect them to have much higher aspirations than boys.

Walter and Marzolf (1961) made a test of boys and girls at several grade and age levels, on the Rotter Aspiration Board. They found that girls had significantly lower scores at all grade levels regardless of being good or poor students.

A study by Bennet and Cohen (1959) sums up the basic differences, that have been corroborated in many other studies as well:

1) Masculine thinking is a modification downward in intensity of feminine thinking. This would give one cause to think that, psychologically, males should be defined relative to females, rather than the other way around.

2) Masculine thinking is oriented more in terms of the self, while feminine thinking is oriented more in terms of

the environment. This is related to their response in problem solving.

3) Masculine thinking anticipates rewards and punishments determined more as a result of the adequacy or inadequacy of the self, while feminine thinking anticipates rewards and punishments determined more as a result of the friendship or hostility of the environment. This shows the attitude of passive-submission adopted by females, and their lack of belief in their own self-determination.

4) Masculine thinking is associated more with a desire for personal achievement, feminine thinking is associated more with a desire for social love and friendship. This is strongly reflected in the choice of values and interests of each of the sexes.

5) Masculine thinking finds more value in malevolent and hostile actions against a competitive society, while feminine thinking finds value more in freedom from restraint in a friendly and pleasant environment. Indicating a lack of fulfilling outlets for female qualities under a harsh capitalist system.

All these findings shed light on the reasons for the great disparity between the actual potentialities of females and their retrograde performance in later life.

Other research into female and male interests has shown males to be more interested in occupations involving physical exertion, machinery and tools, science, physical phenomena, business, commerce, adventure and exploit.

On the last two items some contradictory evidence has shown up in the field of psychobiology. In a test gauging behavior response in males and females to emotion-evoking stimuli, females tended to be more exploratory than males. This would lead one to expect females to be more adventurous. The contradiction between what females are capable of and what they actually do, can be explained by the sex-role concept, and how it affects them. This will be gone into in greater detail later.

Females showed a greater interest in aesthestic objects and occupations, personal affairs, occupations more directly ministrative to the needs of other people, especially the young, helpless, unfortunate or distressed.

The males showed greater aggressiveness and self-assurance, more hardiness and fearlessness, more roughness of manner, language and sentiment.

The females showed and expressed more compassion, sympathy, and aesthetic sensitivity. They were more expressive of emotion in general, severer moralists, yet admitting in themselves more weaknesses.

STABLE PERSONALITY TRAITS

In differences in personality between the sexes, the most stable trait found in females was "passive reaction to frustration". We shall see that this trait shows up markedly in other oppressed groups too, although in these groups its defined differently and referred to as "choking back anger."

The most stable sex characteristic of the male personality is aggression. This indicates that personality traits that are in keeping with the way society expects the members of each sex to act (the sex-role), are more likely to be brought out and reinforced.

Personality traits that don't conform to the sex-role concept, will be frustrated, modified, crushed or atrophied. It is now recognized how great a part sex-roles play in the shaping of a personality. These concepts influence behavior on many different levels and affect all areas of the personality.

Besides directly constraining behavior with discriminatory laws, customs, conventions, unequal education, and opportunities, sex-roles become internalized attitudes people hold about themselves and their capabilities. These attitudes will determine a person's outlook on life, what they learn, how they behave, what they aspire to, and how they interpret life.

A test that will give us an indication of how females are perceived in this society was done by McKee and Sherriffs (1957). A group of boys and girls were asked to vote who possessed each of nineteen good traits and fourteen bad traits. In the older groups both boys and girls ascribed all the good traits to boys. The fact that during these school years girls were behaving better and making better marks, shows that the influence of sex-role concepts outweighs even reality.

In a test of university students 84 per cent of the girls accredited more of the unfavorable traits to women. Another indication of the repugnance of the female image is Grey's finding that for boys perceived similarity to the father went with acceptance by one's peers, but for girls identification with the mother was related negatively to peer acceptance.

We can clearly trace the genesis of aggresssion in boys. It was found that girls showed no more or less aggression, whether they came from homes where the father was present

On the other hand boys who came from homes where the father was absent started showing aggression at the age of five, coinciding with the time they started to leave the home. These boys acquired their concept of the male role at a later age. The father at home started showing aggressive- ness... allowed them to express more aggression at the age of two or three. Their idea of... children, and at an earlier age and girls learn their... that both boys and girls learn their... Because the mother doesn't react... girls as the father does... instrumental...

...because of his instru... goal oriented masculine behavior, shows his boys how to "be a man" by imitating his behavior. The girls trying to please the father adopt the feminine role. This is why girls who are more feminine (passive) have fathers who are more mas- culine (aggressive).

MALADJUSTMENT AND MENTAL ILLNESS

Women tend to be much more maladjusted and neurotic than men. Because this sex difference doesn't occur until high school, it can be directly attributed to the effects of the female sex-role.

The Bernreuter Personality Inventory shows women to be more neurotic, more introverted, more dependent, less self-confident, less self-sufficient and less dominant than men. These differences in contrast to interest differences do not show up until high-school age. The role to be played by women leaves little room for change from the dependent, submissive, obedient child, to an independent, self-assured adult.

The rigidity of this stereotype makes for maladjustment and mental illness. Research shows that women who con- formed were more popular and less neurotic than non- conforming females. Also, conservative girls who were will- ing to go along with accepted standards, even if they thought they might be wrong, were happier and better adjusted than liberal girls who had a tendency to think for themselves.

This is damning evidence that if females don't buckle under, they're broke. The females who accept their roles are just as damaged. These females have given up using their own minds. Even though sex-role concepts do not fit

252 WOMEN'S LIBERATION/VOICES

actual human beings, any deviatio...
psychological punishment, any that ...
Many people argue that this ...
were treated as inferiors only in ...
just how false this assumption ...
the mental and secondly by the ...
research, problems of Southe... and
economic groups, and females ...more malad-
Personality tests show blacks ...ior all the major
justed than whites. Hospitaliza...acks, (Frumkin 1954).
mental disorders are higher an...
These differences become no...cable at higher age levels.

In a study by ...on (1958) Southern blacks had personality differences that were attributable to "caste sanctions" prevalent in the South. The most striking differences were in the area of aggression. There was a denial of aggressive feelings of all kinds. An intuitive choking back of anger. There are many secondary effects in the personality that are an outgrowth of this suppression.

R. E. Clark found that among 12,168 mental patients, those with the lowest income and job prestige got mentally ill at a younger age and their mental disorders were more serious. The better paying the job, and the more prestige, the higher the age at the time of mental breakdown, and the less serious the illness.

Schizophrenia is eight times more prevalent in the lowest socio-economic groups than in the two upper ones (Hollingshead and Redlich 1958).

School children gain or lose in academic achievement according to what class they belong to. The lower-class girls tend to show a loss earlier than the lower-class boys. This can be accounted for by the fact that the lower classes have a less liberal and more rigid view of the place of women in this society.

The oppression of women is still a fact in the twentieth century.

Consciousness Raising

FROM AN UNNAMED LEAFLET

Consciousness raising, in which you will talk about personal experience without broad analysis, will accomplish the following:

Clean out your head
Uncork and redirect your anger
Learn to understand other women
Discover that your personal problem is not only yours

Suggested order of consciousness raising (a topic a week, or month):

1. Discuss your relationships with men as they have evolved. Have you noticed any recurring patterns?
2. Have you ever felt that men have pressured you into having sexual relationships? Have you ever lied about orgasm?
3. Discuss your parents and their relationship to each other and to you.
4. How do you feel about marriage, having children, pregnancy, etc.?
5. Discuss your relationship with other women. Have you ever felt competition for men?
6. Discuss your relationships with women in your family.
7. Problems of growing up as a girl—socialization: Were you treated differently from your brother?
8. How do you feel about getting old (and your mother getting old)? What do you fear most?
9. Sex objects—do you feel like one? If so, how? Do you ever feel invisible?
10. Are you a nice girl? Is your smile like a nervous tic?

11. What would you most like to do in life and what has stopped you?
12. What do you most want this movement to accomplish?

RADICAL FEMINISM

Some Male Responses*

ANNE KOEDT

Here are some male reactions commonly heard when talking to men about women's liberation. They must be pointed
out and exposed for what they are, so that they may no
longer have the effect of keeping women's consciousness
down.

The Laugh: Dismissing the issue without even discussing it.
This puts all the burden of proof on you.

Your Fault: It's your personal problem. Not a social,
political one. "Something in your life must have screwed
you all up so you hate men. See a psychiatrist." This is the
technique of trying to isolate you.

Women Are "Different": The "separate-but-equal" argument based upon biological data. "You're not inferior, just
different. I love women." This technique uses physiology,
which obviously cannot be changed, as proof positive of the
validity of the status quo. Most oppressed groups in the world
have some physiological argument tacked on to them.

Women's Rights were Won 40 Years Ago: Recognizes the
problem as a past one, but denies that it still exists.

The Male Liberal: "I'm all for it, but what about the
children, etc." The technique works to agree there's a "problem," then tries to steer you back to the traditional role by
specific guilt manipulations.

The Super-Feminist: Having accepted the issue superficially
or actually, but still needs to one-up you. So he becomes the
super-feminist, moralizing to you about how you haven't
quite made it yet, etc. Helping the little woman with her

*From *Lilith* #2 (Spring, 1969), © Anne Koedt 1970.

problem. This maintains control over the process and also intimidates the woman.

Seducer: Having been unable to argue or intimidate the woman, he tries to re-establish the conventional role by having sex with her. It's a conquest. This area is very subtle, since he may agree with you verbally, may recognize you as a formidable, strong woman, etc., but that just makes the conquest all the more challenging.

Women Don't Want Freedom: The oppressor turns on the oppressed, blames her for her own oppression. Since one can always find Aunt Toms, scared women, etc., this argument can seem real if one does not distinguish between who is the victim and who is the perpetrator.

I'll Accept Women's Freedom if . . . Women Will Go to Vietnam, Pay Alimony, Etc.: This is a very intimidating tactic because it is a threat that if women want to free themselves the few privileges they have will be taken away from them.

She's Only a Feminist Because She's a Bitch Who Can't Get a Man: And you don't want to be like that, do you? Third-person tactic used to persuade women that the worst thing that could happen is to lose their oppressors.

Karate As Self-defense for Women

REBECCA MOON, LESLIE B. TANNER,

SUSAN PASCALE

Women are attacked, beaten and raped every day. By Men! Women are afraid to walk certain streets after dark, and even afraid to walk into buildings where they live. It's about time that we as Women get strong in order to defend ourselves! Two of us (ages 29 and 43) (along with three children) decided to learn Karate. We went to watch a class before signing up and if we hadn't been so determined, the class (consisting of about twenty-five frighteningly strong men) would have scared us into quitting before we started. We had yet to learn how really weak we were!

One reason for taking Karate, other than strictly learning

self-defense, was a matter of health—women seem to smoke much more than men, and certainly they never give their bodies physical exercise except cleaning house, chasing kids and fucking. Both of us smoked too much and hadn't moved in over ten years. Another reason for one of us getting into Karate was that she has 3 children, and the family structure being what it is—fucked up—she had hopes that it would perhaps relieve some of the emotional bull-shit that goes on between children and between children and parents if they all took Karate together.

In the middle of August, 1969, the two of us (along with the 3 children—a girl aged 15, and two boys, ages 11 and 6) started classes.

PSYCHOLOGICAL OPPRESSION

When we went to our first class we huddled in a corner, feeling inferior and somehow as though we were trespassing. The men stood directly in front of the mirrors, totally unselfconscious, to practice. We, after 3 months, are still self-conscious! Interestingly, the 15-year-old girl is not. She has not been completely conditioned yet to be "feminine." We have discussed this difficulty among ourselves and feel it stems from numerous causes put on us as women: We are conditioned to seeing ourselves other than as tough punchers —we don't really want to see ourselves looking so mean and aggressive, although we do want to, being there. We see our little fists in the mirror, and they look like shit. We punch with our left hands, and they feel like pieces of cooked spaghetti; we are totally unaccustomed to looking in the mirror and praising our gorgeous muscles; it makes us feel like fools. We are conditioned to feel that what we are doing is "unfeminine." We have been taught to be passive all our lives—even for the two of us, who were sports-women and dancers, the punching is just a little too much.

A corollary of this is falling into "female" patterns as a sort of defense against feeling inadequate. When we are instructed in small groups or are working out with each other, we often fall into laughing, playing around and not really doing it seriously. This attitude has become particularly noticeable now that we have begun, after 3 months, to learn Kumite (or free fighting). Up to this time we have really been punching air, and not having to engage in actual combat. This is tremendously difficult; not only do we laugh as defense, but we also tend to do the traditional woman thing—

of backing away and covering our faces. It is our first instinct—not to fight back. It should be mentioned that we will be forced to change these attitudes—the discipline of the Dojo (the place where you learn and practice Karate) does not really allow for fooling around, and no teacher will allow a student to continue backing off in the "feminine" way.

The trouble is, even now, after actually learning how to punch, we don't really want to punch out at men. The first thing that hits your mind is, "But I don't want to hurt him." Then you realize that this is really a traditional feminine cover-up for the truth—which is, we are afraid of men. Women have always really known that to hit a man seriously means risking getting killed.

We have acknowledged these "feminine attributes" that inhibit our Karate progress, and try every day to overcome them. It is clear that the longer our attitudes persist, the less, in fact, we do learn.

MALE CHAUVINISM IN THE DOJO, OR "WE ARE ALL BROTHERS HERE"

NON-TRICKY OBVIOUS FORMS OF MALE CHAUVINISM

Our experiences, as women, at the Dojo have so far been illuminating as to how very deep and very oppressive is the attitude of men toward women. We have been tolerated to the point that we have some times felt like the "Invisible Woman." The men treat us with a patronizing air that seems to say they wish we weren't there.

The first and most obvious example of discrimination is that women are charged only half price. We don't know the actual reason for this. Perhaps it is that we're considered only half-persons, or perhaps the teacher feels guilty because he figures we'll never learn it anyway. We decided to take advantage of this form of oppression however, and have not yet challenged it.

Also, the Sensei (Teacher) originally addressed the class repeatedly as "Gentlemen." Thinking it would probably take him a lesson or two to get used to us, we let this pass for a couple of days. He continued and we confronted him, stating that we didn't care how he wished to address us, just as long as our existence was recognized—either as "ladies" with "gentlemen" or as "women" with "men," or just part of "everybody." The Sensei admitted the oversight and agreed to remedy the situation.

Throughout the next week he continued to address everyone as "gentlemen," and we confronted him again, calling him "Mrs." and explaining that if he did not like that, we did not like being called "gentlemen." He apologized and said he would stop it.

In the next few lessons he occasionally let one or two "gentlemen" slip but usually not more than one a lesson.

Then, quite recently, Sensei got mad at the class and let loose a loud "Don't punch like that. It's too weak. You're punching like girls." (Obviously the very worst insult that can be given to a man.) At one time we probably wouldn't have been insulted by this, knowing that "he couldn't possibly mean us." The 15-year-old girl didn't understand this, and we explained that any insult toward women is an insult to you—since you *are*, in fact, a woman.

Immediately after the class we went to Sensei with the words, "Remember, don't ever punch like a . . ." which he immediately interrupted with a "Yes, I know, I'm sorry. I realized the minute I said it." We replied that "if most women punch weakly, it is precisely because of such male attitudes." He made no comment.

Finally, after three and a half months in the Dojo, attending four to six times a week, a breakthrough came, at least on this issue. Sensei let a "gentlemen" slip from his mouth and after a slight hesitation, followed it with a "and ladies." Whether this will remain a permanent feature in the Dojo remains to be seen, but since more women are now joining our class, it probably will. Our feeling was that you may not be able to change these men's attitudes, but at least you don't have to hear it. This much, at least, is relatively easy to win.

TRICKY, UNOBVIOUS FORMS OF MALE CHAUVINISM

Much more difficult to identify, and hence to combat, is the deep-seated, unobvious male chauvinism in the Dojo. While knowing that close to 100 per cent of the men have traditional attitudes, this is complicated, first, by the fact that apparently the Karate code says that women should be trained on an (almost) equal basis with men. (The only inequality in the rules we have found so far is that women going up for promotions from white to green belt are not required to do free-fighting in the test as the men are.)

There are no obvious distinctions made in instruction between men and women. We are expected to do everything the men do, to learn the positions as fast, and do them as well. We have been rewarded on that basis. We have advanced in rank beyond some men who were ahead of us when we started. We are now advanced white belts (7th kyu), and should have our green belts by the middle of December. It seems to be simply a matter of time spent working in the Dojo. We can say categorically that it is possible to participate in a mixed Dojo on physical considerations. Any woman entering a male dominated Dojo should watch that they are not discriminated against by having less demanded of them than the men. Any woman taking Karate in an all women's group should check her instruction against an all-male or mixed class.

The only real difficulty we had was with push-ups. None of us could do more than one or two when we started. We are now doing about 15 to 20. Twenty to twenty-five are done in every class. We are expected to work up to this number. If anyone tells you that as women you should not do push-ups, you can tell them that you certainly should and will. Or just tell them that they are full of shit.

Second, male chauvinism is masked by the fact that the code of the Dojo is that everyone treat everyone else with great respect and humility, regardless of rank. The unspoken slogan is: "We are all brothers."

Yes, we are treated *very politely*, formally, and "respectfully." In terms of human relationships, however, we are avoided as much as possible because men in the Dojo apparently know how to treat us only in the traditional sense— i.e., as sex objects. Since we have not allowed ourselves to be treated as sex objects, we are not "women" in their eyes. And obviously, we are not "brothers." Hence we are in some undefined, neuter area. We are INVISIBLE!

Our feelings on this were positively confirmed recently when a "radical" male in the Dojo told one of us that she was overdoing the "Women's Liberation business"— that she would be glad to know that not one man in the Dojo found her attractive, and, in fact, most of the men believed she was either a lesbian or had definite sexual problems. They looked upon her, he said, as "non-existent."

Third, it is very difficult to figure out whether we are being treated in a certain manner because we are beginners (and weak) or because we are women.

The men have tried to avoid all physical contact with us.

It's a mind-blower! When you need a partner for sit-ups (which means entangling your legs with theirs), they often try to find someone other than you, using the excuse (when questioned directly) that you're too light-weight or too weak. When Sensei makes the rounds to test your "stance," by touching your "butt" and thigh muscles, he just doesn't touch ours. After three months he finally did touch the 15-year-old's "butt," but he still avoids us like the plague. It seems clear that 25-year-old Sensei cannot see us as other than "females" who can be touched for one purpose, and one purpose only.

Finally, the actual free-fighting exercise we do is ridiculous. One man refused to make any contact at all, and stayed at least five feet away, punching at the air. Nobody can learn to fight if they're INVISIBLE and UNTOUCHABLE. The rationale that would be given is that we're still too weak to defend ourselves.

In addition, one male member of the Dojo told us that a lot of the men will take us as a sort of joke, and yet we must be very careful, for if we think we'll "show them" by really giving them some good strong punches, they then might retaliate far beyond what we are capable of handling at this stage—and really beat us up badly. He advised playing it soft until we really could handle rough dealing. It is the same old story. Men think you're a joke until you prove otherwise, at which point they're out to demolish you.

The 15-year-old girl has had much less trouble adjusting to the Dojo than we have. She has generally been very tough and an excellent fighter. Let her speak for herself:

There are several reasons why I wanted to learn the art of self-defense. The two most important reasons were 1) in the society we live in today I feel a great need for women to be strong, and 2) karate and kata (dance forms) are really most beautiful and exciting. So I, a 15-year-old female joined a Goju Kai Dojo. My mother and one of our friends joined also. In the very beginning I felt inhibited, but not because I am a woman (as did my mother and friend). It was because being a white belt in a Dojo you get treated like a "brand new beginner." I didn't know that much about karate. As the months passed I began to feel confident. At the end of 3 months I was put up against big men to do free-fighting. I felt inferior again, basically because I had never fought before. Again it was the feeling of low rank and lesser experience. All in all I feel I am getting stronger and I feel all women should get strong and learn to fight.

We seem to have only scratched the surface on the male chauvinism in the Dojo. This is so partly because we never intended to make the Dojo an area of attack. It is also very difficult to carry on any fight in the Dojo because of the traditional authoritarianism—something we accepted in order to get our training. Chauvinistic attitudes have been attacked only when *blatant* and we felt directly offended.

We don't know what changes the future will bring. As we get stronger and more confident, issues of chauvinism which are murky to us now, because of our own insecurities, will become clear, and may necessitate a real fight. The men probably will do anything (within reason) to protect the traditional "brotherhood" of the Dojo, if confronted. However it seems unlikely that the Sensei would ever challenge the rules, made in Japan, that are clearly discriminatory to women—such as the rule that women need not free-fight for promotions.

POSITIVE ASPECTS AND IMPLICATIONS FOR WOMEN'S LIBERATION

1. Karate has indeed affected the attitude the children have towards each other, and their mother. They no longer fight and throw sneak punches at each other the way they used to, but use Karate, bowing to each other, therefore being courteous to and thoughtful of each other. The 15-year-old girl is getting very strong and is feeling confident enough to walk the city streets alone, after dark, whereas before she simply wouldn't.

2. Karate has made us feel healthier and stronger than we were before (we've even cut our smoking in half.) Stronger hands and arms enable us to do things that we usually rely on men to do, such as carrying heavy loads from the store. (In fact, you find that you *want* to carry heavy loads, because it makes you stronger.)

3. Karate gets you out of the house three nights (or days) a week, and if you like it, it becomes something you'll do— *no matter what*. It's good for freeing yourself from household chores/waiting around for a man to call/waiting around

for the man to come home/waiting around because the man *is* home/creating a good reason why a man must fit his schedule into yours—i.e., see you when *you're* available/or take care of his own children three nights a week!

4. Karate has mentally increased our confidence in ourselves as human beings. Simone de Beauvoir says, "Not to have confidence in one's body is to lose confidence in oneself." (*The Second Sex*, paperback, Chapter 13, p. 310.) As a result of Karate we are gaining confidence in our bodies and going through some fantastic changes in terms of our self-worth. Our confidence has increased not only in confrontations with "dirty-old-men" on the streets, but in confrontations with our own men and with society in general. We do feel as though we have more control over our own lives because of our new potential physical power.

5. After participating in a few Women's Liberation actions we see more clearly than ever the need for Women to get physically strong. We demonstrated against specific, blatant sexual exploitation of Women in front of the "Electric Circus" on the Lower East Side of New York, and we almost went sprawling a few times as people tried to trip us. We wished then that we were Black Belts so we could really defend ourselves. Recently we helped take over a panel at Cooper Union that was going to discuss "Abortion"—a panel consisting of four Men! The men gave up the stage very quickly to the Women, but shortly after that came on stage and slowly removed four mikes (that were switched off anyway) from the speaker's table, acting all the time as if there were no one there. INVISIBLE again! They (the men) should have been forcibly removed from the scene! The same thing when they turned the lights out on us. We were not strong enough to confront the men, and make them meet our demands.

Women's Liberation has a long tough political fight before it, and our oppression, which is ultimately maintained by Force, can only be overcome by Force. Women will be needed as fighters.

Finally, Simone de Beauvoir says:

Violence is the authentic proof of each one's loyalty to himself, to his passions, to his own will; radically to deny this is to deny oneself any objective truth, it is to

wall oneself up in an abstract subjectivity; anger or revolt that does not get into the muscles remains a figment
of the imagination. It is a profound frustration not to be
able to register one's feelings upon the face of the
world.

(*The Second Sex*)

But she continues: "It remains true that her physical weakness
does not permit woman to learn the lessons of violence . . ."
This we categorically reject. We, once as "physically weak"
as any average female, are learning the "lessons of violence,"
and learning it well. We strongly recommend that anyone
else who is interested, do the same.

Women must get strong!

On Celibacy*

DANA DENSMORE

One hangup to liberation is a supposed "need" for sex.
It is something that must be refuted, coped with, demythi-
fied, or the cause of female liberation is doomed.

Already we see girls, thoroughly liberated in their own
heads, understanding their oppression with terrible clarity
trying, deliberately and a trace hysterically, to make themselves attractive to men, men for whom they have no
respect, men they may even hate, because of "a basic
sexual-emotional need."

Sex is not essential to life, as eating is. Some people
go through their whole lives without engaging in it at
all, including fine, warm, happy people. It is a myth that
this makes one bitter, shriveled up, twisted.

The big stigma of life-long virginity is on women anyway,
created by men because woman's purpose in life is biological and if she doesn't fulfill that she's warped and unnatural and "must be all cobwebs inside."

Men are suspected at worst of being self-centered or
afraid of sex, but do not carry any stigma of being unnatu-

*From *No More Fun and Games*, no. 1.

ral. A man's life is taken as a whole on its merits. He was busy, it may be thought, dedicated, a great man who couldn't spare the time and energy for demanding relationships with women.

The guerillas don't screw. They eat, when they can, but they don't screw. They have important things to do, things that require all their energy.

Every one of us must have noticed occasions when he was very involved in something, fighting, working, thinking, writing, involved to the extent that eating was haphazard, sleeping deliberately cheated. But the first thing that goes is sex. It's inconvenient, time-consuming, energy-draining, and irrelevant.

We are programmed to crave sex. It sells consumer goods. It gives a lift and promises a spark of individual self-assertion in a dull and routinized world. It is a means to power (the only means they have) for women.

It is also, conversely, a means of power for men, exercised over women, because her sexual desire is directed to men.

Few women ever are actually satisfied, of course, but they blame the particular man and nurse the myth that they can be satisfied and that this nirvana is one which a man and only a man can bring her.

Moreover, sexual freedom is the first freedom a woman is awarded and she thinks it is very important because it's all she has; compared to the dullness and restrictiveness of the rest of her life it glows very brightly.

But we must come to realize that sex is actually a minor need, blown out of proportion, misunderstood (usually what passes for sexual need is actually desire to be stroked, desire for recognition or love, desire to conquer, humiliate or wield power, or desire to communicate).

We must come to realize that we don't need sex, that celibacy is not a dragon but even a state that could be desirable, in many cases preferable to sex. How repugnant it really is, after all, to make love to a man who despises you, who fears you and wants to hold you down! Doesn't screwing in an atmosphere devoid of respect get pretty grim? Why bother? You don't need it.

Erotic energy is just life energy and is quickly worked off if you are doing interesting, absorbing things. Love and affection and recognition can easily be found in comrades who love you for yourself and not for how docile and cute and sexy and ego-building you are, a more honest and open love, a love in which you are always subject, never merely object, always active, never merely relative. And if despite all this genital tensions persist you can still masturbate. Isn't that a lot easier anyway?

This is a call not for celibacy but for an acceptance of celibacy as an honorable alternative, one preferable to the degradation of most male-female sexual relationships. But it is only when we accept the idea of celibacy completely that we will ever be able to liberate ourselves.

Until we accept it completely, until we say "I control my own body and I don't need any insolent male with an overbearing presumptuous prick to come and clean out my pipes" they will always have over us the devastating threat of withdrawing their sexual attentions, and worse, the threat of our ceasing even to be sexually attractive.

And that devastating rejection is absolutely inevitable. If you are serious and men realize it they will cease being attracted to you.

If you don't play the game, the role, you are not a woman and they will NOT be attracted. You will be sexless, and worse, unnatural and threatening.

You will be feared and despised and viciously maligned, all by men you know perfectly well you could charm utterly and wrap around your finger just by falling into the female role, even by men who have worshipped you in the past.

How is that possible? Obviously, because they never were worshipping you. That's the bitter truth, and you'd better catch on now.

Whenever they're nice to us, it isn't us they're being nice to but their own solipsistic creations, the versions of us they manufacture for their own amusement and pleasure and purposes. How presumptuous it is of us to accept the love and admiration, to crave it even, as if it were meant for us!

It's their female ideal they adore and they will be resentful and angry if you mar that image and will turn against you to a man if you try to destroy it.

Unless you accept the idea that you don't need them, don't need sex from them, it will be utterly impossible for you to carry through, it will be absolutely necessary to lead a double life, pretending with men to be something other than what you know you are. The strain of this would be unimaginable and could end in any number of disastrous ways.

You, who have had such heady power to charm and arouse and win men's total admiration and respect, must be willing to give it up. You must be willing that they cease to be attracted to you, even find you repulsive, that they cease to respect you, even despise you, that they cease to admire you, even find you unnatural and warped and perverted sexually.

These men who were so tenderly protective will try to destroy you, to stab you in the back, to use any underhanded means to get back at you for posing this threat to them. You have done them the incalculable offense of not deferring to their sex, of daring to be yourself (putting your needs ahead of his), of stepping out of your role, of rejecting the phony sexual differentiations that make each of them feel like a man.

If you don't act like a woman he doesn't see himself as a man, since his sexual identity depends on the differences, and so he feels actually castrated. Expect no love, no desire, no mercy from this man.

You have to be prepared, then, to be not just unattractive but actually sexually repulsive to most men, perhaps including all the men you currently admire.

We've spent many years learning to be appealing to men, to all men, whether we are specifically interested in them or not. We dress, we walk, we laugh, we talk, we move our hands and our heads, we sit, we speak, all in a way carefully cultivated to be feminine and charming.

We need to be thought charming and appealing even by men who bore us or repulse us, by strangers who may be trying to pick us up; we have a horror of appearing vulgar and repulsive even to the most nauseating creep. The creeps must all be brushed off gracefully, in a way that leaves their egos intact and consequently leaves them with a friendly impression of us.

It's so important that our image be favorable, we are willing to put up with the fact that it is false, distorted, that we are being loved for our weaknesses, or for qualities we don't have at all, and our strengths are denied or ridiculed.

If we are going to be liberated we must reject the false image that makes men love us, and this will make men cease to love us.

Unless we can accept this we will crumble under the first look of fear and disgust; or certainly under the first such look from a man we love and admire.

Ultimately, of course, we will cease to love and admire such men. We will have contempt for men who show that they cannot love us for ourselves, men whose egos demand and require falsehoods.

It will be a less friendly world, but there will be no unrequited longing. What we're really after is to be loved for ourselves and if that's impossible, why should we care about love at all? Friends and enemies will be clearly lined up, and the friends will be real friends and the enemies unable to hide behind phony benevolence—nor will we have to toady to them.

An end to this constant remaking of ourselves according to what the male ego demands! Let us be ourselves and good riddance to those who are then repulsed by us!

Goodbye to All That*

ROBIN MORGAN

So. *Rat* has been liberated, for this week, at least. Next week? If the men return to reinstate the porny photos, the sexist comic strips, the "nude-chickie" covers (along with their patronizing rhetoric about being in favor of Women's Liberation)—if this happens, our alternatives are clear. *Rat* must be taken over permanently by women—or *Rat* must be destroyed.

Why *Rat?* Why not *EVO* or even the obvious new pornzines (Mafia-distributed alongside the human pornography of prostitution)? First, they'll get theirs—but it won't be a takeover which is reserved for something at least *worth* taking over. Nor should they be censored. They should just be helped not to exist—by any means necessary. But *Rat,* which has always tried to be a really radical *cum* life-style paper —that's another matter. It's the liberal co-optative masks on the face of sexist hate and fear, worn by real nice guys we all know and like, right? We have met the enemy and he's our friend. And dangerous. "What the hell, let the chicks do an issue; maybe it'll satisfy 'em for a while, it's a good controversy, and it'll maybe sell papers"—runs an unheard conversation that I'm sure took place at some point last week.

*From *Rat* (February 6–23, 1970).

And that's what I wanted to write about—the friends, brothers, lovers in the counterfeit male-dominated Left. The good guys who think they know what "Women's Lib," as they so chummily call it, is all about—and who then proceed to degrade and destroy women by almost everything they say and do: The cover on the last issue of *Rat* (front *and* back). The token "pussy power" or "clit militancy" articles. The snide descriptions of women staffers on the masthead. The little jokes, the personal ads, the smile, the snarl. No more, brothers. No more well-meaning ignorance, no more co-optation, no more assuming that this thing we're all fighting for is the same: one revolution under *man*, with liberty and justice for all. No more.

Let's run it on down. White males are most responsible for the destruction of human life and environment on the planet today. Yet who is controlling the supposed revolution to change all that? White males (yes, yes, even with their pasty fingers back in black and brown pies again). It just could make one a bit uneasy. It seems obvious that a legitimate revolution must be led by, *made* by those who have been most oppressed: black, brown, and white *women*—with men relating to that the best they can. A genuine Left doesn't consider anyone's suffering irrelevant or titillating; nor does it function as a microcosm of capitalist economy, with men competing for power and status at the top, and women doing all the work at the bottom (and functioning as objectified prizes or "coin" as well). Goodbye to all that.

Run it all the way down.

Goodbye to the male-dominated peace movement, where sweet old Uncle Dave can say with impunity to a woman on the staff of *Liberation*, "The trouble with you is you're an aggressive woman."

Goodbye to the "straight" male-dominated Left: to PL who will allow that some workers are women, but won't see all women (say, housewives) as workers (just like the System itself); to all the old Leftover parties who offer their "Women's Liberation caucuses" to us as if that were not a contradiction in terms; to the individual anti-leadership leaders who hand-pick certain women to be leaders and then relate only to them, either in the male Left or in Women's Liberation—bringing their hang-ups about power-dominance and manipulation to everything they touch.

Goodbye to the Weather Vain, with the Stanley Kowalski image and theory of free sexuality but practice of sex on demand for males. "Left Out!"—not Right On—to the

Weather Sisters who, and they know better—they know, reject their own radical feminism for that last desperate grab at male approval that we all know so well, for claiming that the *machismo* style and the gratuitous violence is their own style by "free choice" and for believing that this is the way for a woman to make her revolution . . . all the while, oh my sister, not meeting my eyes because Weather Men chose Manson as their—and your—Hero. (Honest, at least . . . since Manson is only the logical extreme of the normal American male's fantasy (whether he is Dick Nixon or Mark Rudd): master of a harem, women to do all the shitwork, from raising babies and cooking and hustling to killing people on order.) Goodbye to all that shit that sets women apart from women; shit that covers the face of any Weatherwoman which is the face of any Manson Slave which is the face of Sharon Tate which is the face of Mary Jo Kopechne which is the face of Beulah Saunders which is the face of me which is the face of Pat Nixon which is the face of Pat Swinton. *In the dark we are all the same*—and you better believe it: we're in the dark, baby. (Remember the old joke: Know what they call a black man with a Ph.D.? A nigger. Variation: Know what they call a Weatherwoman? A heavy cunt. Know what they call a Hip Revolutionary Woman? A groovy cunt. Know what they call a radical militant feminist? A crazy cunt. Amerika is a land of free choice—take your pick of titles. Left Out, my Sister—don't you see? Goodbye to the illusion of strength when you run hand in hand with your oppressors; goodbye to the dream that being in the leadership collective will get you anything but gonorrhea.

Goodbye to RYM II, as well, and all the other RYMs—not that the Sisters there didn't pull a cool number by seizing control, but because they let the men back in after only *a day or so* of self-criticism on male chauvinism. (And goodbye to the inaccurate blanket use of that phrase, for that matter: male chauvinism is an *attitude*—male supremacy is the *objective reality, the fact*.) Goodbye to the Conspiracy who, when lunching with fellow sexist bastards Norman Mailer and Terry Southern in a bunny-type club in Chicago, found Judge Hoffman at the neighboring table—no surprise: *in the light they are all the same.*

Goodbye to Hip Culture and the so-called Sexual Revolution, which has functioned toward women's freedom as did the Reconstruction toward former slaves—reinstituted oppression by another name. Goodbye to the assumption that Hugh Romney is safe in his "cultural revolution," safe enough to refer to "our women, who make all our clothes" without somebody not forgiving that. Goodbye to the arrogance of power indeed that lets Czar Stan Freeman of the Electric Circus sleep without fear at night, or permits Tomi Ungerer to walk unafraid in the street after executing the drawings for the Circus advertising campaign against women. Goodbye to the idea that Hugh Hefner is groovy 'cause he lets Conspirators come to parties at the Mansion—goodbye to Hefner's dream of a ripe old age. Goodbye to Tuli and the Fugs and all the boys in the front room—who always knew they hated the women they loved. Goodbye to the notion that good ol' Abbie is any different from any other up and coming movie star (like, say Cliff Robertson) who ditches the first wife and kids, good enough for the old days but awkward once you're Making It. Goodbye to his hypocritical double standard that reeks through all the tattered charm. Goodbye to lovely pro-Women's Liberation Paul Krassner, with all his astonished anger that women have lost their sense of humor "on this issue" and don't laugh anymore at little funnies that degrade and hurt them; farewell to the memory of his "Instant Pussy" aerosol-can poster, to his column for *Cavalier,* to his dream of a Rape-In against legislator's wives, to his Scapegoats and Realist Nuns and cute anecdotes about the little daughter he sees as often as any proper divorced Scarsdale middle-aged (38) father; goodbye forever to the notion that he is my brother who, like Paul, buys a prostitute for the night as a birthday gift for a male friend, or who, like Paul, reels off the names in alphabetical order of people in the Women's Movement he has fucked, reels off names in the best locker room tradition—as proof that *he's* no sexist oppressor.

Let it all hang out. Let it seem bitchy, catty, dykey, frustrated, crazy, Solanisesque, nutty, frigid, ridiculous, bitter, embarrassing, man-hating, libelous, pure, unfair, envious, intuitive, low-down, stupid, petty, liberating. WE ARE THE WOMEN THAT MEN HAVE WARNED US ABOUT.

And let's put one lie to rest for all time: the lie that men are oppressed, too, by sexism—the lie that there can be such a thing as "men's liberation groups." Oppression is something that one group of people commits against another group specifically because of a "threatening" characteristic shared by the latter group—skin color or sex or age, etc. The oppressors are indeed *fucked up* by being masters (racism hurts whites, sexual stereotypes are harmful to men) but those masters are not *oppressed.* Any master has the alternative of divesting himself of sexism or racism—the oppressed have no alternative—for they have no power—but to fight. In the long run, Women's Liberation will of course free men —but in the short run it's going to *cost* men a lot of privilege, which no one gives up willingly or easily. Sexism is *not* the fault of women—kill your fathers, not your mothers.

Run it down. Goodbye to a beautiful new ecology movement that could fight to save us all if it would stop tripping off women as earth-mother types or frontier chicks, if it would *right now* cede leadership to those who have *not* polluted the planet because that action implies power and women haven't had any power in about 5,000 years, cede leadership to those whose brains are as tough and clear as any man's but whose bodies are also unavoidably aware of the locked-in relationship between humans and their biosphere—the earth, the tides, the atmosphere, the moon. Ecology is no big *shtick* if you're a woman—it's always been there.

Goodbye to the complicity inherent in the Berkeley Tribesmen being part publishers of Trashman Comics; goodbye, for that matter, to the reasoning that finds whoremaster Trashman a fitting model, however comic-strip far out, for a revolutionary man—somehow related to the same Supermale reasoning that permits the first statement on Women's Liberation and male chauvinism that came out of the Black Panther Party to be made *by a man,* talkin' a whole lot 'bout how the Sisters should speak up for themselves. Such ignorance and arrogance ill befits a revolutionary.

We know how racism is worked deep into the unconscious by our System—the same way sexism is, as it appears in the very name of The Young Lords. What are you if you're a "macho woman"—a female Lord? Or, god forbid, a Young Lady? Change it, change it to The Young Gentry if you must, or never assume that the name itself is innocent of pain, of oppression.

Theory and practice—and the light-years between them. "Do it!" says Jerry Rubin in *Rat's* last issue—but he doesn't, or every *Rat* reader would have known the pictured face next to his article as well as they know his own much-photographed face: it was Nancy Kurshan, the power behind the clown.

Goodbye to the New Nation and Earth People's Park, for that matter, conceived by men, announced by men, led by men—doomed before its birth by the rotting seeds of male supremacy which are to be transplanted in fresh soil. Was it my brother who listed human beings among the *objects* which would be easily available after the Revolution: "Free grass, free food, free women, free acid, free clothes, etc."? Was it my brother who wrote "Fuck your women till they can't stand up" and said that groupies were liberated chicks 'cause they dug a tit-shake instead of a handshake? The epitome of female exclusionism—"men will make the Revolution —and their chicks." Not my brother, no. Not my revolution. Not one breath of my support for the new counterleft Christ —John Sinclair. Just one less to worry about for ten years. I do not choose my enemy for my brother.

Goodbye, goodbye. The hell with the simplistic notion that automatic freedom for women—or non-white peoples—will come about ZAP! with the advent of a socialist revolution. Bullshit. Two evils pre-date capitalism and have been clearly able to survive and post-date socialism: sexism and racism. Women were the first property when the Primary Contradiction occurred: when one half of the human species decided to subjugate the other half, because it was "different," alien, the Other. From there it was an easy enough step to extend the Other to someone of different skin shade, different height or weight or language—or strength to resist. Goodbye to those simple-minded optimistic dreams of socialist equality all our good socialist brothers want us to believe. How liberal a politics that is! How much further we will have to go to create those profound changes that would give birth to a genderless society. *Profound,* Sister. Beyond what is male or female. Beyond standards we all adhere to now without daring to examine them as male-created, male-dominated, male-fucked-up, and in male self-interest. *Beyond all known standards,* especially those easily articulated revolutionary ones we all rhetorically invoke. Beyond, to a species with a new name, that would not dare define itself as Man.

I once said, "I'm a revolutionary, not just a woman," and knew my own lie even as I said the words. The pity of that statement's eagerness to be acceptable to those whose revolutionary zeal no one would question, i.e., any male supremacist in the counterleft. But to become a true revolutionary one must first become one of the oppressed (not organize or educate or manipulate them, but become one of them)—or realize that you *are* one of them already. No woman wants that. Because that realization is humiliating, it hurts. It hurts to understand that at Woodstock or Altamont a woman could be declared uptight or a poor sport if she didn't want to be raped. It hurts to learn that the Sisters still in male-Left captivity are putting down the crazy feminists to make themselves look okay and unthreatening to our mutual oppressors. It hurts to be pawns in those games. It hurts to try and change *each day of your life right now*—not in talk, not "in your head," and not only conveniently "out there" in the Third World (half of which is women) or the black and brown communities (half of which are women) but in your own home, kitchen, bed. No getting away, no matter how else you are oppressed, from the primary oppression of being female in a patriarchal world. It hurts to hear that the Sisters in the Gay Liberation Front, too, have to struggle continually against the male chauvinism of their gay brothers. It hurts that Jane Alpert was cheered when rapping about imperialism, racism, the Third World, and All Those Safe Topics but hissed and booed by a Movement crowd of men who wanted none of it when she began to talk about Women's Liberation. The backlash is upon us.

They tell us the alternative is to hang in there and "struggle," to confront male domination in the counterleft, to fight beside or behind or beneath our brothers—to show 'em we're just as tough, just as revolushunerry, just as whatever-image-they-now-want-of-us-as-once-they-wanted-us-to-be-feminine-and-keep-the-home-fire-burning. They will bestow titular leadership on our grateful shoulders, whether it's being a token woman on the Movement Speakers Bureau Advisory Board, or being a Conspiracy groupie or one of the "respectable" chain-swinging Motor City Nine. Sisters all, with only one real alternative: to seize our own power into our own hands, all women, separate and together, and make the Revolution the way it must be made—no priorities this time, no suffering group told to wait until after.

It is the job of revolutionary feminists to build an ever stronger independent Women's Liberation Movement, so that the Sisters in counterleft captivity will have somewhere to turn, to use their power and rage and beauty and coolness in their own behalf for once, on their own terms, on their own issues, in their own style—whatever that may be. Not for us in Women's Liberation to hassle them and confront them the way their men do, nor to blame them—or ourselves—for what any of us are: an oppressed people, but a people raising our consciousness toward something that is the other side of anger, something bright and smooth and cool, like action unlike anything yet contemplated or carried out. It is for us to survive (something the white male radical has the luxury of never really worrying about, what with all his options), to talk, to plan, to be patient, to welcome new fugitives from the counterfeit Left with no arrogance but only humility and delight, to plan, to push—to strike.

There is something every woman wears around her neck on a thin chain of fear—an amulet of madness. For each of us, there exists somewhere a moment of insult so intense that she will reach up and rip the amulet off, even if the chain tears at the flesh of her neck. And the last protection from seeing the truth will be gone. Do you think, tugging furtively every day at the chain and going nicely insane as I am, that I can be concerned with the puerile squabbles of a counterfeit Left that laughs at my pain? Do you think such a concern is noticeable when set alongside the suffering of more than half the human species for the past 5,000 years —due to a whim of the other half? No, no, no, goodbye to all that.

Women are Something Else. This time, we're going to kick out all the jams, and the boys will just have to hustle to keep up, or else drop out and openly join the power structure of which they are already the illegitimate sons. Any man who claims he is serious about wanting to divest himself of cock privilege should trip on this: all male leadership out of the Left is the only way; and it's going to happen, whether through men stepping down or through women seizing the helm. It's up to the "brothers"—after all, sexism is their concern, not ours; we're too busy getting ourselves together to have to deal with their bigotry. So they'll have to make up their own minds as to whether they will be divested of just cock privilege or—what the hell, why not say it, *say* it?— divested of cocks. How deep the fear of that loss must be, that it can be suppressed only by the building of empires and the waging of genocidal wars!

Goodbye, goodbye forever, counterfeit Left, counterleft, male-dominated cracked-glass-mirror reflection of the Amerikan Nightmare. Women are the real left. We are rising, powerful in our unclean bodies; bright glowing mad in our inferior brains; wild hair flying, wild eyes staring, wild voices keening; undaunted by blood we who hemorrhage every twenty-eight days; laughing at our own beauty we who have lost our sense of humor; mourning for all each precious one of us might have been in this one living time-place had she not been born a woman; stuffing fingers into our mouths to stop the screams of fear and hate and pity for men we have loved and love still; tears in our eyes and bitterness in our mouths for children we couldn't have, or couldn't *not* have, or didn't want, or didn't want *yet*, or wanted and had in this place and this time of horror. We are rising with a fury older and potentially greater than any force in history, and this time we will be free or no one will survive. POWER TO ALL THE PEOPLE OR TO NONE. All the way down, this time.

Free Kathleen Cleaver!
Free Anita Hoffman!
Free Bernadine Dohrn!
Free Donna Malone!
Free Ruth Ann Miller!
Free Leni Sinclair!
Free Jane Alpert!
Free Gumbo!
Free Bonnie Cohen!
Free Judy Lampe!

Free Kim Agnew!
Free Holly Krassner!
Free Lois Hart!
Free Alice Embree!
Free Nancy Kurshan!
Free Lynn Phillips!
Free Dinky Forman!
Free Sharon Krebs!
Free Iris Luciano!
Free Robin Morgan!

FREE VALERIE SOLANIS!

FREE OUR SISTERS!   FREE OURSELVES!

THEORETICAL ANALYSES

Females and Welfare*

BETSY WARRIOR

There are 35 million poor people in this country. A THIRD OF THE POOR LIVE IN FAMILIES HEADED BY FEMALES. Many of these families are on welfare, and more should be getting some kind of welfare supplement added to their income. Many of us think that in the richest nation in the world there should be no poor people at all, and that the political and economic reasons for their existence must come to an end.

Why were the welfare mothers picked by radical organizers to disrupt the political system, with the economic breakdown on a local level, and the change in the whole political structure that their demands might bring?

Since five million of the poor are aged, it isn't likely that these older people would start an active fight against the system that kept them in poverty. Old people are more conservative and lack the energy and determination for a prolonged fight. But other families, a lot of them headed by males—why don't they fight the system that made them poor? They could fight for an adequate income.

What are the special qualities welfare mothers possess, to make them the ones chosen to fight the establishment? The basic reason is mothers will fight for their children, to supply their needs, and they will struggle for as long as it takes for their children to grow up. They possess both the will and sustained determination to demand long and loud that the political structure allow their children enough to live on decently, and in doing so change the political structure.

The fact that most families on welfare are headed by

*From *No More Fun and Games* (November, 1969).

females says just as much about the status of females in this country as it does about the political economy. Females in this country are too often dependent on someone else for their livelihood. Many lack an education good enough to allow them to support a family by themselves; or if they have an adequate education, they don't have the time or energy left after the duties of motherhood, household drudgery and menial tasks, to use it. Women have a status as dependent human beings in this country that doesn't change, whether it's one man or the state that allows them money to live on.

Bringing welfare mothers together to fight for themselves has many positive aspects. It helps them to see their situation isn't caused by personal inadequacy, but the fault of a bad economic system. They find more can be achieved by speaking out and joining together to fight the welfare department than by remaining quiet and alone, or trying to hide the fact that they're on welfare. Of course, this only applies to the women who can be encouraged to join the welfare groups. There are many who are too defeated and afraid to even try to help themselves, these women are even more in need of incentive and help.

The females in the group can become more politically aware of how their lives are run by city hall and demystify the local bureaucracy for themselves. By alleviating some of their more pressing material needs it might give them and their children more energy and hope to tackle some of the many other problems they have as females and human beings.

But the great majority of welfare mothers do not realize what long range effects their actions will have on the system. They're being used as political fodder by men who want the system changed for themselves, and any benefits the mothers receive in the process are purely coincidental or material.

The welfare mothers run the risk of becoming as competitive, aggressive and power-hungry as the males who oppress them. This is because their groups are being patterned after the structure of male organizations, by male organizers, establishing a context of leaders and followers, encouraging competition for recognition and power between the women in the groups.

Though the mothers may change their material and political position, they won't be free until they identify their oppression as being inherent in the role they play as females, and abolish that role. Without consciousness of their inferior status as women they will remain the victims of society and merely tools of the people who wish to use them.

The Political Economy of Women's Liberation*

MARGARET BENSTON

> The position of women rests, as everything in our complex society, on an economic base.
> —Eleanor Marx and
> Edward Aveling

The "woman question" is generally ignored in analyses of the class structure of society. This is so because, on the one hand, classes are generally defined by their relation to the means of production and, on the other hand, women are not supposed to have any unique relation to the means of production. The category seems instead to cut across all classes; one speaks of working-class women, middle-class women, etc. The status of women is clearly inferior to that of the men,[1] but analysis of this condition usually falls into discussing socialization, psychology, interpersonal relations, or the role of marriage as a social institution.[2] Are these, however, the primary factors? In arguing that the roots of the secondary status of women are in fact economic, it can be shown that women as a group do indeed have a definite relation to the means of production and that this is different from that of men. The personal and psychological factors then follow from this special relation to production, and a change in the latter will be a necessary (but not sufficient) condition for changing the former.[3] If this special relation of women to production is accepted, the analysis of the situation of women fits naturally into a class analysis of society.

*From Monthly Review, vol. 21, no. 4 (September, 1969), © 1969 by Monthly Review, Inc.

The starting point for discussion of classes in a capitalist society is the distinction between those who own the means of production and those who sell their labor power for a wage. As Ernest Mandel says:

> The proletarian condition is, in a nutshell, the lack of access to the means of production or means of subsistence which, in a society of generalized commodity production, forces the proletarian to sell his labor power. In exchange for this labor power he receives a wage which then enables him to acquire the means of consumption necessary for satisfying his own needs and those of his family.
>
> This is the structural definition of wage earner, the proletarian. From it necessarily flows a certain relationship to his work, to the products of his work, and to his overall situation in society, which can be summarized by the catchword alienation. But there does not follow from this structural definition any necessary conclusions as to the level of his consumption . . . the extent of his needs, or the degree to which he can satisfy them.[4]

We lack a corresponding structural definition of women. What is needed first is not a complete examination of the symptoms of the secondary status of women, but instead a statement of the material conditions in capitalist (and other) societies which define the group "women." Upon these conditions are built the specific superstructures which we know. An interesting passage from Mandel points the way to such a definition:

> The commodity . . . is a product created to be exchanged on the market, as opposed to one which has been made for direct consumption. *Every commodity must have both a use-value and an exchange-value.*
>
> It must have a use-value or else nobody would buy it. . . . A commodity without a use-value to anyone would consequently be unsaleable, would constitute useless production, would have no exchange-value precisely because it had no use-value.
>
> On the other hand, every product which has use-value does not necessarily have exchange-value. It has an exchange-value only to the extent that the society itself, in which the commodity is produced, is founded on

exchange, is a society where exchange is a common practice. . . .

In capitalist society, commodity production, the production of exchange-values, has reached its greatest development. It is the first society in human history where the major part of production consists of commodities. It is not true, however, that all production under capitalism is commodity production. Two classes of products still remain simple use-value.

The first group consists of all things produced by the peasantry for its own consumption, everything directly consumed on the farms where it is produced. . . .

The second group of products in capitalist society which are not commodities but remain simple use-value consists of all things produced in the home. Despite the fact that considerable human labor goes into this type of household production, it still remains a production of use-values and not of commodities. Every time a soup is made or a button sewn on a garment, it constitutes production, but it is not production for the market.

The appearance of commodity production and its subsequent regularization and generalization have radically transformed the way men labor and how they organize society.[5]

What Mandel may not have noticed is that his last paragraph is precisely correct. The appearance of commodity production has indeed transformed the way that *men* labor. As he points out, most household labor in capitalist society (and in the existing socialist societies, for that matter) remains in the pre-market stage. This is the work which is reserved for women and it is in this fact that we can find the basis for a definition of women.

In sheer quantity, household labor, including child care, constitutes a huge amount of socially necessary production. Nevertheless, in a society based on commodity production, it is not usually considered "real work" since it is outside of trade and the market place. It is pre-capitalist in a very real sense. This assignment of household work as the function of a special category "women" means that this group *does* stand in a different relation to production than the group "men." We will tentatively define women, then, as that group of people who are responsible for the production of simple use-values in those activities associated with the home and family.

Since men carry no responsibility for such production, the difference between the two groups lies here. Notice that women are not excluded from commodity production. Their participation in wage labor occurs but, as a group, they have no structural responsibility in this area and such participation is ordinarily regarded as transient. Men, on the other hand, are responsible for commodity production; they are not, in principle, given any role in household labor. For example, when they do participate in household production, it is regarded as more than simply exceptional; it is demoralizing, emasculating, even harmful to health. (A story on the front page of the *Vancouver Sun* in January 1969 reported that men in Britain were having their health endangered because they had to do too much housework!)

The material basis for the inferior status of women is to be found in just this definition of women. In a society in which money determines value, women are a group who work outside the money economy. Their work is not worth money, is therefore valueless, is therefore not even real work. And women themselves, who do this valueless work, can hardly be expected to be worth as much as men, who work for money. In structural terms, the closest thing to the condition of women is the condition of others who are or were also outside of commodity production, i.e., serfs and peasants.

In her recent paper on women, Juliet Mitchell introduces the subject as follows: "In advanced industrial society, women's work is only marginal to the total economy. Yet it is through work that man changes natural conditions and thereby produces society. Until there is a revolution in production, the labor situation will prescribe women's situation within the world of men."[6] The statement of the marginality of women's work is an unanalyzed recognition that the work women do is *different* from the work that men do. Such work is not marginal, however; it is just not wage labor and so is not counted. She even says later in the same article, "Domestic labor, even today, is enormous if quantified in terms of productive labor." She gives some figures to illustrate: In Sweden, 2,340 million hours a year are spent by women in housework compared with 1,290 million hours spent by women in industry. And the Chase Manhattan Bank estimates a woman's overall work week at 99.6 hours.

However, Mitchell gives little emphasis to the basic economic factors (in fact she condemns most Marxists for being "overly economist") and moves on hastily to superstructural factors, because she notices that "the advent of industrialization has not so far freed women." What she fails to see is that no society has thus far industrialized housework. Engels points out that the "first premise for the emancipation of women is the reintroduction of the entire female sex into public industry. . . . And this has become possible not only as a result of modern large-scale industry, which not only permits the participation of women in production in large numbers, but actually calls for it and, moreover, strives to convert private domestic work also into a public industry."[7] And later in the same passage: "Here we see already that the emancipation of women and their equality with men are impossible and must remain so as long as women are excluded from socially productive work and restricted to housework, which is private." What Mitchell has not taken into account is that the problem is not simply one of getting women into *existing* industrial production but the more complex one of converting private production of household work into public production.

For most North Americans, domestic work as "public production" brings immediate images of Brave New World or of a vast institution—a cross between a home for orphans and an army barracks—where we would all be forced to live. For this reason, it is probably just as well to outline here, schematically and simplistically, the nature of industrialization.

A pre-industrial production unit is one in which production is small-scale and reduplicative; i.e., there are a great number of little units, each complete and just like all the others. Ordinarily such production units are in some way kin-based and they are multi-purpose, fulfilling religious, recreational, educational, and sexual functions along with the economic function. In such a situation, desirable attributes of an individual, those which give prestige, are judged by more than purely economic criteria: for example, among approved character traits are proper behavior to kin or readiness to fulfill obligations.

Such production is originally not for exchange. But if exchange of commodities becomes important enough, then increased efficiency of production becomes necessary. Such efficiency is provided by the transition to industrialized production which involves the elimination of the kin-based production unit. A large-scale, non-reduplicative production unit is substituted which has only one function, the economic one, and where prestige or status is attained by economic skills. Production is rationalized, made vastly more efficient, and becomes more and more public—part of an integrated social network. An enormous expansion of man's productive potential takes place. Under capitalism such social productive forces are utilized almost exclusively for private profit. These can be thought of as *capitalized* forms of production.

If we apply the above to housework and child rearing, it is evident that each family, each household, constitutes an individual production unit, a pre-industrial entity, in the same way that peasant farmers or cottage weavers constitute pre-industrial production units. The main features are clear, with the reduplicative, kin-based, private nature of the work being the most important. (It is interesting to notice the other features: the multipurpose functions of the family, the fact that desirable attributes for women do not center on economic prowess, etc.) The rationalization of production effected by a transition to large-scale production has not taken place in this area.

Industrialization is, in itself, a great force for human good; exploitation and dehumanization go with capitalism and not necessarily with industrialization. To advocate the conversion of private domestic labor into a public industry under capitalism is quite a different thing from advocating such conversion in a socialist society. In the latter case the forces of production would operate for human welfare, not private profit, and the result should be liberation, not dehumanization. In this case we can speak of *socialized* forms of production.

These definitions are not meant to be technical but rather to differentiate between two important aspects of industrialization. Thus the fear of the barracks-like result of introducing housekeeping into the public economy is most realistic under capitalism. With socialized production and the removal of the profit motive and its attendant alienated labor, there is no reason why, *in an industrialized society,* industrialization of housework should not result in better production, i.e., better food, more comfortable surroundings, more intelligent and loving child-care, etc., than in the present nuclear family.

The argument is often advanced that, under neocapitalism, the work in the home has been much reduced. Even if this is true, it is not structurally relevant. Except for the very rich, who can hire someone to do it, there is, for most women, an irreducible minimum of necessary labor involved in caring for home, husband, and children. For a married woman without children this irreducible minimum of work probably takes fifteen to twenty hours a week; for a woman with small children the minimum is probably seventy or eighty hours a week.[8] (There is some resistance to regarding child-rearing as a job. That labor is involved, i.e., the production of use-value, can be clearly seen when exchange-value is also involved— when the work is done by baby sitters, nurses, child-care centers, or teachers. An economist has already pointed out the paradox that if a man marries his housekeeper, he reduces the national income, since the money he gives her is no longer counted as wages.) The reduction of housework to the minimums given is also expensive; for low-income families more labor is required. In any case, household work remains structurally the same—a matter of private production.

One function of the family, the one taught to us in school and the one which is popularly accepted, is the satisfaction of emotional needs: the needs for closeness, community, and warm secure relationships. This society provides few other ways of satisfying such needs; for example, work relationships or friendships are not expected to be nearly as important as a man-woman-with-children relationship. Even other ties of kinship are increasingly secondary. This function of the family is important in stabilizing it so that it can fulfill the second, purely economic, function discussed above. The wage-earner, the husband-father, whose earnings support himself, also "pays for" the labor done by the mother-wife and supports the children. The wages of a man buy the labor of two people. The crucial importance of this second function of the family can be seen when the family unit breaks down in divorce. The continuation of the economic function is the major concern where children are involved; the man must continue to pay for the labor of the woman. His wage is very often insufficient to enable him to support a second family. In this case his emotional needs are sacrificed to the necessity to support his ex-wife and children. That is, when there is a conflict the economic function of the family very often takes precedence over the emotional one. And this in a society which teaches that the major function of the family is the satisfaction of emotional needs.[9]

As an economic unit, the nuclear family is a valuable stabilizing force in capitalist society. Since the production which is done in the home is paid for by the husband-father's earnings, his ability to withhold his labor from the market is much reduced. Even his flexibility in changing jobs is limited. The woman, denied an active place in the market, has little control over the conditions that govern her life. Her economic dependence is reflected in emotional dependence, passivity, and other "typical" female personality traits. She is conservative, fearful, supportive of the status quo.

Furthermore, the structure of this family is such that it is an ideal consumption unit. But this fact, which is widely noted in Women's Liberation literature, should not be taken to mean that this is its primary function. If the above analysis is correct, the family should be seen primarily as a production unit for housework and child-rearing. *Everyone* in capitalist society is a consumer; the structure of the family simply means that it is particularly well suited to encourage consumption. Women in particular *are* good consumers; this follows naturally from their responsibility for matters in the home. Also, the inferior status of women, their general lack of a strong sense of worth and identity, make them more exploitable than men and hence better consumers.

The history of women in the industrialized sector of the economy has depended simply on the labor needs of that sector. Women function as a massive reserve army of labor. When labor is scarce (early industrialization, the two world wars, etc.) then women form an important part of the labor force. When there is less demand for labor (as now under neocapitalism) women become a surplus labor force—but one for which their husbands and not society are economically responsible. The "cult of the home" makes its reappearance during times of labor surplus and is used to channel women out of the market economy. This is relatively easy since the pervading ideology ensures that no one, man or woman, takes women's participation in the labor force very seriously. Women's real work, we are taught, is in the home; this holds whether or not they are married, single, or the heads of households.

At all times household work is the responsibility of women. When they are working outside the home they must somehow manage to get both outside job and housework done (or they supervise a substitute for the housework). Women, particularly married women with children, who work outside the home simply do two jobs; their participation in the labor force is only allowed if they continue to fulfill their first responsibility in the home. This is particularly evident in countries like Russia and those in Eastern Europe where expanded opportunities for women in the labor force have not brought about a corresponding expansion in their liberty. Equal access to jobs outside the home, while one of the preconditions for women's liberation, will not in itself be sufficient to give equality for women; as long as work in the home remains a matter of private production and is the responsibility of women, they will simply carry a double work-load.

A second prerequisite for women's liberation which follows from the above analysis is the conversion of the work now done in the home as private production into work to be done in the public economy.[10] To be more specific, this means that child-rearing should no longer be the responsibility solely of the parents. Society must begin to take responsibility for children; the economic dependence of women and children on the husband-father must be ended. The other work that goes on in the home must also be changed—communal eating places and laundries for example. When such work is moved into the public sector, then the material basis for discrimination against women will be gone.

These are only preconditions. The idea of the inferior status of women is deeply rooted in the society and will take a great deal of effort to eradicate. But once the structures which produce and support that idea are changed, then, and only then, can we hope to make progress. It is possible, for example, that a change to communal eating places would simply mean that women are moved from a home kitchen to a communal one. This *would* be an advance, to be sure, particularly in a socialist society where work would not have the inherently exploitative nature it does now. Once women are freed from private production in the home, it will probably be very difficult to maintain for any long period of time a rigid definition of jobs by sex. This illustrates the interrelation between the two preconditions given above: true equality in job opportunity is probably impossible without freedom from housework, and the industrialization of housework is unlikely unless women are leaving the home for jobs.

The changes in production necessary to get women out of the home might seem to be, in theory, possible under capitalism. One of the sources of women's liberation movements may be the fact that alternative capitalized forms of home production now exist. Day care is available, even if inadequate and perhaps expensive; convenience foods, home delivery of meals, and take-out meals are widespread; laundries and cleaners offer bulk rates. However, cost usually prohibits a complete dependence on such facilities, and they are not available everywhere, even in North America. These should probably then be regarded as embryonic forms rather than completed structures. However, they clearly stand as alternatives to the present system of getting such work done. Particularly in North America, where the growth of "service industries" is important in maintaining the growth of the economy, the contradictions between these alternatives and the need to keep women in the home will grow.

The need to keep women in the home arises from two major aspects of the present system. First, the amount of unpaid labor performed by women is very large and very profitable to those who own the means of production. To pay women for their work, even at minimum wage scales, would imply a massive redistribution of wealth. At present, the support of a family is a hidden tax on the wage earner— his wage buys the labor power of two people. And second, there is the problem of whether the economy can expand enough to put all women to work as a part of the normally employed labor force. The war economy has been adequate to draw women partially into the economy but not adequate to establish a need for all or most of them. If it is argued that the jobs created by the industrialization of housework will create this need, then one can counter by pointing to (1) the strong economic forces operating for the status quo and against capitalization discussed above, and (2) the fact that the present service industries, which somewhat counter these forces, have not been able to keep up with the growth of the labor force as presently constituted. The present trends in the service industries simply create "underemployment" in the home; they do not create new jobs for women. So long as this situation exists, women remain a very convenient and elastic part of the industrial reserve army. Their incorporation into the labor force on terms of equality—which would create pressure for capitalization of housework—is possible only with an economic expansion so far achieved by neocapitalism only under conditions of full-scale war mobilization.

In addition, such structural changes imply the complete breakdown of the present nuclear family. The stabilizing consuming functions of the family, plus the ability of the cult of the home to keep women out of the labor market, serve neocapitalism too well to be easily dispensed with. And, on a less fundamental level, even if these necessary changes in the nature of household production were achieved under capitalism it would have the unpleasant consequence of including *all* human relations in the cash nexus. The atomization and isolation of people in Western society is already sufficiently advanced to make it doubtful if such complete psychic isolation could be tolerated. It is likely in fact that one of the major negative emotional responses to women's liberation movements may be exactly such a fear. If this is the case, then possible alternatives—cooperatives, the kibbutz, etc.—can be cited to show that psychic needs for community and warmth can in fact be better satisfied if other structures are substituted for the nuclear family.

At best the change to capitalization of housework would only give women the same limited freedom given most men in capitalist society. This does not mean, however, that women should wait to demand freedom from discrimination. There *is* a material basis for women's status; we are not merely discriminated against, we are exploited. At present, our unpaid labor in the home is necessary if the entire system is to function. Pressure created by women who challenge their role will reduce the effectiveness of this exploitation. In addition, such challenges will impede the functioning of the family and may make the channeling of women out of the labor force less effective. All of these will hopefully make quicker the transition to a society in which the necessary structural changes in production can actually be made. That such a transition will require a revolution I have no doubt; our task is to make sure that revolutionary changes in the society do in fact end women's oppression.

BIBLIOGRAPHY AND NOTES

[1]Marlene Dixon, "Secondary Social Status of Women." (Available from U.S. Voice of Women's Liberation Movement, 1940, Bissell, Chicago, Illinois 60614.)

[2]The biological argument is, of course, the first one used, but it is not usually taken seriously by socialist writers. Margaret Mead's *Sex and Temperament* is an early statement of the importance of culture instead of biology.

[3]This applies to the group or category as a whole. Women as individuals can and do free themselves from their socialization to a great degree (and they can even come to terms with the economic situation in favorable cases), but the majority of women have no chance to do so.

[4]Ernest Mandel, "Workers Under Neocapitalism," paper delivered at Simon Fraser University. (Available through the Department of Political Science, Sociology and Anthropology, Simon Fraser University, Burnaby, B.C., Canada.)

[5]Ernest Mandel, *An Introduction to Marxist Economic Theory* (New York: Merit Publishers, 1967), pp. 10–11.

[6]Juliet Mitchell, "Women: The Longest Revolution," *New Left Review*, December 1966.

[7]Frederick Engels, *Origin of the Family, Private Property and the State* (Moscow: Progress Publishers, 1968), Chapter IX, p. 158. The anthropological evidence known to Engels indicated

primitive woman's dominance over man. Modern anthropology disputes this dominance but provides evidence for a more nearly equal position of women in the matrilineal societies used by Engels as examples. The arguments in this work of Engels do not require the former dominance of women but merely their former equality, and so the conclusions remain unchanged.

[8]Such figures can easily be estimated. For example, a married woman without children is expected each week to cook and wash up (10 hours), clean house (4 hours), do laundry (1 hour), and shop for food (1 hour). The figures are *minimum* times required each week for such work. The total, 16 hours, is probably unrealistically low; even so, it is close to half of a regular work week. A mother with young children must spend at least six or seven days a week working close to 12 hours.

[9]For evidence of such teaching, see any high school text on the family.

[10]This is stated clearly by early Marxist writers besides Engels. Relevant quotes from Engels have been given in the text; those from Lenin are included in the Appendix.

APPENDIX

Passages from Lenin, *On The Emancipation of Women*, Progress Publishers, Moscow.

Large-scale machine industry, which concentrates masses of workers who often come from various parts of the country, absolutely refuses to tolerate survivals of patriarchalism and personal dependence, and is marked by a truly "contemptuous attitude to the past." It is this break with obsolete tradition that is one of the substantial conditions which have created the possibility and evoked the necessity of regulating production and of public control over it. In particular, . . . it must be stated that the drawing of women and juveniles into production is, at bottom, progressive. It is indisputable that the capitalist factory places these categories of the working population in particularly hard conditions, but endeavors to completely ban the work of women and juveniles in industry, or to maintain the patriarchal manner of life that ruled out such work, would be reactionary and utopian. By destroying the patriarchal isolation of these categories of the population who formerly never emerged from the narrow circle of domestic family relationships, by drawing them into direct participation in social production, . . . industry stimulates their development and increases their independence (p. 15).

Notwithstanding all the laws emancipating women, she continues to be a *domestic slave*, because *petty housework* crushes, strangles, stultifies, and degrades her, chains her to the kitchen and the nursery, and she wastes her labor on barbarously unproductive, petty, nerve-racking, stultifying and crushing drudgery. The real *emancipation of women*, real communism, will begin only where and when an all-out struggle begins (led by the proletariat wielding the state power) against this petty housekeeping, or rather when its *wholesale transformation* into a large-scale socialist economy begins.

Do we in practice pay sufficient attention to this question, which in theory every Communist considers indisputable? Of course not. Do we take proper care of the *shoots* of communism which already exist in this sphere? Again, the answer is *no*. Public catering establishments, nurseries, kindergartens —here we have examples of these shoots, here we have the simple, everyday means, involving nothing pompous, grandiloquent or ceremonial, which can *really emancipate women*, really lessen and abolish their inequality with man as regards their role in social production and public life. These means are not new, they (like all the material prerequisites for socialism) were created by large-scale capitalism. But under capitalism they remained, first, a rarity, and secondly—which is particularly important—either *profit-making* enterprises, with all the worst features of speculation, profiteering, cheating and fraud, or "acrobatics of bourgeois charity," which the best workers rightly hated and despised (pp. 61–62).

You all know that even when women have full rights, they still remain downtrodden because all housework is left to them. In most cases, housework is the most unproductive, the most savage, and the most arduous work a woman can do. It is exceptionally petty and does not include anything that would in any way promote the development of the woman (p. 67).

We are setting up model institutions, dining-rooms and nurseries, that will emancipate women from housework. . . .
We say that the emancipation of the workers must be effected by the workers themselves, and in exactly the same way the emancipation of working women is a matter for the working women themselves. The working women must themselves see to it that such institutions are developed, and this activity will bring about a complete change in their position as compared with what it was under the old, capitalist society (p. 68).

The change in a historical epoch can always be determined by the progress of women toward freedom, because in the relation of woman to man, of the weak to the strong, the victory of human nature over brutality is most evident. The degree of emancipation of women is the natural measure of general emancipation.

—*Charles Fourier*

In education, in marriage, in everything, disappointment is the lot of women. It shall be the business of my life to deepen this disappointment in every woman's heart until she bows down to it no longer.

—*Lucy Stone*

Every socialist recognizes the dependence of the workmen on the capitalist, and cannot understand that others, and especially the capitalists themselves, should fail to recognize it also; but the same socialist often does not recognize the dependence of women on men because the question touches his own dear self more or less clearly.

—*August Bebel*

In no bourgeois republic (i.e., where there is private ownership of the land, factories, works, shares, etc.), be it even the most democratic republic, nowhere in the world, have women gained a position of complete equality. And this, notwithstanding the fact that more than one and a quarter centuries have elapsed since the Great French Revolution. In words bourgeois equality promises equality and liberty. In fact not a single bourgeois republic, not even the most advanced one, has given the feminine half of the human race either full legal equality with men or freedom from the guardianship and oppression of men.

—*Lenin, Pravda, November 8, 1919*

The degree of emancipation of women could be used as a standard by which to measure general emancipation.

—*Marx and Engels, The Holy Family*

Marriage As an Oppressive Institution /

Collectives As Solutions

BARBRA BALOGUN (JACKSON)

Like any political situation, personal relationships do not really change by reform, but only by complete revolution. I feel that the personal relationships of marriage must undergo a revolution to find any real solutions to their problems.

In five years of marriage, my husband and I have been through many discussions, and have come up with many solutions to the problems we have faced in our monogamous legal relationship called marriage. Most of the discussions were fruitless and the solutions, if they worked at all, were short-lived. Some of the problems have been involved with infidelity (on his part), with not sharing in child-care, with not sharing in housework, financial worries, lack of communication, and dishonesty.

Being faced again with the need to "discuss" things, I realize how useless this has been in the past. The problem has always been inherent in the relationship we chose to enter, and only secondarily in our personal response to it. The problem, as I see it, stems from role-playing that is oppressive to both parties, particularly to women.

1. There is monogamy that is naturally assumed to be based on a double standard, which recognizes that the man will run around but, of course, the woman will stay at home being eternally faithful.

Monogamy is, of course, unrealistic for either partner. There is no law that can guarantee that a person can be completely sexually satisfied by one person for the whole of her or his sexual life. Recognizing that most sexual relationships usually improve with time and practice, permanent sexual relationships are to be desired. However, it must be recognized that occasional deviations from this are to be expected, and pose no real danger to the permanent relationship.

2. Most marriages are based on the roles of man as the breadwinner and the woman as keeper of the home and the producer and rearer of the children. This forces the man to measure his success or failure upon his ability to provide for his family. The woman, on the other hand, may help provide for the house, but with full recognition of what her first responsibilities are. And these responsibilities are her trap. This is what gets her up before anyone else in the morning, and gets her to bed after everyone else. These are the duties of the most monotonous, never-ending nature. This is what binds and traps her with children and they with her. Out of this grows the oppressive authoritarianism of parents and the overdependence of children on parents. Because the chil-

dren are such a burden, in attempting to make the job easier by reducing the work they make for her, the mother puts unnatural, over-restricting demands on the children, and tries to get them to conform to her idea of what they should do. There is little recognition of children as people.

The roles of male and female must be completely redefined —NO, eliminated. I do not see this as possible in the present relationships of marriage. For as long as these relationships exist, there is still mainly the role of the man as breadwinner and the woman as mother and housewife. This is so because there is no good alternative present in it for the care and rearing of children. Unfortunately, this is the main purpose of marriage, not a good relationship between two human beings, male and female.

3. For economic reasons, marriage is oppressive to both parties, especially to women. As long as the man has sole, or major, responsibility for the financial support of his family, the women and children, because of their non-contributory roles, are kept dependent and powerless.

a. The man is oppressed just by being forced to bear the sole or major responsibility for the financial support of his family. In addition, the burden is increased because of the exploitative, mind-destroying nature of jobs in a capitalist society. Then, of course, this burden is doubly destructive to those oppressed groups who can't even find work and yet are "expected" to fulfill the "male" functions of society.

b. For women—the economic situation of the family is oppressive because:

(1) Her financial dependence on the man gives her no power in the marriage. The threat of losing economic support if she gets "out-of-line" keeps her "in-line."

(2) In the working world she is exploited with the excuse given that her salary is not as necessary as the man's salary, and therefore can be lower.

(3) Her duties in marriage—i.e., housework and child-care—really constitute slave-labor. There is no economic payment for what is, in fact, real labor—no payment, that is, except whatever money her husband doles out to her for groceries, etc.

The only alternative, as I see it, is communal living, in which the man and the woman enter a collective set-up as individuals, not as "partners" (even though they may continue an on-going sexual relationship). In this collective, the traditional male-female roles—i.e., the sexual, psychological, economic, provider/housewife, mother roles will be eliminated.

CONDUCT OF THE COMMUNITY:

1. Each adult individual is recognized as an equal human being having exactly the same responsibilities and privileges.
2. All household chores are shared equally on a rotating and/or team schedule.
3. Child-care is shared equally by all members on rotating schedules. This recognizes not only the advantages of unburdening the individual parents, but also the privileges they give us, by sharing the love and companionship of their children with other people. This hopefully will eliminate the concept of children as property, not people.
4. All decisions made in the community are collectively discussed and decided upon.
5. Teenagers are to have the privileges and assume the responsibilities as members of the community. Special considerations are to be made for their status as students.
6. Adequate facilities are to be acquired to provide that each adult individual has his or her own private unit. As much privacy as possible is to be provided for the children.

I feel that even between men and women sharing male/female relationships, there should be maintained their own individual units in recognition of the need for privacy, even in such relations.
7. Economically, all people, male and female, will be freed to work if they are able and find this desirable. The specific financial needs will be determined by the individual collective. While all people may not "work" in the recognized job market, this distinction will not be determined by sex, but rather by the needs of the various individuals and the collective.

All that I have proposed goes a long way from what we presently know, but I believe that as long as we try to reform what we have now, we will fail.

I also recognize that conditions being what they are at the present time, most men feel so secure in their oppressive role, that they will not give up their powers willingly. Therefore, male-female communes will be impossible to establish.

It may be that our only solution will be the dissolution of marriages with the formation of all-female communes to eliminate the burdens placed on women.

"Woman As Nigger"*

NAOMI WEISSTEIN

Psychology has nothing to say about what women are really like, what they need and what they want, for the simple reason that psychology does not know. Yet psychologists will hold forth endlessly on the true nature of woman, with dismaying enthusiasm and disquieting certitude.

Bruno Bettelheim, of the University of Chicago, tells us:

We must start with the realization that, as much as women want to be good scientists or engineers, they want first and foremost to be womanly companions of men and to be mothers.

Erik Erikson, of Harvard University, explains:

Much of a young woman's identity is already defined in her kind of attractiveness and in the selectivity of her search for the man (or men) by whom she wishes to be sought.

Some psychiatrists even see in women's acceptance of woman's role the solution to problems that rend our society. Joseph Rheingold, a psychiatrist at Harvard Medical School, writes:

. . . when women grow up without dread of their biological functions and without subversion by feminist doctrine and . . . enter upon motherhood with a sense of fulfillment and altruistic sentiment, we shall attain the goal of a good life and a secure world in which to live it.

*From *Psychology Today* Magazine (October, 1969), © 1969 Communications/Research/Machines/Inc.

These views reflect a fairly general consensus among psychologists, and the psychologists' idea of woman's nature fits the common prejudice. But it is wrong. There isn't the tiniest shred of evidence that these fantasies of childish dependence and servitude have anything to do with woman's true nature, or her true potential. Our present psychology is less than worthless in contributing to a vision that could truly liberate women.

And this failure is not limited to women. The kind of psychology that is concerned with how people act and who they are has failed in general to understand why people act the way they do and what might make them act differently. This kind of psychology divides into two professional areas: academic personality research, and clinical psychology and psychiatry. The basic reason for the failure is the same in both these areas: the central assumption for most psychologists of human personality has been that human behavior rests primarily on an individual and inner dynamic. This assumption is rapidly losing ground, however, as personality psychologists fail again and again to get consistency in the assumed personalities of their subjects, and as the evidence collects that what a person does and who he believes himself to be will be a function of what people around him expect him to be, and what the overall situation in which he is acting implies that he is.

Academic personality psychologists are looking, at least, at the counter evidence and changing their theories; no such corrective is occurring in clinical psychology and psychiatry. Freudians and neo-Freudians, Adlerians and neo-Adlerians, classicists and swingers, clinicians and psychiatrists, simply refuse to look at the evidence against their theory and practice. And they support their theory and their practice with stuff so transparently biased as to have absolutely no standing as empirical evidence.

If we inspect the literature of personality theory that has been written by clinicians and psychiatrists, it is immediately obvious that the major support for theory is "years of intensive clinical experience." Now a person is free to make up theories with any inspiration that works: divine revelation, intensive clinical practice, a random numbers table. He is not free to claim any validity for this theory until it has been tested. But in ordinary clinical practice, theories are treated in no such tentative way.

Consider Freud. What he accepted as evidence violated the most minimal conditions of scientific rigor. In *The Sexual*

Enlightenment of Children, the classic document that is supposed to demonstrate the existence of a castration complex and its connection to a phobia, Freud based his analysis on reports from the little boy's father, himself in therapy and a devotee of Freud. Comment on contamination in this kind of evidence in unnecessary.

It is remarkable that only recently has Freud's classic theory on female sexuality—the notion of the double orgasm—been tested physiologically and found just plain wrong. Now those who claim that 50 years of psychoanalytic experience constitute evidence of the essential truth of Freud's theory should ponder the robust health of the double orgasm. Before Masters and Johnson did women believe they were having two different kinds of orgasm? Did their psychiatrists coax them into reporting something that was not true? If so, were other things they reported also not true? Did psychiatrists ever learn anything that conflicted with their theories? If clinical experience means anything, surely we should have been done with the double-orgasm myth long before Masters and Johnson.

But, you may object, intensive clinical experience is the only reliable measure in a discipline that rests its findings on insight, sensitivity and intuition. The problem with insight, sensitivity and intuition is that they tend to confirm our biases. At one time people were convinced of their ability to identify witches. All it required was sensitivity to the workings of the devil.

Clinical experience is not the same thing as empirical evidence. The first thing an experimenter learns is the concept of the double blind. The term comes from medical experiments, in which one group takes a drug that is supposed to change behavior in a certain way, and a control group takes a placebo. If the observers or subjects know which group took which drug, the result invariably confirms the new drug's effectiveness. Only when no one knows which subject took which pill is validity approximated.

When we are judging human behavior, we must test the reliability of our judgments again and again. Will judges, in a blind experiment, agree in their observations? Can they repeat their judgments later? In practice, we find that judges cannot judge reliably *or* consistently.

Evelyn Hooker of U.C.L.A. presented to a group of judges, chosen for their clinical expertise, the results of three widely used clinical projective tests—the Rorschach, the Thematic Apperception Test (TAT) and the Make-A-Picture Story

Test (MAPS)—that had been given to homosexuals and a control group of heterosexuals. The ability of these judges to distinguish male heterosexuals from male homosexuals was no better than chance. Any remotely Freudian-like theory assumes that sexuality is of fundamental importance in the deep dynamic of personality. If gross sexual deviance cannot be detected, then what do psychologists mean when they claim that "latent homosexual panic" is at the basis of paranoid psychosis? They can't identify homosexual *anything*, let alone "latent homosexual panic."

More astonishing, the diagnoses of expert clinicians are not consistent. In the Kenneth Little and Edwin S. Shneidman study, on the basis of both tests and interviews, judges described a number of normals as psychotic, assigning them to such categories as "schizophrenic with homosexual tendencies," or "schizoid character with depressive trends." When the same judges were asked to rejudge the same test results several weeks later, their diagnoses of the same subjects differed markedly from their initial judgments. It is obvious that even simple descriptive conventions in clinical psychology cannot be applied consistently. These descriptive conventions, therefore, have no explanatory significance.

I was a member of a Harvard graduate seminar to which two piles of TAT tests were presented. We were asked to identify which pile had been written by males and which pile by females. Although the class had spent one and a half months intensively studying the psychological literature on the differences between the sexes, only four students out of 20 identified the piles correctly. Since this result is far below chance, we may conclude that there is a consistency here. Within the context of psychological teaching, the students judged knowledgeably; the teachings themselves are erroneous.

Some might argue that while clinical theory may be scientifically unsound, it at least cures people. There is no evidence that it does. In 1952, Hans Eysenck of the University of London reported the results of an "outcome-of-therapy" study of neurotics that showed that 44 per cent of the patients who received psychoanalysis improved; 64 per cent of the patients who received psychotherapy improved; and 72 per cent of the patients who received no treatment at all improved. These findings have never been refuted, and later studies have confirmed their negative results, no matter what type of therapy was used. In Arnold Goldstein and Sanford Dean's recent book, *The Investigation of Psychotherapy*, five different outcome-of-therapy studies with negative results are reported.

How, in all good conscience, can clinicians and psychiatrists continue to practice? Largely by ignoring these results and taking care not to do outcome-of-therapy studies.

Since clinical experience and tools are shown to be worse than useless when they are tested for consistency, efficacy and reliability, we can safely conclude that clinical theories about women are also worse than useless.

But even academic personality research that conforms to a rigorous methodology has only limited usefulness. As stated above, most psychologists of human personality have assumed that human behavior rests on an individual and inner dynamic, perhaps fixed in infancy, perhaps fixed by genitalia, perhaps simply arranged in a rigid cognitive network. But they have failed repeatedly to find consistency in the assumed personalities of their subjects. A rigid authoritarian on one test will be unauthoritarian on another. The reason for this inconsistency seems to depend more on the social situation in which a person finds himself than on the person himself.

In a series of experiments, Robert Rosenthal and his co-workers at Harvard showed that if experimenters have one hypothesis about what they expect to find and another group of experimenters has the opposite hypothesis, each group will obtain results that are in accord with its hypothesis. Experimenters who were told that their rats had been bred for brightness found that their rats learned to run mazes better than did the rats of experimenters who believed their animals had been bred for dullness. These results would have happened by chance one out of 100 times.

In a recent study, Robert Rosenthal and Lenore Jacobson extended their analysis to the classroom. They found that when teachers expected randomly selected students to "show great promise," the I.Q.s of these students increased significantly.

Thus, even in carefully controlled experiments, our hypotheses will influence the behavior of both animals and people. These studies are extremely important when we assess psychological studies of women. Since it is fairly safe to say that most of us start with hypotheses as to the nature of men and women, the validity of a number of observations on sex differences is questionable, even when these observations have been made under carefully controlled situations. In important ways, people are what you expect them to be, or at least they behave as you expect them to behave. If, as Bruno

Bettelheim has it, women want first and foremost to be good wives and mothers, it is likely that this is what Bettelheim wants them to be.

The obedience experiments of Stanley Milgram point to the inescapable effect of social context. A subject is told that he is administering a learning experiment, and that he is to deal out shocks each time the other "subject" (a confederate of the experimenter) answers incorrectly. The equipment appears to provide graduated shocks ranging from 15 to 450 volts; for each four consecutive voltages there are verbal descriptions such as "mild shock," "danger," "severe shock," and finally, for the 435- and 450-volt switches, simply a red XXX marked over the switches. Each time the stooge answers incorrectly, the subject is supposed to increase the voltage. As the voltage increases, the stooge cries in pain; he demands that the experiment stop; finally, he refuses to answer at all. When he stops responding, the experimenter instructs the subject to continue increasing the voltage; for each shock administered, the stooge shrieks in agony. Under these conditions, about 62.5 per cent of the subjects administered shocks that they believed to be lethal.

No tested individual differences predicted which subjects would continue to obey and which would break off the experiment. When 40 psychiatrists predicted how many of a group of 100 subjects would go on to give the lethal shock, their predictions were far below the actual percentage; most expected only one tenth of one per cent of the subjects to obey to the end.

Even though psychiatrists have no idea how people will behave in this situation, and even though individual differences do not predict which subjects will obey and which will not, it is easy to predict when subjects will be obedient and when they will be defiant. All the experimenter has to do is change the social situation. In a variant of Milgram's experiment, two stooges were present in addition to the "victim"; these worked with the subject in administering electric shocks. When the stooges refused to go on with the experiment, only 10 per cent of the subjects continued to the maximum voltage. This is critical for personality theory. It says that the lawful behavior is the behavior that can be predicted from the social situation, not from the individual history.

Finally, Stanley Schachter and J. E. Singer gave a group injections of adrenalin, which produces a state of physiological arousal almost identical to a state of extreme fear. When they were in a room with a stooge who acted euphoric, they became euphoric; when they were placed in a room with a stooge who acted angry, they became extremely angry.

It is obvious that a study of human behavior requires a study of the social contexts in which people move, the expectations as to how they will behave, and the authority that tells them who they are and what they are supposed to do.

We can now dispose of two biological theories of the nature of women. The first theory argues that females in primate groups are submissive and passive. Until we change the social organization of these groups and watch their subsequent behavior, we must conclude that—since primates are at present too stupid to change their own social conditions—the innateness and fixedness of these sexual differences in behavior are simply not known. Applied to humans, the primate argument becomes patently irrelevant, for the salient feature of human social organization is its variety, and there are a number of cultures in which there is at least a rough equality between men and women.

The second theory argues that since females and males differ in their sex hormones, and since sex hormones enter the brain, there must be innate differences in *psychological nature*. But this argument tells us only that there are differences in *physiological state*. From the adrenalin experiment we know that a particular physiological state can lead to varied emotional states and outward behavior, depending on the social situation.

Our culture and our psychology characterize women as inconsistent, emotionally unstable, lacking in a strong superego, weaker, nurturant rather than productive, intuitive rather than intelligent, and—if they are at all normal—suited to the home and family. In short, the list adds up to a typical minority-group stereotype—woman as nigger—if she knows her place (the home), she is really a quite lovable, loving creature, happy and childlike. In a review of the intellectual differences between little boys and little girls, Eleanor Maccoby has shown that no difference exists until high school, or, if there is a difference, girls are slightly ahead of boys. In high school, girls begin to do worse on a few intellectual tasks, and beyond high school the productivity and accomplishment of women drops off even more rapidly.

In light of the social expectations about women, it is not surprising that women end up where society expects them to; the surprise is that little girls don't get the message that they are supposed to be stupid until they get into high school.

It is no use to talk about women being different-but-equal; all the sex-difference tests I can think of have a "good" outcome and a "bad" outcome. Women usually end up with the bad outcome.

Except for their genitals, I don't know what immutable differences exist between men and women. Perhaps there are some other unchangeable differences; probably there are a number of irrelevant differences. But it is clear that until social expectations for men and women are equal, until we provide equal respect for both sexes, answers to this question will simply reflect our prejudices.

An Argument for Black Women's Liberation As a Revolutionary Force*

Mary Ann Weathers

"Nobody can fight your battles for you; you have to do it yourself." This will be the premise used for the time being for stating the case for Black women's liberation, although certainly it is the least significant. Black women, at least the Black women I have come in contact with in the movement have been expounding all their energies in "liberating" Black men (if you yourself are not free, how can you "liberate" someone else?). Consequently, the movement has practically come to a standstill. Not entirely due however to wasted energies but, adhering to basic false concepts rather than revolutionary principles and at this stage of the game we should understand that if it is not revolutionary it is false.

We have found that Women's Liberation is an extremely emotional issue, as well as an explosive one. Black men are still parroting the master's prattle about male superiority. This now brings us to a very pertinent question: How can we seriously discuss reclaiming our African Heritage—cultural living modes which clearly refute not only patriarchy and matriarchy, but our entire family structure as we know it.

*From *No More Fun and Games* (February, 1969).

African tribes live communally where households let alone heads of households are non-existent.

It is really disgusting to hear Black women talk about giving Black men their manhood—or allowing them to get it. This is degrading to other Black women and thoroughly insulting to Black men (or at least it should be). How can someone "give" one something as personal as one's adulthood? That's precisely like asking the beast for your freedom. We also chew the fat about standing behind our men. This forces me to the question: Are we women or leaning posts and props? It sounds as if we are saying if we come out from behind him, he'll fall down. To me, these are clearly maternal statements and should be closely examined.

Women's Liberation should be considered as a strategy for an eventual tie-up with the entire revolutionary movement consisting of women, men, and children. We are now speaking of real revolution (armed). If you can not accept this fact purely and without problems examine your reactions closely. We are playing to win and so are they. Viet Nam is simply a matter of time and geography.

Another matter to be discussed is the liberation of children from a sick slave culture. Although we don't like to see it, we are still operating within the confines of the slave culture. Black women use their children for their own selfish needs of worth and love. We try to live our lives which are too oppressing to bear through our children and thereby destroy them in the process. Obviously the much acclaimed plaudits of the love of the Black mother has some discrepancies. If we allow ourselves to run from the truth we run the risk of spending another 400 years in self-destruction. Assuming of course the beast would tolerate us that long, and we know he wouldn't.

Women have fought with men and we have died with men in every revolution, more timely in Cuba, Algeria, China, and now in Viet Nam. If you notice, it is a woman heading the "Peace Talks" in Paris for the NLF. What is wrong with Black women? We are clearly the most oppressed and degraded minority in the world, let alone the country. Why can't we rightfully claim our place in the world?

Realizing fully what is being said, you should be warned that the opposition for liberation will come from everyplace, particularly from other women and from Black men. Don't allow yourselves to be intimidated any longer with this nonsense about the "Matriarchy" of Black women. Black women are not matriarchs but we have been forced to live in abandonment and been used and abused. The myth of the matriarchy must stop and we must not allow ourselves to be sledgehammered by it any longer—not if we are serious about change and ridding ourselves of the wickedness of this alien culture. Let it be clearly understood that Black women's liberation is not anti-male; any such sentiment or interpretation as such can not be tolerated. It must be taken clearly for what it is—pro-human for all peoples.

The potential for such a movement is boundless. Whereas in the past only certain type Black people have been attracted to the movement—younger people, radicals, and militants. The very poor, the middle class, older people and women have not become aware or have not been able to translate their awareness into action. Women's liberation offers such a channel for these energies.

Even though middle-class Black women may not have suffered the brutal suppression of poor Black people, they most certainly have felt the scourge of the male-superiority-oriented society as women, and would be more prone to help in alleviating some of the conditions of our more oppressed sisters by teaching, raising awareness and consciousness, verbalizing the ills of women and this society, helping to establish communes.

Older women have a wealth of information and experience to offer and would be instrumental in closing the communications gap between the generations. To be Black and to tolerate this jive about discounting people over 30 is madness.

Poor women have knowledge to teach us all. Who else in this society see more and are more realistic about ourselves and this society and about the faults that lie within our own people than our poor women? Who else could profit and benefit from a communal setting that could be established than these sisters? We must let the sisters know that we are capable and some of us already do love them. We women must begin to unabashedly learn to use the word "love" for one another. We must stop the petty jealousies, the violence that we Black women have for so long perpetrated on one another about fighting over this man or the other. (Black men should have better sense than to encourage this kind of destructive behavior.) We must turn to ourselves and one another for strength and solace. Just think for a moment what it would be like if we got together and internalized our own 24-hour-a-day communal centers knowing our children would be safe and loved constantly. Not to mention what it would do for everyone's egos, especially the children. Women should not have to be enslaved by this society's concept of motherhood through their children; and then the kids suffer through a mother's resentment of it by beatings, punishment, and rigid discipline. All one has to do is look at the statistics of Black women who are rapidly filling the beast's mental institutions to know that the time for innovation and change and creative thinking is here. We cannot sit on our behinds waiting for someone else to do it for us. We must save ourselves.

We do not have to look at ourselves as someone's personal sex objects, maids, baby sitters, domestics and the like in exchange for a man's attention. Men hold this power, along with that of the breadwinner, over our heads for these services and that's all it is—servitude. In return we torture him, and fill him with insecurities about his manhood, and literally force him to "cat" and "mess around" bringing in all sorts of conflicts. This is not the way really human people live. This is whitey's thing. And we play the game with as much proficiency as he does.

If we are going to bring about a better world, where best to begin than with our selves? We must rid ourselves of our own hang-ups, before we can begin to talk about the rest of the world and we mean the world and nothing short of just that. (Let's not kid ourselves.) We will be in a position soon of having to hook up with the rest of the oppressed peoples of the world who are involved in liberation just as we are, and we had better be ready to act.

All women suffer oppression, even white women, particularly poor white women, and especially Indian, Mexican, Puerto Rican, Oriental and Black American women whose oppression is tripled by any of the above mentioned. But we do have female's oppression in common. This means that we can begin to talk to other women with this common factor and start building links with them and thereby build and transform the revolutionary force we are now beginning to amass. This is what Dr. King was doing. We can no longer allow ourselves to be duped by the guise of racism. Any time the White man admits to something you know he is trying to cover something else up. We are all being exploited, even the white middle class, by the few people in control of this entire world. And to keep the real issue clouded, he keeps us at one another's throats with this racism jive. Although Whites are most certainly racist, we must understand that they have been programmed to think in these patterns to divert their attention. If they are busy fighting us, then they have no time to question the policies of the war being run by this government. With the way the elections went down it is clear that they are as powerless as the rest of us. Make no question about it, folks, this fool knows what he is doing. This man is playing the death game for money and power, not because he doesn't like us. He couldn't care less one way or the other. But think for a moment if we all go together and just walked on out. Who would fight his wars, who would run his police state, who would work his factories, who would buy his products?

We women must start this thing rolling.

"Consumerism" and Women*

ELLEN WILLIS

Perhaps the most widely accepted tenet of movement ideology, promulgated by many leftist thinkers, notably Marcuse, is the idea that we are psychically manipulated by the mass media to crave more and more consumer goods, thus powering an economy that depends on constantly expanding sales. It has been suggested that this theory is particularly applicable to women, for women do most of the actual buying, their consumption is often directly related to their oppression (e.g., makeup, soap flakes), and they are a special target of advertisers. According to this view the society defines women as consumers and the purpose of the prevailing media image of women as passive sexual objects is to sell products. It follows that the beneficiaries of this depreciation of women are not men but the corporate power structure.

The consumerism theory has not been subjected to much critical debate. In fact, it seems in recent years to have taken on the invulnerability of religious dogma. Yet further analysis demonstrates that this theory is fallacious and leads to crucial tactical errors. This paper is offered as a critique of consumerism based on four propositions:

*© Ellen Willis 1970.

1. It is not "psychic manipulation" that makes people buy; rather, their buying habits are by and large a rational self-interested response to their limited alternatives within the system.

2. The chief function of media stereotypes of women is not to sell goods but to reinforce the ideology and therefore the reality of male supremacy—of the economic and sexual subordination of women to men, in the latter's objective interest.

3. Most of the "consuming" women do is actually labor, specifically part of women's domestic and sexual obligations.

4. The consumerism theory has its roots in class, sex, and race bias; its ready acceptance among radicals, including radical women, is a function of movement elitism.

First of all, there is nothing inherently wrong with consumption. Shopping and consuming are enjoyable human activities and the marketplace has been a center of social life for thousands of years. The profit system is oppressive not because relatively trivial luxuries are available, but because basic necessities are not. The locus of the oppression resides in the *production* function: people have no control over what commodities are produced (or services performed), in what amounts, under what conditions, or how they are distributed. Corporations make these decisions solely for their own profit. It is more profitable to produce luxuries for the affluent (or for that matter for the poor, on exploitive installment plans) than to produce and make available food, housing, medical care, education, recreational and cultural facilities according to the needs and desires of the people. We can accept the goods offered to us or reject them, but we cannot determine their quality or change the system's priorities. In a truly humane society, in which all the people have personal autonomy, control over the means of production, and equal access to goods and services, consumption will be all the more enjoyable because we will not have to endure shoddy goods sold at exploitive prices by means of dishonest advertising.

As it is, the profusion of commodities is a genuine and powerful compensation for oppression. It is a bribe, but like all bribes it offers concrete benefits—in the average American's case, a degree of physical comfort unparalleled in history. Under present conditions, people are preoccupied with consumer goods not because they are brainwashed but because buying is the one pleasurable activity not only permitted but actively encouraged by the power structure. The pleasure of eating an ice cream cone may be minor compared to the pleasure of meaningful, autonomous work, but the former is easily available and the latter is not. A poor family would undoubtedly rather have a decent apartment than a new TV, but since they are unlikely to get the apartment, what is to be gained by not getting the TV?

Radicals who in general are healthily skeptical of facile Freudian explanations have been quick to embrace a theory of media manipulation based squarely on Freud, as popularized by market researchers and journalists like Vance Packard (Marcuse acknowledges Packard's influence in *One Dimensional Man*). In essence, this theory holds that ads designed to create unconscious associations between merchandise and deep-seated fears, sexual desires, and needs for identity and self-esteem induce people to buy products in search of gratifications no product can provide. Furthermore, the corporations, through the media, deliberately create fears and desires that their products can claim to fulfill. The implication is that we are not simply taken in by lies or exaggerations—as, say, by the suggestion that a certain perfume will make us sexually irresistible—but are psychically incapable of learning from experience and will continue to buy no matter how often we are disappointed, and that in any case our "need" to be sexually irresistible is programmed into us to keep us buying perfume. This hypothesis of psychic distortion is based on the erroneous assumption that mental health and anti-materialism are synonymous.

Although they have to cope with the gyppery inherent in the profit system, people for the most part buy goods for practical, self-interested reasons. A washing machine does make a housewife's work easier (in the absence of socialization of housework); Excedrin does make a headache go away; a car does provide transportation. If one is duped into buying a product because of misleading advertising, the process is called exploitation; it has nothing to do with brainwashing. Advertising is a how-to manual on the consumer economy, constantly reminding us of what is available and encouraging us to indulge ourselves. It works (that is, stimulates sales) *because* buying is the only game in town, not vice versa. Advertising does appeal to morbid fears (e.g. of body odors) and false hopes (of irresistibility) and shoppers faced with indistinguishable brands of a product may choose on the basis of an ad (what method is better—eeny meeny miny mo?) but this is just the old game of caveat emptor. It thrives on naivete and people learn to resist it through experience. The worst suckers for ads are children. Other vulnerable groups are older people, who had no previous experience—individual or historical—to guide them when the consumer cornucopia suddenly developed after World War II, and poor people, who do not have enough money to learn through years of trial, error and disillusionment to be shrewd consumers. The constant refinement of advertising claims, visual effects and so on show that experience desensitizes. No one really believes that smoking Brand X cigarettes will make you sexy. (The function of sex in an ad is probably the obvious one—to lure people into paying closer attention to the ad—rather than to make them "identify" their lust with a product. The chief effect of the heavy sexual emphasis in advertising has been to stimulate a national preoccupation with sex, showing that you can't identify away a basic human drive as easily as all that.) Madison Avenue has increasingly deemphasized "motivational" techniques in favor of aesthetic ones—TV commercials in particular have become incredibly inventive visually —and even made a joke out of the old motivational ploys (the phallic Virginia Slims ad, for instance, is blatantly campy). We can conclude from this that either the depth psychology approach never worked in the first place, or that it has stopped working as consumers have gotten more sophisticated.

The argument that the corporations create new psychological needs in order to sell their wares is similarly flimsy. There is no evidence that propaganda can in itself create a desire, as opposed to bringing to consciousness a latent desire by suggesting that means of satisfying it are available. This idea is supersititious: it implies that the oppressor is diabolically intelligent (he has learned to control human souls) and that the media have magic powers. It also mistakes effects for causes and drastically oversimplifies the relation between ideology and material conditions. We have not been taught to dislike our smell in order to sell deodorants; deodorants sell because there are social consequences for smelling. And the negative attitude about our bodies that has made it feasible to invent and market deodorants is deeply rooted in our anti-sexual culture, which in turn has been shaped by exploitative modes of production and class antagonism between men and women.

The confusion between cause and effect is particularly apparent in the consumerist analysis of women's oppression.

Women are not manipulated by the media into being domestic servants and mindless sexual decorations, the better to sell soap and hair spray. Rather the image reflects women as men in a sexist society force them to behave. Male supremacy is the oldest and most basic form of class exploitation (cf. Engels, *Origin of the Family*); it was not invented by a smart ad man. The real evil of the media image of women is that it supports the sexist status quo. In a sense the fashion, cosmetics and "feminine hygiene" ads are aimed more at men than at women. They encourage men to expect women to sport all the latest trappings of sexual slavery—expectations women must then fulfill if they are to survive. That advertisers exploit women's subordination rather than cause it can be clearly seen now that *male* fashions and toiletries have become big business. In contrast to ads for women's products, whose appeal is "use this and he will want you" (or "if you don't use this, he won't want you"), ads for the male counterparts urge, "you too can enjoy perfume and bright colored clothes; don't worry, it doesn't make you feminine," Although advertisers are careful to emphasize how *virile* these products are (giving them names like "Brut," showing the man who uses them hunting or flirting with admiring women —who, incidentally, remain decorative objects when the sell is aimed directly at men) it is never claimed that the product is *essential* to masculinity (as makeup is essential to femininity), only *compatible* with it. To convince a man to buy, an ad must appeal to his desire for autonomy and freedom from conventional restrictions; to convince a woman, an ad must appeal to her need to please the male oppressor.

For women, buying and wearing clothes and beauty aids is not so much consumption as work. One of a woman's jobs in this society is to be an attractive sexual object, and clothes and makeup are tools of the trade. The chief consumer in this instance is really the man, who consumes woman-as-sexual-commodity. Similarly, buying food and household furnishings is a domestic task; it is the wife's chore to pick out the commodities that will be consumed by the whole family. And appliances and cleaning materials are tools that facilitate her domestic function. When a woman spends a lot of money and time decorating her home or herself, or hunting down the latest in vacuum cleaners, it is not idle self-indulgence (let alone the result of psychic manipulation) but a healthy attempt to find outlets for her creative energies within her circumscribed role.

There is a persistent myth that a wife has control over her

husband's money because she gets to spend it. Actually, she does not have much more financial autonomy than the employee of a corporation who is delegated to buy office furniture or supplies. The husband, especially if he is rich, may allow his wife wide latitude in spending—he may reason that since she has to work in the home she is entitled to furnish it to her taste, or he may simply not want to bother with domestic details—but he retains the ultimate veto power. If he doesn't like the way his wife handles his money, she will hear about it. In most households, particularly in the working class, a wife cannot make significant expenditures, either personal or in her role as object-servant, without consulting her husband. And more often than not, according to statistics, it is the husband who makes the final decisions about furniture and appliances as well as other major expenditures like houses, cars and vacations.

Consumerism is the outgrowth of an aristocratic, European-oriented anti-materialism based on upper-class resentment against the rise of the vulgar bourgeois. Radical intellectuals have been attracted to this essentially reactionary position (Herbert Marcuse's view of mass culture is strikingly similar to that of conservative theorists like Ernest Van Den Haag) because it appeals to both their dislike of capitalism and to their feeling of superiority to the working class. This elitism is evident in radicals' conviction that they have seen through the system, while the average working slob is brainwashed by the media. (Oddly, no one claims that the ruling class is oppressed by commodities; it seems that rich people consume out of free choice.) Ultimately this point of view leads to a sterile emphasis on individual solutions—if only the benighted would reject their "plastic" existence and move to East Village tenements—and the conclusion that people are oppressed because they are stupid or sick. The obnoxiousness of this attitude is compounded by the fact that radicals can only maintain their dropout existence so long as plenty of brainwashed workers keep the economy going.

Consumerism as applied to women is blatantly sexist. The pervasive image of the empty-headed female consumer constantly trying her husband's patience with her extravagant purchases contributes to the myth of male superiority: we are incapable of spending money rationally; all we need to make us happy is a new hat now and then. (There is an analogous racial stereotype—the black with his Cadillac and loud shirts.) The consumer line allows movement men to avoid recognizing that they exploit women by attributing women's oppression solely to capitalism. It fits neatly into already existing radical theory and concerns, saving the movement the trouble of tackling the real problems of women's liberation. And it retards the struggle against male supremacy by dividing women. Just as in the male movement, consumerism encourages radical women to patronize and put down other women for trying to survive as best they can, and maintains individualist illusions.

If we are to build a mass movement we must recognize that no personal decision, like rejecting consumption, can alleviate our oppression. We must stop arguing about whose life style is better (and secretly believing ours is). The task of the women's liberation movement is to collectively combat male domination in the home, in bed, on the job. When we create a political alternative to sexism, the consumer problem, if it is a problem, will take care of itself.

The Man's Problem*

Roxanne Dunbar and Lisa Leghorn

Male supremacy reigns in the United States and Europe. The disease still exists in socialist countries despite a philosophy to the contrary. Men are the oppressors of women in private and public situations. Where men are oppressed, they are oppressed by other men. They fill all the political power positions in this corrupt system. Women form a lower caste in a still rigid caste system, and their economic situation has worsened rather than improved in the past decade (just as it has for black people). Most women come from the working class in the lowest positions in the labor force, or they are domestic servants and mistresses for males (husbands) who possess property, among which property women are counted and highly valued. Like a black person who has "made it," a woman who has "made it" is subject to the same social and economic humiliations as the commonest woman if she leaves the small protective kingdom of her triumph (usually

*From *No More Fun and Games* (November, 1969).

the family). A woman alone on the street or in a public place is fair game for any man, for being the property of none, she becomes the property of all or any.

No man plays a passive role in the oppression of females. The caste system could not function another day unless men vigorously acted out their oppressive roles, took their rewards for granted and stomped on women. Men not only support the caste system; they are terrified of losing any part of it. A bare rumbling from women is exaggerated to the scale of an army of castrating amazons. Men are threatened by women speaking about their freedom just as the racists fear the freedom of black people. To the man, in the absence of social and economic power, woman's freedom literally means his *loss* of freedom. For his only justification for existence lies in his being a man, which means possessing the right to oppress a woman (in the family) and feel superior to women in general.

The history and training of the male develops in him a serious deficiency. But it is difficult to comprehend for one who is not programmed in that way (women and black people in this society). The deficiency can be termed "weakness," "false consciousness," "stupidity" or "paranoia." There are many terms which indicate that men are debilitated and diseased by their training as men (as opposed to the idea that men are oppressed by their programming to the man's role). Many men go insane from the aggressiveness which is trained into them. Almost all acts of violence committed in this society are by men. Women are not the sole receptors of the violence, but they are now the only group of people who do not believe they have the right to defend themselves.

Females or black people who are programmed to a similar aggressiveness are as thoroughly diseased and maddened as males in those roles. So neither racial inferiority nor male genes can account for the white man's sickness.

We must pose the question: "How then does one deal with madness?" Obviously, the person who is the object of aggressive energy, as women are for men, cannot be the therapist. Every action of a woman is a threat to a man. Men are obsessed with their fears of the female—especially femaleness in themselves. Men also have the peculiar problem of dealing with their fears of being tainted with the "blood" of the lower caste, since all males are born of women.

The insane rationale of men's reactions to the slightest objections of women to accept the identities forced upon them (wife, mother, lover, whore, etc.) is the result of their dependence on the inferior role of women for thousands of years. The oppressor is threatened by any hint that women could be regarded equally or even prove superior to him. He responds frantically, fearing the loss of his strength-giving identity. If he is forced to consider the equality of the oppressed he must deal not only with the fact that he is the same as her, but also with his history of oppressing an equal.

There are men who do not appear to be the vicious oppressors of women. Yet any man who is not working consciously to change the inequal relationship of men and women is opposing the interests of women. He is just as guilty as the more blatantly violent man and is actually a great deal more insidious.

Analysis of the man's problem is necessary for women to develop good consciousness, but action is another problem. One thing is certain: Proximity to the male cannot effect cure. The disease is social and must be dealt with politically. We cannot "work out" the problem with a man or men, nor can we transfer the problem to an all female situation. That would mean simply finding comfort there and then returning to our cages. Homosexuality is again no more than a personal "solution."

We should deal with the problem in material terms, not in fantasy terms. Our attitude should lead us to separation from men who are not consciously working for female liberation, not to sectarianism in an all female movement; isolation (desertion) of males, not hate invective; self-defense, not shaming and begging men to stop being brutes (they love being considered brutes). Hatred and resentment for men are not sufficient to give women lasting energy to fight. Yet they are probably inevitable results of increasing awareness of what men have done and do to us. Recognition of the SOCIAL nature of the oppression of females is our first step to consciousness. It might seem that such recognition would free individual men of the burden of guilt. But in fact it makes continued subjugation impossible for the woman. She will begin to fight back and the man will have to confront HIS problem.

A Historical and Critical Essay for Black
Women

PATRICIA HADEN, DONNA MIDDLETON, AND
PATRICIA ROBINSON

It is time for the black woman to take a look at herself, not just individually and collectively, but historically, if she is to avoid sabotaging and delaying the black revolution. Taking a look at yourself is not simply good tactics; it is absolutely necessary at this time in the black movement when even black radical males are still so insecure about their identity and so full of revolutionary phantasies that they cannot reach out to the black woman in revolutionary love—to urge us to begin to liberate ourselves, to tell us the truth: "Black women, you are the most pressed down of us all. Rise up or we as black men can never be free!"

No black man can or should even think he can liberate us. Black men do not have our economic, social, biologic, and historic outlook. We are placed by those who have historically formed and manipulated the values in this society—white males—at the very bottom of all these perspectives. There is so much scorn and fear of WOMEN, ANIMAL and BLACK in this Western culture, and since we are all three, we are simply kept out of history. Except for certain "house women," history is made only by males. The word ANIMAL is used by most males to mean a hated and despicable condition, and anything that is hated is simultaneously feared. Black women get put down as "bitch dogs" and "pussies" by Western white and black men, especially those who so smugly overestimate their brain power flying from campus to campus rapping about reason and SOUL. Their heads blow out this intellectual and educated *spiel* on white and black power. They back it up, like males have always done down through written history, with Gods in their own image. What a come down it is to these males that they so often have to slip away from Harlem and Wall Street—to take "a crap." And how they struggle against the fact that, like so many animals, they are born of the female and from the moment of their leaving our dark wombs, they like all animals, begin to die! Yet we black women in our deepest humanity love and need black men, so we hesitate to revolt against them and go for ourselves.

If we black women got a few of the goodies—and we have bought all that jive put down on us by our field-nigger families, who all our lifetime pushed and hustled to be just simple house niggers—our anger and frustration go underground. We don't dare to endanger what we have been conditioned to accept as making it—a little glass house full of TV crap. We become nervous-nagging-narrow-minded murderers of ourselves and our children. We turn our madness and frustrations into other channels—against other black women and against our oppressed white sisters. We even trip out on smokes. We psyche out on sex with some cat that is as hung-up as we are. Then we got the nerve to break into the bag of cleanliness, godliness, and "I'm better than you are, baby!"

If we are poor black women, one night in the streets we explode. That small razor cupped in our fingers slashes his hated black face, that face that reflects our own. We look at him and see ourselves for what we really are—traitors to ourselves as poor black women and traitors to him, our street-brother, because we let him get to where he's at now—not a man just a jive-time turkey. We did not confront him long ago because our minds were not "wrapped." But now we can hear, see, feel our mistakes through his actions against us, toward his children and his mother. Now he's going to try to prove himself a man—"walk that walk; talk that talk." He's still hanging on to his jive thing. He bops on the corner and raps that he's straight. "I'm coming to my people!" He's still out there *fucking* with his drugs and talking shit. We lunge and sink our knife deep into his chest to blot out this awful truth. His blood oozes and stops while ours gushes from between our legs. Nothing gets born. We just end up murderers of the future of our people.

If we feel ourselves to be college-educated and politically aware, we end up nothing but common opportunists, playing some role of some dreamed-up African Queen, like we "gonna" rule some black country somewhere with some dashiki cat, acting haughty and ending up a tripped out black king. It does not matter to us that it is a historical fact that our own feudal period in Africa was cruelly oppressive to black women and peasants; that in Africa this warring and exploitative period was only interrupted by the landing of the European colonialist and slave trader. The African chiefs and their clique had been selling troublesome relatives and competing tribesmen to Europeans, just as now three-fourths of the so-called African statesmen are wheeling and dealing to sell the riches of their land and the labor of their people under neocolonialism.

We want desperately to feel black, but we also need to feel superior to whitey. We want to take his place. We really want to take over his system and rule over and exploit *every-one*. We want to be black masters and missies and have white maids and big white houses. We want to go to college to get good jobs and bring our learning back to the people in the streets. We're jiving—we're going to college to be social workers, NAACP'ers, teachers, doctors, lawyers, to keep the minds of the poor messed up and confused. We're going to college to be a part of the system.

All of us caught in this white male-jive that was meant to keep us hooked, exploited, and oppressed groove on this big white world of male supremacy, this way-out white capitalism. We hold tight to that little capital, clothes, furniture, and bank account, because if we lose it we'd have to go back to that old feeling of "I ain't nothing." "I ain't nowhere!" We are scared to death of that "big dick," the military-industrial complex. But how we give all praise to its power and tell all our friends how you can't beat the man and his system!

PART II

Myths unite people and steer their culture. They are the dreams and hopes; they are the fears and confusions of a people. They are found in their folktales, customs, in their religious and economic systems. Myths are not about real people, but do express the movement of opposites which is contradiction. The deep thoughts and everyday attitudes of human beings are full of contradictions. Like electrical energy, these thoughts that may oppose each other at times, and may join together as one at other times, move whole peoples into action. They also keep a society steadily moving in one direction or keep it in general peace with itself and its neighbors.

The American Dream is a myth. If you trace it symbolically and historically it is a long route away from the

ANIMAL BODY, away from the LAND, away from the WOMAN, and away from BLACK to condensed wealth (which is capital, and in the American Dream is money, machines and property), to the CITIES, to MAN and to WHITE. It is now the historical time to examine this myth that has made dead things and their creators sacred and overvalued by us.

Black women in the United States are so systematically left out of this society that we do not have an important part in producing the products bought and sold in this economy. We are civil servants, domestic servants, and servants to our families. We have no Gods in our own image, even though South American women, through Catholicism, have the Black Madonna. We are separated from black men in the same way that white women have been separated from white men. But we are even less valued by white and black males because we are not white. The American Dream is white and male when examined symbolically. We are the exact opposite—black and female and therefore carry the stigma, almost religious in nature, of the spurned and scorned and feared outcast.

The Western world was built on much more than colonialism and imperialism. It was also built on a split in the minds of men that thoroughly separated male from female as well as the body from the mind. This mind-blowing phenomenon caused all things having to do with the animal body to be repressed unconsciously. It is a fact of the psyche that repressed feelings, like oppressed peoples, do not stay repressed. Repressed feelings, like living energy, struggle against the force of repression to rise to consciousness. Repression of feelings, which we have learned through the conditioning of myths, is unacceptable, is a constant struggle.

Oppression of unacceptable people—unacceptable to those who rule, reinforced by myths from their imagination—is also a constant struggle between those who oppress and those who are oppressed. The oppressed, like repressed feelings, struggle to rise into the open and freedom. This is an example of the movement of opposites and contradiction.

Men who controlled the making of myths and culture after the overthrow of women managed to banish women and what they had always symbolized to a psychic underworld—a chaotic hell of folktales and fables. ANIMALS, WOMEN, and BLACKS became the underground witches and demons in men's minds. Men's own feminine nature, inherent in their bisexuality, was denied by them. This mental split enabled the male to deny the fact that he was an animal, to struggle against the darkness and toward the light, and to lessen the fact of his dependence on women for his nourishment before and after birth.

Most important, he could deny his dependence on women for his very birth and life. He could now ripple his large muscles and dream of soaring one day to the heavens, where he could be in charge and therefore be worshiped as the God of Light and the Heavens—an Apollo. The woman's body, which receives, hosts, and gives forth the future of the species, is inherently powerful. Her body and power had to be overthrown and suppressed when the male felt overwhelmed by this power and responded with the desperate need to take power from the woman. His desperate need became a living force in his use of external power over others and in the repression of his own soft femininity.

Some thousands of years ago, the female was considered the Goddess of the Universe from which heaven and earth sprang. Certainly this myth conforms to basic reality—out of one comes two. The female births both the male and the female. The Adam and Eve myth that has for so long been an important part of black women's education through our part-time father—the Negro minister—and our devoutly religious black mothers, turns this basic reality on its head and into its opposite. The male gives birth through the magical intervention of an all-powerful male God. The rib of Adam is plucked out and made into woman by this powerful medicine man who resembles in action the African and Asian tribal priest. Indeed, this is a powerful myth, for it grants the role of man in human creation while at the same time utterly denying woman's role. Deep down we black women still believe this clever religious tale that puts us out of creation. The fact that we do exposes our terrible dependence on outside authority and our fear of trusting and thinking for ourselves.

Anthropologists have been able to trace the animal family to the first human family, and they observe that the male's only role early in human history was insemination. Then he drifted off, leaving the female to take care of herself during pregnancy, birth, and the nursing of the young. When men and women began to live together, what can be called culture began. But women controlled the first fruit or surplus, the child, by reason of its long need for protection before it could take care of itself.

This was concrete power over the child and the male in those places with a warm climate and readily available food and water. There was no real need for a male food gatherer, a hunter, in this Garden of Eden. When the male came to live with the female more often, parents and an extended family in a culture began. The children were molded and conditioned by all manner of rituals and folk stories. Their education kept them under control and made them ready to follow the customs and rules set up by parents—first by the female, then the male.

Today in the time of the cities, cybernetics, nuclear power, and space exploration, white men have developed a man-made body, the self-regulating machine. It can operate a whole series of machines and adjust itself much as our human brain is able to readjust to the needs of our body and to operate the human body. It can also do the mental and physical work of men's bodies. At last man has done away with the practical need for his own human form. Now he must turn his attention to the danger the woman's body has always posed to his rule. He struggles to perfect artificial insemination and a machine host for the human fetus. He concerns himself with the biological control of reproduction of the species. Those white males who rule the free world (capitalist world) understand that if they are to keep their rule over women and so-called lesser men, they must stop being dependent on their bodies and must perfect machines which they can control absolutely.

PART III

When any group must be controlled and used, their gods, their religion, their land, and their tools of survival must be taken away from them. These are all reflections of themselves and their inner being as well as practical means to living. This must be done by force at first.

In the days when all the forest was evergreen, before the parakeet painted the autumn leaves red with the color from his breast, before the giants wandered through the woods with their heads above the tree-tops; in the days when the sun and moon walked the earth as man and wife, and many of the great sleeping mountains were human beings; in those far off days witchcraft was known only to the women of Onaland (Tierra del Fuego, South America). They kept their own particular lodge, which no man dared approach. The girls, as they neared womanhood, were instructed in the magic arts, learning how to bring sickness and even death to all those who displeased them.

The men lived in abject fear and subjugation. Certainly they had bows and arrows with which to supply the camp with meat, yet they asked, what use were such weapons against the witchcraft and sickness? This tyranny of the women grew from bad to worse until it occurred to the men that a dead witch was less dangerous than a live one. They conspired together to kill off all the women; and there ensued a great massacre, from which not one woman in human form escaped.

The legend goes on to describe how the men waited for the little girls to grow up so they could have wives. Meanwhile, they plotted how they would have their own lodge or secret society from which all women would forever be excluded. The lowly servant tasks would be performed only by women. They would be frightened into submission by means of demons drawn from men's minds.

This is only one of thousands of such legends taken from all parts of the world that indicate some great crisis did occur where leadership of society was taken away from the women by force. We blacks have a splendid oral tradition and respect for the history that comes to us through our older women. Much of their practical advice on how to doctor our children, make delicious dinners out of scraps the white world throws away, how to get meaning from our dreams, how they felt about the time of slavery, and how they overcame the master, have kept our spirits up. For those of us who want to break out of the subtle oppression of all black women, stories from the past have been used extensively in our research. We have begun to feel sure that before written history there was a great fear of women on the part of males and a sense of being oppressed by their inner and reproductive powers. "The Great Earth Mother" could bring forth life and inexplicably take it away. This was one kind of power—internal power. In all the folktales it could only be overcome through external power —force. It is possible that long ago there was a time when women were murdered in some massive genocide and their ancient God-like reflection destroyed along with their temples. Archaeologists have found such temples in Asia and northern Africa, along with statues of some female goddess. But it is better for women to make the historical connections about these remains, since black and white males still need to rule over us and cannot be depended upon to be free of male prejudice against women. It is enough for now that we note that men were determined at one time in the past to have external power over women, and her symbolic representative nature. . . .

Historical and political understanding of ourselves and our actual place in the American Dream is more important at this time than the gun. We black women look at our backwardness, our colossal ignorance and political confusion, and want to give up. We do not like ourselves or each other. Our contradictory feelings about our black brothers, who seem simultaneously to move forward and backward, are increased by their continual cautioning that we must not move on our own or we will divide the movement. About all that we will mess up will be their black study, black power, cultural nationalism hustle. Forget black capitalism, because when the master offers you his thing, you know it's over! There have been other movements in history when revolutionary males have appeared conservative, opportunistic, or just "stopped at the pass," and revolutionary women have always forged ahead of the males at this time to take the revolution to a deeper stage.

Black revolutionary women are going to be able to smash the last myths and illusions on which all the jive-male oppressive power depends. We are not alone anymore. This country no longer holds one well-armed united majority against an unarmed minority. . . . There is a whole bunch of brown and yellow poor folks out there in the world that the ruling middle-class of this country have used and abused, stolen from and sold their shoddy goods to at way-out prices. They are fighting back now, taking over those U.S. companies that sucked their people and their land. They are putting out the United States Army and capitalist investors as they did in China and Cuba.

But a new stage of history really began when the poor Vietnamese men, women, and children beat up and killed a whole lot of white and black cats who had decided it was easier to fight little, brown, poverty-stricken people than fight the MAN. One-half of these courageous South Vietnamese NLF fighters are women and children, and they have proved that no U.S. male, black or white, got what it takes to destroy a people who have decided in their guts to own themselves and their land. That is power U.S. males have forgotten, but not black women, especially those of us who are poor.

White males are only in the image of God and supernaturally powerful with unbeatable instruments of death, in our own "messed-over" minds—not in the revolutionary world beyond the borders of the United States. All that "Big Daddy" and "head of family" shit is possible because we play the game—

ego-tripping black men and ourselves. If our minds are to-gether, we can work, think, and decide everything for our-selves. It is only a cruel, capitalist system that digs money, property, and white broads more than it digs people, that forces us to be the dependents of men and wards of the state. We recognize that black males are frail human beings, born of women who love them, not for their "Dick power" or their bread, but for their gentle, enduring, and powerful humanity.

It is important for black women to remind themselves oc-casionally that no black man gets born unless we permit it—even after we open our legs. That is the first, simple step to understanding the power that we have. The second is that all children belong to the women because only we know who the mother is. As to who the father is—well, we can decide that, too—any man we choose to say it is, and that neither the child nor MAN was made by God.

Third, we are going to have to put ourselves back to school, do our own research and analysis. We are going to have to argue with and teach one another, grow to respect and love one another. There are a lot of black chicks, field niggers wanting to be house niggers, who will fight very hard to keep this decaying system because of the few, petty privileges it gives them over poor black women. We will be disappointed to lose some house women who will have to revert to their class and who will go with the master, like they did during slavery. Finally, we are going to have to give the brothers a helping hand here and there because they will be uptight, not only with the enemy but with us. But at the same time we've got to do our own thing and get our own minds together.

All revolutionaries, regardless of sex, are the smashers of myths and the destroyers of illusion. They have always died and lived again to build new myths. They dare to dream of a utopia, a new kind of synthesis and equilibrium.

WOMEN RAP

A Woman Scientist Speaks

DIANE NAREK

On July 22, 1969, several of my friends and I were watching the astronauts land on the moon. We watched and asked the same question. "Why aren't there any women astronauts on the moon?" "Why aren't there any women technicians?" "How are we kept from these fields?"

As a woman scientist and someone who wanted to be an astronaut, I feel that I know some of these answers. I have worked as an actuarial trainee, an engineer, a solid state physicist, and a college teacher of mathematics, chemistry, and physics. From these experiences I would like to tell you some of the reasons for the lack of women in technical fields.

As a child I liked to make and build objects. My parents encouraged this interest and my desire to pursue a scientific career. I was also encouraged in school, especially by a woman mathematics teacher in junior high school. This teacher continued to encourage me after I had completed her class. Both my parents and teachers helped me in my personal projects such as breeding fish and plants. This encouragement continued in high school. Several teachers helped me to obtain a National Science Foundation research grant. Following this outside recognition from the NSF, the mathematics department chairman added his help. He coached me in college level mathematics so that I could skip freshmen courses and he also helped me to get research grants. I used one of these grants to study electricity and to build my own radio set. The school where I took this course was normally attended only by men and did not even have a ladies' bathroom. At the time I thought nothing of this, but it was the beginning of the discouragement I was to receive in pursuing my interests. Up to this point I had received only encouragement and help from school and home in learning about science. I wanted to study science because I enjoyed the subject and while I was encouraged I did quite well in this pursuit. Until I graduated from high school, nobody ever questioned my motives or my interest in the subject.

When I began to apply to college I suddenly discovered resistance. I knew that I had to be twice as good as a man to get into college and even better for a scholarship. So I was. I worked hard to graduate first in my class and get 700–800 on the College Boards. In addition I participated in as many school activities as possible. Yet when I applied to college I was told not to indicate my interest in science. I was told that I would not be able to compete with men once I entered college. It was not that I could not, but that I was not allowed. I had already shown that I could. When the scholarships and admissions were given out, I watched as men with poorer grades than my own were awarded the prizes. When I complained I was told that companies and colleges did not want to invest in a woman because she would eventually get married. This was the first time that I learned what it meant to be a woman. But since I did receive offers and was able to go to college I let it slide and the anger passed.

Once I entered college though, I couldn't let the anger pass because I was constantly being reminded that I was a woman and women shouldn't study science and mathematics. Professors told us women that we were not serious enough and we had to prove ourselves. In many science courses the requirements for women were much higher than for men. In my school the course which prospective mathematics majors were required to pass was taught by just such a professor. Many women were denied entrance into the major because he felt they were not serious enough. Once again a woman had to be twice as good to get by. An average man is encouraged to study these subjects but an average woman is denied the same opportunity. I was able to major in mathematics because a visiting woman professor taught the required course one semester. Instead of having to prove myself, I was encouraged to continue. I later switched my major to physics and the pressures on me as a woman became much greater. I was constantly reminded that physics was a man's domain and in order to earn equality and respect for my work I would have to give up my "female privileges." What this meant was that I had to carry my own equipment and open doors for myself. I also had to learn to use tools and although the men knew how they would not give me any of the help they gave to each other. Naturally when a woman learns these things she is laughed at. I was told that I was no longer feminine and ridiculed for this. Many women envy another woman who pursues a scientific career. It is often felt that she will meet many men. The men who are her fellow students do not agree. They do not consider her a woman, but a queer and a threat to themselves. In this way a woman scientist becomes alienated from others very early. Other women are awed by her, men treat her as a freak.

Despite the discouragement I had received, I continued to study. I kept pursuing my interest in science partly to prove that I could do it and partly because I enjoyed it. However, that enjoyment had decreased very much during my college years. The constant discouragement and pressures that I received as a woman had their result. I became less interested and my work suffered. All the energy that I had put into fighting these pressures distracted me from my work. Eventually I believed the belittling, and the quality of my work was lowered. However I managed to finish school and then attempted to apply my skills.

A woman who seeks to continue in her scientific work finds that she has obtained one of the following titles: "the first woman physics graduate in the school's history," "the woman in the mathematics department," "our prettiest engineer," or "the bird-brained scientist." A big fuss is made over her when she gets a job and she is publicly pointed out. However, like every other woman she receives lower salary, lower rank, and less interesting positions than men with the same qualifications. After obtaining the same skills as a man, spending the same time at the same schools, a woman is still treated as an inferior person. On my first job I was not even afforded the common courtesy of being invited to lunch by my co-workers. It is usual to take a new person to lunch. Well, on my first day all my colleagues marched out to lunch leaving me to sit alone in my office. When I was first hired I was told not to expect any favors because I was a woman. Yet every time I turned around my co-workers made a fuss. I cramped the style of the laboratory because they felt they couldn't use curse words in my presence. At the same time every man I worked with expected favors of me because I was a woman. I was told not to use my feminine wiles, but any time I participated in discussions or arguments I was put down as a flighty woman. The men did not respond to my logic but only to my feminine wiles. I wanted to be treated equally in my work but my male co-workers would not allow it. They did not want to follow my logic. They forced me to use my sex "privileges" to get attention for my work and then ridiculed me for it.

There is set up a constant conflict between a woman as a woman and her abilities as a scientist. This conflict is caused by those around her. She is told not to act like a woman but she is always treated like a woman. Her work is belittled and she is constantly asked to prove herself in both her work and her intentions. It is never thought that she is interested in her work. Every man thinks she is interested in him. I was constantly asked why I was wasting my time and told to get married. I was told that their wives preferred homemaking and since I was a woman I wouldn't be happy unless I did the same. My work was considered to be a waste of time, while my co-workers who were doing the same thing were considered to be conducting important research. Even after several years of teaching I find that male students find it necessary to criticize my work as a mathematics teacher.

In addition to being an outcast among my male colleagues I was shunned by other women because I was different. Other women are in awe of the female member of the technical staff and they do not become friends. They also resent any superiority that is held over them and a woman scientist acts superior. The woman scientist feels that she has proven that she is a skilled and accomplished person. She does not receive any recognition from men so she seeks to gain it from the women who are under her. In this way we women are kept divided. The secretaries resent the woman scientist's slight authority, while the woman scientist resents the lack of recognition. At present we are venting these hostilities on each other instead of on the cause, which is men. It is the men who treat us all unequally and do not recognize our individual achievements. As my awareness developed in Women's Liberation, I became less interested in gaining recognition from men and it was no longer necessary to laud my position over other women. When my position was not used this way I became friends with the secretary and we helped and supported each other in our work. I helped her do the mimeographing and she gave me useful information. I used to feel put down when my colleagues suggested that I eat with the secretaries. I not only felt slighted but resentful because I was kept from many fruitful discussions about work. Many ideas and experiments are suggested as a result of social meetings. I felt that I was being deprived of scientific opportunities and did not want to waste this time discussing subjects which I considered to be less important with the secretaries. Since Women's Liberation I actively seek out the secretaries for social company. There is a pleasant atmosphere rather than the competitive hostility I found with men. There is no competition among us for we treat each other equally as women, not as inferiors, while the men treat all women equally, as inferiors.

The only reason that there aren't any more women scientists and technicians is because the men don't allow it. They tell us women that we are not good at mechanical skills. If we disprove their theory by learning these skills, they accuse us of being unfeminine. As a youngster I was encouraged in my scientific pursuits, yet when I tried to achieve these goals I was harassed. I had the confidence in my ability and the desire to study science. The constant pressures that I received caused me to lose both. No wonder a woman who as a child did not receive this encouragement does not enter science. No matter when we feel them, the pressures and discouragement keep us women from becoming scientists. Having the early encouragement I went further but eventually I too lost interest. It was only after my involvement in Women's Liberation that I again found enjoyment in science. I now teach mostly women students who encourage me in my work. In return I encourage them to study mathematics. They are not put down as women and I am not overly criticized and harassed by male students. In this atmosphere, where I am not ill-treated as a woman, I have rediscovered my enjoyment of science.

The Star of Silence

ROBERTA GOOTBLATT

I feel that the poem is quite self-explanatory, but I would like to explain how I came about its title.

As you all know, the symbol of the Jewish religion is the "Star of David," and it is completely centered around the Jewish man.

The Jewish woman is the essence and life force of the Jewish culture. But, while she is destroyed she forever remains "silent"—and never stands up for herself. She has no awareness of who she really is. She has taken all kinds of shit, but still she remains silent, silent, silent. . . .

Therefore, within that man-dominated religion she is "The Star of Silence."

Every woman is born to be;
Like a blossoming flower;
Creative and free.
To give of herself and guide mankind too.
And bring wisdom to the old and nourish
       the new.

But . . .
Woman is kept in her place day by day,
By man who claims he's better and wiser
       so he'll say.
For he is God and from him she must learn,
That he is her master and from him never turn.

Oh, you poor Jewish women,
How blind can you be.
You are one of those billions who has never been
       free.
From the time you are born you are sucked in
       by man,
And silently destroyed as he gently holds your
       hand.

You are told you are nothing when you're a tiny
       child,
You were given a name and a psyche that is filed,
In a small Jewish box labeled *religion for man,*
And the male keeps you there for as long as he can.

The oppression goes on and soon you take your place,
As the mother and housewife in this murderous race.
You cater to the man and bear his children as well,
And soon you feel boredom and the loneliest hell.

But . . .
You remain silent for you can't understand,
That emptiest feeling when he touches your hand.
When those "deeds" of love mean nothing to you,
Life seems so dull and meaningless too.

Wake up my fine sister and raise that head high.
Your heart is as full as that beautiful sky.
Open that mouth and let those thoughts through.
Open those eyes and see yourself too.

A Jewish woman is a person, she is not a toy.
He has no moral right to oppress and destroy.
You owe it to yourself, children and culture
        as well.
To rise from below and escape from your hell.

The Jewish woman is one of so many destroyed
        everyday.
By false and neurotic fantasies that in her
        place she must stay.
And it's so obvious by the state humanity is in,
That all women must unite so femininity can win.

Humanity is lost within man's insecurity and
        self-hate.
And there is only one thing that can save us
        from this destructive fate.
Women fighting together and opening the world's
        eyes,
To the beauty of femininity and the truth about
        those lies.

And, my Jewish sisters, you are a very important
        part it's true,
For you are individuals with your own beauty too.
So think it over within the silence you know,
And I hope with all my heart that with us you
        will go. . . .

Me, Myself and the Middle-class Jew

ROBERTA GOOTBLATT

*I dedicate my story to my daughter Robin, and to all the New
Jewish Women of the future.*
                                        November, 1969

It is not hard to ascertain what it's like to be rich or poor in
the capitalist society. In this respect, you've either got it or
you don't. But, no matter who you are, you're far from heaven,

and much closer to hell, if you are caught in the middle class. And, indeed, if you're a woman—forget it! You are nothing anyway you may look at it. Rich, poor, or in the middle you've had it even before you're born.

Yes, it's a long hard road for any woman in the class society. But, let me tell you, the most deeply and most viciously destroyed woman in this society is none other than the middle-class Jewish woman.

If you are amazed at this fact, yes FACT, let me tell you about 23 years of my life as I have lived them within the Jewish middle class. And, when you finish reading my story, perhaps if you are a Jewish woman with a drop of humanity left within you, you too may realize what a battle we have. And, so, if you are born a female, and Jewish at that, and are raised within the middle class—this may well be your story too. . . .

One thing I can be thankful for is that I was born. And, that is all! I was the first daughter to a lower middle-class Jewish male who was a butcher. My mother, in the same hell, an office worker. My parents, brother, sister and I lived in an ugly building in the East Bronx.

As in all middle-class families, mother and father worked so the kids would have what they *needed*, and the children followed in momma and papa's footsteps. The Jewish kids usually came home with good marks from school. This is about par for an average middle-class Jewish family.

Looking deeper within this class of people, I ask, "What is the Jewish middle-class woman like?" Outwardly, she is just like everyone else. Inwardly, she is not so average. She was born under the Star of David and here is where it all begins.

As the old Jewish saying goes, I was the "Chosen One." I was the female member of the family picked for the scapegoat. For 15 years, I took all the shit the family could dish out. Why? Because if I didn't, I would have been thoroughly rejected, and as a child that was just a little too much to bear. So, I worshiped my father, for the Jewish male is god, and since mother had been in the same boat as I when she was a child, mother just wasn't there. Oh, yes, she worked and cleaned and cooked, but her inner destruction was completed and so she could not comprehend what was being done to me.

The joys of being a child were unknown to me. I wanted only to please god (dear old dad), so I, too, cleaned and cooked and became momala (little mother). You see, a good middle-class Jewish girl's ultimate goal is to be a good cook, and a terrific housewife.

During my so-called childhood there were many times when the loneliness and inner emptiness got so bad that I knew within my imprisoned self that someday I would understand why life seemed so meaningless. Peace and love were unknown within the Jewish middle class. For the tension was beyond control. Everyone existed; life had no true meaning.

At 15 years I had had it! Luckily, I came down with the classical school phobia—and my fight for life had begun.

When I entered therapy, I knew damn well that what was ahead of me was no game. I was either going to completely destroy myself, or I was going to be reborn. You see, I was a hopeless case; at least that's what the society and my family thought. But, within myself I knew that I had to make it. Someone within that damn murderous Jewish neurotic cycle had to break out and lead the way to the birth of the New Jewish Woman. And, perhaps even pave the way toward a new life for all Jews.

I struggled within myself and got back to school. Then I stopped taking shit from everyone. I told my friends that they were going to accept me for who I am or buzz off. (They buzzed off!) I told all my Jewish relatives to go to hell! And, then, I told father to go fuck himself. I refused consciously and subconsciously to be his scapegoat. The family didn't like this, they just couldn't understand. How could any Jewish *good* girl not respect her father!? Where would this poor child be without god!? They actually thought I was completely mad! I was free, and their distorted minds saw my freedom as disrespect and hate!!

So, I picked myself up and moved out. Yep, the little nebbish Jew from the Bronx, at 18 years old went out into the world and left the dead Jewish family. My struggle for freedom continued on. A little while after my rebellious departure, father died! You see, he had lost his scapegoat, so he turned all his anger on himself. It was him or me, and I had to live!!

I obtained for myself a "good" job as a secretary (for most middle-class Jewish girls college is supposedly "unnecessary," so naturally I obtained secretarial skills in high school), and completely enjoyed my individuality. Now, I can go on and on telling about my many experiences while on my ladder to self-liberation, but at this point it is more important to explain something about my Jewishness. For this is the part within me that gave me the strength to overcome any and all stagnations which I faced.

I was resigned to go through all the hell in the world. But, facing it was only part of the struggle. At one time or another there comes the moment to take another step towards rebirth. Now this means continuously growing out of the protective middle-class womb and facing oneself, the middle class and life. Oh, how hard this is! For, as a Jewish woman, you must grow subconsciously away from the father god, and give that supposed *"protector"* up completely. You get caught like a rat in a trap! You're damned if you do, and damned if you don't. In other words, if you take that small, but so important leap toward inner freedom, you don't know what to expect. How terribly frightening the unknown is! And, if you don't take that step, you're still in the same shit and feeling the same hell. Believe me, you feel this bind so deep within your gut—it's the most painful, lonely and frightening feeling. When you are born in the *middle* class, you always find yourself caught in the *middle!*

Here is where my Jewish feminine sensitivity becomes my guiding light. Within this sensitivity I possess, there is the gift of insight. This is my key to the door that has locked all Jewish women out—out of life. And, when I make it all the way, not only will I have opened the door wide, but perhaps if my Jewish sisters wake up, together we shall break that door down—and free all Jewish women from their Yiddish death! This death door is rusty and tight, but I believe that feminine strength can put it to its doom! The Jewish woman has a hell of a lot of inner strength, and it's about time she knew it, and used it!

At 19 I married a very wonderful man. He has also gone through much hell in his struggle for inner freedom. Also, since he too is a Jew, we have much in common. And, with the love we have found together, we have gained a deeper understanding of the Jew as a whole. Understanding one's people is a necessary step to understanding oneself.

Our lovely daughter has been our wisest teacher. She is a free being, knows no contradiction, and the love of life sparkles within her eyes. She is the New Jewish Woman. For I understand. But, do my Jewish sisters understand? Do they give a damn that their kids are caught within a burning hell even before they are born? Do my sisters realize that these innocent babies become a part of a murderous cycle which slowly and quietly destroys their lives?

The Jewish middle class is a death trap. The destruction of a Jewish girl is very, very silently accomplished. And this murder is thorough! Femininity is so deeply oppressed, that scapegoating is easily carried out. The MALE IS GOD! He knows all, and will be obeyed. The Jewish female is property, she cannot, and will not be *who* she is. Just *what* he makes her.

How in the hell can any Jewish woman love herself if she is absolutely nothing within the culture? Therefore, she remains in chains and is destroyed, and destroys her offspring as well. Here is that vicious cycle that continues on and on and on. . . .

When a Jewish woman is destroyed, no one is aware of the viciousness involved; not even she herself. Since she is destroyed from *within*, nothing can shake up that middle-class enslavement. Hitler did outwardly to all Jews, male and female, what the Jewish male does inwardly to the Jewish woman. It's as horrible as that! And this is why the Jewish woman is so caught. What she cannot see, she cannot understand. What she feels she cannot express in words. She has nowhere to go, and no one to turn to. Within that Jewish middle class the women exist in a psychological concentration camp!

It is said that lower-class people have to pull themselves out of the gutter. The middle-class Jewish woman is not only in the gutter, but she is in that gutter in a coffin with the lid nailed down! This is the hell she has to fight her way out of. That is exactly what I have done. And, I am damn proud of myself, indeed!

Here I sit. I am asking myself whether there are any women out there who understand what I have said above, and how I feel? I have completely given up all relationships with the middle-class Jews. They are a pack of destroyed girls who care about no one, not even themselves. They exist day by day, and haven't the slightest conception of life. They cannot think or feel, and therefore I will not waste my time and energy trying to relate to brick walls!

So, where do I belong? A lonely nebbish Jew with a hell of a lot to give, but to who? Will the women of the liberation movement accept me? Or, will they laugh and turn away? Am I good enough? I want so much to be accepted, so that I can give of my self to a cause so worthy of life—the liberation of all women all over the world!

My story, of course, does not end here. An individual revolution must continue and become a part of a larger revolution. This society may isolate everyone, but life does not!

My sisters, I need you, and I believe you need me. The Woman's Liberation Movement must grow and gain recognition. It is about time the world got a taste of femininity! Indeed, it is certainly about time women realized how beautiful and strong they really are.

The Politics of Housework

PAT MAINARDI

(1968, revised 1970)

Though women do not complain of the power of husbands,
each complains of her own husband, or of the husbands of her
friends. It is the same in all other cases of servitude; at least
in the commencement of the emancipatory movement. The
serfs did not at first complain of the power of the lords, but
only of their tyranny.
        —John Stuart Mill, *On the Subjection of Women*

Liberated women—very different from Women's Liberation!
The first signals all kinds of goodies, to warm the hearts (not
to mention other parts) of the most radical men. The other
signals—HOUSEWORK. The first brings sex without marriage,
sex before marriage, cozy housekeeping arrangements ("You
see, I'm living with this chick") and the self-content of knowing that you're not the kind of man who wants a doormat
instead of a woman. That will come later. After all, who wants
that old commodity anymore, the Standard American Housewife, all husband, home and kids. The New Commodity, the
Liberated Woman, has sex a lot and has a Career, preferably
something that can be fitted in with the household chores—
like dancing, pottery, or painting.

On the other hand is Women's Liberation—and housework.
What? You say this is all trivial? Wonderful! That's what I
thought. It seemed perfectly reasonable. We both had careers,
both had to work a couple of days a week to earn enough to
live on, so why shouldn't we share the housework? So I suggested it to my mate and he agreed—most men are too hip to
turn you down flat. You're right, he said. It's only fair.

Then an interesting thing happened. I can only explain it by
stating that we women have been brainwashed more than even

we can imagine. Probably too many years of seeing television women in ecstasy over their shiny waxed floors or breaking down over their dirty shirt collars. Men have no such conditioning. They recognize the essential fact of housework right from the very beginning. Which is that it stinks.

Here's my list of dirty chores: buying groceries, carting them home and putting them away; cooking meals and washing dishes and pots; doing the laundry, digging out the place when things get out of control; washing floors. The list could go on but the sheer necessities are bad enough. All of us have to do these things, or get some one else to do them for us. The longer my husband contemplated these chores, the more repulsed he became, and so proceeded the change from the normally sweet considerate Dr. Jekyll into the crafty Mr. Hyde who would stop at nothing to avoid the horrors of—housework. As he felt himself backed into a corner laden with dirty dishes, brooms, mops and reeking garbage, his front teeth grew longer and pointier, his fingernails haggled and his eyes grew wild. Housework trivial? Not on your life! Just try to share the burden.

So ensued a dialogue that's been going on for several years. Here are some of the high points:

"I don't mind sharing the housework, but I don't do it very well. We should each do the things we're best at."

MEANING unfortunately I'm no good at things like washing dishes or cooking. What I do best is a little light carpentry, changing light bulbs, moving furniture (how often do you move furniture?).

ALSO MEANING Historically the lower classes (Black men and us) have had hundreds of years experience doing menial jobs. It would be a waste of manpower to train someone else to do them now.

ALSO MEANING I don't like the dull stupid boring jobs, so you should do them.

"I don't mind sharing the work, but you'll have to show me how to do it."

MEANING I ask a lot of questions and you'll have to show me everything everytime I do it because I don't remember so good. Also don't try to sit down and read while I'M doing my jobs because I'm going to annoy hell out of you until it's easier to do them yourself.

"We used to be so happy!" (Said whenever it was his turn to do something).

MEANING I used to be so happy.

MEANING Life without housework is bliss. No quarrel here. Perfect agreement.

"We have different standards, and why should I have to work to your standards. That's unfair."

MEANING If I begin to get bugged by the dirt and crap I will say "This place sure is a sty" or "How can anyone live like this?" and wait for your reaction. I know that all women have a sore called "Guilt over a messy house" or "Household work is ultimately my responsibility." I know that men have caused that sore—if anyone visits and the place is a sty, they're not going to leave and say, "He sure is a lousy housekeeper." You'll take the rap in any case. I can outwait you.

ALSO MEANING I can provoke innumerable scenes over the housework issue. Eventually doing all the housework yourself will be less painful to you than trying to get me to do half. Or I'll suggest we get a maid. She will do my share of the work. You will do yours. It's women's work.

"I've got nothing against sharing the housework, but you can't make me do it on your schedule."

MEANING Passive resistance. I'll do it when I damned well please, if at all. If my job is doing dishes, it's easier to do them once a week. If taking out laundry, once a month. If washing the floors, once a year. If you don't like it, do it yourself oftener, and then I won't do it at all.

"I hate it more than you. You don't mind it so much."

MEANING Housework is garbage work. It's the worst crap I've ever done. It's degrading and humiliating for someone of *my* intelligence to do it. But for someone of *your* intelligence.
. . .

"Housework is too trivial to even talk about."

MEANING It's even more trivial to do. Housework is beneath my status. My purpose in life is to deal with matters of significance. Yours is to deal with matters of insignificance. You should do the housework.

"This problem of housework is not a man-woman problem. In any relationship between two people one is going to have a stronger personality and dominate."

MEANING That stronger personality had better be *me*.

"In animal societies, wolves, for example, the top animal is usually a male even where he is not chosen for brute strength

but on the basis of cunning and intelligence. Isn't that interesting?"

MEANING I have historical, psychological, anthropological and biological justification for keeping you down. How can you ask the top wolf to be equal?

"Women's Liberation isn't really a political movement."

MEANING The Revolution is coming too close to home.

ALSO MEANING I am only interested in how I am oppressed, not how I oppress others. Therefore the war, the draft and the university are political. Women's Liberation is not.

"Man's accomplishments have always depended on getting help from other people, mostly women. What great man would have accomplished what he did if he had to do his own housework?"

MEANING Oppression is built into the system and I as the white American male receive the benefits of this system. I don't want to give them up.

POSTSCRIPT

Participatory democracy begins at home. If you are planning to implement your politics, there are certain things to remember.

1. He *is* feeling it more than you. He's losing some leisure and you're gaining it. The measure of your oppression is his resistance.

2. A great many American men are not accustomed to doing monotonous repetitive work which never issues in any lasting let alone important achievement. This is why they would rather repair a cabinet than wash dishes. If human endeavors are like a pyramid with man's highest achievements at the top, then keeping oneself alive is at the bottom. Men have always had servants (us) to take care of this bottom strata of life while they have confined their efforts to the rarefied upper regions. It is thus ironic when they ask of women—where are your great painters, statesmen, etc. Mme Matisse ran a millinery shop so he could paint. Mrs. Martin Luther King kept his house and raised his babies.

3. It is a traumatizing experience for someone who has always thought of himself as being against any oppression or

exploitation of one human being by another to realize that in his daily life he has been accepting and implementing (and benefiting from) this exploitation; that his rationalization is little different from that of the racist who says "black people don't feel pain" (Women don't mind doing the shitwork); and that the oldest form of oppression in history has been the oppression of 50% of the population by the other 50%.

4. Arm yourself with some knowledge of the psychology of oppressed peoples everywhere, and a few facts about the animal kingdom. I admit playing top wolf or who runs the gorillas is silly but as a last resort men bring it up all the time. Talk about bees. If you feel really hostile bring up the sex life of spiders. They have sex. She bites off his head.

The psychology of oppressed peoples is not silly. Jews, immigrants, black men and all women have employed the same psychological mechanisms to survive: admiring the oppressor, glorifying the oppressor, wanting to be like the oppressor, wanting the oppressor to like them, mostly because the oppressor held all the power.

5. In a sense, all men everywhere are slightly schizoid—divorced from the reality of maintaining life. This makes it easier for them to play games with it. It is almost a cliché that women feel greater grief at sending a son off to war or losing him to that war because they bore him, suckled him, and raised him. The men who foment those wars did none of those things and have a more superficial estimate of the worth of human life. One hour a day is a low estimate of the amount of time one has to spend "keeping" oneself. By foisting this off on others, man has seven hours a week—one working day more to play with his mind and not his human needs. Over the course of generations it is easy to see whence evolved the horrifying abstractions of modern life.

6. With the death of each form of oppression, life changes and new forms evolve. English aristocrats at the turn of the century were horrified at the idea of enfranchising working men—were sure that it signalled the death of civilization and a return to barbarism. Some workingmen were even deceived by this line. Similarly with the minimum wage, abolition of slavery, and female suffrage. Life changes but it goes on. Don't fall for any line about the death of everything if men take a turn at the dishes. They will imply that you are holding back

the Revolution (their Revolution). But you are advancing it (your Revolution).

7. Keep checking up. Periodically consider who's actually *doing* the jobs. These things have a way of backsliding so that a year later once again the woman is doing everything. After a year make a list of jobs the man has rarely if ever done. You will find cleaning pots, toilets, refrigerators and ovens high on the list. Use time sheets if necessary. He will accuse you of being petty. He is above that sort of thing—(housework). Bear in mind what the worst jobs are, namely the ones that have to be done every day or several times a day. Also the ones that are dirty—it's more pleasant to pick up books, newspapers, etc. than to wash dishes. Alternate the bad jobs. It's the daily grind that gets you down. Also make sure that you don't have the responsibility for the housework with occasional help from him. "I'll cook dinner for you tonight" implies it's really your job and isn't he a nice guy to do some of it for you.

8. Most men had a rich and rewarding bachelor life during which they did not starve or become encrusted with crud or buried under the litter. There is a taboo that says that women mustn't strain themselves in the presence of men—we haul around 50 pounds of groceries if we have to but aren't allowed to open a jar if there is someone around to do it for us. The reverse side of the coin is that men aren't supposed to be able to take care of themselves without a woman. Both are excuses for making women do the housework.

9. Beware of the double whammy. He won't do the little things he always did because you're now a "Liberated Woman," right? Of course he won't do anything else either. . . .

I was just finishing this when my husband came in and asked what I was doing. Writing a paper on housework. Housework? he said, *Housework?* Oh my god how trivial can you get. A paper on housework.

LITTLE POLITICS OF HOUSEWORK QUIZ

The lowest job in the army, used as punishment is a) working 9–5 b) kitchen duty (K.P.).

When a man lives with his family, his a) father b) mother does his housework.

When he lives with a woman, a) he b) she does the housework.

a) His son b) His daughter learns preschool how much fun it is to iron daddy's handkerchief.

From the N. Y. *Times*, 9/21/69: "Former Greek Official George Mylonas pays the penalty for differing with the ruling junta in Athens by performing household chores on the island of Amorgos where he lives in forced exile." (With hilarious photo of a miserable Mylonas carrying his own water.) What the *Times* means is that he ought to have a) indoor plumbing b) a maid.

Dr. Spock said (*Redbook* 3/69): "Biologically and temperamentally, I believe, women were made to be concerned first and foremost with child care, husband care, and home care." Think about a) *who* made us b) why? c) what is the effect on their lives d) what is the effect on our lives?

From *Time* 1/5/70: "Like their American counterparts, many housing project housewives are said to suffer from neurosis. And for the first time in Japanese history, many young husbands today complain of being henpecked. Their wives are beginning to demand detailed explanations when they don't come home straight from work and some Japanese males nowadays are even compelled to do housework." According to *Time*, women become neurotic a) when they are forced to do the maintenance work for the male caste all day every day of their lives or b) when they no longer want to do the maintenance work for the male caste all day every day of their lives.

The Bar As Microcosm*

SHULAMITH FIRESTONE

THE FUNCTION OF THE BAR

The bar is the male kingdom. For centuries it was the bastion of male privilege, the gathering place for men away from their women, a place where men could go to freely indulge in The Bull Session—which, like the Hartyhar Clubcar Joke, the running down of the latest shifty tricks of the blacks or the Jews, has a serious political function: the release of the guilty anxiety of the oppressor class. In this case, the bar functioned as an even more sorely needed refuge, for, unlike the racial caste system, the sexual caste system suffered from an intolerable, yet unavoidable, flaw: The intimate nature of sexploitation, unlike the easy segregation of undesirable races, had continual psychological boomerang effects on the oppressor class. For women took advantage of their close and constant physical proximity to their oppressors to make men's lives miserable, paying them back in nasty little ways (gossip, nagging), rubbing their noses in their own arrogance, making them feel guilty, and so on—forcing men to seek (usually a daily) release in "the bar scene." Thus the bar became a necessary buttress institution to male supremacy, a place where men could go to get their own back, and reshore a constantly battered-upon privilege.

Today, thanks to the early feminist movement, this essentially anti-woman function of the bar has been soft-pedaled, blurred over, and combined with other social functions (café, dance or music hall, restaurant) to form the modern bar. But, especially in working-class neighborhood bars, the more open bigotry of the nineteenth century still lingers. For example, a classic bar sign I saw there recently listed the drinker's weekly budget: beer, $10.00, dog food, $2.00, and wife, $1.68, in that order. The appeal to nineteenth-century women of the temperance movement that led to Prohibition, that it drained off so much of the potential radical feminist, or even just the suffrage movement, is attributable to the sheer economics of the problem: In a day when women had no civil or legal rights, when even the basest service jobs were closed to them, male alcoholism-chauvinism became a serious threat to their survival —of far more immediate importance than an abstract equality with men, or even than the concrete issue of the vote. In this light, Swinging Carrie was not ludicrous or puritan at all: she was simply attacking a foremost bastion of male supremacy, which kept millions of women in wracking economic poverty.

AND HOW THE BAR FUNCTIONS

The hierarchy of The Bar is that of the larger male world. At the top is the Owner(s). In his pocket is the Clientele; but The Customer Is Always Right. The Boss, if he is smart, does not hang around his own place too much, coming in only on big nights, or when The Help is getting slack. For that would expose his nervous anxiety about how well his Establishment is being run—making him appear vulnerable—as well as making everyone below him nervous. So he hires a decoy, a tough Bartender(s) to do his dirty work for him—who, because he has no vested interest, can generally do it better. The bartenders are ranked on the basis of experience, toughness, "smarts"; they must be able to handle many situations rougher than mixing a good drink, though they must be skilled at that too. Below the bartenders are the Bouncers, the Doormen, and any other (usually transient) male personnel. Then, on the outer edge of the Establishment, are the Musicians—when there are any—treated well only if they are bringing in lots of money. And finally, the Waitress, everyone's whipping girl.

In this male hierarchy, the waitress is at the bottom. Her job is transient, fly-by-night. In some places, she can make a lot of money. But the risks are great. Sound familiar? It is. The Cocktail Waitress in relation to The Bar holds the same position as the prostitute class in the larger male world. In fact, much of her function is literally that of the prostitute, minus (though very often including) actual sex: the doling out of sympathy and small ego-buildups to men wanting to repair their bruised Egos away from Home. Yet she is not only Whore, member of the sexual service class; she is also literally service class. She is, after all, a waitress. She has to serve people. Like the geisha, she has a rough job to do, while appearing to be at ease. The glamour is only an added work function, essentially packaging, to spare the male the unpleasantness of watching his work-horse grow dull and complaining under his eyes. And this glamour, while seemingly only dressing, has a specific political function: It stereotypes the woman into her Bunny role, making her all but invisible as an individual human being. A man may vaguely recollect a soft bosom or a pretty smile as he lurches out the door, but essentially *he never saw her:* She has been successfully transformed into her role. This is most clearly revealed when she accidentally messes up her service function—"There goes *her* tip!" The minute she accidentally spills something on his pants, she is no longer even "that cute little waitress," but rather "the lousy service in this place."

Also in the category of women within the male establishment are the literal prostitutes, to be found in abundance especially in the lower type bars. Though held in contempt, they too at least have a definite place in the male hierarchy; in fact, the male world could not function without them: Not only is the presence of some "chicks" necessary at all times to maintain cockmanship and other Male Ego trips, but they function politically as a buffer to keep the sexual caste system running smoothly, by repairing and erasing the daily petty attacks on the Male Ego executed by the Wives. Because of these essential functions, the hustler feels secure enough at the bar to drink heavily, be loud or conspicuous in manner, imperious with waitresses, friendly (flirtatious) enough with the bartender to wheedle free drinks or sob on his shoulder.

But, how do women in general relate to this male establishment? In our time women are—in most places—admitted to The Bar. But only on certain conditions: That is, on the arm of an Escort, on the strength of the man who accompanies them, much as the black is allowed into an exclusive club if accompanied by a card-carrying member. Even this occasional excursion into the male domain is a recent innovation, as we have seen. And, ironically, like the "sexual revolution" in general, all these first signs of breakdown of the sexual caste system have been converted by men into supports for that very system. In the case of wives, Lets-Have-a-Drink has been found to be a useful appeasement tactic ("You see, dear, I don't do anything more glamorous out here than you do at home," or "You see, dear, how you are included in all aspects of my life"), and in the case of "dates," it is useful in snowing them with all the power and glamour of the male world ("See how at ease I am in this important and frightening world" . . . . the better to seduce you with, my dear . . .), or to show them off, a rather more important function. (A beautiful girl is brought up to the bar at a canter. "Isn't she a beaut? Now I ask you. . . ." "Magnificent!" agrees the bartender. "Honey, soon as you get tired of this old man of yours, I'm waiting with open arms. . . ." The girl blushes, and is trotted out. "The old son-of-a-bitch," mumbles the bartender under his breath. "I don't know where he finds them.")

Then there are the less respectable women, those not leashed to clearcut owners. These women occupy a peculiar limbo, for they are neither of the women's world, nor are they the women of the men's world (like the Waitress-Whore). They vary in "looseness" from the Occasional Pickup Girls—who, scared and shy, come in pairs to huddle at darkened corner tables, wavering in their choice of a drink—to (a few months or years later) their more experienced sisters, the hardened Pickups, who, still young enough to "get laid," are by now old enough to know they won't find love. Often they have the beginnings of that weary look, like a whore's ("Not bad in the sack, if you put a bag over her head").

The female "bar-fly" is a modern phenomenon which mirrors the position of the modern woman who has tried, against all male resistance, to carve a place for herself in the male world. Most women instinctively feel uncomfortable in The Bar; seeing that they are not wanted there, they stay away. But there are always those few obdurate ones who resist their own emotional vibes and all warnings (from her mother on down to Helen Gurley Brown, every girl has been told that, though bars are male watering places rich in prey, a girl who meets her man there can expect only the most limited and exploitative relationships) to insist that this world belongs to them as much as to any man. These women pay a stiff price for ignoring the unwritten sexual caste taboos: they become a peculiar hybrid, accepted by neither men nor women. Eventually the constant rejection begins to tell: they lose all humanity—much less desirability.

THROUGH THE EYES OF THE COCKTAIL WAITRESS

Of all these supplementary roles that women play vis-à-vis The Bar—the respectable wife, hidden safely away except for an occasional jaunt, the loose "chick," gradually becoming "shopworn" and contemptible, the literal hustler, hardnosed and generally ignored, when not in use, that is, and finally the service-class waitress-whore—the Cocktail Waitress perhaps best exemplifies woman's role in the male world.

Like the black domestic, the cocktail waitress sees more of what goes on than anyone ever realizes. Her job depends on her knowing the mechanics of The Bar—and on seeming not to know them. She keeps a trained eye on brawls and marital spats. She watches uptight couples in careful clothes exchange polite date talk—all the while knowing that the man is worrying about the price of the drink, the woman about the choice of the drink (the perennial question of the Woman at The Bar: What sort of drink shall I choose to make me appear neither an experienced drinker, nor a virginal one?). She must be hip to all the little intricacies of personal taste: which sort of people go for the Casual Beer Stein approach, and which for the Fancy Napkin Treatment; which get annoyed at a cluttered table, and which like to keep empty glasses for show. She has to guess who is secretly craving extra maraschinos, and who is searching for the john. Her tips, her very job, depends upon her thus psyching out her Customers.

She must understand all the different games of the male world, some of which include her directly (the various types of flirtation) and some of which do not (such as the Fight-for-the Check Game, in which it is up to her to size up who is bluffing most). She must act as a go-between, using her feminine charm as a neutralizer in male power struggles (to a poor jazz buff cringing at a corner table: "I'm sorry, sir, if this were my place, believe me, I'd say to hell with the two-drink minimum . . . because I respect people who come just for the music, I really do . . . but (Wry Smile) it's this *job*. . . .")

Diplomat, servant, worker, whore, she must have her eyes everywhere at once, keep a firm grip on her tips (yes, they do steal candy from babies and tips from waitresses), and always maintain a coolly practical head. (Ironically, perhaps the *most* practical aspect of her exceedingly down-to-earth job is her simulated giddy appearance.) Though she may have been holding the place up singlehandedly for years, she must never get familiar with her job (asking for free drinks), instead blushing constantly grateful. She must never say what she *really* thinks at any time: She must never really like any of her customers, nor, say, really dig the music; she must *pretend* to. (The difference is immediately detectable to The Management.) Any mistake made must be immediately acknowledged as hers. If the cash didn't tally, it must be her fault. If a drink is spilled, she did it. If her feet are aching, her bills sloshed with beer, her head buzzing with too many orders at once, she must still *smile*. And she must smile equally at everyone, for they are all important, because they are all above her.

Like the girls of the brothel, The Management wants its girls *fresh*. A major requirement of her job is that she tease and turn on the customers—yet at the same time remain unavailable. Thus, she must also learn how to deal with the resulting perverted lust—lewd words, gestures, propositions—without insulting or appearing insulted; indeed, she soon learns to control it by appearing charmed, flattered. (All the while thinking, "You unoriginal bastard, you think you're the only one who ever noticed my cleavage when I bend over. . . . Seven different tables clamoring for drinks—from Singapore Slings to Black Russians with cream on the side—and I got to put up with this bullshit . . . trip to Florida, my eye, I'll be lucky to get a tip out of you. . . .")

But even more important than titillating the customers, she must keep the management charmed. Very often the price of her job is intercourse, or at least heavy petting and dope in the backroom with one or more of those above her; but this is dangerous, even if she didn't have to keep it balanced with the more drudge aspects of her job, for the easing of friction between the various levels of the male power structure is difficult enough to handle without creating new sexual rivalries. Unless she is making it with the Big Boss himself—but then her time is measured, for eventually he will tire of her in favor of another—and will be glad to let the others go for her throat, thereby neatly getting rid of her and guilt at once. The loss of erotic appeal in becoming the Big Boss' "old lady" is something few waitresses survive.

So that many waitresses, instead of tampering with the high explosive of Sex-with-the-Management, prefer to take their chances with the Hard-to-Get Approach, appearing susceptible to propositions from The Management, yet keeping them dangling, somehow always managing to remain unavailable. ("Gee, Larry, you know I'd adore having breakfast with you, only I'm a . . . just a teeny bit *involved* now . . . you know how it is. . . . But you're the first to know the minute it's through (Embrace). . . .") But this too is dangerous. Eventually they catch on. Whichever why she becomes Unavailable, losing her erotic appeal, she has had it.

So whatever she does about Sex, it is only a question of time. Even when she truly succeeds at her job, even when she is tough, experienced, shrewd under a stupid exterior, diplomatic, supersexy (and clever at handling it), there is always the day when someone above her takes a shine to a cute little piece of ass who just walked in (shyly) looking for her job. Because a fresh piece is better than a tired one beginning to blend into The Bar.

And then one day it's, "Um, Carol, see me before you punch out, ok. I've been meaning to speak to you about . . ." or, "Look, Linda, we won't be needing you anymore on Thursday nights" . . . and then on Friday nights, and then on Saturday nights. The spell has worn off. She finds herself changed from "glamorous" cocktail waitress to poor domestic: Don't bother to come in.

Lesbians Are Sisters

Nanette Rainone, Martha Shelley, Lois Hart

An interview with Martha Shelley and Lois Hart on the WBAI-New York radio program Womankind. *The discussion is the relationship between lesbianism and feminism. The interviewer is Nanette Rainone, creator of the radio program* Womankind.

NANETTE: This week I've invited two women here. They are Martha Shelley and Lois Hart. They are lesbians and members of the Gay Liberation Front. They are also involved in the Women's Liberation movement. What we're going to get into today is the relationship between lesbianism and feminism. When I called Lois last week about this program, I displayed in a very short time that I was particularly ignorant about this relationship and, more important than that, that I was afraid of it. I think that I am typical of women who are in the women's movement and that my response might be typical of what theirs would be.

I think, and Lois you can say whether this is fair or not, that what I was expressing was confusion over whether lesbianism can be considered a choice that a person makes and in that sense a political position, comparable, let's say, to some women as feminists separating from men or having less relationships with men or a different relationship than they had had previously. And that I wasn't sure that it was a choice and therefore whether it was open to discussion as a political position on feminism. Is that a fair expression?

LOIS: Well, that was part of what happened to us on the phone. We can talk about that part and I'll sort of repeat myself, and then Martha can say what she wants to say. I see two levels to this. At one level you can discuss it as something political. At another level, loving another woman is no more a choice than a man loving a woman. It's spontaneous, emotional, physical sensuality, and at that level I don't think we have choices. I think we just respond and are. At another level, there is a political aspect to it. And that is, in living with another woman, and in developing a relationship with another woman, there's a whole different set of dynamics. I don't have to deal with a lot of my own feelings of oppression as when I'm with a man. I don't have to deal with that part of me that's been trained to respond to men in certain ways and to have certain emotional reactions toward men. It's very clear to me, when I'm with another woman, that I am responsible for myself. Totally responsible for myself. I experience myself that way. I see that as a political thing.

NANETTE: Are you then saying that you feel yourself freer in a relationship with another woman than you could feel in a relationship with a male?

LOIS: Yes. I think a lot of women accept their ego identity and accept their lot. The woman feels that if the man is successful, somehow she's successful. She never experiences herself other than through him. You can call this political or psychological. You can call it anything you want. But it is an extremely important stance for a woman to remove herself from that.

MARTHA: I see this as political in the same sense; for instance, you take an older black person living in the South, who all his life has adopted a shuffle, an obsequious attitude towards white people in a certain series of relationships with them, and a corresponding series of relationships with black people. Now, this person isn't aware of himself making choices in a certain situation, but nevertheless, looked at from the outside, it's obvious that he's adopted certain roles for the sake of survival. He's living those roles. His whole self-image is bound up in those roles. He's never seen alternative choices. And yet the whole process goes on unconsciously. Within that same culture you can find a certain number of black people who are somewhat rebellious, who either come North or end up being martyrs or lynched, or start organizing a local chapter of the NAACP or of CORE or start something else. I think you can see the lesbian in a political sense as unconsciously propelled by whatever hidden motivations—say as a rebel against the accepted mores of society. This is a political decision, even if it happens on an unconscious level.

NANETTE: Well, I've been at feminist meetings where the subject of lesbianism has come up. And my response, spoken or not, has often been that lesbian relationships—woman-to-woman relationships—often take on the pattern of dominance-submission, so that one woman will play a male role and the other a female role. I cannot see this as an alternative. It seems to me this takes on a greater distortion in a sense than it does in a normal man-woman relationship.

LOIS: Why do you say a greater distortion? Why is it a greater distortion among two women than between a man and a woman?

NANETTE: Well, because the woman who is taking on the male role is going beyond the conventional role that society forces the man into, and—I don't know why. I'll tell you. No, I don't know why I said that.

MARTHA: Because somehow it seems more natural for a man to take on a man's role in society. If a woman takes it on, it seems a gross distortion and unnatural.

LOIS: But there is a distortion. There's no question about it. I can't think it's any more distorted in one case than in the other. Male homosexuals and female—they're part of a society that dictates patterns of submission and domination. I mean, that's the hang-up right there. People pick up on models of behavior. It's the root of women's oppression. It's the root of gay oppression. These heterosexual images of male domination and female submission. So you respond in terms of these rules, because people lack alternatives, until you grow to a point where you can throw off these rules and start being yourself.

NANETTE: Are you suggesting that for a woman who is heterosexual—and for many women the choice never appears . . .

LOIS: . . . on a conscious level.

MARTHA: I would say that there are many heterosexual women who are as independent as any women you can find and whose rebelliousness or whose challenge to the established system comes out in another direction than, let's say, in the choice of lovers. I would say that this is one particular area—there are other areas, too—where you can rebel, where you can express yourself. There are other patterns of behavior where you can challenge the system. Some people have to challenge in one area but maintain security and a connection to their culture in another area.

LOIS: There is something, though, in the fact that if a woman has so totally taken on the psychological taboo of not loving another woman, it's . . . it's a hang-up for her. It's one of the things that alienates her from other women. I was in a Women's Liberation group that finally began to deal with our feelings for each other in terms of just warmth and sensuality. Most of the women said this caused them—it was just terrifying for them. It was so much easier to put your arms around a man, you know, than around each other. It doesn't mean that there are no feelings there. We broke through this one night. There were tears. There was reaching out. There was closeness. The group parted shortly thereafter. We've met individually and talked about it, but there's a lot of terror there. It doesn't mean that you're not going to be a strong woman, not going to be a radical woman. Yet I think all of us, if our sensuality and responses were totally freed, would be that much stronger and that much more creative.

NANETTE: Tell me something. All and all in the feminist movement, what are the vibrations you have felt? Have you felt they will accept lesbianism in the movement? Or do you think that there is fear? And what do you think this means to the movement if they will not accept it?

MARTHA: Well, from what I've seen, I've observed various groups of women with different attitudes on the subject. In New York, I've found quite a number of women who are willing to accept lesbians into the movement, but who are themselves cut off from experiencing this for themselves. I've also found a number of other women who are pretty panicky about lesbians. I think outside New York you get a lot more panic. I just got a letter from a girl in Minneapolis who's in a Women's Liberation group, who's just discovered she's a lesbian and who knows very well that she couldn't possibly tell the other women in the group because they would all panic, and throw her out. So she wrote to me asking for help.

I told her what information I had about other Women's Liberation groups and tried to somehow help her adjust to being a lesbian.

NANETTE: Well, sometimes the fear is an image fear. I was at, the taping of a program the other day, and a man had been on the panel. He was not attacked by a group of feminists but they asked him some hard questions and were critical of him, and after the program was over he stood up and he said, "Those sick dikes!" You see, I was among them and this was the response, and there is a fear to that response, that you're going to be cut off from any legitimacy. But somehow we are going to have to deal with that in ourselves.

LOIS: Think of what you just said: "Cut off from any legitimacy." And it's true, the whole basis of your sense of yourself as a woman is being responsive to a man as a sexual object. You have no legitimacy unless you let yourself be fucked by a man. And that's like the whole male thing coming down on us again. The *horror* of being a dike. The *horror* of being a lesbian. Cosmically, we're damned. It's a terrible fear to deal with. Let me just say one thing in terms of the dichotomy—the kinds of experience I've had in Women's Liberation. It's again an *age* kind of dichotomy. You see it in life styles of the older woman, the professional woman, the NOW [National Organization for Women] woman. As Women's Liberation gets younger and more radical, the life style will change. It's a kind of expansion thing—as you go closer toward the younger end of the spectrum.

Let me tell you what I got from women at Atlantic City who shied away because of my masculine attire. You could just see them cringe at the word "lesbianism"—like it had no room in their middle class houses at all. Then you get from a woman who intellectually understands that there is nothing wrong, but she still can't deal with it emotionally— to some of the younger women who don't have to deal with these things, like virginity. Virginity used to be a terribly, terribly crucial problem. I mean it's laughable now. I think the same kind of thing is happening in other areas. I saw young women at one of the Women's Liberation meetings of Redstockings talking openly about how they're trying to deal with these things and saying that, if they could only get together sexually, they wouldn't have some of the many problems that they're having. I feel that it's something that's changing in and of itself, somehow, as part of our total consciousness changes.

MARTHA: I think also that if a man stands up and he gives opinions which are, say, counter to the general silent majority type of opinions, it's pretty rare that he'll be called a homosexual. Or that somehow he'll be required to prove his manhood. It happens. But it doesn't happen quite that frequently. As soon as a woman stands up independently, immediately she has to prove, quote, her "womanhood," . . . that's it, that's the legitimacy thing.

NANETTE: Well, I was covering a story the other day which involved a Puerto Rican community. There was the insurgent group of young men, Spanish men. Then there was the establishment figure, who was also Spanish. And the way they dealt with him was by calling him "faggot." Now, the Spanish culture has more of what they always refer to as *machismo*, a more masculine image. So I think that there is that assault, but I think you're right, that it's more frequent to women. And I suppose that I know it, because when I'm going to someplace to speak as a feminist, I go out of my way to look feminine. One thing that puzzles me is: can a woman make the choice? Is lesbianism something that you can make a choice about? Can a woman who has been heterosexual all her life, but honestly enters this problem in a feminist organization, for example, if you're going to be warm with people, it might become a physical relationship. Can one make a choice? Is there a point where you make a choice? Or does it just happen?

LOIS: Let's say you're going into a feminist organization and you realize you're having problems getting close. So you're entering sensitivity groups together, and you start touching, and essentially you're having feelings. You keep talking about it as if you can make some sort of political choice. If you have as few feelings toward women as you're expressing, well, let's say forget it. Or maybe you can, but I don't think it's going to work out as a human relationship. Well, ask yourself: have you experienced feelings towards women? That's the only way a woman can answer that. If she realizes that she does have warm feelings toward a woman, but that there's a lot of fear, a lot of blockage there. I mean you can make a choice, just like freeing yourself up in a certain direction. But if you look at yourself and you totally register no feelings, that area of sensuality is totally blocked in you. Then, it seems to me if you make that kind of decision on the head level, you're being destructive to yourself.

NANETTE: But wouldn't it be true the other way around? Let's say, if a woman is only having relationships with other women and not with men, then doesn't it apply the other way? Doesn't that become its own block?

MARTHA: Well, yes, I think so. If I found myself completely blocked off from being able to appreciate a man physically or relate normally to a man, I call that a block too. On the other hand, I do feel that in the current society I will be much more comfortable and happy being blocked off from men, who I consider my oppressors, than from being blocked off from women, who I consider my equals in the struggle. So, if I can't relate to my equals, that's important to me.

NANETTE: May I ask both of you what you discovered about yourselves that attracted you to women to the extent of having a sexual relationship with them?

LOIS: I can think back now to my fantasizing, even as a child, where I took on a male identification, and I was making love. I was having sexual fantasies. I was the aggressor. I was making love to the woman and . . .

NANETTE: Was there a third party? Was there a man present in the fantasy?

LOIS: I was the man.

NANETTE: I see. So that it was just two of you present. [Laughter] That interests me, because I have talked with other people about this, and I think sometimes a woman will have a fantasy where the man is present and another woman is present. In other words, she has the two parties, yet she will act the aggressor toward the woman. And that's a way of handling fantasizing.

LOIS: Yes, but at what age does that fantasizing start? I would think that would be an older fantasy. I don't think a grade school girl would fantasize that way. But an older woman, and by older, I mean someone in her teens, starts having those feelings. You start knowing because you know you're feeling in a certain way. It's how in touch you are with your own body, really. If you start feeling those things and you don't want to do them, they would start coming out on the fantasy level, and you start—or you know that threesomes are a sexual possibility. That's how you might make it all right for yourself to start thinking about balling another woman.

MARTHA: The presence of the man legitimizes your being allowed to play with the other woman. As long as there's a man present, then you're not homosexual. It's just sort of a swinger's game.

NANETTE: I think it's a way of loving yourself, too. Because women have a special problem of feeling that the sexual parts of their body are ugly and dirty in some sense, and so by a fantasy expressing love to another woman, you thereby express a love for yourself or an acceptance of yourself.

LOIS: Sure. And what a good political decision to make. To suddenly learn to make love to yourself or to another woman and to realize the beauty of your own body.

MARTHA: When I was a kid I used to go to the Brooklyn Museum. There was a statue of Hercules there. I don't remember whether he was standing there with a club or shooting a huge bow or something, and I was really enthralled by it, because I wanted to grow up to be big and strong and powerful like that. I wasn't interested in the statues of women because they were done sexy, and that was sort of against my Puritanical upbringing. But I really dug this power image. Later, when we grew up, it was a strange experience for me to find that I was attracted to women physically.

NANETTE: How does it occur to you? Does it just occur to you suddenly? Or is it something that you fight in yourself before you become aware of it?

MARTHA: Well, it started as a fantasy. For example, there was this German instructor. You know, the usual story of the German instructor. Fantasizing about her, partly because she was a powerful woman.

NANETTE: The identity is almost to get out of being what a woman is defined of in this society. In other words, it's not *not* to be a woman, but not to be what she has been defined as. So that when you identify with men, one way is to become a male, or rather, to take on the male role.

MARTHA: And this is kind of a bad bag. It's a bad trip. Because if you start identifying with men or rejecting yourself as a woman, what you are essentially doing is putting yourself down. Let's face it, unless you go through a sex change, you're born a woman and that's what you are. The thing to do is to become the kind of woman you want to be, rather than to become a man, and to realize that the role scene is for the birds.

NANETTE: Now, I suppose the way most women handle it is, they also want to be men in the sense that they want that identity with power and with the male ego—which is the only ego that exists, because, I guess, women don't have it. So the way they do that is by marrying and taking on his identity, his name—my husband is a doctor, sort of thing.

MARTHA: It's like becoming yes-man to the White House. I mean there you are standing around the center of power. A woman will do that with her husband or some other man. And a lot of guys will do that to some guy they consider a strong leader. Basically, it's a refusal to face the fact that you want to be stronger than you are.

NANETTE: We ought to get back to more general statements of the relationship between the Gay Liberation Front and the feminist movement, or just the relationship between lesbians and feminists. And maybe you'd like to make a general statement about that?

MARTHA: Well, the way I see it is that in order for women to liberate themselves they have to be liberated from their sexual roles. One of the ways they have to confront the oppression they get in their sexual roles is to confront alternatives, such as homosexuality. Part of the oppression is structured on the basis of homosexual versus heterosexual. Natural—what you're supposed to be—as opposed to unnatural. And this has got to be dealt with psychologically. So, I think that Gay Liberation is very important to Women's Liberation.

LOIS: I would just repeat what Martha said. The homosexual taboo is really like a last gateway. If you push Women's Liberation, and follow its logic to the end, what we're saying is to end all sexual roles. What we're saying is sexual freedom for everyone.

NANETTE: Well, it's an objection to sex casting in both cases.

LOIS: Exactly.

NANETTE: Of being told what you should be because you've been born this sex, and for women this takes on an especially degrading position, because the role is passive, non-intelligent, etcetera, etcetera, which we've said on any number of these programs. But the whole question is a sex-role and it's not being able to make free choices among a number of alternatives that realistically exist for people.

LOIS: More than that. I mean, we're talking about human liberation. And basically, what we're talking about is completely rejecting imposed definitions upon our humanity. I mean, we believe we're endless and infinite, in some kind of sense, and that we have the right to be ourselves, whatever that might be. It's human liberation, and it's for men and women, regardless of how they turned out, heterosexual or homosexual.

MARTHA: Yes, I think what we're fighting, in its broadest sense, is a form of racism, where, because you are born with a particular color, shape, sex, nationality, into a family with a particular religious orientation, you are automatically forced into a certain pattern. And with the gay thing, it's because of certain things that come up a bit later in life. But, nevertheless, it's ultimately a form of racism.

NANETTE: You see, I still get hung up in the same problem. Because the way I see the future, the post-revolutionary future, is a kind of bisexuality.

MARTHA: Okay with me.

NANETTE: But does that mean that I am therefore rejecting that a person be either heterosexual or homosexual? You see, I still see homosexual as being derivative of heterosexual, under the present circumstances. Because, when I say that the future will be bisexual, what I'm saying is that everybody will be that way, and I still see homosexuality now as a response to the heterosexual condition. I don't, I cannot see it, as growing of itself. I have to see it as a response, as a rejection of heterosexuality.

MARTHA: Frankly, I see heterosexuality as growing out of homosexual rejection in this society. I don't see how you can separate the two. Even if you look at the animal kingdom there's plenty of natural homosexuality around. And if you take either Sullivan's theory, or Freud's theory, homosexuality begins at an earlier stage of development. If you accept their theories, the problem is that homosexuality exists. The problem is that most people reject it and don't feel what they feel at a stage of development.

LOIS: Nanette, your assumption is that the heterosexual condition is the natural condition and anyone who is homosexual has to react against a bad . . .

NANETTE: No, I'm not assuming that, I'm assuming only that the conditioning for sexuality is so strong that under those circumstances . . .

LOIS: No, that's a false premise. Because, what it is, is the programming for heterosexuality has to be so strong, because people's sexual responses *are* so strong. I mean, why do you have to lay such a strong thing on people, not to be homosexual? I mean, there's a whole negative . . .

NANETTE: But are you saying that . . . ?

LOIS: Let me just talk about programming. The programming is to make you heterosexual, which has got to be a reaction against something. Why do you have to watch on your TV screen over and over again these rules, reinforced and reinforced? Why do homosexuals have to be painted in the kind of colors they are? Why did I know even as a child that there was something hideous and evil and ugly about homosexuality? That was put there for a reason. That was a conscious decision to create a society that worked. A society of workers and producers, with division of labor that maybe at one time was spiritually valid. But, even in those times when it was spiritually valid, I don't think it was ever considered the kind of threat that it has been, let's say, in the last hundred years—in this particular society, maybe a couple of hundred years. But I would say that heterosexuality is almost the other way, that it is a reaction against your sexuality. Your total sexuality.

MARTHA: It's a way of excluding part of your sexuality.

LOIS: And you and I both learned the same way. I mean we were born the same kind of sensual beings, and we both had a series of experiences. One turned you out more comfortable in your heterosexual responses—because of the people you met and the kinds of experiences. I was raised in the same society, with a different set of experiences, but I came out homosexual because, maybe I met groovier, more sensual women, or whatever, or because I've made the strong male identification. I don't know the whole complexity of it.

NANETTE: But you're not suggesting in all this that homosexuality would be a preference . . .

MARTHA: Why not?

NANETTE: . . . if there were open sexuality. It might be a preference to some people, but why would either type be a preference to anybody?

LOIS: Because of the people involved. Now, what you love is not necessarily the body. That's part of it. I mean, what you're responding to are the things you said, his or her way of life, their mind, their spiritual stand. I mean, we're not just bodies. So, what we're talking about, if we ever get through this prehistoric age, are human beings in relationships that could be much more fluid than what we're experiencing now. And we're going to be responding to a total person and what that person is into. And what's between the person's legs will probably have very little to do with it.

NANETTE: You might not even describe it that way. I mean you might say I love so-and-so, or I'm having an affair with so-and-so. But, you see, that's one of the problems of the pronouns. You always have to describe to somebody "she said," or "he said," and I've thought about that a lot and I can't think of what information it gives except prejudice. Because, if I was talking about Lois and I continued to say, "she said, she said," what information am I conveying? And so under total freedom, it wouldn't be important to describe the sex of the person. That would be incidental to the love of the person.

MARTHA: Right. Supposing in the future, where the people will be more free, you decided to spend a lot of your time investigating, say, theoretical math and neglected, say, poetry or music or something else. That would not necessarily mean that you were stuck in a particular bag, but that you were particularly interested in relating in this way. And whether you happen to choose at that point in your love life to be relating to one sex or the other wouldn't mean that you were stuck in a bag but that you were relating in a particular area and a particular style.

LOIS: I imagine our language—this point that you brought up—is going to change totally. Our names are an immediate indication of our sex, Miss, Mrs. or Mr.

NANETTE: And your marital status.

MARTHA: I think that if our consciousnesses get to the point where we realize that human beings are pretty much one kind of thing, a lot of words are going to drop out. Our consciousness will start being reflected in our language.

NANETTE: Thank you both very much.

ANALYSES OF THE MOVEMENT

Toward a Female Liberation Movement

BEVERLY JONES and JUDITH BROWN

PART I, *by Beverly Jones*

*Woman's steady march onward, and her growing desire
for a broader outlook, prove that she has not reached
her normal condition, and that society has not yet conceded all that is necessary for its attainment.*
    (Introduction, *A History of Woman Suffrage*, 1889)

THE MANIFESTO

For a middle-aged female accustomed to looking to militant
youth for radical leadership it was a shock to read the
Women's Manifesto which issued from the female caucus of
the national SDS convention last summer (1967; Manifesto
printed in *New Left Notes* of 10 July 1967). Here were a
group of "radical women" demanding respect and leadership
in a radical organization and coming on with soft-minded
NAACP logic and an Urban League list of grievances and
demands. One need only substitute the words "white" and
"black" for "male" and "female" respectively, replace references to SDS with the city council, and remember all the
fruitless approaches black groups made and are still making
to local white power groups to realize how ludicrous this
manifesto is.

To paraphrase accordingly,

1. Therefore we demand that our brothers on the city
council recognize that they must deal with their own prob-

lems of white chauvinism in their personal, social, and political relationships.

2. It is obvious from this meeting of the city council that full advantage is not being taken of the abilities and potential contributions of blacks. We call upon the black people to demand full participation in all aspects of local government from licking stamps to assuming leadership positions.

3. People in leadership positions must be aware of the dynamics of creating leadership and are responsible for cultivating all of the black resources available to the local government.

4. All University administrations must recognize that campus regulations discriminate against blacks in particular and must take positive action to protect the rights of black people.

And so on. The caucus goes on to charge *New Left Notes* with printing material on the subject, developing bibliographies, and asks the National Council to *set up a committee to study* the subject and report at a future date!

There is also a rather pathetic attempt on the part of the caucus to prove its credentials by mimicking the dominant group's rhetoric on power politics. Thus there ensues some verbiage about the capitalist world, the socialist world, and the third world in which it is implied that women are somehow better off under socialism.

It must have been disappointing indeed to the women who drew up the "analysis of women's role" and insisted it be printed verbatim in *New Left Notes* to find Castro quoted the following month in the *National Guardian* to the effect that he is assuredly grateful to the women of Cuba for having fought in the hills and otherwise aided the revolution, but now all that is past and women's place is once again servant to husband and children, in the home.

In a plea to the Women's Federation to hold down its goals of female integration into the greater Cuban society, he said, "But who will do the cooking for the child who still comes home for lunch? Who will nurse the babies or take care of the preschool child? Who will cook for the man when he comes home from work? Who will wash and clean and take care of things?"

The Women's Manifesto ends, and again we will substitute "white" for male and "black" for female:

"We seek the liberation of all human beings. The struggle for the liberation of blacks must be part of the larger fight for freedom. (A line which could better have been uttered by the city commission.) We recognize the difficulty our brothers will have in dealing with white chauvinism and we assume our full responsibility (as blacks) in helping to resolve the contradiction."

And lest the men get upset by all this wild talk, or even think of taking it seriously, the women add a reassuring note.

"Freedom now! We love you!"

What lessons are to be learned from this fantastic document, the discrimination which preceded it, and the unchanging scene which followed? I think the lessons are several and serious. I'd like to list them first and discuss each one separately.

1. People don't get radicalized (engaged with basic truths) fighting other people's battles.

2. The females in SDS (at least those who wrote the Manifesto) essentially reject an identification with their own sex and are using the language of female power in an attempt to advance themselves personally in the male power structure they are presently concerned with.

3. That for at least two reasons radical females do not understand the desperate condition of women in general. In the first place, as students they occupy some sexy, sexless, limbo area where they are treated by males in general with less discrimination than they will ever again face. And in the second place, few of them are married or if married have children.

4. For their own salvation and for the good of the movement, women must form their own group and work primarily for female liberation.

1. PEOPLE DON'T GET RADICALIZED FIGHTING OTHER PEOPLE'S BATTLES

No one can say that women in the movement lack courage. As a matter of fact they have been used, aside from their clerical role, primarily as bodies on the line. Many have been thrown out of school, disowned by their families, clubbed by the cops, raped by the nuts, and gone to jail with everyone else.

What happened to them throughout the movement is very much what happened to all whites in the early civil rights days. Whites acted out of moral principles, many acted courageously, and they became liberalized but never radicalized. Which is to say, they never quite came to grips with the reality of anybody's situation. It is interesting to speculate on why this should be the case. At least one reason, it seems to me, is that people who set about to help other people generally manage to maintain important illusions about our society, how it operates, and what is required to change it. It is not just that they somehow manage to maintain these illusions, they are compelled to maintain them by their refusal to recognize the full measure of their own individual oppression, the means by which it is brought about, and what it would take to alter their condition.

Any honest appraisal of their own condition in this society would presumably lead people out of logic, impulse, and desire for self-preservation, to shoot at the guys who are shooting at them. Namely, first of all, to fight their own battles.

No one thinks that poor whites can learn about their own lives by befriending black people, however laudable that action may be. No one even thinks that poor whites can help black people much, assuming some might want to, until they first recognize their own oppression and oppressors. Intuitively we grasp the fact that until poor whites understand who their enemies are and combine to fight them they can not understand what it is going to take to secure their freedom or anyone else's. And no one seriously doubts that if and when the light dawns upon them collectively, it will be, in the first instance, their battle they will fight.

We understand this intuitively but white students in the early civil rights days would not have done so. They thought they were really getting a thorough education in the movement, that they were really helping, that they knew in what limited ways the society needed changing and what was necessary to obtain those limited changes, and they were thoroughly shaken by Black Power, which said in effect: you don't understand anything. They also thought in those dim days of the past, that they as white students had no particular problems. It was more or less noblesse oblige. Enlightment soon followed, at least for some white male students.

One of the best things that ever happened to black militants happened when they got hounded out of the stars-and-stripes, white-controlled civil rights movement, when they started fighting for blacks instead of the American Dream. The best thing that ever happened to potential white radicals in civil rights happened when they got thrown out by SNCC and were forced to face their own oppression in their own world. When they started fighting for control of the universities, against the draft, the war, and the business order. And the best thing that may yet happen to potentially radical young women is that they will be driven out of both of these groups. That they will be forced to stop fighting for the "movement" and start fighting primarily for the liberation and independence of women.

Only when they seriously undertake this struggle will they begin to understand that they aren't just ignored or exploited —they are feared, despised, and enslaved.

If the females in SDS ever really join the battle they will quickly realize that no sweet-talking list of grievances and demands, no appeal to male conscience, no behind-the-scenes or in-the-home maneuvering is going to get power for women. If they want freedom, equality, and respect, they are going to have to organize and fight for them realistically and radically.

2. RADICAL FEMALES ESSENTIALLY REJECT AN IDENTIFICATION WITH THEIR SEX AND USE THE LANGUAGE OF FEMALE LIBERATION IN AN ATTEMPT TO ADVANCE THEMSELVES IN THE MALE POWER STRUCTURE OF THE MOVEMENT

It is hard to understand the women's manifesto in any other way. It reeks of the bourgeois black who can't quite identify with the lame and mutilated casualties of the racist system; who doesn't really see himself as an accidental over-sight but as a genetic mutation; who takes it upon himself to explain problems he doesn't understand to a power structure that could care less; who wants to fight for blacks but not very hard and only as a member of the city council or perhaps one of its lesser boards.

If the women in SDS want study committees on the problems of women, why don't they form them? If they want bibliographies, why don't they gather them? If they want to protest University discrimination against women, why don't they do so? No one in SDS is going to stop them. They can even use SDS auspices and publish in *New Left Notes*, for a while anyway.

But that isn't what they want. They want to be treated like "white people" and work on the problems important to white people like planning, zoning, and attracting industry, or in this case the war, the draft, and university reform.

The trouble with using the language of black or female liberation for *this* purpose—essentially demanding a nigger on every committee—is two-fold. In the first place it is immoral—a Tom betrayal of a whole people. In the second place it won't work.

There is an almost exact parallel between the role of women and the role of black people in this society. Together they constitute the great maintenance force sustaining the white American male. They wipe his ass and breast feed him when he is little, they school him in his youthful years, do his clerical work and raise his and their replacements later, and all through his life in the factories, on the migrant farms, in the restaurants, hospitals, offices, and homes, they sew for him, stoop for him, cook for him, clean for him, sweep, run errands, haul away his garbage, and nurse him when his frail body falters.

Together they send him out into his own society, shining and healthy, his mind freed from all concern with the grimy details of living. And there in that unreal world of light and leisure he becomes bemused and confused with ideas of glory and omnipotence. He spends his time saving the world from dragons, or fighting evil knights, proscribing and enforcing laws and social systems, or just playing with the erector sets of manhood—building better bridges, computers, and bombs.

Win or lose on that playground, he likes the games and wants to continue playing—unimpeded. That means that the rest of the population, the blacks and females, who maintain this elite playboy force, must be kept at their job.

Oh, occasionally it occurs to one or another of the most self-conscious, self-confident, and generous white men that the system could be changed. That it might be based on something other than race or sex. But what? Who would decide? Might not the change affect the rules of the game or even the games themselves? And where would his place be in it all? It becomes too frightening to think about. It is less threatening and certainly less distracting simply to close ranks, hold fast, and keep things the way they are.

This is done by various techniques, some of which are: sprinkling the barest pinch of blacks and women over the playground to obscure the fact that it is an all white male facility; making a sacred cow out of home and family; supporting a racist and antifeminist church to befuddle the minds of the support force and to divert what little excess energy is available to it; and most importantly, developing among white men a consensus with regard to blacks and females and a loyalty to each other which supersedes that to either of the other groups or to individual members of them, thus turning each white man into an incorruptible guard of the common white male domain.

The gist of that consensus which is relevant to the point at issue here is,

1. Women and blacks are of inherently inferior and alien mentality. Their minds are vague, almost inchoate, and bound by their personal experiences (scatterbrained, or just dumb). They are incapable of truly abstract, incisive, logical, or tactical thinking.

2. Despite or perhaps because of this inferior mentality women and blacks are happy people. All they ask out of life is a little attention, somebody to screw them regularly, second-hand Cadillacs, new hats, dresses, refrigerators, and other baubles.

3. They do not join mixed groups for the stated purposes of the groups but to be with whites or to find a man.

3. RADICAL WOMEN DO NOT REALLY UNDERSTAND THE DESPERATE CONDITIONS OF WOMEN IN GENERAL—AS STUDENTS, THEY OCCUPY SOME SEXY, SEXLESS LIMBO WHERE THEY ARE TREATED BY MALES WITH LESS DISCRIMINATION THAN THEY WILL EVER AGAIN FACE

It may seem strange, but one of the main advantages of a female student, married or unmarried, with or without children, is that she is still public. She has in her classes, in her contacts on campus, the opportunity to express her ideas publicly to males and females of all rank. Indeed, she is expected to do so—at least in good schools, or in good seminars. Anyway, she has this opportunity on an equal basis with men.

Moreover, her competition with men, at least scholastically, is condoned—built into the system. This creates in the girl an illusion of equality and harmony between the sexes very much as a good integrated school (where students visit each other's homes even for weekends and are always polite) creates in the black the illusion of change and the faith in continued good relations upon graduation.

These female illusions are further nurtured by the social life of students. Since many live in dorms or other places where they can not entertain members of the opposite sex, most social intercourse of necessity takes place in public. I mean that people congregate in coffee houses, pubs, movies, or at parties of the privileged few with off-campus apartments or houses. And since most students are unmarried, unsure of themselves, and lonely, they are constantly on the make. Thus they dance with each other and talk with each other. The conversation between the sexes is not necessarily serious or profound but it takes place, and, as we have said, takes place, in the great main, publicly. Each tries to find out more about the other, attempts to discover what future relations might be possible between them, tries to impress the other in some way.

So that the female student feels like a citizen, like an individual among others in the body politic, in the civil society, in the world of the intellect. What she doesn't understand is that upon graduation she is stripped of her public life and relegated to the level of private property. Enslavement is her farewell present. As things stand now, she is doomed to become someone's secretary, or someone's nurse, or someone's wife, or someone's mistress. From now on if she has some contribution to make to society she is expected to make it privately through the man who owns some part of her.

If as a secretary she has a criticism of the firm she works for and a money-making idea of improvement for the company, she certainly doesn't express her view publicly at the board meeting of the firm, though she may be there taking minutes. Nor does she speak to her boss about it at an office party or in any other public place. She is expected rather to approach him in private, in a self-effacing manner, indicating that she probably doesn't really know what she is talking about but it seems to her . . .

He then proposes the idea to the board and receives both the credit and the raise or promotion. And the peculiar twist is that this holds equally true even if in passing he mentions that the idea was brought to him by his secretary. For in the eyes of the board, as in the eyes of all male society, the female employee has no independent identity. She belongs to the boss as a slave belongs to his master. If slaves are exceptionally productive, the slave holder is given credit for knowing how to pick them and how to work them. Slaves aren't promoted to free men and female secretaries aren't promoted to executive positions.

But slavery is an intricate system. As an institution it cannot be maintained by force alone. Somehow or other slaves must be made to conceive of themselves as inferior beings and slave holders must not be permitted to falter in the confidence of their superiority. That is why female secretaries are not permitted to offer public criticism. How long, after all, could the system survive if in open *public* exchange some women, even in their present downtrodden position, turned out to be smarter than the men who employ them?

What is feared most is that women, looking out at their natural surroundings, will suffer a reversal of perspective like that one experiences looking at optically balanced drawings where background suddenly becomes subject. That one day looking at men and women in full blown stereotype a woman will suddenly perceive individuals of varying ability, honesty, warmth, and understanding. When that day comes her master stands before her stripped of his historical prerogative—just another individual with individual attributes. That has ponderous implications for their relationship, for all of society.

In the world of the graduated and married, this situation is forestalled in perhaps the most expeditious way. Men simply refuse to talk to women publicly about anything but the most trivial affairs: home, cooking, the weather, her job, perhaps a local school board election, etc. In these areas they are bound to be able to compete and if they fail—well, men aren't supposed to know anything about those things anyway. They're really just trying to give the girls a little play.

But even that routine has its dangers. Women are liable to change the topic, to get to something of substance. So generally to be absolutely safe men just don't talk to women at all. At parties they congregate on one side of the room, standing up as befits their condition and position (desk workers in the main) and exhausted women (servants and mothers) are left propped up by girdles, pancake make-up, and hair spray, on the couch and surrounding chairs. If the place is big and informal enough, the men may actually go into another room, generally under the pretext of being closer to the liquor.

Of course, most women don't understand this game for what it is. The new-comer to it often thinks it is the women who withdraw and may seek out what she imagines to be the more stimulating company of the men. When she does, she is quickly disillusioned. As she approaches each group of men the conversation they were so engrossed in usually dies. The individual members begin to drift off—to get a refill, to talk with someone they have just noticed across the room, etc. If she manages to ensnare a residual member of the group in conversation, he very soon develops a nervous and distressed look on his face as though he had to go to the bathroom; and he leaves as soon as possible, perhaps to make that trip.

There is another phenomenon not to be confused here. Namely, men being stimulated to show off in the presence of an attractive female, to display in verbal exchange what they imagine to be their monstrous cleverness. But the rules of this game require the women to stand by semi-mute, just gasping and giggling, awed, and somewhat sexually aroused. The verbal exchange is strictly between the men. Any attempt on the woman's part to become a participant instead of a prize breaks up the game and the group.

This kind of desperate attempt by men to defend their power by refusing to participate in open public discussion with women would be amusing if it were not so effective. And one sees the beginnings of it even now, while still students, in SDS meetings. You are allowed to participate and to speak, only the men stop listening when you do. How many times have you seen a woman enter the discussion only to have it resume at the exact point from which she made her departure, as though she had never said anything at all? How many times have you seen men get up and actually walk out of a room while a woman speaks, or begin to whisper to each other as she starts?

In that kind of a hostile, unresponsive atmosphere, it is difficult for anyone to speak in an organized, stringent manner. Being insulted, she becomes angry; in order to say what she wanted to say and not launch an attack upon the manners of her "audience", she musters the energy to control her temper, and finally she wonders why she is bothering at all since no one is listening. Under the pressure of all this extraneous stimulation she speaks haltingly, and if she gets to the point at all hits it obliquely.

And thus the male purpose is accomplished. Someone may comment, "Well, that is kind of interesting but it is sort of beside the main point here." Or, whoever is in charge may just look at her blankly as if, "What was that all about?" The conversation resumes and perhaps the woman feels angry, but she also feels stupid. In this manner the slave relationship is learned and reinforced.

Even if the exceptional case is involved—the woman who does sometimes get up front—the argument holds. I know whom you are thinking about. You are thinking about the girl who has thirty IQ points over almost anyone in the group and therefore can't be altogether put down. She is much too intelligent, much too valuable. So she is sometimes asked by the male leadership to explain a plan or chair a meeting and since it is obvious that she is exercising *male*-delegated authority and because she is so bright people will sometimes listen to her. But have you ever known the top dog in an SDS group to be a woman, or have you ever known a woman to be second in command? Have you ever seen one argue substance of tactics with one of the top males *in front* of the full group? She may forget her place and do so, but if she does she receives the same treatment as all other females. The rules may and sometimes have to be stretched for the exceptional, but never at the price of male authority and male control.

Of course, being a student, having not as yet come under the full heel of male domination, and not identifying with women in general, you may view SDS group dynamics somewhat differently. You may grant the male domination but think it is a function of the particular males in command, or you may grant its existence but blame the women for not asserting themselves.

With regard to the first assumption, let me point out that almost all men are involved in the male mystique. No matter how unnecessary it may be, particularly for the bright and most able among them, each rests his ego in some measure on the basic common denominator, being a man. In the same way white people, consciously or unconsciously, derive ego support from being white and Americans from being American.

Allowing females to participate in some group on the basis of full equality presents a direct threat to each man in that group. And though an individual male leader may be able to rise above this personal threat he cannot deviate from the rules of the game without jeopardizing his own leadership and the group itself. If he permits the public disclosure in an irrefutable manner of the basic superiority of half of the women to half the men, of some of the women to some of the men, he breaks the covenant and the men will not follow him. Since they are not obliged to, they will not suffer this emasculation and the group will fall apart.

To think that women by asserting themselves individually in SDS, can democratize it, can remove the factor of sex, is equally silly. In the first place the men will not permit it and in the second place, as things stand now, the women are simply incapable of that kind of aggressive individual assertion. The socialization process has gone too far, they are already scrambled. Meeting after meeting their silence bears witness to their feelings of inferiority. Who knows what they get out of it? Are they listening, do they understand what is being said, do they accept it, do they have reservations? Would urging them to speak out have any effect other than to cut down their numbers at the next meeting?

The limbo

Though female students objectively have more freedom than most older married women, their life is already a nightmare. Totally unaware they long ago accepted the miserable role male society assigned to them: help-mate and maintenance worker. Upon coming to college they eagerly and "voluntarily" flood the great service schools—the college of education, the college of nursing, the departments of social work, physical therapy, counseling, and clinical psychology. In some places they even major in home economics.

Denied most of them forever is the great discovery, the power and beauty of logic and mathematics, the sweeping syntheses, the perspective of history. The academic education in these service schools varies from thin to sick—two semester courses in history of Western civilization, watered down one-quarter courses on statistics for nurses, and the mumbo-jumbo courses on psychoanalysis.

It is no wonder that women who may have come to college with perfect confidence in themselves begin to feel stupid. They are being systematically stupefied. Trying to think without knowledge is just a cut above trying to think without language. The wheels go around but nothing much happens.

The position of these women in college is very much like the position of black kids in the black public schools. They start out with the same IQ and achievement scores as their white counterparts but after the third year they begin to lag further and further behind in both measurements. Those blacks still around to graduate from high school usually measure at least two years below graduating whites. Of course, black kids blame the discrepancy on the schools, on the environment, on all kinds of legitimate things. But always there is the gnawing doubt. It is hard to believe the schools could be so different; white women, being at the same school and from the same families, understand that they are simply, though individually, inferior.

But that is not the only reason female students are scrambled. They are also in a panic, an absolute frenzy, to fulfill their destiny: to find a man and get married. It is not that they have all been brainwashed by the media to want a husband, split level house, three children, a dog, a cat, and a station wagon. Many just want out from under their parents. They just can't take the slow slaughter any more but they don't have the courage to break away. They fear the wrath of the explosion but even more they fear the ensuing loneliness and isolation.

Generally a single girl's best friend is still her family. They are the only people she can rely upon for conversation, for attention, for concern with her welfare, no matter how misdirected. And everyone needs some personal attention or they begin to experience a lack of identity. Thus the big push to find the prince charming who will replace the chains with a golden ring.

But that is not as simple as it may seem. It is not proper for women to ask men out. They are never permitted the direct approach to anything. So women must set traps and, depending upon their looks and brains, that can be terribly time-consuming, nerve-racking, and disappointing. Thus the great rash of nose jobs, the desperate dieting, the hours consumed in pursuit of the proper attire. There is skin care, putting up one's hair each night, visits to the hairdressers, keeping up with, buying, applying, and taking off make-up, etc. The average American woman spends two hours a day in personal grooming, not including shopping or sewing. That is one-twelfth of her whole life and one-eighth of the time she spends awake. If she lives to be eighty, a woman will have spent ten whole years of her time awake in this one facet of the complex business of making herself attractive to men. It is staggering to think what that figure would be if one were to include the endless hours spent looking through fashion magazines, shopping and window shopping, discussing and worrying about clothes, a hair style, diet, and make-up. Surely one-fourth of a woman's waking time would be a conservative estimate here. Twenty years of wakeful life!

So, one-fourth of a female student's day goes down the drain in this manner, another one-fourth to one-half is spent getting brainwashed in school and studying for the same end. What does she do with the rest of the time? Often, she must work to support herself and she must eat, clean, wash clothes, date, etc. That leaves her just enough time to worry about her behavior on her last date and her behavior on her next one. Did she say and do the right thing, should she change her approach? Does he love her or does he not? To screw or not to screw is often a serious question. It is taken for granted amongst the more sophisticated that it helps to nail a man if one sleeps with him. Still, it is no guarantee and there are only so many men with whom a woman can cohabit in the same circle and still expect a proposal. Movement men seem prone to marry the "purer" non-movement types. And at that age and stage, when girls are worried about being used, about pregnancy and privacy, still ignorant of the potentials of their bodies, and hung-up by the old sexual code which classifies so much as perversion and then demands it, sex usually offers only minimal gratification anyway. Given the girls' hang-ups and the insecurity and ineptness of young men, even that gratification is more often psychological than sexual.

Sex becomes the vehicle for momentary exchanges of human warmth and affection. It provides periods in which anxiety is temporarily allayed and girls feel wanted and appreciated, periods in which they develop some identity as individuals. It is ironic indeed that a woman attains this sense of identity and individuality through performing an act common to all mankind and all mammals. It bespeaks her understanding that society as it is presently organized will not permit her to function at all expect through some male. The church used to say that "husband and wife are as one, and that one is the husband," or, "The husband and wife are as one body and the husband is the head." As though fulfilling a prophecy unmarried women go about like chickens with their heads cut off.

In this terrible delirium between adolescence and marriage the friendship of female to female all but disappears. Girls, because they are growing duller, become less interesting to each other. As they slip into the role of submissiveness or respondent to male initiative, male intelligence, they also become increasingly uneasy with one another. To be the benefactor of female intelligence and to respond with warmth and affection brings with it anxieties of "homosexual tendencies." To initiate, direct, or dominate brings with it the same apprehensions. To insure a female for every male (if he wants one), to insure his freedom and his power through the enslavement of our sex, males have made of homosexuality *the* abomination. Everyone knows what happens to them: they go crazy and get buried at some intersection. It is too terrible to think about; it can only be feared.

And that fear, initiated by men, is reinforced by both men and women. Perform a simple spontaneous act like lighting another woman's cigarette with the same match you've just lit your own and there is panic on all sides. Women have to learn to inhibit these natural, asexual gestures. And any close and prolonged friendship between women is always suspect.

So women use each other as best they can under the circumstances, to keep out the cold. And the blood-pacts of childhood where one swore not to reveal a secret on penalty of death turn into bargains about not leaving each other until both are lined up for marriage. Only these later pacts are never believed or fulfilled. No woman trusts another because she understands the desperation. The older a woman becomes the more oppressive the syndrome. As one by one her contemporaries marry she begins to feel the way old people must when one by one their friends and relatives die. Though an individual in the latter condition is not necessarily burdened with a sense of failure and shame.

So there you have the typical coed—ignorant, suffering from a sense of inferiority, barely perceiving other women except as mindless, lonely, and terrified. Hardly in any condition to aggressively and individually fight for her rights in SDS. It seems, in a way, the least of her problems. To solve them all she is fixated on marriage. Which brings us to the second arm of this discussion, the point we raised earlier.

4. RADICAL WOMEN DO NOT REALLY UNDERSTAND THE DESPERATE CONDITIONS OF WOMEN IN GENERAL—BECAUSE SO FEW ARE MARRIED, OR IF MARRIED HAVE NO CHILDREN

No one would think to judge a marriage by its first hundred days. To be sure there are cases of sexual trauma, of sudden and violent misunderstandings, but in general all is happiness; the girl has finally made it, the past is but a bad dream. All good things are about to come to her. And then reality sets in. It can be held off a little as long as they are both students and particularly if they have money, but sooner or later it becomes entrenched. The man moves to insure his position of power and dominance.

There are several more or less standard pieces of armament used in this assault upon wives, but the biggest gun is generally the threat of divorce or abandonment. With a plucky woman a man may actually feel it necessary to openly and repeatedly toy with this weapon, but usually it is sufficient simply to keep it in the house undercover somewhere. We all know the bit, we have heard it and all the others I am about to mention on television marital comedies and in night club jokes; it is supposed to be funny.

The husband says to the wife who is about to go somewhere that doesn't meet with his approval, "If you do, you need never come back." Or later, when the process is more complete and she is reduced to frequent outbreaks of begging, he slams his way out of the house claiming that she is trying to destroy him, that he can no longer take these endless, senseless scenes; that "this isn't a marriage, it's a meat grinder." Or he may simply lay down the law that God damn it, her first responsibility is to her family and he will not permit or tolerate something or other. Or if she wants to maintain the marriage she is simply going to have to accommodate herself.

There are thousands of variations on this theme and it is really very clever the way male society creates for women this pre-marital hell so that some man can save her from it and control her ever after by the threat of throwing her back. Degrading her further, the final crisis is usually averted or postponed by a tearful reconciliation in which the wife apologizes for her shortcomings, namely the sparks of initiative still left to her.

The other crude and often open weapon that a man uses to control his wife is the threat of force or force itself. Though this weapon is not necessarily used in conjunction with the one described above, it presupposes that a woman is more frightened of returning to an unmarried state than she is of being beaten about one way or another. How can one elaborate on such a threat? At a minimum it begins by a man's paling or flushing, clenching his fists at his sides or gritting his teeth, perhaps making lurching but controlled motions or wild threatening ones while he states his case. In this circumstance it is difficult for a woman to pursue the argument which is bringing about the reaction, usually an argument for more freedom, respect, or equality in the marital situation. And of course, the conciliation of this scene, even if he has beat her, may require his apology, but also hers, for provoking him. After a while the conditioning becomes so strong that a slight change of color on his part, or a slight stiffening of stance, nothing observable to an outsider, suffices to quiet her or keep her in line. She turns off or detours mechanically, like a robot, not even herself aware of the change, or only momentarily and almost subliminally.

But these are gross and vulgar techniques. There are many more subtle and intricate which in the long run are even more devastating. Take for instance the ploy of keeping women from recognizing their intelligence by not talking to them in public, which we mentioned earlier. After marriage this technique is extended and used on a woman in her own home.

At breakfast a woman speaks to her husband over or through

the morning paper, which he clutches firmly in his hands. Incidentally, he reserves the right to see the paper first and to read the sections in order of his preference. The assumption is, of course, that he has a more vested interest in world affairs and a superior intelligence with which to grasp the relevance of daily news. The Women's Section of the paper is called that, not only because it contains the totality of what men want women to be concerned with, but also because it is the only section permitted to women at certain times of the day.

I can almost hear you demur. Now she has gone too far. What super-sensitivity to interpret the morning paper routine as a deliberate put-down. After all, a woman has the whole day to read the paper and a man must get to work. I put it to you that this same situation exists when they both work or when the wife works and the husband is still a student, assuming he gets up for breakfast, and on Sundays. What we are describing here is pure self-indulgence. A minor and common, though none the less enjoyable, exercise in power. A flexing of the male prerogative.

Perhaps the best tip-off to the real meaning of the daily paper act comes when a housewife attempts to solve the problem by subscribing to two papers. This is almost invariably met with resistance on the part of the man as being an unnecessary and frivolous expense, never mind whether they can afford it. And if his resistance doesn't actually forestall the second subscription he attempts to monopolize the front sections of both papers! This is quite a complicated routine, but, assuming the papers are not identical, it can be done and justified.

However, we were talking about conversation and noted that it was replaced by the paper in the morning. In the evening men attempt to escape through more papers, returning to work, working at home, reading, watching television, going to meetings, etc. But eventually they have to handle the problem some other way because their wives are desperate for conversation, for verbal interchange. To understand this desperation you have to remember that women before marriage have on the whole only superficial, competitive, and selfish relationships with each other. Should one of them have a genuine relationship it is more likely with a male than a female. After marriage a woman stops courting her old unmarried or married female side-kicks. They have served their purpose, to tide her over. And there is the fear, often well founded, that these females will view her marriage less as a sacrament than a challenge, that they will stalk her husband as fair game, that they will outshine her, or in some other way lead to the disruption of her marriage.

Her husband will not tolerate the hanging around of any past male friends, and that leaves the woman isolated. When, as so often happens, after a few years husband and wife move because he has graduated, entered service, or changed jobs, her isolation is complete. Now all ties are broken. Her husband is her only contact with the outside world, aside, of course, from those more or less perfunctory contacts she has at work, if she works.

So she is desperate to talk with her husband because she must talk with *someone* and he is all she has. To tell the truth a woman doesn't really understand the almost biologic substructure to her desperation. She sees it in psychological terms. She thinks that if her husband doesn't talk to her he doesn't love her or doesn't respect her. She may even feel that this disrespect on his part is causing her to lose her own self-respect (a fair assumption since he is her only referent). She may also feel cheated and trapped because she understood that in return for all she did for him in marriage she was to be allowed to live vicariously, and she cannot do that if he will not share his life.

What she does not understand is that she cannot go on thinking coherently without expressing those thoughts and having them accepted, rejected, or qualified in some manner. This kind of feed-back is essential to the healthy functioning of the human mind. That is why solitary confinement is so devastating. It is society's third-rung "legal deterrent," ranking just below capital punishment and forced wakefulness, or other forms of torture that lead to death.

This kind of verbal isolation, this refusal to hear a woman, causes her thought process to turn in upon itself, to deteriorate, degenerate, to become disassociated from reality. Never intellectually or emotionally secure in the first place, she feels herself slipping beyond the pale. She keeps pounding at the door.

And what is her husband's response? He understands in some crude way what is happening to her, what he is doing to her, but he is so power-oriented that he cannot stop. Above all, men must remain in control; it's either him or her. The worse she becomes the more convinced he is the coin must not be turned. And from thence springs anew his fear of women, like his fear of blacks.

We tend to forget that witches were burned in our own country not too long ago, in those heroic days before the founding fathers. That each day somewhere in our country women are raped or killed just for kicks or out of some perverted sense of retribution. And we never even consider the ten thousand innocent women annually murdered by men who refuse to legalize abortion. The fear and hatred must be deep indeed to take such vengeance.

But back to the husband. We all know that marriage is far from solitary confinement for a woman. Of course, the husband talks to her. The questions are, how often, what does he say, and how does he say it? He parries this plea for conversation, which he understands thoroughly, until bedtime or near it and then exhausted and exasperated he slaps down his book or papers, or snaps off the TV, or flings his shoe to the floor if he is undressing and turns to his wife, saying, "Oh, for Christ sake, what is it you want to talk about?"

Now he has just used all of his big guns. He has showed temper which threatens violence. He has showed an exasperated patience which threatens eventual divorce. He has been insulting and purposely misunderstanding. Since she is not burning with any specific comments, since she is now frightened, hurt, angry, and thoroughly miserable, what is she to say? I'll tell you what she does say: "Forget it. Just forget it. If that's the way you are going to respond I don't want to talk with you anyway."

This may bring on another explosion from him, frightening her still further. He may say something stupid like, "You're crazy, just crazy. All day long you keep telling me you've got to talk to me. O.K., you want to talk to me, talk. I'm listening. I'm not reading. I'm not working. I'm not watching TV. I'm listening."

He waits sixty silent seconds while the wife struggles for composure and then he stands up and announces that he is going to bed. To rub salt in the wound, he falls to sleep blissfully and instantly.

Or, playing the part of both cops in the jailhouse interrogation scene he may, after the first explosion, switch roles. In this double-take he becomes the calm and considerate husband, remorseful, apologizing, and imploring her to continue, assuring her he is interested in anything she has to say, knowing full well the limitations of what she can say under the circumstances. Predictably, done in by the tender tone, she falls in with the plot and confesses. She confesses her loneliness, her dependence, her mental agony, and they discuss *her* problem. Her problem, as though it were some genetic defect, some personal shortcoming, some inscrutable psychosis. Now he can comfort her, avowing how he understands how she must feel, he only wished there were something he could do to help.

This kind of situation if continued in unrelieved manner has extreme consequences. Generally the marriage partners sense this and stop short of the brink. The husband, after all, is trying to protect and bolster his frail ego, not drive his wife insane or force her suicide. He wants in the home to be able to hide from his own inner doubts, his own sense of shame, failure, and meaninglessness. He wants to shed the endless humiliation of endless days parading as a man in the male world. Pretending a power, control, and understanding he does not have.

All he asks of his wife, aside from hours of menial work, is that she not see him as he sees himself. That she not challenge him but admire and desire him, soothe and distract him. In short, make him feel like the kind of guy he'd like to be in the kind of world he thinks exists.

And by this time the wife asks little more really than the opportunity to play that role. She probably never aspired to more, to an equalitarian or reality-oriented relationship. It is just that she cannot do her thing if it is laid out so baldly; if she is to be denied all self-respect, all self-development, all help and encouragement from her husband.

So generally the couple stops short of the brink. Sometimes, paradoxically enough, by escalating the conflict so that it ends in divorce, but generally by some accommodation. The husband encourages the wife to make some girl friends, take night courses, or have children. And sooner or later, if she can, she has children. Assuming the husband has agreed to the event, the wife's pregnancy does abate or deflect the drift of their marriage, for a while anyway.

The pregnancy presents to the world visible proof of the husband's masculinity, potency. This visible proof shores up the basic substructure of his ego, the floor beyond which he cannot now fall. Pathetically his stock goes up in society, in his own eyes. He is a man. He is grateful to his wife and treats her, at least during the first pregnancy, with increased tenderness and respect. He pats her tummy and makes noises about mystic occurrences. And since pregnancy is not a male thing and he is a man, since this is cooperation, not competition, he can even make out that he feels her role is pretty special.

The wife is grateful. Her husband loves her. She is suffused with happiness and pride. There is, at last, something on her side of the division of labor which her husband views with respect, and delight of delights, with perhaps a twinge of jealousy.

Of course, it can't last. After nine months the child is bound to be born. And there we are back at the starting gate. Generally speaking, giving birth must be like a bad trip with the added feature of prolonged physical exhaustion.

Sometimes it takes a year to regain one's full strength after a messy Caesarian. Sometimes women develop post-parturational psychosis in the hospital. More commonly, after they have been home awhile they develop a transient but recurring state called the "Tired Mother Syndrome." In its severe form it is, or resembles, a psychosis. Women with this syndrome complain of being utterly exhausted, irritable, unable to concentrate. They may wander about somewhat aimlessly, they may have physical pains. They are depressed, anxious, sometimes paranoid, and they cry a lot.

Sound familiar? Despite the name one doesn't have to be a mother to experience the ailment. Many young wives without children do experience it, particularly those who, without an education themselves, are working their husband's way through college. That is to say, wives who hold down a dull eight or nine hour day job, then come home, straighten, cook, clean, run down to the laundry, dash to the grocery store, iron their own clothes plus their husband's shirts and jeans, sew for themselves, put up their hair, and more often than not type their husband's papers, correct his spelling and grammar, pay the bills, screw on command, and write the in-laws. I've even known wives who on top of this load do term papers or laboratory work for their husbands. Of course, it's insanity. What else could such self-denial be called? Love?

Is it any wonder that a woman in this circumstance is tired? Is it any wonder that she responds with irritability when she returns home at night to find her student husband, after a day or half day at home, drinking beer and shooting the bull with his cronies, the ring still in the bathtub, his dishes undone, his clothes where he dropped them the night before, even his specific little chores like taking out the garbage unaccomplished?

Is it any wonder that she is tempted to scream when at the very moment she has gotten rid of the company, plowed through some of the mess, and is standing in a tiny kitchen over a hot stove, her husband begins to make sexual advances? He naively expects that these advances will fill her with passion, melting all anger, and result not only in her forgetting and forgiving but in gratitude and renewed love. Ever hear the expression, "A woman loves the man who satisfies her"? Some men find that delusion comforting. A couple of screws and the slate is wiped clean. Who needs to pay for servants or buy his wife a washing machine when he has a cock?

And even the most self-deluded woman begins to feel depressed, anxious, and used, when she finds that her husband is embarrassed by her in the company of his educated, intellectual, or movement friends. When he openly shuts her up saying she doesn't know what she is talking about or emphasizes a point by saying it is so clear or so simple even his wife can understand it.

He begins to confuse knowledge with a personal attribute like height or a personal virtue like honesty. He becomes disdainful of and impatient with ignorance, equating it with stupidity, obstinacy, laziness, and in some strange way, immorality. He forgets that his cultivation took place at his wife's expense. He will not admit that in stealing from his wife her time, energy, leisure, and money he also steals the possibility of her intellectual development, her present, and her future.

But the working wife sending her husband through school has no monopoly on this plight. It also comes to those who only stand and wait—in the home, having kiddy after kiddy while their husbands, if they are able, learn something, grow somewhere.

In any case, we began this diversion by saying that women who are not mothers can also suffer from the "Tired Mother Syndrome." Once a mother, however, it takes on a new dimension. There is a difference of opinion in the medical and sociological literature with regard to the genesis of this ailment. Betty Friedan, in the sociological vein, argues that these symptoms are the natural outgrowth of restricting the mind and body of these women to the narrow confines of the home. She discusses the destructive role of monotonous, repetitive work which never issues in any lasting, let alone important, achievement. Dishes which are done only to be dirtied the same day; beds which are made only to be unmade the same day. Her theory also lays great emphasis on the isolation of these women from the larger problems of society and even from contact with those concerned with things not domestic, other than their husbands. In other words, the mind no more than the body can function in a straitjacket and the effort to keep it going under these circumstances is indeed tiring and depressing.

Dr. Spock somewhat sides with this theory. The main line medical approach is better represented by Dr. Lovshin who

says that mothers develop the "Tired Mother Syndrome" because they are tired. They work a 16-hour day, 7 days a
week. Automation and unions have led to a continuously
shortened day for men but the work day of housewives with
children has remained constant. The literature bears him out.
Oh, it is undoubtedly true that women have today many
time-saving devices their mothers did not have. This advantage is offset, however, by the fact that fewer members of the
family help with housework and the task of child care, as it
is organized in our society, is continuous. Now the woman
puts the wash in a machine and spends her time reading to
the children, breaking up their fights, taking them to the playground, or otherwise looking after them. If, as is often said,
women are being automated out of the home, it is only to be
shoved into the car chauffering children to innumerable lessons and activities, and that dubious advantage holds only for
middle and upper class women who generally can afford not
only gadgets but full or part-time help.

One of the definitions of automation is a human being acting
mechanically in a monotonous routine. Now as always the
most automated appliance in a household is the mother. Because of the speed at which it's played, her routine has not
only a nightmarish but farcical quality to it. Some time ago
the *Ladies Home Journal* conducted and published a forum
on the plight of young mothers. Ashley Montague and some
other professionals plus members of the *Journal* staff inter-
viewed four young mothers. Two of them described their
morning breakfast routine.

One woman indicated that she made the breakfast, got it out,
left the children to eat it, and then ran to the washing machine.
She filled that up and ran back to the kitchen, shoved a little
food in the baby's mouth and tried to keep the others eating.
Then she ran back to the machine, put the clothes in a wringer
and started the rinse water.

The other woman stated they had bacon every morning, so
the first thing she did was to put the bacon on and the water
for coffee. Then she went back to her room and made the
bed. "Generally, I find myself almost running back and forth.
I don't usually walk. I run to make the bed." By that time the
pan is hot and she runs back to turn the bacon. She finishes
making the children's breakfast and if she is lucky she gets to
serve it before she is forced to dash off to attend to the baby,
changing him and sitting him up. She rushes back, plops him
in a little canvas chair, serves the children if she has not already done so, and makes her husband's breakfast. And so it

goes through the day. As the woman who runs from bed to bacon explains, "My problem is that sometimes I feel there aren't enough hours in the day. I don't know whether I can get everything done."

It's like watching an old time movie where for technical reasons everyone seems to be moving at three times normal speed. In this case it is not so funny. With the first child it is not as severe.

What hits a new mother the hardest is not so much the increased work load as the lack of sleep. However unhappy she may have been in her childless state, however desperate, she could escape by sleep. She could be refreshed by sleep. And if she wasn't a nurse or airline stewardess she generally slept fairly regular hours in a seven to nine hour stretch. But almost all babies returning from the hospital are on something like a four-hour food schedule, and they usually demand some attention in between feedings. Now children differ, some cry more, some cry less, some cry almost all of the time. If you have never, in some period of your life, been awakened and required to function at one in the morning and again at three, then maybe at seven, or some such schedule, you can't imagine the agony of it.

All of a woman's muscles ache and they respond with further pain when touched. She is generally cold and unable to get warm. Her reflexes are off. She startles easily, ducks moving shadows, and bumps into stationary objects. Her reading rate takes a precipitous drop. She stutters and stammers, groping for words to express her thoughts, sounding barely coherent—somewhat drunk. She can't bring her mind to focus. She is in a fog. In response to all the aforementioned symptoms she is always close to tears.

What I have described here is the severe case. Some mothers aren't hit as hard but almost all new mothers suffer these symptoms in some degree and what's more, will continue to suffer them a good part of their lives. The woman who has several children in close succession really gets it. One child wakes the other, it's like a merry-go-round, intensified with each new birth, each childhood illness.

This lack of sleep is rarely mentioned in the literature relating to the Tired Mother Syndrome. Doctors recommend to women with new born children that they attempt to partially compensate for this loss of sleep by napping during the day. With one child that may be possible; with several small ones it's sort of a sick joke. This period of months or years of forced wakefulness and "material" responsibility seems to have a long-range if not permanent effect on a woman's sleeping habits. She is so used to listening for the children she is awakened by dogs, cats, garbage men, neighbors' alarm clocks, her husband's snoring. Long after her last child gives up night feedings she is still waking to check on him. She is worried about his suffocating, choking, falling out of bed, etc. Long after that she wanders about opening and closing windows, adjusting the heat or air conditioning, locking the doors, or going to the bathroom.

If enforced wakefulness is the handmaiden and necessary precursor to serious brainwashing, a mother—after her first child—is ready for her final demise. Too tired to comprehend or fight, she only staggers and eventually submits. She is embarrassed by her halting speech, painfully aware of her lessened ability to cope with things, of her diminished intellectual prowess. She relies more heavily than ever on her husband's support, helping hand, love. And he in turn gently guides her into the further recesses of second class citizenship.

After an extended tour in that never-never land, most women lose all capacity for independent thought, independent action. If the anxiety and depression grow, if they panic, analysis and solution elude them.

The return from the never-never land

Women who would avoid or extricate themselves from the common plight I've described and would begin new lives, new movements, and new worlds, must first learn to acknowledge the reality of their present condition. They have got to reject the blind and faulty categories of thought foisted on them by a male order for its own benefit. They must stop thinking in terms of "the grand affair," of the love which over-comes, or substitutes for, everything else, of the perfect moment, the perfect relationship, the perfect marriage. In other words, they must reject romanticism. Romance, like the rabbit of the dog track, is the illusive, fake, and never-attained reward which for the benefit and amusement of our masters keeps us running and thinking in safe circles.

A relationship between a man and a woman is no more or less personal a relationship than is the relationship between a woman and her maid, a master and his slave, a teacher and his student. Of course, there are personal, individual qualities to a particular relationship in any of these categories but they are so overshadowed by the class nature of the relationship, by the volume of class response as to be almost insignificant.

There is something horribly repugnant in the picture of women performing the same menial chores all day, having almost interchangeable conversations with their children, engaging in standard television arguments with their husbands, and then in the late hours of the night, each agonizing over what is considered her personal lot, her personal relationship, her personal problem. If women lack self-confidence, there seems no limit to their egotism. And unmarried women cannot in all honesty say their lives are in much greater measure distinct from each other's. We are a class, we are oppressed as a class, and we each respond within the limits allowed us as members of that oppressed class. Purposely divided from each other, each of us is ruled by one or more men for the benefit of all men. There is no personal escape, no personal salvation, no personal solution.

The first step, then, is to accept our plight as a common plight, to see other women as reflections of ourselves, without obscuring, of course, the very real differences intelligence, temperament, age, education, and background create. I'm not saying let's now create new castes or classes among our own. I just don't want women to feel that the movement requires them to identify totally with and moreover love every other woman. For the general relationship, understanding and compassion should suffice.

We who have been raised on pap must develop a passion for honest appraisal. The real differences between women and between men and women are the guideposts within and around which we must dream and work.

Having accepted our common identity the next thing we must do is to get in touch with each other. I mean that absolutely literally. Women see each other all the time, open their mouths and make noises, but communicate on only the most superficial level. We don't talk to each other about what we consider our real problems because we are afraid to look insecure, because we don't trust or respect each other, and because we are afraid to look or be disloyal to our husbands and benefactors.

Each married woman carries around in her a strange and almost identical little bundle of secrets. To take, as an example, perhaps the most insignificant, she may be tired of and feel insulted by her husband's belching or farting at the table. Can you imagine her husband's fury if it got back to him that she told someone he farted at the table? Because women don't tell these things to each other the events are considered personal, the woman may fantasize remarriage to mythical men who

don't fart, the man feels he has a personal but minor idio-
syncrasy, and maledom comes out clean.

And that, my dear, is what this bit of loyalty is all about. If
a man made that kind of comment about his wife, he might
be considered crude or indiscreet; she's considered disloyal—
because she's subject, he's king, women are dominated and
men are the instruments of their domination. The true objective nature of men must never become common knowledge lest
it undermine in the minds of some males—but most particularly in ours—the male right-to-rule. And so we daily participate in the process of our own domination. For God's sake,
let's stop!

I cannot make it too clear that I am not talking about group
therapy or individual catharsis (we aren't sick, we are oppressed). I'm talking about movement. Let's get together to
decide in groups of women how to get out of this bind, to
discover and fight the techniques of domination in and out of
the home. To change our physical and social surroundings to
free our time, our energy, and our minds—to start to build for
ourselves, for all mankind, a world without horrors.

Women involved in this struggle together will come to respect, love, and develop deep and abiding friendships with each
other. If these do not thoroughly compensate for losses that
may be ours, they will carry us through. For different ages
and different stages there are different projects. Young married or unmarried women without children are sympathetic
to the problems of mothers but do not pretend to fully understand them. In all honesty, as a middle-aged mother I cannot
really grasp the special quality of life of an unmarried young
woman in this generation. Her circumstance is too distinct
from mine, and my memories of youth are by this time too
faded to bridge the gap. Youth has available to it perspectives
and paths not destined to be shared by many in the older
generation. We must work together but not presuppose for
each other. It is, then, the younger author who will speak to
the young. Before this part of the paper is ended, however, I
would like to mention briefly projects I think women my age
must undertake as part of the overall movement. If they have
any relevancy for young women, so much the better.

1. Women must resist pressure to enter into movement activities other than their own. There cannot be real restructuring
of this society until the relationships between the sexes are
restructured. The inequalitarian relationship in the home is
perhaps the basis of all evil. Men can commit any horror, or

cowardly suffer any mutilation of their souls and retire to the home to be treated there with awe, respect, and perhaps love. Men will never face their true identity or their real problems under these circumstances, nor will we.

If movement men were not attempting to preserve their prerogative as men while fighting "the system", they would welcome an attack launched upon that system from another front. That they do not shows how trapped they are in the meshes of the very system they oppose. Our vision must not be limited by theirs. We must urge in speech and in print that women go their own way.

2. Since women in great measure are ruled by the fear of physical force, they must learn to protect themselves. Women who are able ought to take jujitsu or karate until they are proficient in the art. Certainly they ought to organize and enroll their daughters in such courses. Compare the benefits young girls would derive from such courses with those they attain from endless years of ballet. As an extra added goodie, we could spare ourselves the agony of those totally untalented recitals, and later, the sleepless nights worrying about our daughter's safety.

3. We must force the media to a position of realism. Ninety percent of the women in this country have an inferiority complex because they do not have turned-up noses, wear a size ten or under dress, have "good legs", flat stomachs, and fall within a certain age bracket. According to television no man is hot for a middle-aged woman. If she is his wife he may screw her but only because he is stuck with her. More important that that, women are constantly portrayed as stupid. The advertisements are the worst offenders. Blacks used to be left out of TV altogether except for occasional Tom roles. Women are cast on every show and always Tom. From such stuff is our self-image created, the public and accepted image of women. The only time my daughter saw a woman on TV who gave her pride in being a woman was when she saw Coretta King speak to the poor people's march. And as my son said, "It was almost like he had to die before anyone could know she existed." Let's not simply boycott selected products; let's break up those television shows and refuse to let them go on until female heroines are portrayed in their total spectrum. And let's make sure that every brilliant heroine doesn't have a husband who is just an eentsy teentsy bit more brilliant than she is.

4. Women must share their experiences with each other until they understand, identify, and explicitly state the many psychological techniques of domination in and out of the home. These should be published and distributed widely until they are common knowledge. No woman should feel befuddled and helpless in an argument with her husband. She ought to be able to identify his strategems and to protect herself against them, to say, you're using the two-cop routine, and premature apology, the purposeful misunderstanding, etc.

5. Somebody has got to start designing communities in which women can be freed from their burdens long enough for them to experience humanity. Houses might be built around schools to be rented only to people with children enrolled in the particular school, and only as long as they were enrolled. This geographically confined community could contain cheap or cooperative cafeterias and a restaurant so that mothers would not have to cook. This not only would free the woman's time but would put her in more of a position of equality with Daddy when he comes home from work. The parents could both sit down and eat at the same time in front of and with the children, a far different scene from that of a conversing family being served by a harassed mother who rarely gets to sit down and is usually two courses behind. These geographic school complexes could also contain full-time nursuries. They could offer space for instrument, dance, and self-defense lessons. In other words, a woman could live in them and be relieved of cooking, childcare for the greater part of the day, and chauffeuring. The center might even have nighttime or overnight babysitting quarters. Many women will be totally lost to us and to themselves if projects like this are not begun. And the projects themselves, by freeing a woman's time and placing her in innumerable little ways into more of a position of equality, will go a long way toward restructuring the basic marital and parental relationships.

6. Women must learn their own history because they have a history to be proud of and a history which will give pride to their daughters. In all the furor over the *Ramparts* article, I have heard women complain of the photographs and offer unlikely stories of trickery. I've heard them voice resentment toward coalitions like the Jeanette Rankin Brigade and toward *Ramparts* for pushing them. But I have yet to hear a cry of outrage to the real crime of that article. It purposely, maliciously, and slanderously rewrote, perverted, and belittled our

history—and most of us weren't even aware of it. What defense is there for a people so ignorant they will believe anything said about their past? To keep us from our history is to keep us from each other. To keep us from our history is to deny to us the group pride from which individual pride is born. To deny to us the possibility of revolt. Our rulers, consciously, unconsciously, perhaps intuitively, know these truths. That's why there is no black or female history in high school texts, *Ramparts'* reference to its location there notwithstanding. Courageous women brought us out of total bondage to our present improved position. We must not foresake them but learn from them and allow them to join the cause once more. The market is ripe for feminist literature, historic and otherwise. We must provide it.

7. Women who have any scientific competency at all ought to begin to investigate the real temperament and cognitive differences between the sexes. This area has been hexed with a sort of liberal taboo like the study of race differences. Presumably, we and blacks were being saved from humiliation by a liberal establishment which was at least in pretense willing to grant that aside from color and sexual anatomy we differed from white men in no significant aspect. But suppose we do? Are we to be kept ignorant of those differences? Who is being saved from what?

8. Equal pay for equal work has been a project poo-pooed by the radicals but it should not be because it is an instrument of bondage. If women, particularly women with children, cannot leave their husbands and support themselves decently, they are bound to remain under all sorts of degrading circumstances. In this same line college entrance discrimination against females, and job discrimination in general, must be fought, no matter what we think about the striving to become professional. A guaranteed annual income would also be of direct relevance to women.

9. In what is hardly an exhaustive list, I must mention abortion laws. All laws relating to abortion must be stricken from the books. Abortion, like contraceptives, must be legal and available if women are to have control of their bodies, their lives, and their destiny.

PART II, *by Judith Brown*

We are determined to foment a rebellion, and will not hold ourselves bound to obey any laws in which we have no voice or representation.

(Abigail Adams, to her husband, John Adams, then in the Continental Congress, 1776)

5. FOR THEIR OWN SALVATION, AND FOR THE GOOD OF THE MOVEMENT, WOMEN MUST FORM THEIR OWN GROUPS AND WORK FOR FEMALE LIBERATION

In the previous sections we have attempted to refute the erroneous assumptions of the female caucus at the 1967 SDS Convention. We have emphasized the plight of the married woman in her relationship with a power-oriented representative of the master caste. Here, we will take up the situation in which the younger, typical radical female finds herself, and talk about some of the hassles in the emerging liberation movement.

We do not wish to belabor the classic statements in the literature which affirm the slave status of women in Western culture. There is sufficient evidence of our economic, political, psychological, and physiological subjugation. For radical women we will propose radical solutions; let the fainthearted cling to the "desegregation" model.

First, it requires only a cursory glance at history to recall that men have played the games of war, racial taboo, mastery, and conspicuous production and consumption for thousands of years. While we do not question the courage of radical men who now confront most of the manifestations of imperialism, we do recognize that like their brave predecessors in other eras, they expect and require that women—*their* women— continue to function as black troops—kitchen soldiers— in *their* present struggle.[1] Radical men are not fighting for female liberation, and in fact, become accountably queasy when

[1] "It was in Fayerweather that a male leader asked for girls to volunteer for cooking duty and was laughed down . . ." "The Siege of Columbia", *Ramparts*, 15 June 68.

the topic is broached. Regrettably the best—radical men and their black counterparts—do not even have a political interest in female liberation.[2]

And indeed, this is not peculiar. We cannot expect them to relinquish, by our gentle persuasion, the power their sex knows and takes for granted. They do not even know how. Few can say, "The only honorable course, when confronted with a just revolt against yourself or political territory in which you have a vested interest, is to yield gracefully." Yet we, like radical men, have only one life we know of. It is a serious question whether we should live it as slaves to the rhetoric, the analysis, and the discipline of the movement we have come to be a part of, if that movement, that analysis, and that discipline systematically deprive us of our pride, genuine relationships with free women, equal relationships with men, and a sense that we are using our talents and dedication to a committed life as fully and as freely as possible.

The SDS experience—a female view

For a moment it will be helpful to review the experience of a young woman who enters a radical movement, unmarried, in order to appreciate her position, against the backdrop of male movement behavior. For we should recognize clearly the conditions under which we live as oppressive in order to identify ourselves with other women in a common struggle.

The typical "radical" woman goes to college and is well-endowed intellectually, physically, and sexually. She has most likely excelled somewhere in high school, whether as a scholar, politico, or artist. She is fully capable of competing with men in college work, and simultaneously, she has already learned that it pays to restrain those overt displays of her competency which men feel no shame in exercising. In exclusively female circles she has held leadership positions and felt bored there, and she has remarked, at least once in her life, that she "prefers the more stimulating company of men." She is not a homosexual, and she usually echoes the fraternity brand of contempt for "fags" and "dikes." She thinks she is turned off to women and is secretly relieved that she passed through the "stage" of homosexuality without "becoming one." Yet,

[2]In response to what is hopefully the last stand of women *in* SDS, at the 1968 National Convention, June 13: "The feeling in the room was, well, those Women have done their silly little thing again." *Guardian*, 28 June 68.

she may quietly recognize that she has loved at least one woman somewhere along the way.

At the same time, she is unusually adroit at the sophisticated forms of putting down men, and more than once she watched a movement male explaining tactics or leading a demonstration with personal knowledge that he is a bad screw or privately panders to his parents. Her nearly subliminal review of these failings would stop at mere insight were it not also true that she has, on occasions she can recall, savored her knowledge and derived malicious pleasure from it. It is this idle malicious pleasure, which in adult life finds fuller expression in a petty, indirect, consistent, and fruitless attack on men, which should be the litmus for why the woman ought to concern herself with female liberation first.

Because she knows that equality between the sexes in the movement is nonexistent. She knows, as we have said, that women are silent at meetings, or if they speak, it is slightly hysterical and of little consequence to all the others. Men formally or informally chair the meeting. Women, like all good secretaries, take notes, circulate lists, provide ashtrays, or prepare and serve refreshments. They implement plans made by men through telephoning, compiling mailing lists, painting picket signs, etc. In some quarters, now that written analysis seems to have supplanted organizing as the status movement work, women are promoted to fill that void. More often than not, however, radical women sit through meetings in a stupor, occasionally patting or plucking at "their" men and receiving, in return, a patronizing smile, or as the case may be, a glare. In demonstrations they are conspicuously protected, which does not always mean however, that they are spared the club or the jailhouse, but they are spared *responsibility* for having made the direct confrontation.

In the jailhouse, they experience perhaps the only taste of independent radical female expression given them. There, they are segregated by sex, and the someone who always assumes leadership is this time a woman. They find out about each other, probably for the first time. They learn that the others, like themselves, are generally brave, resourceful, and militant. If they stay in jail long enough, they begin to organize themselves and others in the cell-block for prison reform, etc. They get up petitions, smuggle out protest letters and leaflets, mount hunger strikes, and other forms of resistance. They manage very adequately to sustain the abuses, self-imposed disciplines, the loss of status, and the fear, which their brothers face. Outside, of course, jailhouse reminiscence is dominated by the men. And the women desegregate themselves, recalling only rarely a faint affection for their former cell-mates. It is little wonder then that for some women, jail may be the first time that they know their sisters and work with them in radical organizing *where they're at.* A very militant white woman remarked to me that after 34 years, a husband, and three children, an earlier two-month stint in jail was the first time she felt at home in organizing.

The radical woman lives off-campus, away from her parents, and often openly with one man or another. She thinks this is "freedom." But if she shares a place with a man, she "plays marriage," which means that she cooks, cleans, does the laundry, and generally serves and waits. Hassles with parents or fear of the Dean of Women help to sustain the excitement —the romantic illusions about marriage she brought to the domicile.

If she shares an apartment with other women, it is arranged so that each may entertain men for extended visits with maximum privacy. Often, for the women, these apartments become a kind of bordello; for the men, in addition to that, a good place to meet for political discussion, to put up campus travelers, to grab a free meal, or sack out. These homes are not centers for female political activity; and rather than being judged for their interior qualities—physical or political—they are evaluated by other women in terms of the variety and status of the radical men who frequent them.

But women in general are becoming healthier, better educated, more independent, and as the years go by, more experienced movement personnel. The movement itself is growing up. The one-time single female organizer marries, and her younger sisters are beginning to see that movement participation will not save them from essentially the same sexual and marital styles they reject in their parents. The older, now married radical woman goes on trips—to visit the parents; may live in a larger, less free apartment; or may even live in a home she and her husband buy. She is "protected" by her husband, and generally she stays at home when he goes out to move the world. The marital pattern sets in, and he lapses from a sloppy courtship to ordering her to get the drinks, cut the grass, etc. The tremendous political investments made by the older radical women (now 25–30) didn't make a way for the younger; newcomer female radicals have fewer illusions these days about what is in store for them anyway, and the lifestyles of their predecessors offer little inspiration. Is it surprising then that we read in radical journals that they are dropping out of the movement in droves?

The female radical, or old-timey civil rights activist, is soon "cooled out" of the movement in one of several ways and for several reasons: (1) if she is too competent and threatens male dominance (perhaps her credentials are too impeccable), she is given a high-level secretarial post (forceably ejected), or she is co-opted and perhaps even impregnated by a male honcho; (2) if she has suffered for several years, consistently being handed menial tasks, she may find, since she has been around so long, that she is one of the "old guard," and she wonders why she isn't invited to steering committee meetings—she quietly drops out; (3) some men are more direct; in squelching a paper questioning the role of black women, Stokely Carmichael said, "The only position for women in SNCC is prone." Most women are not long-suffering for the movement; they never really get in, and their brief passing is hardly noted. The radical female is cooled out, very simply, because she is not wanted politically, and she cannot proffer her secretarial skills as payment for inclusion in traditionally male activity—political decision-making.

More sophisticated male leadership, a year or two ago, began to sense the rumblings of discontent. An effort was made to buy off female militants. They were included in some photographs of the "leadership," given titles in the organization, or consistently laid by the second in command. Those who were married were advised by their husbands to take a year off and do research into the problems of women (meaning take off), or urged to enter one of the new, female "coalition" groups. The last resort, winningly argued, is the We Need You; and, of course, everybody knows that those who fight for peace are the best, anyway. It parallels the Johnsonian whine to blacks, and it goes like this: there is a war; radical men are being cut down on all sides; we know there must be merit in what you say, but for the *good of the movement,* we ask you to wait, to defer to the higher aim of draft resistance; besides, if you will fight along with us in our battles, you will receive equality when we return from the serious front.

The weak position paper of the 1967 female caucus brought an anonymous response (*New Left Notes,* 4 December 67) from a male, a response we are still hearing and from both sexes. He suggested (and see how this would sound if the word "black" were substituted) that: (1) there is danger in placing an underdeveloped woman in a position of leadership because her certain failure would only reinforce her sense of innate inferiority; (2) it is not possible for females to separate themselves from the oppressor class; (3) women must be more accepting and understanding than men; (4) women must first educate themselves and develop their capabilities; and finally, (5) when they marry, they should keep their maiden names. Translation: Nigger, you can't be an officer in our white civil rights group until you are properly educated; if you intend to challenge white racists, best do it lovingly, you have no identity of your own, so forget combinations in your own interests; but, we do think an Afro would be advisable.

On Southern plantations in the "days of slavery," each member of a wealthy white family had attached to him, often for life, at least one black person who "did for him." In turn, the black derived from the master a commensurate status. Our analysis should be that it is the destiny of most women— no less the radical—to become, finally, some man's nigger. If these be harsh words they only bespeak a desperate future for the young radical female.

She is dehumanized and politically turned off and turned out. The *Ramparts* issue on Woman Power featured exceptional niggers who had attained positions of power formerly held by men. If one imagines a substitution of that article for one in *Ebony* on successes of black businessmen, our objection is clear. *Ramparts* on female liberation is Urban League logic.

Marilyn Webb's article in *New Left Notes* ("Women: We Have a Common Enemy," 10 June 68) deserves more space. It is dangerous because in its description of the female's lot in the movement it hits the mark perfectly, which only makes its damaged conclusion the more tempting. Marilyn tells it like it is with respect to women in the movement but she refuses to name the representatives of the sexual domination system, refuses to acknowledge that for a time at least, men are the enemy, and that radical men hold the nearest battle position. Instead, she emphasizes that "In building a woman's movement, we clearly see that we have to be active within other, co-ed (if you will) movement organizations and action." She attacks the mini-culture correctly because "We are forced to view ourselves as commodities to be sold sexually," but she hastens to add that we aren't masculine, but instead we are attired in the "colorful dress of a turned-on generation"—the movement has baubles too. She is dismayed that movement marriages rarely last more than two years, but cannot elucidate the obvious reason. Lots of marriages last less than two years, and we assume that radical women catch on a little more quickly to the game, just at that crucial juncture when it's time to "begin raising a family"; they want out before it's too late.

Finally, she invokes the experience of Vietnamese women as her only real programmatic suggestion—the Third World Hang-up, with which we will deal later; to paraphrase: they have their "freedom" because they took up arms to support an ideology they never developed, a political framework in which they never participated, and—get this—because they "could not but identify (their struggle) with the common struggle for liberation." Remember Fidel!

A movement of women which speaks to their needs, and which can mobilize their full political energies, may very well, as we shall propose, look quite different from SDS, SNCC, or the NLF. Any thorough radical analysis would, of course, incorporate a stance vis-a-vis the war, racism, and the Savage Society. But it may be a long and dark passage before ours should risk co-educational alliances or actions.

So the young radical woman does her secretarial tour of duty for the movement, drops out, or, finding that she is getting older, marries. If she marries out of the movement, she's in a position similar to that described in Part I. If she marries within the movement, she is faced with a comparable life style except that (1) she thinks she is already liberated by virtue of marriage to a movement guy, and (2) the movement man has, in addition to the standard male ploys, some extras, even more oblique, confusing, and "convincing." Since they married, in good part, on the basis of a shared and serious commitment, the movement itself then becomes reason for male domination. A radical woman, after all, is more likely to give in when the issue is draft resistance than when it is impressing the boss, although some of that goes on too. It may take two years before she ceases to hand out rhetoric about a "liberated marriage which began several years before the license" and recognizes that the style of her days is more nearly like that of her non-movement sisters than like her husband's. And female liberation literature, so far, offers her no alternative way to go.

Women must work For female liberation first, and now

A respectable canon of new left philosophy to which we turn is that central theme that human beings, by combining in organizations, by seeking to participate in decision-making which affects their lives, can achieve a democratic society, and hence, a life-experience perhaps approximating their potentiality.

> Social life imposes on the consanguineous stocks of mankind an incessant traveling back and forth, and family life is little else than the expression of the need to slacken the pace at the crossroads and to take a chance to rest.
>
> (Levi-Strauss)

We want to make a few tentative comments about the form of the marriage institution, for we hope that radical women will begin to turn from psychiatry to anthropology for insight about their oppressive sexual relationships. Family arrangements, as we all know, vary from culture to culture. While the female has a biological requirement for some support immediately after child-birth, anthropology suggests that the form of this support is not always that which we find institutionalized in the West—namely, one man providing economic aid so that one female can be a full-time mother, with this relationship extended then, perhaps for a lifetime.

The institution of marriage, given us in the United States, was the pawn of other, more powerful, institutions. It is a potent instrument for maintaining the status quo in American Society. It is in the family that children learn so well the dominance-submission game, by observation and participation. Each family, reflecting the perversities of the larger order and split off from the others, is powerless to force change on other institutions, let alone attack or transform its own. And this serves the Savage Society well.

The family owes its characteristic features to the economic necessities of frontier America (nation building), its monogamous form to a statistical and cultural happenstance (monogamy seems to prevail where the sex ratio is about 50/50 and there is a pretense to democracy), and the monogamy is sustained by the Puritan ethic. The particular division of labor was designed to contribute to the industrial revolution, a requirement of the most powerful national institution. Levi-Strauss suggests that "like the form of the family, the division stems more from social and cultural considerations than from natural ones." He recalls the "Nambikwara father nursing his baby and cleaning it when it soils itself" as a contrast to the European nobleman who rarely sees his children. And he notes that the "young concubines of the Nambikwara chieftain disdain domestic activities and prefer to share in their husband's adventurous expeditions." In the absence of household servants, most American émigré men first subdued one woman, and with her aid produced a family of servants sufficient at least to manage the homestead and offer him the leisure to participate in town politics and even revolutions.

Now, with birth control, higher education for women, and the movement itself, it is becoming clear to some women that the marriage institution, like so many others, is an anachronism. For unmarried women it offers only a sanctional security and the promise of love. The married woman knows that love is, at its best, an inadequate reward for her unnecessary and bizarre heritage of oppression. The marriage institution does not free women; it does not provide for emotional and intellectual growth; and it offers no political resources. Were it not for male-legislated discrimination in employment, it would show little economic advantage.

Instead, she is locked into a relationship which is oppressive politically, exhausting physically, stereotyped emotionally and sexually, and atrophying intellectually. She teams up with an individual groomed from birth to rule, and she is equipped for revolt only with the foot-shuffling, head-scratching gestures of "feminine guile." We conceptualize the significance of the marriage institution this way:

$$\frac{\text{Marriage}}{\text{Integration}} \qquad \frac{\text{Women}}{\text{Blacks}}$$

Marriage, as we know it, is for women as integration is for blacks. It is the atomization of a sex so as to render it politically powerless. The anachronism remains because women won't fight it, because men derive valuable benefits from it and will not give them up, and because, even given a willingness among men and women to transform the institution, it is at the mercy of the more powerful institutions which use it and which give it its form.

We would return to our relational model and suggest that some women will have to remove themselves totally from the marriage arrangement which insists that they love, in a predetermined style, their own personal masters. And married women will have to do this periodically to revitalize their commitment to their sex and to the liberation movement.

All-female communes for radical women

Many younger, unmarried women live in all-female groups now. The problem, as we have mentioned earlier, is that these domiciles are not self-consciously arranged to serve political as well as personal needs. They are not a temporary stopping off place for women who need to re-evaluate their lives. They are no sanctuary from destructive male-female encounters. They are no base for female liberation work.

Some radical women, in deciding to live together, ought to fashion homes which have definite political goals. A woman, married or unmarried, could move into such a center for a period of time and be relieved of the terrible compulsion to one-up her sisters in dating, grooming, etc. The commune should decide on house rules, experiment with sexual relationships on an equal basis with men (that is, remove the bordello element from the place). The commune should be a center for women to live during decision periods in their lives. We all know about these crisis periods; most of the time we manage to suffer through them while at the same time carrying all the burdens of "keeping face," maintaining some sexual life, etc. The commune would define itself as a female place. Innumerable experiments in living, political forays and serious and uninterrupted thinking could center in the commune.

While sexual and emotional alliances with men may continue to be of some benefit the peculiar domestic institution is not. Only women can define what "womanhood" might best be, and likewise men might better redefine themselves in the absence of a daily reminder of their unwarranted experience of masterdom. Theoretically, such women and men might, in the future, liberated from this master-slave hang-up, meet and work out a new domestic institution which better serves the interest of free men and free women. We do not feel compelled to offer any Utopian model for that institution, but we are certain that it will be designed most rapidly, and most reasonably, by liberated souls. Some women, then, and perhaps some men, will have to reject the present domestic model given us, destroy it, and build another.

And we consider this operation worthy of the time of radical women. Let us review briefly why this program at least parallels in importance the anti-draft, anti-imperialistic movements we all know. (1) People Get Radicalized Fighting Their Own Battles. For women, these are her chains, and she will ultimately invest more energy and in the process become radicalized, breaking them than attacking the other forms of colonialism men urge us to fight. (2) Pace of History Making. Men have accelerated their rate of history-making beyond humane proportions. With their slaves secure at home, they have the time to play abstractly and inhumanly with their technology and to make history more rapidly than they can effectively comprehend or control. Robbed of a faithful custodial class (women, blacks, etc.), they will be less effective, and time may finally overtake them so that where they're at is also where it's at. Women who organize other women to slow male history-making are functioning, in this country, at their political best. (3) Benefits Accrue to the Movement. The goal of the new left is to dismantle outworn institutions and replace them with better arrangements. Presently, the energies of radical women are not wholeheartedly with this effort because it has no program which speaks to their needs. Women mobilized where they stand against the nearest oppressor, will make their most effective contribution to this process.

We cannot cover all the bases in such a paper. A few, perhaps the most pressing, deserve attention here.

Long-term goals vs. short-term tactics

One of the serious flaws in most radical male thinking is the substitution of goals for tactics. The Columbia sit-ins, with all of their attendant anti-feminism, were guerrilla plays. It was a good show, and we all applauded from in front of our television sets. It lacked a tone, however, an important tone and thrust, which should accompany any such further operations. Women make the same mistake when they perform guerrilla theater at SDS conventions, and so it is important to look for a moment at the Columbia scene.

Everybody inside the buildings knew that they remained there only because the administration hesitated, foolishly, to mount its police attack. Nobody thought the students would actually hold Columbia, and subsequently administrators have dropped the guise of dialogue and moved in immediately with their troops. The action was groovy, but the retrospective analysis is misleading. That operation at Columbia cannot be cast parallel with sieges on Saigon, etc. But most movement men are unable to see it as merely a "royal finger" given the establishment. Instead, they talk about occupation and sieges. And because they up the ante on their behavior, attempt to make it look like something it was not, women are pulled along as support troops, taken in by the rhetoric. A play is a play however you cut it. And if the men cannot admit that the movement cannot take tangible territory, women shouldn't fall into the trap. In radical journals, the tone of analysis should be: "Well, we really shook them up for a while—they fell for our revolutionary language and provided a good forum. The next operation, however, can't take the same form because they're on to our game." A lot of movement men would prefer a Columbia "siege" to telling their parents when to shove it. And I imagine that most of the women who perform guerrilla theater protests against male chauvinism would find it far more scary to, let us say, refuse to perform their traditional domestic tasks for movement men. Demonstrations in this country are still limited to two functions: (1) radicalizing the participants, and (2) getting a point across to the media or a constituency. As long as we remember this, men in the movement won't claim the prerogatives of participation in a real "third world" battle, and women won't feel obligated, by falling into the analogy, to limit themselves to loading the metaphorical guns.

From looking around these days, it becomes obvious that the radicals of the early '60s do grow older. Most of them are still alive, much to their own surprise. And the wiser men among them are beginning to talk about programs which will keep the older troops in touch and in action. Women must do the same. When we begin to go about organizing, we will have to recognize that we are dealing with a number of constituencies and design our tactics accordingly. A radical confrontation for one group would be an unavailable option to another. I would like to cover briefly some topics which may serve in the overall strategy for female liberation.

Integration: the central problem

Most women are integrated with men in an ongoing institutionalized setup. One or two all-female meetings, or even one a month, will not begin to solve our problems or guide our programming intelligently. The particular need to get together is shared by the youngest and the older, married women who have children. We are all separated from each other. This does not mean that the constituency should meet together—there is no little hostility among older women toward what they imagine to be their more liberated younger sisters, and the problems differ. The tactics will differ. But both groups need to plan programs in which women can meet for extended periods to talk about the political issues of female liberation. And this meeting, this talking, in itself, is more difficult than we had imagined.

But women are beginning to meet, and they are beginning to talk to each other. That some of these discussions produce ideas or actions at which male radicals giggle, and Aunt Thomasinas cat-call, is a measure of what we are up against.

Children

The big push to have children, whether we are married or not, should be viewed as one of the strong links in the chain which enslaves us. Biological arguments are romantically blown out of proportion by men and their "Dr. Joyce Brothers" spokesmen in the female ghetto of the mind. We have plenty of so-called biological needs which we have learned to control or rechannel for political purposes. Let us remember that many of us have been willing to exchange, for principle, what are bound to be even more basic needs: food, during hunger strikes; and our lives, in police battles and the more extended confrontations on dirt roads in the civil rights South. We were willing to face being shotgunned to death for black voter registration; I think we can defer dropping children on cultural command for our own thing, if we think that necessary. I am not making a call for eternal celibacy, but for intelligent birth control and a rethinking of the compulsion to have children, a compulsion, I am sure, which still troubles even the most "liberated" of women. The same radical woman who thinks draft resistance is more important than female liberation ends up having a baby, and then she is immobilized for both battles. If we take seriously our role in history, we will plan to have or not have children on a political basis.

Sexuality and celibacy

Control over our own sexuality is another short-term goal. We all believe in birth control and legalized abortion. However, there is little talk of periodic, self-imposed celibacy. We are brainwashed by the media with sexy commercials and talk in the movement about screwing as often as possible; many of us have already been on the pill for longer than we can medically afford. And a good many of us, I would suspect, are desperately screwing some guy because we think we should and wonder what our friends would think if we didn't at all for a while. Celibacy has always been a tool for those who wish, for a time, to "stop the world and get off." It requires, for an unmarried woman, a lot more time to maintain a sexual relationship than it does for her male partner; many of these relationships are mind-blowers as well. Radical women could gain a lot in time, energy, and getting themselves together if they would avail themselves of this tactic occasionally. We must stop being pawns in the media's sexuality game and reconsider the whole scene.

Emergency tactics for non-separatists

Those radical females already married, but without children, should be prepared to make a decision about how they will live their lives in order to have time for their political activities. Regardless of who is working, going to school, etc., you should demand equal time for your own things. This requires your husband to assume half of the burden of maintaining a home: in terms of cooking, cleaning, laundering, entertaining, etc. If he can't do these things now, you can teach him. If you plan to live with your husband, you will have to begin making changes in the marital pattern. And the chances are that unless he has a radical analysis which is pretty thorough, your marriage will end in divorce if you take this route.

If you have children already, the most devastating pattern of the male-female relationship has set in long ago. If you are serious about political activity and female liberation, you may have to make important adjustments in your life. Presently you work from daybreak until the time when your husband falls asleep. He will have to assume enough of the child-caring and housekeeping chores so that you each have equal time off during each day. His posture of dominance will be threatened, his time consumed, and his ability to live in "maleville" decimated by such a plan. Stop-gap measures such as communal evening-care centers and communal eating are short-term tactics which serve the long-term goal of freeing women up for first class personal and political behavior. What is central to our problem is our complete alienation from other women. We will have to get out of our houses and meet with them on serious issues. The most serious for the moment is not the war, the draft, the presidency, the racial problem, but our own problem. We will need each other's support and advice to achieve liberation. We will need time to read, to study, to write, to debate, among ourselves. And when we act politically, we will need time for organizing, etc.

No woman can go this alone. The territory ahead is new, frightening, and appears lonely. We must begin by forming organizations which will provide emotional support and an intellectual base for framing action. If we are to enter the struggle, and in addition, attempt to preserve our marriages, it will require group approaches. It will require a realistic appraisal of the history of women, which we must research and compile. It may require new programs for economic self-help, in anticipation of male retribution.

Underlying much of the evasiveness, the apparent lack of self-confidence, and even the downright silliness among women when confronted with the possibility of a female liberation movement, is the big male gun—the charge of homosexuality. Before turning to some current hassles in our movement, many of which at least partially derive from this question, we want to begin an open discussion of homosexuality in the hope that future conferences and private thinking will consider the issue.

Homosexuality

The radical woman, for very specific reasons, is probably more up tight about homosexuality than other women. This is one of the curious paradoxes in the movement; in many ways, movement people tend to maintain some Puritan mores to excess. Most of us entered the movement on the basis of simple, middle class, idealistic hangups. Our parents taught us all the tenets of "clean living," including equality for the races and humanity among men, and when we got to college we recognized that this was science fiction. Our minds were momentarily blown, we went to a meeting somewhere, got involved, and a few of us got radicalized along the way. While younger radicals tend to be more cynical, perhaps have freer life-styles, all of us have a heritage which is essentially Puritanical. Homosexuality is "wrong."

There are political considerations. Those who are actually organizing disapprove of drug use which becomes so extensive that the user drops out politically. We look upon homosexuals who will not protest openly against mores as cop-outs. And while we are willing to combat the social order, while we accept ostracism from our families and live in that twilight zone which is at once inside and outside of the system, for self-protection we have learned a thousand tricks to forestall the ultimate bust—legal or psychological. Homosexuality, we imagine, would be too much to add to an already strained relationship with the society in which we dwell.

And there are practical considerations. We don't carry with us, as part of our movement baggage, an understanding of homosexual technique, so our childhood excursions appear bland in comparison with even the clumsiest heterosexual referent.

The movement places no premium on homosexuality. While everybody clamors for more meaningful relationships, more self-expression, more affection, and less inhibition in our social styles, nobody suggests in radical journals that we mean homosexuality. Anything but that; what we say is that we wish people would not define as homosexual the new human forms of relationship we want to enjoy. This must have been what the SDS men were playing at the convention when they complained to radical women that they "aren't supposed to cry or to express their love for each other physically" (*Guardian*, 28 June 68). For once they were caught in their own bag.

Women who turn from men for a time, to look to each other for political relationships, movement thinking, and an organizational milieu, are bound to see here and there someone they love. The slightest measure of female liberation will bring with it an ability to perceive again the precise qualities and degree of responsivity which inhere in other women. For those in serious communes or political trenches, a continued fear of homosexuality may be the one last strand by which the male order can pull us back into tow. It has been our past error to repress the political attraction we have for our own kind. It would be equally wrong to turn female communes into anything less than a tentative experiment with a new domestic arrangement; political content will not suffice to fill the need every human has for that place where one "slackens the pace at the crossroads, and takes a chance to rest." It will be in these communes, or their less rigorous counterparts in female rediscovery, that we may learn to design new living arrangements which will make our co-existence with men in the future all the more equal and all the more humane. And exploring the possibilities of non-elitist, non-colonial love may teach us forms of political strength far more valuable than guerrilla theater.

We have got to stop throwing around terms like "fag," "pimp," "queer," and "dike" to reassure men of our absolute loyalty to them. This is the language which helps to insure that each man has his female slave, and that each woman eventually becomes one.

Indirect male sniping, insinuating homosexuality is a horror which is bound to attend female liberation activity, has some interesting analogies in our movement experience. It's like the signals Southern Whites put out: "If you leave a white and a black alone for five minutes, there's no telling what might happen." And it's a lot like Red-baiting. Our answers to Red-baiting will serve us well here. The charge of homosexuality—which will be more openly voiced by non-movement males—stands for a fear of something greater, as did the charge of communism against Southern blacks and whites getting together: that they might get together. An indigenous movement of any people determined to gain their liberation is a more serious threat than "Communism" or "homosexuality," and the charge is merely a delaying tactic to obstruct organization.

We should begin to talk about homosexuality; be prepared to defend against male sniping on the issue. Most importantly, we should not couch the issue in the language of "affection" until we can define affection through the experience of our liberation and then stand by our knowledge, whatever that may come to be.

6. SOME CURRENT HASSLES IN THE DEVELOPMENT OF THE MOVEMENT

The co-ed model

Several thoughtful writers have recently suggested that all-female groups be organized to fight corporate liberalism on the early Black Power model. That is, these new groups formed to attack the draft, racism, etc., would be distinguishable from traditional movement groups only in their all-female composition. Presumably, these groups would negotiate with others on a coalition, or as Marilyn Webb puts it, a co-ed basis. If there is any need at all for solely female political groups, this purposeful segregation by sex must then mean that some women consider themselves—if not an oppressed class—at least different from men in a politically relevant way. If men are to be permitted to continue defining the movement for us while we operate in these co-ed arrangements, why segregate at all, since we all agree that they do their thing better than we do, for now, anyway. I suspect that even the formation of such groups as Coretta King's implies something about the female condition other than anatomy.

Women should combine politically and define for themselves their enemy and describe the machinery of their oppression. We should not promise in advance that we will join any specific issue. We think that well organized women, supportive of each other, will carry their share.

The third world analogy

The third world analogy has caused plenty of trouble in the radical male left. Looking to revolutionary movements in underdeveloped countries has encouraged a sort of one-upmanship desperation to act; and, much to its detriment, the left usually only mimics in what are essentially theatrical performances, the real life blood and guts scene of revolutionary movements in action.

What is so important for women is that we not become trapped in this frenzied, often irrational behavior. The Third World Analogy is inappropriate to us. First, the conditions under which people live in ongoing revolutions are simply different from ours and call for different activity. Second, radical women who invoke the Third World Analogy are unaware of the role women have actually played in the Cuban, Vietnamese, and Algerian struggles; or, if they describe these roles accurately, they then romanticize, misquote, and generally push them off as something desirable, when in fact these roles are pawns of a historical circumstance—imperialism—not chosen by those in revolt.

In female liberation literature we hear about three groups of women who allegedly "won their freedom" or are winning equality by picking up guns and fighting for the national liberation of one or another country. Cuba, the most often cited case, did use women as troops, much as they are used in SDS. In the war, women had much the same status as the female in SDS, and now that the Cuban revolution has moved into its cultural phase, we know what Castro wants them to do: go home, cook, take care of the kids. It is true that many women are becoming doctors (Russia has more female physicians than male; this is the highest rank in the "caring for" professions). Certainly a few are executives in the nationalized Ford Motors to the South. But the largest female group, the Women's Federation, "does not crusade for the emancipation of women." Of course, "its main function is to implement government work policies" ("Cuban Women," by Mary Nel-

son, *Voice of the Women's Liberation Movement,* June 1968).
Mary Nelson, who has just returned, tells us that nothing
basic has changed in patterns of dominance between the
sexes. OEO may provide public nurseries for working women
before Castro gets hep. What's the big hangup with Cuba?
Men still run it their own way, for their own ends.

Socialism, or even a commitment to socialism, is viewed
by many American women as the panacea for their problems.
Why doesn't anybody ever talk about the plight of women in
the socialized Mid-Eastern or African nations?

Now Marilyn Webb is cool. She can strain the analogy
between the US left and the NLF just enough to make it
look reasonable for the American women, who can't be in
the black thing, and want to do something, to think of themselves as Vietnamese. What we have got to recognize is that
women living in Viet Nam face very different circumstances
than our own. Their children, and they themselves, are being
murdered daily, and a third of the population goes about
missing a limb. Under constant military attack, it is necessary
to defer designing new institutions in order to preserve life
itself; Vietnamese women have no choice. We should admit
that we are not in the same position. We who support draft
resistance are not being literally shelled out of existence. And
more to the point, women who *merely* support draft resistance
are not doing all they can in what is an essentially revolutionary movement. In the United States, women ought to be
organizing women, as their proper constituency, to add to
the growing number of disaffected quarters. In a country
which is on the offensive in the world, our job is to reorganize
our institutions so that they are no longer viable instruments
of colonialism and war. Marilyn tells us that Vietnamese
women found out that the only way they can get equality
is to participate in the national political struggle. The strict
analogy between Viet Nam and the United States is more
realistically phrased: American women would get a lot more
equality if they gave militant support to our *national* struggle:
to colonize, to murder, to enslave. The most proper third
world analogy I have heard is the "eerie, high pitched wail
of the Algerian women." That is already our own.

Male chauvinism

Somebody very courageously put this phrase into the female manifesto at last year's SDS Convention, and ever since,
women have been taking it back or redefining it to spare the

male ego. There is great value in naming your enemy. The definition of the phrase goes: Surname of Nicolas Chauvin, soldier of Napoleon I, notorious for his bellicose attachment to the lost imperial cause: militant, unreasoning devotion to one's race, sex, etc., with contempt for other races, the opposite sex, etc.: as, male chauvinism. The phrase makes some sense, and if you apply it to men in general, rather than to the nice guy you're living with (this comes later), that's more or less where it's at.

The argument over terminology really stands for a much more important proposition, one to which Carl Oglesby addressed himself some time ago. He presented a very significant speech in which he kept repeating to this effect: Let's stop talking about General Motors, the Poverty Program, or the Justice Department; let's call it by its name; it has a name, and that name is the System. We're not going to solve the problem by attacking General Motors; the system is the enemy, let's call it by its name. The drive for domination, be it genetic or learned, which so aptly characterizes the male sex, finds larger expression in our national posture. We may decide later, as the female liberation movement matures, that our real job is to dethrone the king—an entire sex bred for mastery—and replace it with an order which more closely corresponds with the traditional female approach: attention to personal needs, caring for others, making decisions on the basis of a multitude of human data. If this be our goal, we must, as must all oppressed people, assume for a time an adversary stance (unaccustomed for women) toward our oppressors. Since such a stance places a premium on winning, we are going to have to name what it is that we want to win, and against whom; that requires naming goals and the enemy.

In the life of each woman, the most immediate oppressor, however unwilling he may be in theory to play that role, is "the man." Even if we prefer to view him as merely a pawn in the game, he's still the foreman on the big plantation of maleville. And that plantation has a name. While "male chauvinism" isn't sacred, if we're searching for a better name for the enemy, let's not de-escalate.

So-called female elitism and male liberation groups

It turns out that men at the SDS convention this summer got hacked off having to drink beer waiting for the women to return from political discussion. They started talking about the oppressive aspects of the male roles given them. Like when a white person first realizes that racism hurts him too. Well, fine, if men want to form male liberation groups, they should go ahead. But what we must understand is that in the area of sex, a male liberation group *could* be to female liberation what "SPONGE" is to the black revolution. That is, I wonder if these male groups will focus on supporting us, when we want them, in our attacks on the male order; or, will they attempt to liberate themselves at our further expense. From Susan Sutheim's report ("Women Shake Up SDS Session," *Guardian*, 28 June 68), the impulse for male liberation groups sounds reactionary, and in our community, when the term is used, it is often accompanied by a particularly vengeful smirk.

However, as we have already suggested, with a separation of the sexes, real or political, some men might come to a more humane understanding of what it means to be a man. And if this is the program the men intend to pursue, let them go it alone. We must remember that there is a great difference between an organization of the dominant and an organization of the oppressed, whatever sweet language attempts to fuse the two (as, for example, Johnson's grunting out "We Shall Overcome").

Susan Sutheim, who wants to invite men to female liberation meetings, and who supports the idea of male liberation groups, assumes that the problem is limited to psychological flaws in sexual roles; in fact, the problem is political and does not call for desegregated soul searching. We don't need T-groups. And as one of the Canadian women has observed, men will not participate democratically in decisionmaking that disrupts their lives.

The hysterical and reactionary responses of men at the SDS convention this summer—the charges of female elitism and the call for male liberation groups—will serve their function with women who insist upon an NAACP approach to their condition: half-assed attempts to recapture some half-assed female territory.

7. SOME URGENT PRIORITIES

As we begin talking to women about female liberation, most of them accept our description of our lot with little argument. But they do come on with honest fears about engaging in the movement, and they tell us how incompetent (inferior) they feel, how they lack self-confidence (have been brainwashed), how they don't have much time (got a lot of custodial tasks on the home front), and most important how they're scared.

Being afraid has been a genuine response of oppressed people to their initial encounter with a vision of liberation. As is always the case, discipline and organization are the antidote, the means by which the exploited are drawn out of the routine of their ghettos. We cannot meet fear with rhetoric or statistics. We must become ready to organize, support, and act.

As radical women, we must set the tone, and there are several things we can begin doing now. We can discuss the problems of organizing uncommitted women and designing for them support facilities which will free them up for political behavior. We can get clear about our own history. We should elevate our own, and there really are some groovy women in the movement. We can begin to think about our proper relationships to our derivative movements, to the men we know and to men as a class. The professionals among us can look into legal discrimination and the lies about our history. We can support the newsletter and the journal and write out and exchange our thoughts in these media. And, we can begin to think about organizing projects, pacing and fashioning them, so that they speak to American women about their condition and encourage them to join the movement.

A good U.S. newsletter, *Voice of the Women's Liberation Movement,* has already started. It serves well the functions of rapid communication, morale-building, and reporting of organizational activity. Dee Ann Pappas has begun a journal which offers a forum for larger organizational issues, studies on women, the history of women, and female art. Marilyn Webb and others have already initiated some fascinating organizing projects.

A Personal Summary

June 17, 1968

I had saved this particular evening for reviewing our paper, perhaps to add and change a word or two. But I cannot approach the task properly, because today I witnessed once more that sort of oppression which drives one back into the thick of the movement. And as I sit here in poorly controlled rage, I realize that there is one thing we have omitted from our paper which I must try to fill in now.

The media warn us daily of a national and even international Apocalypse. We who have experienced the movement—even as troops in the battles of others—know so well that for many people the Day of Doom has been the measure of their years and the only Revelation of their lives. Political and emotional devastation are the weird bread and wine—the vinegared communion—of the Damned. Our experience attunes us to these people, their lives, but they move among us, except when we know rage, only as metaphors for our understanding of the social order.

And in our paper we have not yet spoken of that indignation, that rage—perhaps the essence of militancy—which almost never finds its way into movement writing but which surely must be the impetus of our commitment. Tonight I am with the rage, an old friend now. And since for me, at any rate, that rage has always been the maelstrom in which I come to recall again my own alienation, my own political powerlessness, the peculiar prison of my female days, as well as my passion for my comrades, I want to share it in this context.

The occasion is one we all have known. I was writing earlier of a friend who had spent several months in jail. This morning I watched while a Southern judge racked her again on another charge, and this one carrying a big penalty. No bail, no appeal—off to the prisonhouse with one of the best and most beautiful of my generation and my sex. Can we allow this to be our Coda?

We gathered up her children and sent them to safety, out of reach of the greedy juvenile officers. My husband and I reordered her now silent house, locked the doors again. Because this rare, rare, white woman had become a sort of Che in another land than her own, the black community will pop off tonight. But we worry very little about our safety now, for this kind of rage makes one brave and negligent of the usual curious defenses. Carol Thomas felt it so often, herself moving with the doomed, was brave so often, was enraged so often, and now is racked by the Savage Society, as she so often had been before. Carol, my sister, they have got you again in that ugly place they build as a refuge from themselves.

We have not conned ourselves into political paralysis as an excuse for inaction—we are a subjugated caste. We need to develop a female movement, most importantly, because we must fight this social order with all of the faculties we have got, and those in full gear. And we must be liberated so that we can turn from our separate domestic desperation—our own Apocalypse of the Damned—toward an exercise of social rage against each dying of the light. We must get our stuff together, begin to dismantle this system's deadly social and military toys, and stop the mad dogs who rule us every place we're at.

"I am my brother's keeper" is the cautious altruism of those who are themselves enchained. Rather: "I Am My Brother's Brother, My Sister's Sister." Women together, sustaining each other politically, restored to an affection for each other, and unburdening themselves of their struggle with men, must move to take that Savage Society apart.

Bread and Roses*

KATHY MCAFEE and MYRNA WOOD

A great deal of confusion exists today about the role of women's liberation in a revolutionary movement. Hundreds of women's groups have sprung up within the past year or two, but among them, a number of very different and often conflicting ideologies have developed. The growth of these movements has demonstrated the desperate need that many women feel to escape their own oppression, but it has also shown that organization around women's issues need not lead to revolutionary consciousness, or even to an identification with the left. (Some groups mobilize middle class women to fight for equal privileges as businesswomen and academics; others maintain that the overthrow of capitalism is irrelevant for women.)

Many movement women have experienced the initial exhilaration of discovering women's liberation as an issue, of realizing that the frustration, anger, and fear we feel are not a result of individual failure but are shared by all our sisters, and of sensing—if not fully understanding—that these feelings stem from the same oppressive conditions that give rise to racism, chauvinism and the barbarity of American culture.

*From *Leviathan #3* (June, 1969).

But many movement women, too, have become disillusioned after a time by their experiences with women's liberation groups. More often than not these groups never get beyond the level of therapy sessions; rather than aiding the political development of women and building a revolutionary women's movement, they often encourage escape from political struggle.

The existence of this tendency among women's liberation groups is one reason why many movement activists (including some women) have come out against a women's liberation movement that distinguishes itself from the general movement, even if it considers itself part of the left. A movement organized by women around the oppression of women, they say, is bound to emphasize the bourgeois and personal aspects of oppression and to obscure the material oppression of working class women *and men*. At best, such a movement "lacks revolutionary potential" (Bernadine Dohrn, *N.L.N.*, V.4, No. 9). In SDS, where this attitude is very strong, questions about the oppression and liberation of women are raised only within the context of current SDS ideology and strategy; the question of women's liberation is raised only as an incidental, subordinate aspect of programs around "*the* primary struggle," anti-racism. (Although most people in SDS now understand the extent of black people's oppression, they are not aware of the fact that the median wage of working women, (black and white) is lower than that of black males.) The male domination of the organization has not been affected by occasional rhetorical attacks on male chauvinism and most important, very little organizing of women is being done.

Although the reason behind it can be understood, this attitude toward women's liberation is mistaken and dangerous. By discouraging the development of a revolutionary women's liberation movement, it avoids a serious challenge to what, along with racism, is the deepest source of division and false consciousness among workers. By setting up (in the name of Marxist class analysis) a dichotomy between the "bourgeois," personal and psychological forms of oppression on the one hand, and the "real" material forms on the other, it substitutes a mechanistic model of class relations for a more profound understanding of how these two aspects of oppression depend upon and reinforce each other. Finally, this anti-women's liberationist attitude makes it easier for us to bypass a confrontation of male chauvinism and the closely related values of elitism and authoritarianism which are weakening our movement.

Before we can discuss the potential of a women's liberation movement, we need a more precise description of the way the oppression of women functions in a capitalist society. This will also help us understand the relation of psychological to material oppression.

(1) *Male Chauvinism—the attitude that women are the passive and inferior servants of society and of men—sets women apart from the rest of the working class.* Even when they do the same work as men, women are not considered workers in the same sense, with the need and right to work to provide for their families or to support themselves independently. They are expected to accept work at lower wages and without job security. Thus they can be used as a marginal or reserve labor force when profits depend on extra low costs or when men are needed for war.

Women are not supposed to be independent, so they are not supposed to have any "right to work." This means, in effect, that although they do work, they are denied the right to organize and fight for better wages and conditions. Thus the role of women in the labor force undermines the struggles of male workers as well. The boss can break a union drive by threatening to hire lower paid women or blacks. In many cases, where women are organized, the union contract reinforces their inferior position, making women the least loyal and militant union members. (Standard Oil workers in San Francisco recently paid the price of male supremacy. Women at Standard Oil have the least chance for advancement and decent pay, and the union has done little to fight this. Not surprisingly, women formed the core of the back to work move that eventually broke the strike.)[1]

In general, because women are defined as docile, helpless, and inferior they are forced into the most demeaning and mindrotting jobs—from scrubbing floors to filing cards—under the most oppressive conditions where they are treated like children or slaves. Their very position reinforces the idea, even among the women themselves, that they are fit for and should be satisfied with this kind of work.

(2) *Apart from the direct, material exploitation of women, male supremacy acts in more subtle ways to undermine class consciousness.* The tendency of male workers to think of themselves primarily as men (i.e., powerful) rather than as workers (i.e., members of an oppressed group) promotes a false sense of privilege and power, and an identification with the world of men, including the boss. The petty dictatorship which most men exercise over their wives and families enables them

to vent their anger and frustration in a way which poses no challenge to the system. The role of the man in the family reinforces aggressive individualism, authoritarianism, and a hierarchical view of social relations—values which are fundamental to the perpetuation of capitalism. In this system we are taught to relieve our fears and frustrations by brutalizing those weaker than we are: a man in uniform turns into a pig; the foreman intimidates the man on the line; the husband beats his wife, child, and dog.

(3) *Women are further exploited in their roles as housewives and mothers, through which they reduce the costs (social and economic) of maintaining the labor force.* All of us will admit that inadequate as it may be American workers have a relatively decent standard of living, in a strictly material sense, when compared to workers of other countries or periods of history. But American workers are exploited and harassed in other ways than through the size of the weekly paycheck. They are made into robots on the job; they are denied security; they are forced to pay for expensive insurance and can rarely save enough to protect them from sudden loss of job or emergency. They are denied decent medical care and a livable environment. They are cheated by inflation. They are "given" a regimented education that prepares them for a narrow slot or for nothing. And they are taxed heavily to pay for these "benefits."

In all these areas, it is a woman's responsibility to make up for the failures of the system. In countless working class families, it is mother's job that bridges the gap between week to week subsistence and relative security. It is her wages that enable the family to eat better food, to escape their oppressive surroundings through a trip, an occasional movie, or new clothes. It is her responsibility to keep her family healthy despite the cost of decent medical care; to make a comfortable home in an unsafe and unlivable neighborhood; to provide a refuge from the alienation of work and to keep the male ego in good repair. It is she who must struggle daily to make ends meet despite inflation. She must make up for the fact that her children do not receive a decent education and she must salvage their damaged personalities.

A woman is judged as a wife and mother—the only role she is allowed—according to her ability to maintain stability in her family and to help her family "adjust" to harsh realities. She therefore transmits the values of hard work and conformity to each generation of workers. It is she who forces her children to stay in school and "behave" or who urges her husband not to risk his job by standing up to the boss or going on strike.

Thus the role of wife and mother is one of social mediator and pacifier. She shields her family from the direct impact of class oppression. She is the true opiate of the masses.

(4) *Working class women and other women as well are exploited as consumers.* They are forced to buy products which are necessities, but which have waste built into them, like the soap powder, the price of which includes fancy packaging and advertising. They also buy products which are wasteful in themselves because they are told that a new car or TV will add to their families' status and satisfaction, or that cosmetics will increase their desirability as sex objects. Among "middle class" women, of course, the second type of wasteful consumption is more important than it is among working class women, but all women are victims of both types to a greater or lesser extent, and the values which support wasteful consumption are part of our general culture.

(5) *All women, too, are oppressed and exploited sexually.* For working class women this oppression is more direct and brutal. They are denied control of their own bodies, when as girls they are refused information about sex and birth control, and when as women they are denied any right to decide whether and when to have children. Their confinement to the role of sex partner and mother, and their passive submission to a single man are often maintained by physical force. The relative sexual freedom of "middle class" or college educated women, however, does not bring *them* real independence. Their sexual role is still primarily a passive one; their value as individuals still determined by their ability to attract, please, and hold on to a man. The definition of women as docile and dependent, inferior in intellect and weak in character cuts across class lines.

A woman of any class is expected to sell herself—not just her body but her entire life, her talents, interests, and dreams —to a man. She is expected to give up friendships, ambitions, pleasures, and moments of time to herself in order to serve his career or his family. In return, she receives not only her livelihood but her identity, her very right to existence, for unless she is the wife of someone or the mother of someone, a woman is nothing.

In this summary of the forms of oppression of women in this society, the rigid dichotomy between material oppression and psychological oppression fails to hold, for it can be seen that these two aspects of oppression reinforce each other at every level. A woman may seek a job out of absolute necessity, or in order to escape repression and dependence at home. In either case, on the job she will be persuaded or forced to accept low pay, indignity and a prison-like atmosphere because a woman isn't supposed to need money or respect. Then, after working all week turning tiny wires, or typing endless forms, she finds that cooking and cleaning, dressing up and making up, becoming submissive and childlike in order to please a man is her only relief, so she gladly falls back into her "proper" role.

All women, even including those of the ruling class, are oppressed as women in the sense that their real fulfillment is linked to their role as girlfriend, wife or mother. This definition of women is part of bourgeois culture—the whole superstructure of ideas that serves to explain and reinforce the social relations of capitalism. It is applied to all women, but it has very different consequences for women of different classes. For a ruling class woman, it means she is denied real independence, dignity, and sexual freedom. For a working class woman it means this too, but it also justifies her material super-exploitation and physical coercion. Her oppression is a total one.[2]

II.

It is true, as the movement critics assert, that the present women's liberation groups are almost entirely based among "middle class" women, that is, college and career women; and the issues of psychological and sexual exploitation and, to a lesser extent, exploitation through consumption, have been the most prominent ones.

It is not surprising that the women's liberation movement should begin among bourgeois women, and should be dominated in the beginning by their consciousness and their particular concerns. Radical women are generally the post war middle class generation that grew up with the right to vote, the chance at higher education and training for supportive roles in the professions and business. Most of them are young and sophisticated enough to have not yet had children and do not have to marry to support themselves. In comparison with most women, they are capable of a certain amount of control over their lives.

The higher development of bourgeois democratic society allows the women who benefit from education and relative equality to see the contradictions between its rhetoric (every boy can become president) and their actual place in that society. The working class woman might believe that education could have made her financially independent but the educated career woman finds that money has not made her independent. In fact, because she has been allowed to progress halfway on the upward-mobility ladder she can see the rest of the distance that is denied her only because she is a woman. She can see the similarity between her oppression and that of other sections of the population. Thus, from their own experience, radical women in the movement are aware of more faults in the society than racism and imperialism. Because they have pushed the democratic myth to its limits, they know concretely how it limits them.

At the same time that radical women were learning about American society they were also becoming aware of the male chauvinism in the movement. In fact, that is usually the cause of their first conscious verbalization of the prejudice they feel; it is more disillusioning to know that the same contradiction exists between the movement's rhetoric of equality and its reality, for we expect more of our comrades.

This realization of the deep-seated prejudice against themselves in the movement produces two common reactions among its women: (1) a preoccupation with this immediate barrier (and perhaps a resultant hopelessness), and (2) a tendency to retreat inward, to buy the fool's gold of creating a personally liberated life style.

However, our concept of liberation represents a consciousness that conditions have forced on us while most of our sisters are chained by other conditions, biological and economic, that overwhelm their humanity and desires for self fulfillment. Our background accounts for our ignorance about the stark oppression of women's daily lives.

Few radical women really know the worst of women's condition. They do not understand the anxious struggle of an uneducated girl to find the best available man for financial security and escape from a crowded and repressive home. They have not suffered years of fear from ignorance and helplessness about pregnancies. Few have experienced constant violence and drunkenness of a brutalized husband or father. They do not know the day to day reality of being chained to a house and family, with little money and lots of bills, and no diversions but TV.

Not many radical women have experienced 9–11 hours a day of hard labor, carrying trays on aching legs for rude customers who may leave no tip, but leave a feeling of degradation from their sexual or racist remarks—and all of this for $80–$90 a week. Most movement women have not learned to blank out their thoughts for 7 hours in order to type faster or file endless numbers. They have not felt their own creativity deadened by this work, while watching men who were not trained to be typists move on to higher level jobs requiring "brain-work."

In summary: because male supremacy (assumption of female inferiority, regulation of women to service roles, and sexual objectification) crosses class lines, radical women are conscious of women's oppression, but because of their background, they lack consciousness of most women's class oppression.

III.

The development of the movement has produced different trends within the broad women's liberation movement. Most existing women's groups fall into one of the four following categories:

(1) *Personal Liberation Groups.* This type of group has been the first manifestation of consciousness of their own oppression among movement women. By talking about their frustrations with their role in the movement, they have moved from feelings of personal inadequacy to the realization that male supremacy is one of the foundations of the society that must be destroyed. Because it is at the level of the direct oppression in our daily lives that most people become conscious, it is not surprising that this is true of women in the movement. Lenin once complained about this phenomenon to Clara Zetklin, leader of the German women's socialist movement: "I have been told that at the evening meetings arranged for reading and discussion with working women, sex and marriage problems come first."

But once women have discovered the full extent of the prejudice against them they cannot ignore it, whether Lenin approves or not, and they have found women's discussions helpful in dealing with their problems. These groups have continued to grow and split into smaller, more viable groups, showing just how widespread is women's dissatisfaction.

However, the level of politicization of these groups has been kept low by the very conditions that keep women underdeveloped in this society; and alienation from the male dominated

KATHY MCAFEE AND MYRNA WOOD 423

movement has prolonged the politicization process. These groups still see the source of their oppression in "chauvinist attitudes," rather than in the social relations of capitalism that produce those attitudes. Therefore, they don't confront male chauvinism collectively or politically. They become involved solely in "personal liberation"—attempts to create free life styles and define new criteria for personal relations in the hoped for system of the future. Bernadine Dohrn's criticism of these groups was a just one: "Their program is only a cycle that produces more women's groups, mostly devoted to a personal liberation/therapy function and promises of study which are an evasion of practice" (*N.L.N.*, V. 4, No. 9).

(2) *Anti-Left Groups.* Many women have separated from the movement out of bitterness and disillusionment with the left's ability to alter its built-in chauvinism. Some are now vociferously anti-left; others simply see the movement as irrelevant. In view of the fate of the ideal of women's equality in most socialist countries, their skepticism is not surprising. Nor is it surprising that individuals with leadership abilities who are constantly thwarted in the movement turn to new avenues.

These women advocate a radical feminist movement totally separate from any other political movement. Their program involves female counter-institutions, such as communes and political parties, and attacks upon those aspects of women's oppression that affect all classes (abortion laws, marriage, lack of child care facilities, job discrimination, images of women in the media).

The first premise of the theory with which these radical feminists justify their movement is that women have always been exploited. They admit that women's oppression has a social basis—*men as a group oppress women as a group*— therefore, women must organize to confront male supremacy collectively. But they say that since women were exploited before capitalism, as well as in capitalist and "socialist" societies, the overthrow of capitalism is irrelevant to the equality of women. Male supremacy is a phenomenon outside the left-right political spectrum and must be fought separately.

But if one admits that female oppression has a social basis, it is necessary to specify the social relations on which this condition is based, and then to change those relations. (We maintain that the oppression of women is based on class divisions; these in turn are derived from the division of labor which developed between the stronger and weaker, the owner and the owned; e.g., women, under conditions of scarcity in primitive society.) Defining those relations as "men as a group *vs.* women as a group," as the anti-left groups seem to do, is ultimately reducible only to some form of biological determinism (women are inherently oppress-able) and leads to no solution in practice other than the elimination of one group or the other.

(3) *Movement Activists.* Many radical women who have become full time activists accept the attitude of most men in the movement that women's liberation is bourgeois and "personalist." They look at most of the present women's liberation groups and conclude that a movement based on women's issues is bound to emphasize the relatively mild forms of oppression experienced by students and "middle class" women while obscuring the fundamental importance of class oppression. "Sure middle class women are oppressed," they say, "but how can we concentrate on making our own lives more comfortable when working class women and men are so much more oppressed." Others point out that "women cannot be free in an unfree society; their liberation will come with that of the rest of us." These people maintain that organizing around women's issues is reformist because it is an attempt to ameliorate conditions within bourgeois society. Most movement activists agree that we should talk about women's oppression, but say we should do so only in terms of the super-exploitation of working women, especially black and brown working women, and not in terms of personal, psychological, and sexual oppression, which they see as a very different (and bourgeois) thing. They also say we should organize around women's oppression, but only as an aspect of our struggles against racism and imperialism. In other words, there should not be a separate revolutionary women's organization.

Yet strangely enough, demands for the liberation of women seldom find their way into movement programs, and very little organizing of women, within or apart from other struggles, is actually going on:

—In student organizing, no agitation for birth control for high school and college girls; no recognition of the other special restrictions that keep them from controlling their own lives; no propaganda about how women are still barred from many courses, especially those that would enable them to demand equality in employment.

—In open admissions fights, no propaganda about the channeling of girls into low-paying, deadend service occupations.

—In struggles against racism, talk about the black man's

loss of manhood, but none about the sexual objectification and astounding exploitation of black women.

—In anti-repression campaigns, no fights against abortion laws; no defense of those "guilty" of abortion.

—In analysis of unions, no realization that women make less than black men and that most women aren't even organized yet. The demands for equal wages were recently raised in the Women's Resolution (at the December SDS, NC), but there are as yet no demands for free child care and equal work by husbands that would make the demand for equal wages more than an empty gesture.

It is clear that radical women activists have not been able to educate the movement about its own chauvinism or bring the issue of male supremacy to an active presence in the movement's program any more than have the personal liberation groups.

The failure of the movement to deal with male supremacy is less the result of a conscious evaluation of the issue's impact than a product of the male chauvinism that remains deeply rooted in the movement itself. Most full-time women organizers work in an atmosphere dominated by aggressive "guerilla" street fighters and organizers (who usually have a silent female appendage), of charismatic theoreticians (whose ability to lay out an analysis is not hampered by the casual stroking of the girl's hair while everyone listens raptly), of decision-making meetings in which the strong voices of men in "ideological struggle" are only rarely punctuated by the voice of one of the girls more skilled in debate, and of movement offices in which the women are still the most reliable (after all, the men are busy speaking and organizing).

"Bad politics" and "sloppy thinking" baiting is particularly effective against women who have been socialized to fear aggressiveness, who tend to lack experience in articulating abstract concepts. And at the same time, a woman's acceptance in the movement still depends on her attractiveness, and men do not find women attractive when they are strong-minded and argue like men.

Many of the characteristics which one needs in order to become respected in the movement—like the ability to argue loud and fast and aggressively and to excel in the "I'm more revolutionary than you" style of debate—are traits which our society consistently cultivates in men and discourages in women from childhood. But these traits are neither inherently male nor universally human; rather they are particularly appropriate to a brutally competitive capitalist society.

That most movement women fail to realize this, that their ideal is still the arrogant and coercive leader-organizer, that they continue to work at all in an atmosphere where women are consistently scorned, and where chauvinism and elitism are attacked in rhetoric only—all this suggests that most movement women are not really aware of their *own* oppression. They continue to assume that the reason they haven't "made it" in the movement is that they are not dedicated enough or that their politics are not developed enough. At the same time, most of these women are becoming acutely aware, along with the rest of the movement, of their own comfortable and privileged backgrounds compared with those of workers (and feel guilty about them). It is this situation that causes them to regard women's liberation as a sort of counter-revolutionary self-indulgence.

There is a further reason for this; in the movement we have all become aware of the central importance of working people in a revolutionary movement and of the gap between their lives and most of our own. But at this point our understanding is largely an abstract one; we remain distant from and grossly ignorant of the real conditions working people face day to day. Thus our concept of working class oppression tends to be a one-sided and mechanistic one, contrasting "real" economic oppression to our "bourgeois hang-ups" with cultural and psychological oppression. We don't understand that the oppression of working people is a total one, in which the "psychological" aspects—the humiliation of being poor, uneducated, and powerless, the alienation of work, and the brutalization of family life—are not only real forms of oppression in themselves, but reinforce material oppression by draining people of their energy and will to fight. Similarly, the "psychological" forms of oppression that affect all women —sexual objectification and the definition of women as docile and serving—work to keep working class women in a position where they are super-exploited as workers and as housewives.

But because of our one-sided view of class oppression, most movement women do not see the relationship of their own oppression to that of working class women. This is why they conclude that a women's liberation movement cannot lead to class consciousness and does not have revolutionary potential.

(4) *Advocates of a Women's Liberation Movement.* A growing number of radical women see the need for an organized women's movement because: (1) they see revolutionary potential in women organizing against their direct oppression, that is, against male supremacy as well as their

exploitation as workers; and (2) they believe that a significant movement for women's equality will develop within any socialist movement only through the conscious efforts of organized women, and they have seen that such consciousness does not develop in a male chauvinist movement born of a male supremacist society.

These women believe that radical women must agitate among young working class girls, rank and file women workers, and workers' wives, around a double front; against their direct oppression by male supremacist institutions, and against their exploitation as workers. They maintain that the cultural conditions of people's lives is as important as the economic basis of their oppression in determining consciousness. If the movement cannot incorporate such a program, these women say, then an organized women's liberation movement distinguished from the general movement must be formed, for only through such a movement will radical women gain the consciousness to develop and carry through this program.

The question of "separation" from the movement is a thorny one, particularly if it is discussed only in the abstract. Concretely, the problem at the present time is simply: should a women's liberation movement be a caucus within SDS, or should it be more than that? The radical women's liberationists say the latter; their movement should have its own structure and program, although it should work closely with SDS, and most of its members would probably be active in SDS (or other movement projects and organizations) as individuals. It would be "separate" *within* the movement in the same sense that say, NOC is separate, or in the way that the organized women who call themselves "half of China" are separate within the Chinese revolution.

The reason for this is not simply that women need a separate organization in order to develop themselves. The radical women's liberationists believe that the true extent of women's oppression can be revealed and fought only if the women's liberation movement is dominated by working class women. This puts the question of "separation" from SDS in a different light. Most of us in the movement would agree that a revolutionary working class movement cannot be built within the present structure of the student movement, so that if we are serious about our own rhetoric, SDS itself will have to be totally transformed, or we will have to move beyond it, within the coming years.

The radical women's liberationists further believe that the American liberation movement will fail before it has barely begun if it does not recognize and deal with the elitism, coerciveness, aggressive individualism, and class chauvinism it has inherited from capitalist society. Since it is women who always bear the brunt of these forms of oppression, it is they who are most aware of them. Elitism, for example, affects many people in the movement to the detriment of the movement as a whole, but women are always on the very bottom rung of participation in decision-making. The more they are shut out, the less they develop the necessary skills, and elitism in the movement mirrors the vicious circle of bourgeois society.

The same characteristics in the movement that produce male chauvinism also lead to class chauvinism. Because women are politically underdeveloped—their education and socialization have not given them analytic and organizational skills—they are assumed to be politically inferior. But as long as we continue to evaluate people according to this criterion, our movement will automatically consider itself superior to working class people, who suffer a similar kind of oppression.

We cannot develop a truly liberating form of socialism unless we are consciously fighting these tendencies in our movement. This consciousness can come from the organized efforts of those who are most aware of these faults because they are most oppressed by them, i.e. women. But in order to politicize their consciousness of their own oppression, and to make effective their criticisms of the movement, women need the solidarity and self-value they could gain from a revolutionary women's liberation movement involved in meaningful struggle.

What is the revolutionary potential of women's liberation?

The potential for revolutionary thought and action lies in the masses of super-oppressed and super-exploited working class women. We have seen the stagnation in New Left women's groups caused by the lack of the *need to fight* that class oppression produces. Unlike most radical women, working class women have no freedom of alternatives, no chance of achieving some slight degree of individual liberation. It is these women, through their struggle, who will develop a revolutionary women's liberation movement.

A women's liberation movement will be necessary if unity of the working class is ever to be achieved. Until working men see their female co-workers and their own wives as equal in their movement, and until those women see that it is in their own interests and that of their families to "dare to win," the position of women will continue to undermine every working class struggle.

The attitude of unions, and of the workers themselves, that women should not work, and that they do not do difficult or necessary work, helps to maintain a situation in which (1) many women who need income or independence cannot work, (2) women who do work are usually not organized, (3) union contracts reinforce the inferior position of women who are organized, and (4) women are further penalized with the costs of child care. As a result, most women workers do not see much value in organizing. They have little to gain from militant fights for better wages and conditions, and they have the most to risk in organizing in the first place.

The position of workers' wives outside their husbands' union often places them in antagonism to it. They know how little it does about safety and working conditions, grievances, and layoffs. The unions demand complete loyalty to strikes—which means weeks without income—and then sign contracts which bring little improvement in wages or conditions.

Thus on the simple trade union level, the oppression of women weakens the position of the workers as a whole. But any working class movement that does not deal with the vulnerable position of totally powerless women will have to deal with the false consciousness of those women.

The importance of a working class women's liberation movement goes beyond the need for unity. A liberation movement of the "slaves of the slave" tends to raise broader issues of people's oppression in all its forms, so that it is inherently wider than the economism of most trade union movements. For example, last year 187 women struck British Ford demanding equal wages (and shutting down 40,000 other jobs in the process). They won their specific demand, but Ford insisted that the women work all three rotating shifts, as the men do. The women objected that this would create great difficulty for them in their work as housekeepers and mothers, and that their husbands would not like it.

A militant women's liberation movement must go on from this point to demand (1) that mothers must also be free in the home, (2) that management must pay for child care facilities so that women can do equal work with men, and that (3) equal work *with* men must mean equal work *by* men. In this way, the winning of a simple demand for equality on the job raises much broader issues of the extent of inequality, the degree of exploitation, and the totality of the oppression of all the workers. It can show how women workers are forced to hold an extra full time job without pay or recognition that this is necessary work, how male chauvinism allows the capitalist class to exploit workers in this way, how people are treated like machines owned by the boss, and how the most basic conditions of workers' lives are controlled in the interests of capitalism.

The workplace is not the only area in which the fight against women's oppression can raise the consciousness of everybody about the real functions of bourgeois institutions. Propaganda against sexual objectification and the demeaning of women in the media can help make people understand how advertising manipulates our desires and frustrations, and how the media sets up models of human relationships and values which we all unconsciously accept. A fight against the tracking of girls in school into low-level, deadend service jobs helps show how the education system channels and divides us all, playing upon the false self-images we have been given in school and by the media (women are best as secretaries and nurses; blacks aren't cut out for responsible positions; workers' sons aren't smart enough for college).

Struggles to free women from domestic slavery which may begin around demands for a neighborhood or factory child care center can lead to consciousness of the crippling effects of relations of domination and exploitation in the home, and to an understanding of how the institutions of marriage and the family embody those relations and destroy human potential.

In short, because the material oppression of women is integrally related to their psychological and sexual oppression, the women's liberation movement must necessarily raise these issues. In doing so it can make us all aware of how capitalism oppresses us, not only by drafting us, taxing us, and exploiting us on the job, but by determining the way we think, feel, and relate to each other.

IV.

In order to form a women's liberation movement based on the oppression of working class women we must begin to agitate on issues of "equal rights" and specific rights. Equal rights means all those "rights" that men are supposed to have: the right to work, to organize for equal pay, promotions, better conditions, equal (and *not* separate) education. Specific rights means those rights women must have if they are to be equal in the other areas: free, adequate child care, abortions, birth control for young women from puberty, self-defense, desegregation of all institutions (schools, unions, jobs). It is not so much an academic question of what is correct theory as an inescapable empirical fact; women must fight their conditions just to participate in the movement.

The first reason why we need to fight on these issues is that we must serve the people. That slogan is not just rhetoric with the Black Panthers but reflects their determination to end the exploitation of their people. Similarly, the women's liberation movement will grow and be effective only to the extent that it abominates and fights the conditions of misery that so many women suffer every day. It will gain support only if it speaks to the immediate needs of women. For instance:

(1) We must begin to disseminate birth control information in high schools and fight the tracking of girls into inferior education. We must do this not only to raise the consciousness of these girls to their condition but because control of their bodies is the key to their participation in the future. Otherwise, their natural sexuality will be indirectly used to repress them from struggles for better jobs and organizing, because they will be encumbered with children and economically tied to the family structure for basic security.

(2) We must raise demands for maternity leave and child-care facilities provided (paid for, but not controlled) by management as a rightful side benefit of women workers. This is important not only for what those issues say about women's right to work but so that women who choose to have children have more freedom to participate in the movement.

(3) We must agitate for rank and file revolt against the male supremacist hierarchy of the unions and for demands for equal wages. Only through winning such struggles for equality can the rank and file *be* united and see their common enemies—management and union hierarchy. Wives of workers must fight the chauvinist attitudes of their husbands simply to be able to attend meetings.

(4) We must organize among store clerks, waitresses, office workers, and hospitals where vast numbers of women have no bargaining rights or security. In doing so we will have to confront the question of a radical strategy towards established unions and the viability of independent unions.

(5) We must add to the liberal demands for abortion reform by fighting against the hospital and doctors boards that such reforms consist of. They will in no way make abortions

more available for the majority of non-middle class women or young girls who will still be forced to home remedies and butchers. We must insist at all times on the right of every woman to control her own body.

(6) We must demand the right of women to protect themselves. Because the pigs protect property and not people, because the violence created by the brutalization of many men in our society is often directed at women, and because not all women are willing or able to sell themselves (or to limit their lives) for the protection of a male, women have a right to self-protection.

This is where the struggle must begin, although it cannot end here. In the course of the fight we will have to raise the issues of the human relationships in which the special oppression of women is rooted: sexual objectification, the division of labor in the home, and the institutions of marriage and the nuclear family. But organizing "against the family" cannot be the basis of a program. An uneducated working class wife with five kids is perfectly capable of understanding that marriage has destroyed most of her potential as a human being—probably she already understands this—but she is hardly in a position to repudiate her source of livelihood and free herself of those children. If we expect that of her, we will never build a movement.

As the women's liberation movement gains strength, the development of cooperative child care centers and living arrangements, and the provision of birth control may allow more working class women to free themselves from slavery as sex objects and housewives. But at the present time, the insistence by some women's liberation groups that we must "organize against sexual objectification," and that only women who repudiate the family can really be part of the movement, reflects the class chauvinism and lack of seriousness of women who were privileged enough to avoid economic dependence and sexual slavery in the first place.

In no socialist country have women yet achieved equality or full liberation, but in the most recent revolutions (Vietnam, Cuba, and China's cultural revolution) the women's struggle has intensified. It may be that in an advanced society such as our own, where women have had relatively more freedom, a revolutionary movement may not be able to avoid a militant women's movement developing within it. But the examples of previous attempts at socialist revolutions prove that the struggle must be instigated *by* militant women; liberation is not handed down from above.

FOOTNOTES

[1] *See Movement,* May 1969, pp. 6–7.
[2] We referred above to "middle class" forms of oppression, contrasting the opportunity for wasteful consumption among relatively affluent women, and superficial sexual freedom of college women to the conditions of poor and uneducated working women. Here "middle class" refers more to a life style, a bourgeois cultural ideal, than to a social category. Strictly speaking, a middle class person is one who does not employ other people but also does not have to sell his labor for wages to live, e.g., a doctor or owner of a small family business. Many people who think of themselves as "middle class," and who can afford more than they need to live on are, strictly speaking, working class people because they must sell their labor, e.g., high school teachers and most white collar workers. There is, of course, a real difference in living conditions as well as consciousness between these people and most industrial workers. But because of the middle class myth, a tremendous gap in consciousness can exist even where conditions are essentially the same. There are literally millions of female clerical workers, telephone operators, etc., who work under the most proletarianized conditions, doing the most tedious female-type labor, and making the same wages, or even less, as sewing machine factory workers, who nevertheless think of themselves as in a very different "class" from those factory women.

The Women's Rights Movement in the U.S.: A New View*

SHULAMITH FIRESTONE

What does the word "feminism" call to mind? A granite-faced spinster obsessed with the vote? A George Sand in bloomers with cigar, a woman "against Nature"? Whatever the image, chances are it is a negative one. To be called a feminist has become an insult. Even many contemporary women radicals go to great lengths to deny connection with the old feminism, calling it kop-out, reformist, bourgeois, without having bothered to examine the little and usually slanted or false information there is on the subject. (The few historians of the Woman's Rights Movement[1] in the U.S. complain that the records have been lost, damaged, or scattered due to the little value placed on them.)

I think this is because the struggle for women's rights is in itself a revolutionary struggle. In this article I shall attempt to show that the WRM was a radical movement from its very beginning, in the early nineteenth century, and that a strong radical wing of the movement existed up to and through the bitter end in 1920—the last to die, and that the history of this radical strain has been buried for political reasons. Let's review the WRM in America from this perspective.

The early women's movement was a radical movement. To attack the Family, the Church, and the State was no small thing in the Victorian Era. Few people today realize what a grass roots movement it was, nor do they know of the tortuous journeys made by dedicated feminists into frontiers and backwoods to speak about the issues to a few huddled women, or to collect signatures for endless petitions which were laughed right out of the assemblies. The meagre funds that kept the WRM going were the nickels and dimes of housewives and laundresses. For from the beginning the WRM identified itself with the poorest, most abused women, working women, prostitutes and criminals. In 1868, long before any official female trade unionism had begun, Susan B. Anthony and Elizabeth Cady Stanton, the most militant feminists in the movement, formed the Working Women's Association —remembered for its championship of the case of Hester Vaughn, a destitute victim of seduction and abandonment, falsely accused and sentenced to be hanged for infanticide. (Appearing as delegates to the National Labor Union Convention in the same year, they later fell out over the male chauvinist policies of the male-dominated labor movement.) Other early female labor organizers, such as Kate Mullany or Augusta Lewis, were feminists.

The theory of the WRM was solidly based in the ideas of the abolitionist movement and in those of such utopian/ socialists and freethinkers as Fanny Wright or Ernestine Rose. This movement was built by women who literally had no civil status under the law, who were pronounced civilly dead upon marriage, or who remained legal minors if they didn't marry, who could not even sign their own wills or have custody of their own children upon divorce, who were not allowed to

[1]The Woman's Rights Movement, hereafter abbreviated WRM, is often confused with one of its branches, the Suffrage Movement.

go to school at all, let alone college, who were, at best, equipped with a little knowledge of embroidery, French, or harpsichord as their sole political education, who had no political status or weapons whatever. And yet, today, we hardly remember that less than a century ago, even after the Civil War, more than half of this country's population were still slaves, under the law women not owning even the bustles on their backs.

The women's movement from the first was tied up with anti-slavery forces, the most important radical movement in 19th-century America. It was due to their work in the abolitionist movement that many women first developed the courage to fight their own slavery. (It is an irony that the first Women's Rights Convention at Seneca Falls in 1848 came about as a result of the ire felt by Lucretia Mott and Elizabeth Cady Stanton when they were denied seating at the World Anti-Slavery Convention in England in 1840.)

Today again, women are beginning to move largely on the inspiration and impetus from the black movement of the sixties. And indeed the black struggle and the feminist struggle always seem to run parallel in this country. Both were aborted, their energy drained off, at about the same time; and it is only recently that both have begun to question and demand, to analyze what went wrong and why.

And, just as with black history, there is a suspicious blank in the history books when it comes to the WRM, one of the greatest struggles for freedom this country has known. Little girls are taught to believe that all their rights were won for them a long time ago by a silly bunch of ladies who carried on and made a ridiculous display, all to get a piece of paper into a ballot box.

Why is this? Why are little girls familiar with Louisa May Alcott rather than Margaret Fuller, with Scarlett O'Hara and Myrtilla Miner, with Florence Nightingale and not Fanny Wright? Why have they never heard of the Grimké Sisters, Sojourner Truth, Inez Milholland, Prudence Crandall, Ernestine Rose, Abigail Scott Duniway, Harriet Tubman, Clara Lemlich, Alice Paul, and many others, a long list of brilliant, courageous people? Something is fishy when, scarcely fifty years after the vote was won, the whole WRM has been forgotten—remembered only by a few "eccentric" old ladies.

I submit that women's history has been hushed up for the same reason that black history has been hushed up—so that the black child learns, not about Nat Turner, but about the triumphs of Ralph Bunche, or George Washington Carver and the peanuts—and that is that a feminist movement poses a direct threat to the establishment. From the beginning it exposed the hypocrisy of the male power structure, its very existence and long duration proof of massive large-scale inequality in a system that pretended to democracy. Both the abolitionist movement and the WRM, working at times together, at times separately, threatened to tear the country apart, and very nearly did during the Civil War. (If the feminists then hadn't been persuaded to abandon their cause for "more important" issues, i.e., other, men's issues, the history of the WRM might have been different.)

The history of the struggle for suffrage alone is an account of tooth and nail opposition from the most reactionary forces in America. The work involved to achieve the vote was staggering. Carrie Chapman Catt estimated that:

> To get the word "male" out of the Constitution cost the women of this country 52 years of pauseless campaign. . . . During that time they were forced to conduct 56 campaigns of referenda to male voters, 480 campaigns to get legislatures to submit suffrage amendments to voters, 47 campaigns to get state constitutional conventions to write woman suffrage into state constitutions, 277 campaigns to get state party conventions to include woman suffrage planks, 30 campaigns to get presidential party conventions to adopt woman suffrage planks in party platforms and 19 campaigns with 19 successive Congresses.
>
> (Carrie Chapman Catt and Nettie Rogers Shuler, *Woman Suffrage and Politics,* New York, 1923, Chas. Scribners Sons, pg. 107)

Defeat was so frequent and victory so rare, and then achieved only by the skin of the teeth, that even to read about it is grueling, let alone to have lived through it, or to have devoted life to the struggle.

Was male chauvinism the sole cause? Certainly it was the most fundamental cause, underlying all the other forces obstructing the movement. Remember that in that period, male power was as taken for granted as once was the Divine Right of Kings; it was so entrenched, unquestioned, and absolute that even demands for the mildest reforms seemed ludicrous.

Eleanor Flexner, in *Century of Struggle* (Harvard University Press, paperback, Atheneum) examines the anti-suffrage forces that fought to such great lengths, pinpointing those (male) institutions most resistant to women's liberation:

1. *Capitalism:* The big industrial states of the North were among the last to give in. Oil, manufacturing, and railroad lobbies worked secretly against suffrage, not only because the big liquor interests were threatened by an early alliance of the Women's Christian Temperance Union with the Suffrage cause, but also because the WRM had from the beginning been identified with the labor reform, and "creeping socialism" in general. Let's not forget that women were—and still are— a source of cheap labor. The vote could have worked against that. (Flexner notes in this connection that the women's anti-suffrage committees were a female front for big money interests. Records show that ⅘ of their contributions came from *Men,* generally in quite substantial sums.)

2. *Racism:* The second large bloc to fight woman suffrage to the bitter end was, you guessed it, the Southern States. In those days the connection between the black struggle and the feminist struggle was more obvious than it is today. And, to grant the vote to women would not only enfranchise another *Half* of the Negro race, but would call attention to the fact that suffrage was *Not* universal. With 51% of the population looking out for corruption at the polls, the 14th amendment might get enforced as well as the 19th.

3. *Government:* The political machines of government itself, maintaining the interests of the upper classes and repressing the lower, were still only a superstructure on top of an even deeper exploitation—that of women and children in the "private" institutions. Should this foundation give way the whole thing would topple. As the *Albany Advocate* predicted after the first feminist convention at Seneca Falls, N.Y. in 1848, "the order of things established at the creation of mankind, and continued 6,000 years, would be completely broken up."

4. *The Church:* Judaeo-Christianity has always espoused the inferiority of women, pointing to Genesis for proof of women's temptress nature, her special role, her mission to be fruitful and multiply, and after Eden, to multiply in pain and submission to man.

5. *The Family:* The family unit, based on women's responsibility for childrearing, on male supremacy and the sexual double standard, was severely threatened at its core by any talk of women's liberation. After all, who knew at that time that the movement could be stopped with only partial or surrogate freedoms? They saw clearly that to follow through on women's rights would mean abolition of the traditional family

structure, which provided every man—powerful or power-less—with his deepest privilege.

6. *The Law:* The facade which reinforced and guaranteed the status quo.

Thus the first modest demands of women for equal rights were recognized by the men in power as a revolutionary threat—the beginning of the end of their system—and, as so often happens, this was recognized more clearly by the enemy than by some of the crusaders themselves. Even with the Suffrage Association later turning conservative in their obsession with getting the vote at all cost, and in their zeal practically assuring the male power structure that if they were granted the vote they wouldn't *use* it, the establishment wasn't convinced. It took 53 years from the first state suffrage referendum in Kansas in 1867 to the final ratification of the 19th amendment in 1920. And even then there was so much stalling that from January 10, 1918, when the amendment was finally passed (by the *exact* ⅔ majority required), it took two years and nine months to get it ratified. And then it passed by only a miraculous two votes. When all else had failed, the losing minority even tried the desperate tactic of crossing the state line into Alabama to prevent a quorum until they could undermine the majority vote.

But though these forces finally appeared to give in, they did so in name only. They never lost. For by that time, after the barrage of campaigns, the concentration of all energy into the limited goal of suffrage (which in the beginning after all, had been seen only as a preliminary, a weapon with which to wrest real political power) had depleted the WRM. The monster of the vote had swallowed everything else. Three generations had come and gone, the masterplanners were all dead. The women who had joined later to work for the clear cut issue of the vote had never had time to develop a broader consciousness, to see where the vote fit in. By that time they could hardly remember that there had been anything else to fight for. By the time the Suffrage Movement disbanded the WRM was dead. The opposition had had its way.

For what is the vote worth finally if the voter is manipulated? Every American husband now has two votes instead of one. For today, some 50 years later, women still vote as wives, just as they can govern only as wives. Lurleen Wallace symbolized the puppet political position women have in this country. Margaret Chase Smith has been the only woman Senator elected independently of any connection with husband or father. And where are the woman mayors? In 1968, Jackie

Kennedy correctly told a reporter that "in my family politics are left to the men," while Lady Bird, the highest lady of the land, provided an exemplary model for the young ladies with her concern for Easter outfits and beautiful highways.

Though, as often quoted to show progress, one third of all women work, they have merely added a new exploitation to the old one. For they are concentrated in the service occupations, at the bottom rung of the employment ladder, in jobs that no one else will take. As for earnings, only 2% of the jobs with salaries of over $10,000 annually are held by women.

The average woman earns approximately $2,827 annually, a little over half the average man's earnings ($4,466). Despite the talk about bitchy businesswomen, how many businesswomen do you ever see? How many women in any managerial or decision-making position? How many professionals? Ninety-five per cent of all professionals are still male. Academic opportunities are shrinking, not growing; even the women's colleges and magazines are run by men. Nor does anyone mention the fact that future prospects look even dimmer. The routine jobs that were granted to women, a lollipop to appease their hunger for real and important work, will be the first to go, come automation. Perhaps men will have their way after all, and women will go back to the home they never should have left.

What went wrong? Why did the Women's Rights Movement fail?

1. *By Selling Out the Cause for "More Important" Issues:* Women, more than any other oppressed group, were easy to convince that their concern for their own needs was "selfish," their own sufferings "trivial" compared with others. This may be due to the special conditioning which women undergo from the beginning—to put the interests of the male or the child above their own—to please rather than disturb.

First, in the Civil War, the back of the tough little WRM was broken when the energy of women was channelled into abolitionism or war work. After the war the movement had to be built up again from scratch. Only the staunchest feminists insisted that the word *sex* as well as *color* go into the 14th amendment. The abolitionists, who had been glad to accept the aid of women all along, suddenly decided that now it was "the Negro's hour"—that the cause of women was too unimportant to delay for a minute any advances in the liberation of the blacks. But they had forgotten that the newly freed slaves were *half* female. Once again it had been proved that unless oppressed groups stick together, and on alliances of self-interest rather than do-goodism, nothing can be accomplished in the long run to dismantle the apparatus of oppression—as long as it remains to be used on one group, it can just as easily be employed on another.

Later in World War I the same thing happened. Sensitive to the charge that they cared more about their own interests than the good of the country most of the suffragists turned from feminism to peace and then war work. Only the militant feminists kept at it, acknowledging the war only by such slogans as "Freedom Begins at Home." Baited for this, and vilified, they proved right in knowing that if they gave up now they would never get the vote. For once, they were needed in the labor force—if only temporarily for the "war effort"—and thus they had a bargaining position. They knew that then their citizenship could be questioned by no one, whereas after the war there would be the usual backlash, the attempt to put them back in the home. And indeed it is no accident that the amendment finally passed when it did, right before the end of the war, in 1918.

In this regard we should keep in mind that revolutions anywhere are always glad to use any help they can get—even from women. But unless women also use the revolution to further their own interests as well as everyone else's, unless they make it consistently clear that all help given now is expected to be returned, both now and after the revolution, they will be sold out again and again—as, for example, they were in Algeria.

2. *By Single Issue Organizing As Opposed to Organizing to Raise the General Consciousness:* Many organizers believe that they can "use" an existing, already "hot" issue to build up their own cause. I think this is a delusion, that in fact it does not save time or effort, but can really set a movement back or even destroy it. To reach the people "where they are at" when they are in the wrong place, is a false approach. Rather, we should be concerned with educating them at all times to the real issues involved. If they *are* real issues, people will catch on soon enough.

An example of this failing in the WRM was the alliance with the Women's Christian Temperance Union. After the Civil War, when the solid base of the WRM had been broken, it seemed opportune to use whatever women's organizations there were as a platform to promote genuine women's issues. The staunchest feminists were against this alliance. Others, notably Frances Willard, argued that she could "use" the temperance issue to further women's rights, since temperance was "where the women were at." It not only failed, but it set back the vote fifty years. Once the WRM became allied in the public mind with the unpopular temperance issue, once it was associated, not with freer women, but with puritanism, once the big liquor interests stepped in—the rest is history.

Again, Stanton and Anthony made a mistake merging their radical feminist National Suffrage Association with the timid provincial American Suffrage Association. The National was concerned with the vote only as the means to a much broader end. Their strategy reflected this: they were against any type of partial suffrage, favoring instead the application of pressure on Washington to amend the Constitution. But Stanton and Anthony, with many misgivings, finally were forced to merge the National with the "better organized" American, a single issue organization, devoted strictly to suffrage, and working on the state level. Again, they might have saved fifty years.

For once the pressure was taken off Washington, the Suffrage issue sank into the "doldrums" until years later, when Harriet Stanton Blatch, Elizabeth Cady Stanton's daughter, returned from the militant feminist movement in England with a set of new tactics, and a renewed pressure for the National Amendment, a strategy unused since her mother's time. The later militants were not single-issue oriented like the others. Their strategy was better because they approached the problem fearlessly from a broader perspective.

Again, we can see how this principle operates on the international level as well. Women in socialist countries or situations, such as Russia or the Kibbutz, have been used in the economy, but because a profound raising of consciousness did not occur during the revolutionary period, because they were too concerned with *the* Revolution and not *their* Revolution, because their definition of themselves did not change radically but was only reformed on specific issues like labor, they found themselves later not only not free, but perhaps in an even worse position. They simply had added a new job to their old one. Now they work harder.

I conclude, that contrary to what most historians would have us believe, women's rights were never won. The Women's Rights Movement did not fold because it accomplished its objectives, but because it was defeated. *Seeming* freedoms appear to have been won. Let's investigate these briefly:

1. *Sexual:* Though it's true that women wear shorter skirts than they used to, I would suggest that this happened not so much in their interest as because *men* preferred it that way.

After all, girls are still sent home from high school in winter for wearing pants to keep their legs warm. Mini skirts are impractical, requiring constant attention to one's sitting posture, constant emphasis on one's sexual nature. High heels, girdles, garter belts, nylons and all the changing trappings of modern fashion may appear more natural, but in fact are not so different in function from the corsets and bustles our grandmothers had to wear. For even when a "natural" look is in style, women are expected to work to achieve it (blush-on, hair straighteners). Girls today are as concerned about "image" as ever. And they are still sexual objects. Only the styles have changed.

As for sex itself, I would argue that any changes were as a result of male interests and not female—any benefits for women only incidental. A relaxing of the mores concerning female sexual behavior was to *his* advantage; it increased the sexual supply and lowered its cost. But his attitudes haven't changed much since the days of the professional whore.

2. *Labor:* Though one third of the women are employed, they have merely taken over the shit jobs. Even when they earn as much as their husbands do, the equal work does not grant them a new equal status in the family; rather, they are considered to be "helping out." And when they come home, there's still that housework to do, the child care, the cooking of supper. ("Woman's work is never done.") So that here again, the change resulted in male advantage; that is, the woman took over the menial jobs he didn't like, jobs that she had no commitment to, and would give up in favor of marriage or babies, any time he so desired. (Then as her employer he would argue that he couldn't hire her for the good jobs, train or promote her, or give her equal wages for equal work when she'd just turn over and get married.)

3. *Women and Money:* This is the one you never hear the end of: how the women control all the bread and spend it on whatever they please. But though in their personal lives they will be the first to berate their wives for spending so much money, the advertisers and manufacturers want it that way. Because this is a consumer economy, one that needs full-time consumers of useless products for its very existence. What better target than a class of semi-educated semi-conscious unhappy people, who also have some access to the budget money? So instead of all those tedious cartoons depicting Irate Husband chewing out Big Mama for always going shopping whenever she's unhappy let's start putting the

blame where it belongs: on that same husband when he's in his office doing market research.

4. *Legal Rights:* A Canadian documentary on the Women's Rights Movement, *Women on the March,* showed that the Canadian Supreme Court had once handed down a decision declaring that, no, women were *not* people. Later, there was a lot of fanfare when the decision was reversed. A plaque was even presented to someone, I forget who. And that's about where it's at. Now we are declared human in certain books, but though some legal rights have been won, as with black people, it's quite another thing to have them actually enforced. More often legal gains are, ironically, used as grounds for more severe exploitation, i.e., "See what you've done now that we've given you your freedom?"

But even these superficial advances, so hard won, and yielded with such ill grace, turned out to be a hoax, and we're finally catching on. There are several important lessons to be learned if this time around we don't want to be subtly subverted yet again.

To capitulate briefly, these are:

1. Never compromise basic principles for political expediency.

2. Agitation for specific freedoms is worthless without the preliminary raising of consciousness necessary to utilize these freedoms fully.

3. Put your own interests first, then proceed to make alliances with other oppressed groups. Demand a piece of that revolutionary pie before you put your life on the line.

TOOTH & NAIL
P.O. Box 4137
Berkeley, California 94704

REDSTOCKINGS
c/o The Group Center
42½ St. Marks Place
New York, New York 10003
(List of literature available on request.)

SOUTHERN FEMALE RIGHTS UNION
1024 Jackson Avenue, Room 3
New Orleans, Louisiana 70130

LILITH
Women's Majority Union
2021 Elynn
Seattle, Washington 98102

NO MORE FUN AND GAMES
Female Liberation
371 Somerville Avenue
Somerville, Massachusetts 02143
(Issues $1 each.)

WOMEN: A Journal of Liberation
3011 Guilford Avenue
Baltimore, Maryland 21218
($1.25/issue $5/5 issues $3/3 remaining issues)

NOTES FROM THE FIRST YEAR
P.O. Box AA
Old Chelsea Station
New York, N. Y. 10011
(This is out of print, but NOTES FROM THE SEC-
OND YEAR (covering radical feminist writings of
1969) is available for $1.50.)

THE GROUP
42½ St. Marks Place
New York, N. Y. 10003
(List of literature available on request.)

N.Y. RADICAL FEMINISTS
P.O. Box 621
Old Chelsea Station
New York, N.Y. 10011

CHICAGO WOMEN'S LIBERATION UNION
2875 W. Cermak
Room 9
Chicago, Illinois 60623

WOMEN'S LIBERATION COMMUNE
5224 19th Street, NE
Seattle, Washington

SOJOURNER TRUTH'S DISCIPLES
1515 Cherry Street (B. Woodford)
Philadelphia, Pennsylvania 19102

UP FROM UNDER
399 Lafayette Street
New York, N.Y. 10012
(60¢ issue/$3—5 yr. sub.)

AIN'T I A WOMAN?
Women's Liberation Front
P.O. Box 1169
Iowa City, Iowa 52240
(25¢ issue)

IT AIN'T ME BABE
1126 Addison Street
Berkeley, California 94702
($3—6 mos./$6—1 year.)

RAT
241 E. 14th Street
New York, N.Y.
($6—1 yr.)

Ø

SIGNET Titles of Current Interest

☐ **AMERICA VS. AMERICA: The Revolution in Middle-Class Values by James A. Michener.** Written out of concern for the rebellion of the younger generation against the values of their parents, this Broadside explores present middle-class guidelines and the contradictions between what many Americans say they believe and what they actually do. (#P3819—60¢)

☐ **CONFRONTATION ON CAMPUS: THE COLUMBIA PATTERN by Joanne Grant.** A revealing day-by-day account of the Columbia University rebellion which serves as a prototype for student revolts across the country. (#Q3883—95¢)

☐ **ON DISOBEDIENCE AND NON-VIOLENCE by Tolstoy.** One of the world's greatest writers speaks with renewed relevance to our own generation in this first collection of his essays on the power of non-violence and the necessity for civil disobedience. (#Q3501—95¢)

☐ **MIAMI AND THE SIEGE OF CHICAGO: An Informal History of the Republican and Democratic Conventions of 1968 by Norman Mailer.** From the pen of "the best writer in America" (Book Week), comes a unique and deeply moving report of the shame of Miami and the shambles of Chicago during the 1968 presidential conventions. (#W4736—$1.50)

THE NEW AMERICAN LIBRARY, INC.,
P.O. Box 999, Bergenfield, New Jersey 07621

Please send me the SIGNET BOOKS I have checked above. I am enclosing $_____(check or money order—no currency or C.O.D.'s). Please include the list price plus 15¢ a copy to cover mailing costs.

Name_____

Address_____

City_____State_____Zip Code_____
Allow at least 3 weeks for delivery